Deposition
1940–1944

Deposition
1940–1944

A Secret Diary of Life in Vichy France

LÉON WERTH

EDITED AND TRANSLATED
BY DAVID BALL

OXFORD
UNIVERSITY PRESS

OXFORD
UNIVERSITY PRESS

Oxford University Press is a department of the University of Oxford. It furthers
the University's objective of excellence in research, scholarship, and education
by publishing worldwide. Oxford is a registered trade mark of Oxford University
Press in the UK and certain other countries.

Published in the United States of America by Oxford University Press
198 Madison Avenue, New York, NY 10016, United States of America.

Originally published as *Déposition: Journal 1940–1944*
© Éditions Viviane Hamy, Paris, 2000
English translation © Oxford University Press 2018

First issued as an Oxford University Press Paperback in 2021

Library of Congress Cataloging-in-Publication Data
Names: Werth, Léon, 1878–1955 author. |
Ball, David, 1937– translator.
Title: Deposition 1940–1944 : a secret diary of life in Vichy France / Léon Werth ;
edited and translated by David Ball.
Other titles: Déposition. English
Description: New York : Oxford University Press, 2018. |
Includes bibliographical references and index.
Identifiers: LCCN 2017047180 (print) | LCCN 2017048650 (ebook) |
ISBN 9780190499556 (updf) | ISBN 9780190499563 (epub) |
ISBN 9780190499549 (hardcover : alk. paper) | ISBN 9780197602966 (paperback)
Subjects: LCSH: Werth, Léon, 1878–1955—Diaries. |
World War, 1939–1945—Personal narratives, French. |
France—History—German occupation, 1940–1945.
Classification: LCC D811.5 (ebook) | LCC D811.5 .W471613 2018 (print) |
DDC 940.53/44092—dc23
LC record available at https://lccn.loc.gov/2017047180

1 3 5 7 9 8 6 4 2

Paperback printed by Marquis, Canada

Frontispiece: Léon Werth, ca. 1920. *Centre de la Mémoire, Médiathèque Albert-Camus, Issoudun.*

CONTENTS

ACKNOWLEDGMENTS

I wish to thank Mme Stéphanie Gelfi, the archivist at the Centre de la Mémoire of the Médiathèque Albert-Camus in Issoudun where the Léon Werth collection is housed, for her gracious, knowledgeable help in leading me through the archives to find photographs and documents relating to Werth. The riches of the collection made me wish I were writing his biography and not simply annotating a translation. I am indebted to the director of the médiathèque, Mme Anne-Marie L'Hour-Chambenoit, and to Mme Sylvaine Werth for welcoming me there. My special thanks to Mme Werth, who kindly granted me the right to use the photographs.

Thanks, too, to Werth's French publisher, Mme Viviane Hamy, for taking time to share her extensive knowledge of Léon Werth and his family with me.

For the translation, I owe so much to the linguistic knowledge and critical sense of Nicole Ball, my frequent collaborator and best critic, that it would take too much space to express it adequately. And I'm grateful to my colleagues Betsey Harries and Thalia Pandiri for letting me try out different versions of various passages on them and bringing me back to English when I was thinking in French. My gratitude to Tom Raworth for the same reason—sad, belated gratitude, as he did not live to read this.

Elizabeth Vaziri managed to find some unfindable photos, and I am grateful to her.

And thanks once again to Nancy Toff for her support and wisdom—and for her always prompt, smart answers to my concerns, even when we didn't agree. I am lucky to have such an editor.

TRANSLATOR'S INTRODUCTION

DAVID BALL

Deposition is the diary of a Jewish writer in Nazi-occupied France, a man with
an uncommon gift for observation and a passion for the truth. From June 1940
to January 1944, Léon Werth, who had published ten novels, several political
essays, and many articles of cultural criticism for Parisian journals, lived in his
wife's country home outside a small village in the southeast: Saint-Amour, in
the Jura.[1] He normally lived in Paris most of the year. If he had stayed there, he
might well have been one of the fifty thousand Jews deported from the city and
exterminated.[2] Alone in his house, with the habit of writing, no other work, and
the obvious impossibility of publishing during the war, he made entries in his
diary almost every day: noting what people said, what he saw, and what he heard
on the radio and read in the press, often with comments like this:

> "Monsieur de Gaulle (that's what the paper calls him) and General
> Catroux have been stripped of their French nationality."
> So has France.[3]

He followed the war the way most people did in occupied Europe: from afar, day
by day, week by week, noting what he learned and could guess from the radio
(English, French, sometimes Swiss) and the press. It is typical of this diarist to
be aware of that distance—the distance most of us have from terrible events
taking place in the world—and to comment on it with self-irony:

> The radio. Bombs, shells, bullets, cannons, planes, machine guns:
> Stalingrad, the Indian Ocean, the Pacific, Libya; English planes over
> Italy and Germany. Real men, not men made of communiqués and news
> flashes, kill and die. I'm alone in my room in front of the big radio. The

war comes to me stripped down, cleaned up. The wounded don't bleed. The corpses are statistical. I'm above the war like an old, tired god.[4]

Paradoxically, an added pleasure for us as we read this book today is to follow the progress of the war step by step, not like a historian but like a contemporary. But unlike Werth in 1942, we know the story ends well.

Above all, Werth recorded daily life in Vichy France, including what the peasants and townspeople and railwaymen were saying, with all their contradictions— on the farm, in the shops, at the market, or in the café at the railway station. Another great diary of life during the Occupation, Jean Guéhenno's *Diary of the Dark Years: 1940–1944*, deals with occupied Paris and cultural collaboration and resistance in the capital.[5] Werth's diary is very different. He takes note of state and cultural collaboration, but also of resistance of a different kind in the countryside— derailments of German supply trains, for example—along with growing repression: arrests, torture, deportation, and execution by firing squad. Mostly, we see how Vichy and the Occupation affect ordinary life in the French countryside and village, the markets and the surrounding towns (especially Bourg-en-Bresse) and nearby city (Lyon). Werth's ear for dialogue and novelist's gift for the creation of character serve him well: we meet French peasants and shopkeepers, railroad men and the *patronne* of the little café at the station, schoolteachers and gendarmes. They come alive off the page, and the French countryside and villages come alive with them.

The last section of the diary has descriptions of occupied Paris at night (the only time Werth could venture out) and of life in Werth's Paris apartment where the passing "guests" are *résistants* on the run or British aviators hiding there until they could be smuggled out of France. The last pages of the diary give us an account of the fighting in the Latin Quarter during the insurrection that liberated the capital. Unlike the rest of the war, that happened before Werth's very eyes, and his reporting makes us see it with ours. Finally, in a lyrical close to this otherwise precise and factual diary, we witness Charles de Gaulle's triumphal walk down the free Champs-Élysées on August 26, 1944. Characteristically, one day earlier Werth noted the troubling sight of women with shaved heads accused of "horizontal collaboration" and even, just before "tears of deliverance" come into his eyes, his pity for German prisoners "with their hands clasped over the nape of their necks . . . in the posture of the damned. One of them, barely in his teens, has let his head fall on his neighbor's chest. He's sleeping." He is full of joy at the victory, he's glad the German soldiers are now prisoners, but their humiliation, he notes, "makes me suffer." Werth's self-portrait has all the complexity that Jean-Pierre Azéma applauds in his portraits of others.

Jean-Pierre Azéma, the foremost French historian of the period, and Lucien Febvre,* one of the most influential historians of the twentieth century, agree: Léon Werth's *Deposition* is both a remarkable historical document and an extremely enjoyable read. Azéma notes that "the historical interest of [Werth's] testimony is sustained by the pleasure of reading it. The humor is often ferocious, well served by a fine, tough, precise style—a style that is always lively." Febvre praises its "admirable sincerity" and applauds the way Werth reports "all the talk . . . exactly, without dressing it up or filling it out," and "the constant care [he] takes to interpret peasant reactions correctly and sensitively." He concludes that "*Deposition* is one of the most direct and precious pieces of testimony historians can find to reconstruct the development of people's thinking in one corner of France from the nauseating time of the stagnant Armistice to the great year of the Liberation." Speaking of Werth's testimony, Azéma notes, "He is perpetually sensitive to ambivalences. . . . That quest for ambivalence, that complexity of portraits nonetheless composed with such ferocious clarity, that weighing of all the elements, even those that can appear paradoxical in retrospect, is just what historians now seek . . .—the quest for the average Frenchman, the one outside the committed minorities, the one who had to live through both the Occupation and the constraints of an undemocratic emergency regime. . . . That's what makes this text so singularly modern in all ways."

When Viviane Hamy republished the diary in 1992, it was unanimously hailed by the French press: "An essential witness . . . an absolutely independent mind"; "One of the richest pieces of testimony of 'the dark years.' Werth paints the changing moods of the French population by observing the microcosm [of a village]"; "An acerbic chronicler of Pétainism . . . this subtle writer's journal, the diary of a pariah in Vichy, [is] a true document of a dark France seen through the slots in the shutters." Pierre Vidal-Naquet, an eminent and courageous historian, said, "The gaze [Werth] turns on the world" is simply "astounding."[6]

Léon Werth is not well known to English-speaking readers, although his memoir *33 Days* was published recently;[7] what kind of man was he, and what kind of writer?

The beginning of Antoine de Saint-Exupéry's dedication in *The Little Prince* is as good a place to start as any:

> TO LÉON WERTH. I apologize to children for having dedicated this book to a grownup. I have a good excuse: this grownup is the best friend I have in the world. I have another excuse: this grownup can understand anything, even books for children. I have a third excuse: this grownup lives in France, where he is cold and hungry. He needs consolation.[8]

Saint-Exupéry was writing in 1943, when France had been occupied by Nazi Germany through three exceptionally cold winters.

Léon Werth was born in 1878, into an assimilated Jewish family in a small town in Lorraine in eastern France. Despite his rebellious nature, he did so well in his secondary school in Lyon that he was able to come to Paris in 1896 for a postgraduate year at the elite Lycée Henri-IV to prepare for the competitive entrance exam to the still more elite École Normale Supérieure. Typically, he then refused to take the exam. He became the personal secretary and friend to the novelist Octave Mirbeau (*Diary of a Chambermaid*) and actually finished Mirbeau's last book when the aging novelist became too sick to do so.

After Mirbeau died, he lived off odd jobs and then, increasingly, his writing—novels, but also newspaper journalism and essays for distinguished left-wing political and cultural journals: mainly literary, art, and cultural criticism. Werth was close to the anarchists and Communists in the pre-war years, but he was far too independent-minded to belong to any political party. Thus, he was denied entrance to the Soviet Union when he wanted to write a story about it.

A common adjective applied to Léon Werth is "unclassifiable."[9] In 1913, his first novel, *La Maison Blanche*, narrowly missed winning the most prestigious literary prize in France, the Prix Goncourt. His two semi-autobiographical novels about the First World War, a war in which one might call him an anti-patriotic volunteer,[10] were highly praised by critics and writers alike. In addition to his ten novels, the ninety-plus titles bearing his name in the Bibliothèque Nationale catalogue include art criticism (he was the first to "give a philosophical basis to Cubism," says one scholar),[11] travel writing, personal essays, and a great deal of political journalism: his *Cochinchine* was a denunciation of French rule in what is now Vietnam, the fruit of a visit there in 1926, well before most intellectuals became anti-colonialists. It was so scandalous that French intelligence services investigated his possible contacts with dangerous Indochinese revolutionaries (he didn't have any). Readers will find scathing entries in this diary, too, about French colonial rule in Vietnam, Algeria, and elsewhere during the war years: Werth was reading behind the lines of news items about the colonies in the Vichy press. Immediately after the war, Werth wrote an account of Marshal Pétain's trial for treason that transcends the genre of courtroom reporting, with its incisive irony, literary style, and constant sense of the inadequacy of the poorly conducted hearings.[12]

Werth's 2006 French biography is called *L'Insoumis* ("Permanent Rebel" gives the sense),[13] appropriately enough for a man who was proud of maintaining his anarchistic spirit in the midst of the terrible events of 1940—proud even of being frivolous. Consider this, for example: "I have never voted. Not out of principle or laziness. Nor, as one might think, because of my police record. But every time I thought of registering, I was stopped by my horror of the corridors in barracks, prisons, or administrative office buildings. Those Parisian buildings are just too depressing. If I'm not a registered voter, it's the architects' fault."[14] That a Jew in Nazi-occupied France could make this light-hearted comment tells us much about the man. This spirit—along with his high moral seriousness and novelist's gift for observation—infuses his diary.

Werth was sixty-two, caught in the exodus of panicked refugees heading south,[15] when on June 17, 1940, after just six weeks of fighting, Marshal Philippe Pétain, a renowned eighty-four-year-old World War I general and the newly appointed premier of France, announced that French forces had to lay down their arms: he had asked Germany for peace.[16] Never in its long history had France known such a humiliating defeat.

Pétain's delegates signed the Armistice on June 22, in direct violation of France's agreement with England but to the delight of Adolf Hitler, who was present for part of the ceremony. Like Poland, Belgium, the Netherlands, and Luxembourg, France was now going to be occupied by Nazi Germany—directly occupied as far south as the Massif Central (roughly three-fifths of France), but with a "Free Zone" below it governed by the new French regime, whose authority theoretically extended all over what remained of France. So a line drawn across the middle of southern France was now a border guarded by German troops— the "Demarcation Line," often simply shortened to "the Line." The French could not cross without German authorization. Moreover, Alsace and Lorraine were annexed to Germany, and there were smaller "forbidden zones" along the Atlantic and in the north.[17] Above all—though few saw it at the time—since an armistice is a peace agreement that goes well beyond a simple ceasefire, officially Germany was no longer France's enemy: the foundations for French collaboration with their Nazi occupiers had been laid.

Despite the mortifying defeat and Armistice, most French people were probably relieved that the slaughter had stopped. In those six weeks, the French had lost between 50,000 and 90,000 men, with at least twice that number of wounded.[18] Their army was cut into disorganized pieces and millions of civilian refugees were clogging the roads, fleeing the German advance. The situation aroused memories of the more than 1.3 million dead and 4 million casualties France had suffered in the First World War, which had ended just twenty-two years before. Nonetheless, for Werth and many French men and women, the main feeling was no doubt one of shame and confusion. We can see the utter confusion of that time in the very first pages of this diary. Everyone has a different explanation for the disaster, most of them wildly improbable. The humiliation of the crushing, incomprehensible military defeat had been followed by the total capitulation of the new leaders of France and, increasingly, by their collaboration with the Nazi occupiers.[19]

Roughly two weeks after the Armistice was signed, the panicked deputies and senators, meeting in the south-central resort town of Vichy, voted overwhelmingly to invest Pétain with "full powers," and the military defeat turned into the end of the French Republic. The "French State," as Pétain now called it, would have its capital down in Vichy. "An unregulated authoritarian regime was substituted for the structures of parliamentary democracy," as the historian H. R. Kedward summed it up.[20] For the next four years, Werth was to live in the so-called Free Zone not directly occupied by German troops (until November 1942, when they crossed the Demarcation Line and occupied all of France directly, violating the terms of the Armistice). Luckily for Werth, they were not a terribly important presence in the village of Saint-Amour.

Pétain's explanation for the disastrous defeat was simple: France's lack of military preparedness and the decadence of France under the Third Republic. Vichy constantly hammered away at these themes. "Too few children, too few weapons, too few allies. These are the causes of our defeat," said Pétain in June 1940. "Our defeat came from our laxity. The spirit of pleasure destroys what the spirit of sacrifice has built," he moralized on June 25.[21]

Today we know that these "explanations" were self-serving myths. The Germans had roughly 3 million men under arms; the French, 5.7 million; the Germans had 2,800 tanks, the Allies, 3,000—and so on.[22] As for "laxity," the military defeat came so quickly and was so complete that factors like France's supposed "decadence" had no chance to come into play.[23] The causes for the fall of France are many, but most can be summed up in two words: military incompetence. France had built its Maginot Line, an impressive series of state-of-the-art defenses along its eastern borders, and waited to be attacked. The Germans went around it and attacked from the north, through Belgium. The French high command was stupefied when German forces attacked through the forest of the Ardennes: Pétain had called it "impenetrable" in 1934, and the doctrine did not change until masses of German tanks had actually crashed through it.[24] French military leaders had no conception of how war was waged in 1940, as distinguished from 1914—particularly how fast troops could move—and thus were unable to come up with a suitable response to the attack. French military intelligence was also outmoded and inefficient. All of this made the struggles of their troops hopeless.[25] Although Werth's friend Marc Bloch, the brilliant medieval historian who served as a French army officer in that short war, perceived these factors quite clearly, few saw it at the time; de Gaulle was a great exception, as he also was in predicting the disastrous effects of the Armistice.[26]

The Vichy government used Pétain's myths to justify his political, cultural, and moral program for France: his call for a "National Revolution," a "Moral Order," a "New Order," and "regeneration."[27] This thoroughgoing reform of French society was to be accomplished in a country where the real power lay in the hands of Nazi Germany, with its soldiers and Gestapo there to enforce its power if necessary. But France could do whatever it wanted, as far as the occupiers were concerned, as long as it kept quiet (sparing them the task of policing the country themselves),[28] turned over a large part of its economic and agricultural production to Germany, furnished German factories with cheap labor, and helped the Nazis get rid of the Jews. Vichy began the latter job on its own initiative by forcing the Jews to identify themselves and removing them from all aspects of public life. Werth being Werth, he records even this with irony—but also anger.

The rest of Pétain's plan for France had nothing that could bother the Nazis either—far from it. It was essentially a program for a hierarchical regime in which all "real Frenchmen" (but not Jews or Masons) had their assigned place, as in an imagined Middle Ages: peasants happily tilling the soil, craftsmen plying their age-old trades, workers at their machines under the unquestioned authority of their bosses (the fact that the fruit of their toil was going to Germany was, of course, ignored), families—as large as possible—under the authority of the father, and all under the benign authority of Marshal Philippe Pétain, head of the French State: "Chef de l'État Français" was his official title. No parliament, none of the disorderly disagreements that had soiled and weakened the old republic, according to Vichy, none of the freewheeling individualism that was the very essence of Werth's character. All that was to be replaced by a vague "community" and absolute submission to the chief.[29] The propaganda for the New Order was tirelessly repeated on the radio and in the press, controlled by Vichy down in the Free Zone where Werth lived and directly by the Nazis in the Occupied Zone, where the big Paris dailies were not only censored but subsidized by the German *Propagandastaffel*. As Werth was to discover in January 1944, the occupiers' propaganda squad had French Nazi enthusiasts doing their work for them in Paris. So did the radio.

This was the France that Léon Werth lived in for four years.

He would remain in Saint-Amour (no one denounced him, although everybody must have known he was Jewish) until January 1944, when he went back to their apartment in Paris—clandestinely, of course.

The French edition of this journal is more than 730 pages long, and this edition is an abridgement. As with any abridgement, some tough choices had to be made. Werth made entries in his diary almost every day, often including descriptions of the landscape, sometimes reflections on the Church, on science, on his reading (Pascal, Spinoza, Saint-Simon, La Fontaine, the Bible, etc.), criticism of contemporary novelists and essayists (some obscure today), and sometimes his dreams. Most of these have been cut. I have kept the greater part of Werth's testimony on life in Vichy France, especially in the countryside, while cutting some of the repetition; I have retained enough of the landscape descriptions to give us a feel for where he was and the passing seasons, and just one dream, where he sees Jean Guéhenno, who at that moment was writing his own diary of life under German occupation. Above all, I tried to retain enough of Werth's irony and shifting tones to convey a sense of what his diary is like in the original. This translation strives to render Werth's varied style in French—a style that is, as Azéma notes, "always lively"—into a similarly varied and, I hope, lively English.[30]

Some of the critical apparatus of the French edition has been cut. Lucien Febvre divided the diary into chapters and invented titles for them; this heavy-handed editorial intervention made little sense in an abridgement, and many of his chapter titles will not mean much to a non-French reader, so they have been eliminated. The 1992 Viviane Hamy edition is preceded by Febvre's 1947 article on *Deposition* from the historical journal *Les Annales'*, introduced and annotated by Jean-Pierre Azéma. A few lines in these introductory essays would have required lengthy explanation for today's non-French readers, so I took the liberty of cutting them. Similarly, while some of Azéma's scholarly notes to the French edition were perfect for non-French readers, others required adaptation; still others would have required explanation themselves, so they were cut. When I felt a note was needed for today's readers, I added it. Both my notes and my adaptations of Azéma's are unsigned, except when leaving them unsigned might be confusing. Those of his notes that are faithfully translated are signed J.-P. A., and Febvre's, in his essay, L. F.

Names followed by an asterisk can be found in the biographical dictionary in the back of the book.

Notes

1. Not to be confused with Saint-Amour Bellevue in the Beaujolais region, which produces the good Beaujolais called "Saint-Amour."
2. United States Memorial Holocaust Museum website, https://www.ushmm.org/wlc/fr/article.php?ModuleId=201.
3. December 12, 1940.
4. October 25, 1942.
5. Jean Guéhenno, *Diary of the Dark Years, 1940–1944: Collaboration, Resistance, and Daily Life in Occupied Paris*, trans. David Ball (New York: Oxford University Press, 2014).
6. *Le Figaro Littéraire*, December 4, 1992; *Le Monde*, December 3, 1992; *Le Nouvel Observateur*, December 31, 1992 (Mona Ozouf); *Le Nouveau Politis*, January 1993. Similar praise was voiced by *Le Canard Enchaîné*, December 9, 1992; by *Le Quotidien des Livres*, November 25, 1992; and by many, many other publications.
7. *33 Days*, trans. Austin D. Johnston (Brooklyn, NY: Melville House, 2015).
8. My translation. Among the dozen affectionate entries about his friend Saint-Exupéry in Werth's diary, the one on October 15, 1940, stands out (Lucien Febvre appreciated it, too): "That restaurant in the Bois de Boulogne, where we had dinner together last year. How did we come to judge some of the men who were then leading France—in other words, ministers? We ascribed projects to them, a grand plan. And suddenly Tonio murmured: 'I think we're indulging in anthropomorphism.'"
9. "Applied" by the French: *inclassable*.
10. This is the sense of the chapter Gilbert Heuré devotes to Werth in the First World War in *L'Insoumis: Léon Werth 1878–1955* (Paris: Éditions Viviane Hamy, 2006).
11. John Shannon Hendrix, *Platonic Architectonics: Platonic Philosophies and the Visual Arts* (New York: Peter Lang, 2004), 208.
12. Consider these sentences from the conclusion: "In this court, impoverished events emptied of their substance were randomly thrown together, as in a bad student essay. The real marshal and the legendary marshal grew indistinct, like a fading photograph eaten by the light." Léon Werth, *Impressions d'audience* (Paris: Éditions Viviane Hamy, 1995), 146–47; my translation. Originally published as a series of articles in the newspaper *Résistance*, 1945.
13. Heuré, *L'Insoumis*.

14. December 12, 1940.

15. *L'exode* is what the French call it. It took Werth and his wife thirty-three days to drive from Paris to their country home, normally a five-hour trip. He describes the experience in *33 Days*.

16. This account largely borrows from my introduction to Jean Guéhenno's *Diary of the Dark Years*.

17. It was also agreed that France would pay Germany "the tidy sum of 400 million French francs [per day]" for the costs of occupying it. Allan Mitchell, *Nazi Paris: The History of an Occupation, 1940–1944* (New York: Berghahn, 2008), 14, citing German sources. Finally, the armistice signed with Italy two days later stipulated that Italy would occupy a good part of the Côte d'Azur.

18. Julian Jackson, *The Fall of France: The Nazi Invasion of 1940* (Oxford: Oxford University Press, 2003), 180. Estimates of the number vary; some historians put it much higher.

19. Jacques Debû-Bridel, who played an important role in the Resistance, quotes one of the first underground leaflets to appear in occupied France: "In 1940, France lived through two calamities: defeat and shame." Despite appearances, this summed up the sentiments of the majority, he affirms. *La Résistance intellectuelle en France* (Paris: Juillard, 1970), 15.

20. H. R. Kedward, *Occupied France: Collaboration and Resistance 1940–1944* (Oxford: Basil Blackwell, 1985), 2.

21. Philippe Pétain, *Discours aux Français: 17 juin 1940–20 août 1944*, edited and presented by Jean-Claude Barbas (Paris: Albin Michel, 1989), 60, 66. (My translation.)

22. Serge Berstein and Pierre Milza, *Histoire de la France au XXe siècle*, vol. 2, *1930–1945* (Paris: Éditions Complexe, 1991), 310.

23. Julian Jackson makes this point, *Fall of France*, 213.

24. Jackson, *Fall of France*, 32. He cites Pétain's testimony before the Senate Army Committee: "If any enemy attacked he would be pincered as he left the forest. This is not a dangerous sector." He also quotes General Gamelin, who said in 1937 that the Ardennes "never favored large operations." While David Chuter claims Pétain is often "selectively quoted" and "was not so obtuse as to imagine [the forest] was 'impenetrable'" (*Humanity's Soldier: France and International Security 1912–2001* [New York: Berghahn, 1996], 125), the full quotation shows he thought an enemy going through it would be caught in a very bad position indeed. At any rate, it is absolutely certain that the French generals were not expecting a German tank attack through the forest and were incapable of reacting quickly to it when it happened.

25. Jackson, *Fall of France*, 221. Jean-Pierre Azéma puts it succinctly: "Le haut commandement français fut au-dessous de tout." Freely translated: "The French high command was absolutely useless." *Nouvelle histoire de la France contemporaine*, vol. 14, *De Munich à la Libération, 1938–1944*, 2nd ed. (Paris: Éditions du Seuil, 1979, 1992), 57. There is ample contemporary evidence for this judgment in Claude Paillat, *Dossiers secrets de la France contemporaine*, vol. 5, *Le Désastre de 1940: La Guerre éclair 10 mai–24 juin 1940* (Paris: Robert Laffont, 1985). In his chapter on the decisive German breakthrough, a German military scholar outlines "The French Army's six fatal mistakes at Sedan," among them "neglecting the Sedan Sector," notably "the Gaulier Gap": ("One is . . . astonished to find not a single bunker at the most endangered point . . . [precisely] where the breakthrough was later located!"). Karl-Heinz Frieser with John T. Greenwood, *The Blitzkrieg Legend: The 1940 Campaign in the West* (Annapolis, MD: Naval Institute Press, 2005), 148. But these were mistakes in *preparation*; what followed was even worse.

26. For Marc Bloch, see his *Strange Defeat*, trans. Gerald Hopkins (New York: Octagon, 1969) (*L'Étrange Défaite* was written in 1940 and posthumously published in 1946 with five subsequent re-editions). For Charles de Gaulle in June 1940, see "The Call of June 18" in the appendix. It is a famous piece of rhetoric, but also a lucid analysis of the situation.

27. "The Moral Order" (*l'Ordre moral*) is one of the terms used to describe the Vichy government's cultural and "moral" program, the values it preached in its effort to control

the lives of the French people. It is one aspect of Pétain's "new order" (*ordre nouveau*). In his speech of June 25, 1940, Pétain announced, "A new order is beginning. . . . I am urging you, first of all, to intellectual and moral regeneration [*redressement*]." *Discours aux Français, op. cit.* p. 66. In April 1941 four members of Pétain's government sent Hitler a "Plan for a New Order in France," ending, "We beg the Führer to trust us." In Henry Rousso, *Un Château en Allemagne: Siegmaringen, 1944-1945* (Paris: Fayard/ Pluriel, 2012), 70-71. In August 1941 Pétain deplored the slow pace of "building, or more exactly imposing, a new order." *Discours, op. cit.* p. 166.

28. "The manpower of the German police force in all of France probably exceeded no more than 3,000 [in 1940] and was never to become far more numerous." Mitchell, *Nazi Paris*, 7.

29. There was also a technocratic side to Vichy—the various Metro companies in Paris, for example, were centralized into the RATP we know today—but this was not part of its cultural program. Robert O. Paxton's *Vichy France: Old Guard and New Order, 1940-1944* (New York: Knopf, 1972), which illuminates this dual aspect of Vichy, is still a classic; it revolutionized French studies of the regime.

30. Two choices may require some explanation. First, I have almost invariably translated *paysan* as "peasant," not "farmer." The difference between a French *paysan* in the 1940s and what comes to mind when we hear the word "farmer" is so great that I thought "peasant" gave a better picture of the truth. Second, I have kept Werth's use of gendered terms that today's writers might avoid (though rarely in French): *les hommes* ("men"), for example, when "humanity" is intended. Trying to avoid them would have occurred to no one in Werth's day, and I wanted to keep the sense of a "deposition" written at that time.

INTRODUCTION

JEAN-PIERRE AZÉMA, JULY 1992

If there is one kind of writing today's historians are insufficiently fond of using, it is the genre of the diary, those logbooks or family account books even more interesting when they are written in hard times, like this one. And it probably is not enough simply to publish them, since *Déposition*, which Grasset published in 1946, was neglected by practically everyone who was interested in this period, for whatever reason.

Now, this text by Léon Werth has an obvious interest for the specialist and the general reader both. First—and this is essential—its author, who died in 1955, hardly revised it at all. The journal had only been very slightly trimmed by Lucien Febvre, a longtime friend. Secondly, the diary covers the whole period of the dark years: it begins at the end of July 1940 and ends on August 26, 1944; the pages near the end on the liberation of the capital are written as an eyewitness report. Finally, the field of observation is not negligible. First, Saint-Amour, a village located in the Southern Zone in the region of the Jura Mountains, where the Werths owned a vacation home; Léon Werth took refuge there after thirty-three days of "exodus." There is also Bourg-en-Bresse, where he lived for several months in a hotel from which he took a few trips to Lyon; and finally Paris, where he regained his apartment on Rue d'Assas in January 1944. So there is diversity, but with a focal point—that town of two thousand souls that Werth scrutinizes, undresses, and dissects for almost three years.

The historical interest of his testimony is sustained by the pleasure of reading it. The humor is often ferocious, well served by a fine, tough, precise style—always lively: a style that avoids both boring lyrical flights and pedantry.

The diary is not written by a politician or an important man who wants to carve out his statue for eternity. The author does not have an ax to grind or a case to argue. But it is not a naïve piece of testimony either, the conventional life-of-a-simple-man-caught-in-turmoil. At sixty-two, Werth already had a creditable career behind him as an essayist, novelist, and journalist. He regularly contributed to magazines, particularly *Marianne*, a distinguished literary and political journal sponsored by Gallimard.[1]

Although the word "intellectual" probably would not have pleased him, that is how Werth must be classified, while giving the word a particular meaning: one of those intellectuals who do not exclusively contemplate their navel, who keep a completely independent mind, and who do not bow down to any intellectual or political chapel. The more we read him, the more we like to recall that in 1943 he was the one to whom Saint-Exupéry* dedicated *The Little Prince*.

He certainly needed all his independence of mind to live as an "occupied" man and remain so methodically tuned in to a France that was occupied itself, first partially and then totally. It was almost voluntarily that he became a kind of refugee despite himself, "reduced to a kind of idleness" and solitude. Until January 1944, he preferred to live apart, in his vacation home. And when he decided to regain his Parisian apartment, trusting the discretion of his concierge, he only went out at night and a suspicious ring at the doorbell made him climb, at the price of some acrobatics, down into the courtyard next door, which belonged to a Catholic youth center. The reason: Léon Werth was Jewish.

Born into a middle-class family in the Vosges, he considered himself what historians will call an assimilated Jew, perfectly agnostic. There is no trace of any Judeocentrism in this diary. Not that he denies his origins. Quite the contrary. When Vichy's second Statute Regulating the Jews is promulgated,[2] he writes, nobly:

> I'm going to Lons to declare that according to the terms of the Law of June 2, 1941, I am Jewish. I feel humiliated. It's the first time society has humiliated me. I feel humiliated, not because I'm Jewish, but because I am presumed to be of inferior quality because I'm Jewish. . . . I made my declaration at the prefecture. I threw out the word "Jew" as if I was about to sing the Marseillaise.[3]

But that is what explains why he is in hiding, counting on his wife: she returned to Paris and was able to go back to her activities as an interior decorator in

[1] Gallimard is the largest quality publishing house in France. *Voyages avec ma pipe* (1920) is a highly personal account of his travels across France, Holland, and other parts of Europe.

[2] The two Statuts des Juifs were anti-Semitic measures taken on Vichy's own initiative: Jews had to officially register as Jews and were excluded first from the liberal professions, the civil service and military, the media, and the like and then from all public places. Mass deportation to concentration camps came later, under German orders.

[3] July 9, 1941.

the Banque Nationale pour le Commerce et l'Industrie. She would cross the Demarcation Line thirteen times at her own risk.

Surprisingly enough, in this situation, the man was extremely well informed. As he had time on his hands, he was able to get a relatively precise idea of how the situation was developing in France and in the world. He regularly read the Lyon press, listened to Radio Nationale but also to the BBC; he caught the Gaullist programs on Radio-Brazzaville at least once, and sometimes Swiss radio; he was familiar with underground leaflets and "newspapers," particularly *Cahiers du Témoignage Chrétien*, from which he quotes many excerpts.[4] So we are not surprised that after a speech by Churchill, he could talk, precociously, about Auschwitz and the concentration camps.

Yet his "deposition" remains hard to analyze. He himself feels some difficulty in defining his position as a witness; he, who loathes lukewarm people, wavers between the pessimistic retreat, on the one hand, into a tower not of ivory but of books and paintings and on the other the wish to be useful and thus to get involved. But, perhaps because of his age, past disillusions, or even because of his lack of knowledge about resistance movements, he remains what he always was: a kind of unclassifiable sniper. In Paris he watches—through his wife—the actual work of what is apparently an effective escape network, and we can presume he helped out. But that is all. He is, in sum, a kind of committed spectator, whose ambivalence puts him in one of those many variants of the "wait-and-see" position to which today's historians have become very sensitive. What is certain is that he absolutely and continuously refuses to put what he knows is his talent at the service of Vichy—of what he calls Hitlerian fascism—as Emmanuel Berl did, for example, a writer to whom Werth can be compared in many ways.[5] As for him, he refuses to howl with the wolves.

We can call him a free man, a man whose skepticism keeps him at a healthy distance from anything that might tempt him. He was drafted in 1914, and his fifteen months in the trenches before he was discharged naturally made him an antimilitarist, just as his stay in Indochina in 1924 made him an anti-colonialist. Enthusiasm for the Bolshevik revolution and its revolutionary perspectives even turned him into a kind of fellow traveler, but during his two years as editor of *Le Monde* (Barbusse was the editor in chief) he became resolutely anti-Stalinist, reinforced in this by the imprisonment of Victor Serge.[6] He was deeply left-wing

[4] Literally "Notebooks of Christian Witness," an underground journal. *Témoignage Chrétien* was founded by a Jesuit priest in 1941 in Lyon. It was one of the first underground publications in France and denounced anti-Semitism and Vichy itself.

[5] Emmanuel Berl (1892–1976) was a well-known Jewish essayist, journalist, and historian. He helped write Pétain's speeches at the beginning of the Vichy regime.

[6] *Le Monde* was a left-wing journal (not to be confused with today's well-known daily) edited from 1928 to 1935 by Henri Barbusse (1873–1935), a Communist journalist and writer whose World War I novels, particularly *Le Feu* (*Under Fire*), are still read today. So are the novels of Victor Serge (1890–1947), a Russian revolutionary who died in exile.

because he was revolted by injustice and systematically anticlerical; one can see his libertarian reflexes without suspecting him of being a devoted anarchist for all of that. He can easily be classified among the nonconformists, but he belongs to none of the chapels of the thirties who were obsessed by what they called the established disorder. Some of them were to end badly. And we have not -reached the end of the list of what he rejects: he is profoundly irritated by the caste of parliamentary politicians, which sold out the republic; by the local dignitaries, great and small, whom he calls "the bourgeois"; and by pedants, semi-intellectuals, and all those who think they are cultivated because they passed the Baccalauréat.[7]

Did the war modify all his resentments? Certainly not all of them. For many of his enemies wallowed, bowed, and scraped before the occupier. The local dignitaries do not make his skin crawl any less after 1940 than before and politicians do not find more favor with him either, especially since they rallied to the regime—and how! Thus he calls someone like Bergery a "hideous little politician, spindly scum with no resonance whatsoever."[8] Nor does he forgive even the men who have gone to London with the Free French, finding in a former cabinet minister "the banality of clichés, the vulgarity of the voice"; he spots the ones who are trying to save their marbles, betting opportunistically on a third force in 1943 and thus in reality reinvigorating Pétain's French State.

But sometimes he is of two minds. First about the Catholics, for example. He suspects the Church hierarchy of serious wrongdoing, the worst ulterior motives, and attentively notes their small-mindedness and genuflections, whether before Pétain or others. But the multiple activities of Father Fanget in the Resistance and, still more, the writing in *Témoignage Chrétien* lead him to refine his judgment. In the same way, while Stalin remains "the Red czar" in his eyes, he recognizes him as "a true Marshal . . . the marshal of freedom" in December 1943. He admires the commitment of a ranking officer, Colonel Vendeur, while continuing to distrust the great majority of generals, and quickly sees in Giraud* "a swollen rural policeman."

He often returns to the idea that he does not want to become a living-room strategist and a fight-to-the-ender in bedroom slippers, but he now rejects all absolute pacifism. What irritates him the most is that "France is asleep," letting others wage her war for her: in April 1944, he lambastes "the petty bourgeoisie, just waiting for the English, the Americans, or the Russians or anyone who'll give them back the pleasures of the belly and freedom of comfort." That is why he is all for immediate action, indeed, for actions called "terrorist," and mistrusts

---

[7] The examination at the end of secondary school. Those who pass it are automatically admitted to the university.

[8] Gaston Bergery (1892–1974) moved from the anti-fascist left to the pro-fascist right. Vichy's ambassador to Russia and then to Turkey, he was tried for treason after the Liberation and acquitted. He remained an ardent Pétainist until his death.

"soft *Résistants*," the ones who "hope for deliverance through the evaporation of the Germans and an [Allied] landing in bedroom slippers."[9] That Jacobinism, which hardens week after week, likes to view itself as ultimately irenic. In 1944, Werth the nonconformist expresses the wish to see "Communists, Catholics, and a column of Paris cops all parading by." But he knows it will be harder to have better tomorrows than the statements you could read here and there suggest.

It is rather remarkable that Werth progressively becomes a Gaullist: we mean that what interests him is actually the personality of Charles de Gaulle. As early as September 1940, he is intrigued by that military man who is classified as a far-right royalist. Little by little, he feels increasingly drawn to him. Despite his general's epaulettes, he is cleared of any "pandering Boulangism," so much so that he affirms—and the comparison carries weight—that "the hatred some bourgeois have for de Gaulle is of the same order as the hatred that assassinated Jaurès" (August 23, 1943).[10] This, because he contrasts sharply with the old bunch of politicians and because he says aloud what he should say, without trickery and without half measures: "Could de Gaulle be the statesman who breaks with the diplomatic style at last, the style that puts a people to sleep?"[11] And, finally, he recognizes a quality in him that is far from negligible: he does not sell himself. "De Gaulle is distant—I was going to say discreet. He doesn't speak to the crowd but to a people."[12]

Conversely, Werth rages against everyone who thinks they are on the side of power. Against his colleagues, first of all, who have lost all dignity in his eyes: Giraudoux is a "pedant in disguise," Morand a "sequined nothing," Montherlant* "a Sciences-Po grad who wants to make us think he went to a whorehouse";[13] and as for Henriot,* "the timbre [of his voice] is coarse. A voice to sell dirty postcards with." And then, against the little political world. He did not know the Parisian collaborationists very well; he only became familiar with their press at the end of February 1944, which was also when he heard Hérold-Paquis,* one of the stars of Radio-Paris, for the first time:[14] "He sounds like an

---

[9] April 17, 1944.

[10] The ultranationalist General Georges Boulanger (1837–1891) was so popular during the Third Republic that he almost became dictator of France. Jean Jaurès (1859–1914), one of the great figures of French socialism, was assassinated because of his pacifism during World War I. His assassin was acquitted when the war was over.

[11] June 11, 1944.

[12] May 2, 1944.

[13] Jean Giraudoux (1882–1944) is generally considered the most important French playwright between the two world wars; Paul Morand (1888–1976) was a writer of some renown; and Henry de Montherlant (1895–1972), a novelist and dramatist still read and produced today. "Sciences-Po," the nickname of the Institut des Études Politiques, counts several French presidents among its alumni.

[14] Collaborators in Paris were more violently pro-Nazi than in Vichy, which explains Azéma's Germanized spelling further on.

agitated monkey, a monkey breaking words."[15] He is not much interested in him. All the more so as there is, in his eyes, no difference in the nature of the Paris Kollaborators and Vichy's collaboration—an attitude characteristic of his era. Indeed, he sees "Hitlerian fascism" in Vichy, a fief of the far right and specifically the henchmen of Maurras,* whom he utterly detests.

He states at the outset: "In principle, all governmental 'reforms' seem shameless to me, since two-thirds of France is occupied." He will ceaselessly denounce the "childishness" of Pétain's "National Revolution," a term he does not use. Behind its obsession with order, he quickly becomes sensitive to the growth of police repression—true, he overestimates the role of the Légion des Combattants, strictly speaking.[16] The Militia, for him, is composed of "Laval's SS." But it is Vichy in its entirety that horrifies him, its supporters in the media, its syrupy yes-men. He hates those sluggish ministers who like to think they're virtuous: Laval*, of course, too wily and deceitful not to bring the country to catastrophe, and above all Pétain, to whom he leaves the dignity of marshal but refuses to capitalize the word. In page after page, he denounces his vanity, his disastrous impotence, and regularly calls him a "sinister old man," a vain country policeman who swallowed his badge, the ghost of Papa Ubu.[17]

While systematically informing himself about world events, he uses his forced solitary exile to engage in conversations, to listen and note his observations. It is this double register—his gaze on the world and on his village—that makes this "deposition" a decisive document, irreplaceable testimony. He takes notes on everything—the chatter, the rumors, the speeches, and the reactions of every man and woman. Of course he chooses among them, but he does not change them.

There are, of course, masses of notations to be gleaned here about the Paris of 1944, about its sadness, its lassitude, its incontrollable rumors, and about the functioning of what seems to be—without giving us enough detail—an escape network. Or about the breathless days of the Liberation, strictly speaking. But the main part of his annotations concerns a small corner of the Jura region, Saint-Amour. It is a town of two thousand souls, which lives from agriculture but prides itself on a railroad station whose café is a refuge for our narrator (ah, the heat of the stove!), a precious source of information and the place—through

---

[15] June 6.

[16] This relatively benign organization, created in 1941, would evolve first into the more violent Service d'Ordre Légionnaire (SOL) under Joseph Darnand* and then into the pro-Nazi, militarized Milice Française, the Militia.

[17] Ubu is the grotesque protagonist of Alfred Jarry's farcical, proto-Dadaist play *Ubu the King* (1896).

the intermediary of railroad workers—for epistolary exchange.[18] It is a relatively active market town, with its four butcher shops, five grocery stores, and two pharmacies. The population seems to be rather left-wing and hardly influenced by the Church.

Werth listens to all of them; people trust him enough to talk in front of him, doubtless prudently but meaningfully. Note that the priest and the school-teacher are almost absent from these exchanges.[19] What he pays attention to is what a chair mender, Old François, and peasants of all conditions are saying. The feelings he has about them are, to tell the truth, ambivalent. His initial assessment is that at a time of complete intellectual breakdown, they have a kind of common sense, for "they have the sense of doubt." But little by little, he comes to wonder if they are not "going too far in what is purely material," and in the last analysis, he adds, "you can't progress like that." But that doesn't stop him from listening to them and talking with them. He is irritated by a common hostility: the resentment toward cities, against workers and paid vacations, and the certainty that "whatever happens, *they're* not going to die of hunger."

This said, he is very careful to note individual reactions: what he shows us is not "the peasantry" but individual trajectories. He is particularly concerned to understand "Laurent," a former tenant farmer who has rounded off his nest egg by becoming a small-scale dealer in farm animals. He goes to country markets and brings back the rumors. Laurent became a real Anglophile when he thought the Germans were going to confiscate his animals; after that, we see him much more wait-and-see because he trusts the Marshal[20] and because he is afraid of revolution—the Red one. But from the end of 1942 on, we can feel his hostility to the government, even if it is extremely prudent.

What everyone pays most attention to is, of course, food supplies, taxes, and requisitions. Léon Werth is a consumer: the question of prices opposes him to the peasants, who are suppliers. But they are all on the same side when it comes to tricking the inspectors and other bureaucrats—spoilsports, or rather, spoilfarms—and frustrating their raids, despite the letters of denunciation. Werth confirms that home-produced food and secret slaughtering of animals increased on the farms, and we see Laurent kill—without having fattened it—a 130 kilo pig, following a discreet, nocturnal ritual.[21] Necessity does not prevent the impression of culpability: when a calf's heart leaves

---

[18] Saint-Amour was in the "Free," or Southern, Zone, and correspondence with the Occupied Zone, where Werth's wife was working in Paris, was legally limited to prescribed formulas on postcards.

[19] Priest and schoolteacher were the traditionally influential figures in small towns, respectively on the right and the left.

[20] Since Azéma makes a point of Werth's not capitalizing "marshal," we have respected that as well as Azéma's capitalization of the word, unusual in English when separated from the name.—DB.

[21] 130 kilos is about 306 pounds.

stains on Werth's pants, he feels like an assassin. When the peasants think a tax is exorbitant, they simply go on strike, a strike of fowls brought to market, and this as early as December 1940. Besides, they more or less do whatever they want and soon engage in the gray market—the expression is well known—with normal prices (almost bargains!): country prices, in between the prices fixed by the government and the black market. Werth gives us points of reference: 1,000 francs for a goose in 1942, 200 francs a rabbit. Of course, as months go by and middlemen come in, prices soar: in November 1943, a pound of butter is traded at the train station café for 100 francs, in June '44—true, in Paris—a kilo of the same commodity is worth 850 francs (we recall that the salary of a skilled worker in the Paris region at that time is evaluated at 4,500 francs).

What strikes Werth is that aside from the game of dodging taxation and requisitions, the peasants—and the village as a whole—are "absolutely indifferent to everything the Vichy government says and does." Except for a few isolated cases, Pétain's "National Revolution" simply slides over them, and its hymns to the upstanding peasant find no echo whatsoever. We should probably take better stock of this indication in analyzing public opinion. And if there is any movement on this point, it is negative. Although he still admires Marshal Pétain, Laurent thinks 95 percent of the people are "against the government" as early as May '42. Two correctives must be added, however. First of all, *maréchalisme*, the cult of the Marshal, is still strong, and the government probably serves as a fuse when the current stops passing completely; and then, in the summer of '43, Werth notices that "they look down on the government but still respect its gendarmerie and its police." But we can feel these instruments of power losing their effectiveness too. As for the gendarmerie, it progressively cuts its losses: in '41, a sergeant sees fit to turn in a woman in town who listens to English radio, but in '43 we see two gendarmes who were supposed to arrest a work-draft dodger let him escape.

That's how life was progressively coded until the fall of '43. From then on, we enter another sequence: fear clamps down on the population. Fear of the occupying forces, which, however, entered the Southern Zone discreetly in November 1942 and only left twenty-odd soldiers in place, often young and inexperienced; they hardly bother the population. In 1944, with the rise of sabotage on the railroads and attacks on militiamen, fear of reprisals becomes intense; it is also a fear of arrest (Werth himself is very careful where he sets his feet at night) when the most committed men and women are captured. More than the Germans, people fear the Militia, who are downright detested, which is, when all is said and done, normal. They find no excuses for the few men who choose to strut around under the sign of the gamma so as not to go to Germany for Compulsory Work

Service[22] or to supplement their income. Ultimately, through letters, Werth will learn that the maquis occupied the village for almost two weeks; it would be recaptured by German forces because of the importance of the railroad station.

On the whole, the village has a wait-and-see attitude, but it develops in a way we may judge as positive. As for confirmed collaborators who support state collaboration and perhaps a little more, we can barely count twenty or so. Only four are openly active: a sergeant turned grocer, a pastry maker, a pharmacist, and a man who owns a hardware store. They are absolutely detested, all the more so as one of them is seen denouncing the mayor for his hostile attitude toward the regime, by means of an anonymous letter. We can sense heavy clouds rising, the settling of scores to come—but little by little: Werth is surprised the detested shopkeepers have not lost more than ten customers in all. Two of these collaborators will be taken away by the maquis; the women will meet various fates in town. Moreover, attacks against militiamen are reported regularly.

We can also see some rather spectacular about-faces, scorned as a general rule. But overall, this village behaves honorably despite its wait-and-see attitude, neatly confirming Pierre Laborie's hypotheses about public opinion.[23] Let us outline its development: the village was not absolutely hostile to Germany in 1940: German troops were "correct" and their discipline contrasted, for many people, with the messy debacle of French forces. Still, as early as September 1940, Werth notes that the village expresses a wish for the survival of the British. For it is less a question of Anglophilia than of Britainophilia, a point that must be emphasized. A Britainophilia that never fades, expressed particularly around the funeral of nine aviators burnt to cinders in their plane shot down by flak (November 1, 1942). According to an eyewitness Werth trusts, two thousand people attend the funeral: "The coffins were covered with flowers. Never have I seen so many flowers." Let us also note the great divide that marks the rebirth of hope that occurs after the success of Operation Torch.[24] And if the peasants are not sure what to think about the Compulsory Work Service, they nonetheless cover the Work Service evaders hiding out in the area. Later—and this observation is important because things are not necessarily the same in other

---

[22] The paramilitary Militia used the Greek letter gamma instead of the swastika as their emblem. The Compulsory Work Service—the Service du Travail Obligatoire (STO)—which obliged young men to go work in German factories was decreed in February 1943. As Germany and Vichy increased the quotas, growing numbers of young men, faced with the choice of either working in Germany or "disappearing," joined the maquis, the armed resistance groups in the countryside.

[23] In his *L'Opinion française sous Vichy* (Paris: Le Seuil, 1990), Laborie analyzes Prefects' reports on opened private correspondence (standard practice under Vichy) and concludes that widespread hostility to the regime began well before Germany seemed likely to lose the war.

[24] The Allied landing in North Africa, November 1942.

regions—if we are to believe Werth, they are favorable to the maquis, which will occupy the village and control it for ten days or so after June 7, 1944. For the maquis is theirs, not a foreign excrescence. All of which does not prevent the villagers from maintaining their trust in the Old Man for quite some time. And certainly this point distresses the narrator. Laval may be scorned, but Pétain remains a mythical figure, following a kind of reasoning typical of the Marshal's supporters: without him, it would be worse, and some people are ready to endow him with the virtues of playing a double game. How long does this trust in the Marshal continue? Werth notes that the first insulting inscription against him, "Pétain = sold out," appears in October 1942—graffiti in the urinal of the café at the railroad station.

On the whole, in any case, the village behaved well, with a few exceptions. Moreover, on November 11, 1942, some three hundred of them hold a silent demonstration in front of the War Monument; Werth stresses that these peasants "don't revolt," they calculate, they examine, they hesitate. But they refuse to be accomplices, even if there are a few letters of denunciation. Village solidarity against the outside turns out to be still more virulent against the occupier and creates a relatively protective circle around the people—peasants, and still more craftsmen, more or less on the left—who are actively committed to resistance.

Traces of the Resistance can be found, but not massively, which is to be expected. Reading this diary, we can easily make out what may be happening under cover. The first leaflet or paper Werth reads, called *Liberté*, quite likely appeared in August 1941, issued by one of the very first *mouvements de Résistance* of the Southern Zone, the one that will become one of the constitutive elements of *Combat*. After this, Werth will read texts from *Combat*, *Libération*, and *Franc-Tireur*, the major Resistance trio of the Southern Zone, and also a copy of *Défense de la France*, which was expanding its activities toward the south, and above all the *Cahiers du Témoignage Chrétien*, and even—passionately—the *Courrier du TC*. True, André Mandouze* is teaching literature in the higher classes of the lycée in Bourg, and he was not a man to remain inactive, even if he finally had to go into hiding.[25] There are few traces of the Communists in the diary (except for a leaflet); on the other hand, Werth observes that the card-carrying *Résistants* are socialists or close to it. While the town has a rather wait-and-see attitude—although it does lean to the correct side—the republic is still at home in Saint-Amour.

---

[25] Literally "Journal of Christian witness" and "Letters from CW." Bourg, the nearest city to Saint-Amour, was where Werth's son was a boarding student in the lycée (the secondary school).

What happens after an arrest is well known, and rumors go around about torture. Werth admires the action of those men. Which does not stop him from taking note of the criticisms he hears: people deplore their imprudence, vanity, and internal rivalries.

And everybody imagines they can see the light at the end of the tunnel; but the wait is long. This is a recurrent observation: "People are losing patience," he writes as early as July 30, 1942. After November 1942: "We thought it would all be over through enchantment, with a wave of a magic wand." Later, people begin to believe in Churchill's promise: France will supposedly be liberated before the leaves fall from the trees. In Paris, it is still worse: the dominant feeling, he says, is "weariness and disappointment." " 'Let them come quickly!' say the street, the concierge's lodge and the shop" (May 7, 1944). And in the spring, they even begin to express "a kind of resentment toward the Anglo-Americans, because of the postponed landing." By June 5, Werth himself is so weary that he indulges— and he notes it as a form of decline—in a game of solitaire!

"Will we forget the unbelievable atrocities, too? Yes, like everything else. What can we do so as not to forget?" he writes on August 22, in the midst of the Parisian insurrection. Put markers in your memory, but also give yourself the justification you need to be a committed spectator, not an actor. That is how Werth wrote this *Deposition*. Thanks to Lucien Febvre, his friend and neighbor, he has discovered, he says, what a bad historian might be: "His history is the defendant in a criminal trial. The bad historian is the judge." As for him, Werth is careful not to function in a Manichaean way. He is perpetually sensitive to ambivalences, and in February 1944 he could note:

> It seems to me collaboration and resistance are as different as black and white. And it's true that a few people found certainty deep inside themselves as early as June 1940. But how many have wavered! And it's impossible to know if they gave in to self-interest, to the pressures of propaganda, or if they were reeling from the shocks of the times.

He keeps this formulation of Febvre's in mind: "At the bottom of history, there are feelings." That quest for ambivalences, that complexity of portraits none-theless composed with such ferocious clarity, that weighing of all the elements, even those that can appear paradoxical in retrospect, is just what historians working on this period now look for. One of the great advances in French histo-riography is precisely the quest for the average Frenchman, the one outside the committed minorities, the one who had to experience both the Occupation and the constraints of an undemocratic emergency regime contrary to decades of republican spirit. That is what makes this text so singularly modern in all ways.

In the review he wrote in the *Annales* in January–March 1948, Febvre, always critical of his profession, wondered: "Historians . . . will they actually read these books?" He seemed convinced that this one would hardly be read. As we said, he was not entirely wrong, since this fine, extraordinary text had been forgotten. Congratulations to Viviane Hamy for having rediscovered it, with the complicity of Claude Werth, and offering it not only to historians but to all those who will read it with profit and pleasure.

ON *DÉPOSITION*

LUCIEN FEBVRE

I am going to surprise, nay, scandalize Léon Werth. But there you are, I can't do a thing about it, it's a fact: his *Déposition*—not the deposition of a Vichy minister or of one of Pétain's admirals, or of a diplomat playing both ends against the middle—his *Déposition* is an admirable historical document. And I know of few documents more precious in everything that has been published up to now on the France of 1940–1944.

Léon Werth, a historian: Shall I reveal a terrible secret? Will I confide to readers of this historical journal the last contact the author of *La Maison Blanche* and *Voyages avec ma pipe* had with the muse of history?[1] It was in Lyon, so long ago I do not want to recall the date. The Concours Général was in full swing.[2] The teacher broke the seals of the big envelope in front of the competitors and in a rather solemn voice announced: "Historical essay: The Estates General of 1614." It was very warm out, a lovely day. A swim in the river. Cut through the violent waters of the Rhône or float in the nonchalant waters of the Saône . . . How could one resist?

Léon Werth did not. On the fine sheet of paper he had been given, he copied out the topic like a good student. Drew a line beneath it. And in his large, clear handwriting, inscribed this lapidary text: "The Estates General of 1614 was a trivial little estates general of no importance whatsoever." Signed: "Léon Werth." This was his last contact with history.

Or so he thought. For I solemnly swear that this *Deposition* he has just published is a book of history, and a first-rate work of history at that.

---

[1] Both *La Maison Blanche* and *Voyages avec ma pipe* were republished by Viviane Hamy in the early 1990s.

[2] A nationwide competitive exam taken by the best lycée students toward the end of their secondary-school careers.

Among other things—for in this big volume there are so many riches!—two contrasting themes: the countryside and the war. The countryside, unfolding and folding again to the rhythm of the seasons, rolls up and unrolls its splendors and desolations and lives its natural life, completely indifferent to the suffering of the "occupied." And all through the book there is a series of often exquisite notations, never indifferent, thrown onto paper with an astonishing sureness of touch. Like colorful sketches. Except that Werth always shows himself in a corner of the paper. He cannot not put himself there. He does not set out with a light heart each morning on a disinterested hunt for images. Who in 1940, in 1941, in 1942, could have a light heart? Léon Werth notes things down—and then thinks, What's the use?

> The world outside. Beak to beak, two turkeys are fighting. Each of them eats the other's skull and squeezes his beak. They make a little warlike jump and lift up their heads again with a look of stupid indignation: "What d'you think you're doing . . . What d'you think you're doing . . ." They're ferocious and ridiculous.
>
> How beautiful the spring is! A faded black of Chinese silk overlaid with ash, ochre dust, and a dull whiteness, washed with all the bourgeois cleanliness of white. Nuances of batik, still more discreet and more precious. . . . But those pleasures—I no longer know where to put them. All this touches me—and suddenly, it seems to me that I'm mad.

A blank line. And then: "I'm civilization-sick the way you can get homesick. Am I going to die of this sickness?"

Thus, "Nature," as they say in the Sorbonne ("Compare the feeling for nature in the work of Léon Werth to the feeling for nature in . . .")—thus: Nature and War. The latter uniformly captured through Vichy spokesmen, London radio, and above all the rumors that rise from the neighboring village to the hermit's observatory. When he does not walk down "to town" to "make contact" with the natives . . .

Two themes, three milieus:

First, the observatory. Chantemerle, his country home. But it is merely indicated. Suggested by a word here and there. Never painted full-size, for itself. And in fact that is a pity.

Next, the town. The administrative center of the district, like all such district centers. With its church steeple. Its factory. Its town hall from the Restoration, in rather fine stone, so the building can be called a town hall. Its war monument, alas, and its esplanade planted with admirable linden trees. The traces of a military past, the past of a border village—stormed, sacked, violated, and burned twenty times over. About which, naturally, neither the two doctors, nor the two pharmacists, nor the two notaries, nor the justice of the peace and the registrar, nor the people of the shops that line the main street care at all.

The town, then. And thirty kilometers away, the administrative center of the *département*, Bourg-en-Bresse, since Werth does not hesitate to spell out its name in this journal. "That city of soft cheese," he writes, on a day of nausea. Indeed, one of the ugliest, gloomiest, and most boring. Bourg, capital of the fattened chicken, academy of the quenelle, temple of indigestion.[3] But joyless, since it has no wine, no vines, no winegrowers.

Now, in this setting, the two protagonists give each other their cues, the one who leads the game and the one who plays it: the observer and the subject, Werth and the Peasant. To whom I give a capital letter, for symmetry. But the capital letter is not capital. For Werth does not prostrate himself before the Peasant, that wonder, that incarnation of virtue.[4] He does not revile him either, nor abhor him. For him, he is a peasant, no more and no less. But Werth knows him well.

When I classify the themes, settings, and actors in this way, I am arranging things. And I am doing a great injustice to Werth, who does not arrange them. He has other things to do. He is at work. He sets up his easel outside or in, according to his moods and those of the weather. He paints Léon Werth and he paints the peasant. "If I write nothing here [in the country]," writes Guéhenno in his diary, "It's because outside of my work, my life in this village is completely empty."[5] He could say that because he only came to his village as a passerby, only for a few days of rest and inaction. Werth found himself pinned down there for a time he couldn't measure: he had to fill that emptiness in his life or perish. And examine himself, observe himself, take his temperature every day, and, in the absence of an interlocutor, talk to himself. Which he did.

And throughout the book there is a remarkable series of reflections in the margins of his readings, in the margin of the thoughts of a hermit to whom nothing people say is indifferent: from Pascal* to Saint-Simon,* from Voltaire to Bossuet,* from Diderot to Flaubert, he never stops seeking "that other world, which is man."[6]

---

[3] Thirty kilometers is about 18.5 miles. France is divided into administrative regions called *départements*, each headed by a prefect appointed at the national level. Bresse chickens are renowned in France.

[4] Vichy propaganda glorified the French Peasant and the Soil in contrast to the "decadent" cities.

[5] Jean Guéhenno, *Diary of the Dark Years, 1940–1944: Collaboration, Resistance, and Daily Life in Occupied Paris*, trans. David Ball (New York: Oxford University Press, 2014), 173. Guéhenno was on summer vacation when he wrote this.

[6] A phrase well known in France, from Rabelais's chapter on the education of Gargantua. The *Memoirs* of Louis de Rouvroy, Duc de Saint-Simon (1675–1755) are still read today. Proust loved them, and Werth quotes them often in this diary. Jacques-Bénigne Bossuet was a seventeenth-century bishop whose sermons and other writings are classics of French prose. Most of Werth's literary commentary has been cut in this edition, as has the rest of Febvre's sentence about it.

And what a critical mind, never satisfied on the cheap! A visit from Saint-Exupéry* to Chantemerle. Evocation of shared memories: "That restaurant in the Bois de Boulogne, where we had dinner together last year. How did we come to judge some of the men who were then leading France—in other words, cabinet ministers? We ascribed projects to them, a grand plan. And suddenly Tonio murmured: 'I think we're indulging in anthropomorphism.'"[7] Werth stops a moment. Smiles at his memory. Just a remark, a witty remark of the kind people used to make . . . But he adds immediately: "And now I'm betraying our friendship. One should not write down what was said. A double betrayal, for I'm turning a smile into a cut-and-dried thought, and I'm not reproducing the lightness of the evening, the lamps in the trees. . ."

I told you there was a historian in Léon Werth. But how many historians should ask him for lessons in critical thinking!

There is something else in this book, too. An unease that always analyzes itself. A sense of justice that ceaselessly feels the need to justify itself.[8] A distrust, an instinctive horror, a lucid hatred of commonplaces: "I distrust those who talk of *La France éternelle* all the time . . . If France is eternal in essence, all you have to do is stand there with your arms folded."[9] And elsewhere (October 21, 1940): "'France cannot disappear,' they say. It's not true. . . Like all figures on the earth, France changes and can die. . . . In how many centuries will a Germanized France be resuscitated? And who says it will be?"

Nothing is more moving than these extremely simple meditations on great, complicated problems: "When I saw a German regiment marching over French ground for the first time, near Montargis, that regiment insulted both my feeling for the nation and my internationalism. Both equally wounded. But I didn't know yet that under German occupation and Pétain's occupation, France would become a myth more distant and more elusive than internationalism."[10]

The homeland. Liberty, too. Which immediately evokes, in Werth's thought, the name of Michelet:[11] "We can understand the hatred for Michelet that all

---

[7] October 15, 1940.

[8] Thus on Pierre Pucheu,* see October 9, 1943; March 4, 1944; and March 21, 1944. On Marcel Déat,* this meditation, April 9, 1944: "What is he hoping for? Is he hoping for something? Is he slipping down a slope he can no longer climb? Perhaps, as all he got out of the university was a formalist culture, a mechanical intellectual agility. He plays with ideas like a child playing with jacks. Many men called cultured come to an ignominious end because they manipulated their ideas like boxes without having the slightest idea of their contents." Etc.—L. F.

[9] April 4, 1944.

[10] October 21, 1940.

[11] Jules Michelet (1798–1874) was a historian who was also a great writer, still read over a century after his death.

deniers of liberty feel for Michelet. For him, liberty is not a myth, it is France itself. They call him a poet or a rhetorician lost in history. They don't forgive him for having discovered the signs they use, signs they divert from their real meaning."[12] And this, which in fact sums it all up: "He invented Joan of Arc. That is the miracle. The miracle of Joan of Arc is Michelet's miracle. Who, before him, even talked about her?"

And thus the portrait of a man is drawn, with little touches, little pencil strokes, never premeditated, but attentive, moving ever closer to the true portrait. A man—a man in a tragedy. The person all of us were between 1940 and 1944, each in our own way, in those years of solitary meditation, of exaltation and disgust, of enthusiasm and nausea. With sudden temptations to give up everything . . . Does this mean "when Greece disappears, Hellenists remain"? Come on, let history run its course. Let history run its course. And avoid getting hit. Take shelter and "don't give in, that's all that counts."[13] "I was going to detach myself from the world. But Andrée François has come back from town: 'General de Gaulle spoke on the radio yesterday. He said the Italians were done for and the Germans would be done for soon.'"[14]

A translation of the speech not guaranteed by the government (especially not the government of that period). But it is enough to clear away the fog. To drive away the nightmare. To put to flight the devils that always prowl around hermits. And who was not a hermit, in those years when man had learned, once again, to fear man?

But above all, there is something else in Werth's book. Which, as far as I know, can be found only there. Something else, which for us, historians that we are, carries a singular weight. What is it? The peasant, the small craftsman, the village shopkeeper, and the humble folk of farms and market towns. With their slowness, their ruminations. The surprising susceptibilities of their protocol. Their inability to accept, for weeks and months, what does not immediately

---

[12] November 7, 1940.

[13] December 9, 1940.

[14] Werth, who has such little regard for contingencies and prudence, is careful not to dodge around the great figure of Charles de Gaulle. And his observations, as always, are original. And lucid. From the first, September 23, 1940: "What is General de Gaulle hoping for? . . . Is he a prisoner of his own resistance, of his first refusal? That is, of an attitude he decided on, but will govern all his decisions despite what happens?"—to the last, August 26, 1944, which ends the book: "De Gaulle is walking down the Champs-Élysées. A lapping of shouts and murmurs rises from the waiting crowd. When he appears, all those cries and all those murmurs fuse into one wave, hardly oscillating at all and filling the whole space between earth and heaven." But passing through many others—this one, for example, May 16, 1941: "General de Gaulle, England wins and you land in France. All we ask of you is a little genius."—L. F.

xxxvi   On *Déposition*

fit into the framework of their moral doctrine and way of reasoning.[15] But also their derisive irony. Their refusal to read what was written for their consumption. The strange disdain they show for the nice little dishes cooked up for them by Laval* or Otto Abetz:* they all boil down to the same thing.[16] The townspeople and still more the peasants make their own truths for themselves. Their successive Pétains. From Good Papa Pétain and his syrupy aphorisms to Daddy Defeat, a traitor and a killer. All that, drifting over the enormous sea of events with the slowness of an iceberg, while the Vichy regime is also evolving from inanity to cruelty, under the impetus of global catastrophes.[17]

In sum, a prodigious gallery of sketches, a magnificent collection of recordings made at the time, at the moment Werth takes them out of his collection so we can hear them. The little Bourg watchmaker in October 1940, talking about the war dispassionately. As if it did not touch him at all:

> He puts English victory and German victory on two pans of the scale. He doesn't try to tip the scales through prayers or wishes. . . . This isn't some unhinged intellectual talking, but a craftsman. . . . Zigzagging and badly informed, G's thought, craftsman though he is, resembles the specious dialectic [of] the Drieus* and Montherlants* of this world. "Germany is vacant, Nazism is vacant. They are all empty constructions. We can put whatever we want into them, we can put their opposites into them." . . . [However,] "I'm playing the German card," says a neighborhood squire to whoever will listen to him. An odd confession: he's playing cards with his country. . . . [But] from the town, this piece of news: "The people are saying there'll be a revolution."

[15] There is admirable lived material in *Deposition* to follow the evolution of the people's feelings about Pétain. At the beginning, the people construct the marshal they wished for—a good, disinterested tyrant. As for his ugly words, the people simply annul them. They repress the odious acts of his ministers: "The government," Laurent says as he loads manure onto a wheelbarrow, "Maybe the government agrees with de Gaulle. It's trying to fool Germany." And when Werth protests: "Not Laval, of course, but the others" (December 12, 1940). There are countless passages showing how shameful acts are dumped onto Laval. (See, for example, December 4, 1940)—L. F.

[16] For example: "The papers are full of 'the indignation aroused in France' by the bombing of Marseilles by English planes. A farmer is laying manure on his field. Hardly have we exchanged a few words about the wind and weather: 'The planes in Marseilles,' he tells me, 'were Italian planes disguised as English. That's what they're saying in town and it wouldn't surprise me a bit'" (November 27, 1940).—L. F.

[17] On its inanity: "Young people are asked to pick chestnuts. The regeneration of France through Aunt Annette's recipes." "Agricultural technique: it is forbidden to kill a pig weighing less than a hundred kilos. Forbidden to feed potatoes to pigs. 'We'll fatten them up on clear water,' the peasants say" (October 17, 1940). Or, "Vichy, neglecting the regeneration of our souls for the day, turns its attention to our bellies and advises us to pick acorns" (November 23, 1940).—L. F.

And Werth notes: "They don't say: 'We'll make a revolution' but 'There will be a revolution.'"[18]

For a long time, morons kept stubbornly repeating like angry turkeys: "Neither German nor English: French." Hypocrisy or stupidity? In April '41, the phrase was still reappearing. A phrase fit for the brains of Legionnaires.[19]

I cannot go on with this presentation of the book. At the end, the whole journal would go into it. I will simply say that through its admirable sincerity, the probity of a logic that surrounds all the facts, all the people, all the talk—reported exactly, without dressing it up or filling it out—through the constant care it takes to interpret peasant reactions correctly and sensitively, *Deposition* is one of the most direct and precious pieces of testimony historians can find to reconstruct the development of people's thinking in one corner of France from the nauseating time of the stagnant Armistice to the great year of the Liberation.

Werth did not, unfortunately, see it rise in the sky of the town, at the reddish gleam of village fires over there in Bresse. At the edge of that sinister meadow where seventeen patriots fell under German bullets during the night of June 24. One of them was called Marc Bloch.*[20]

Historians . . . Will they actually read these books? I am afraid they will come to them with a satisfied smile—the smile they put on when they explained to us—to us, who haven't understood a thing—that France of 1900 they draw with features none of us had ever seen. What strange picture of "Occupied France" will they draw for us in their textbooks? The real one dragged itself painfully along over a terrain constantly furrowed with new borders, constantly dotted with new ruins—a France that month after month rose one day and fell the next, a little lower, and began its depressing march again. The France that said, with that woman quoted by Léon Werth (October 8, 1941): "If I had the slightest doubt, it would be all over for me. But I don't have any doubt and everything is still solid inside me . . ." That France, the real one—they will have to go to *Deposition* to find it.

---

[18] September 29, 1940.

[19] Parisian collaborationists created the Légion des volontaires français contre le bolchévisme (LVF) on July 18, 1941, with the approval of the Occupying Authorities. Some seven thousand French volunteers would eventually join a regiment of the Wehrmacht to fight on the Eastern Front.—J.-P. A.

[20] With Lucien Febvre, the medieval historian Marc Bloch founded *Les Annales*, the influential historical journal where this review of *Déposition* first appeared.

PREFACE

This is the preface Werth wrote for the 1946 edition of Deposition, *published by* Grasset.

All you'll find in this book is little notes and ruminations from the time of the Occupation. I responded to stimuli that came to me from the newspaper or the radio. I noted what I heard people saying in town and on the farms. Often in total solitude, I struggled with the gravest problems. As if this were my profession. I gave in to a trend that is already out of fashion and noted down a few dreams as well. I retained tiny things, things to be forgotten, slight feelings. Today, if I confront that attention to my "self," it seems indecent to me. But I knew almost nothing about the torture bureaus and the extermination camps.

I have not cut the passages where I spoke harshly of writers who have died since then.[1] My judgment or my bad mood did not concern what they did but what they wrote. There is nothing they could do to win me over if they were alive today.

A strange mixed pudding. I corrected nothing in it. It would have been too easy to add touches when it was all over, emphasize my premonitions, and erase my mistakes.

This explains many uncertainties in the diary. Others, too, will recognize themselves in them. This explains the importance given to insignificant facts. It explains this or that opinion about Germany at a time when I knew nothing of its atrocities.

It explains the dry tone of these notes, written without taking care to perfect them. Thus, on Antoine de Saint-Exupéry, the simple notes of a datebook, unrevised. So don't be surprised if you don't see him here, immobilized in "the perfection of death." Don't be surprised to discover nothing here of a sorrow that will never heal.

---

[1] Many of these are cut in the present edition, as are all of Werth's dreams, with one exception.

1940

A market town. The Free Zone. Between the Jura and the Ain.[1] Three weeks have gone by since we learned of the Armistice.

It's a market day. Not many animals. But the souk is just as it always is on a fine summer's day. The sun is licking the canvas covers of the stands and turns the shirts, cotton dresses, and back braces into magnificent "items."

I ask about the hidden reasons for what happened. "Well . . . I mean . . . what happened?" I ask a local squire—landed gentry. He answers unhesitatingly: "We were sold out." "By whom?" "By whom? By the government, by Daladier* . . ."

But a retired general, one of his friends, heard our brief conversation and relieves my uncertainty with a broader explanation: "It's all because of the automobile and the wireless." I suppose he's accusing mechanization and the whole modern world. But Germany, too, was infected with automobiles and radios.

Two minutes later, a road worker points to the general: "They say he's in the Fifth Column."

"It was a setup. That's what they wanted," the butcher tells me, "To prevent revolution."

"The English," says an old lady, a Parisian who took refuge in the town, "the English are selfish and treacherous . . . General de Gaulle is just pretentious." The first time I heard the name of General de Gaulle I was still in Paris, when he was called up by General Weygand.[2] I was in Montargis at the beginning of July when I learned, through an issue of the morning paper (*Le Matin*) written by the *Kommandatur*, that he had been "dismissed because of his attitude and should

---

[1] The Jura and the Ain are *départements* (administrative divisions) in southeastern France; the "market town" is Saint-Amour, in the Jura mountain region, not far from the Swiss and German borders.

[2] A mistake: Prime Minister Paul Reynaud appointed de Gaulle undersecretary of defense on June 5, 1940. General Maxime Weygand, who was instrumental in surrendering and signing the Armistice with Germany, distrusted him.—J.-P. A.

1

be tried by a military tribunal." I'm not sure what details I put together, or what breaking news I heard to form an image of General de Gaulle in my mind.

Alone, a captive in our summer home.

I'm getting to know the Empire clock under a glass cover. Its face is surrounded by a strange gilded construction: columns ending in sphinx heads, cherubs carrying palms, an eagle with wings outspread, and swans drinking in a fountain with three basins. Very surrealist. It rings out hours from former times. Its timbre is reminiscent of small church bells and music boxes from old albums or dancing dolls.

I take refuge in my room, like zoo animals in their little den.

Old house, old library. All of Voltaire, all Rousseau, all Balzac.

I read Voltaire in the evenings. His octosyllabic verses aren't always very amusing. Acrobats in prosody have done better since then. However, there's this:

> The kindly strumpet had a lay
> With an actor in the play
> Who got her pregnant in the wings.

Chantemerle (literally "sing, blackbird"), the country house on a hill outside Saint-Amour where Werth wrote most of *Déposition*. *Centre de la Mémoire, Médiathèque Albert-Camus, Issoudun*

I'm not sure he's as mediocre a philosopher as people have said. True, he doesn't swim around in systems. He measures their every centimeter. But he has flashes. When he makes fun of theoretical debates on liberty, when he makes fun of the faculties of the soul—already—when he says (in the *Philosophical Dictionary*, I think), that there is no such thing as man's thought or man's will, but only men thinking and men wanting, isn't he anticipating the "concrete psychology" of recent years?

A visit to the R——s. An old family, where they like traditions. The men farm, and not always disdainfully; they're officers, and sometimes priests. A provincial family, which does not like to think the world is mutable. All the women are pious, but the grandfathers were often Voltairians.

I had every reason to believe that in this conservative, patriotic milieu, they would be crushed by France's misfortune and at least wouldn't take it lazily, as an effect of this or that policy or of fate. All of them, young and old, felt sorry for our skimpy meals, our fatigue, and the danger we were in during the "exodus." But our astonishment at the debacle appeared to them a prehistoric sentiment.[3] Our sadness was foreign to them. They had accepted the event, as if it belonged to the oldest collection of historical facts. They merely expressed their satisfaction that the small town near which they lived had not resisted the Germans and had not been shelled. And Madame R—— didn't hide her feeling that selfishness had always been the dominant trait of the English.

I felt like a traveler who'd come back from China after a ten-year absence and expressed pity for a dead man long forgotten.

September 6

Fear has been resolved. Into acceptance, even attraction. The German has become a magician, who possesses the secret of order. I remember that Rauschning has Hitler say, "The petit bourgeois Frenchman will greet me as a liberator."[4]

In a first-page headline in big capital letters, a Lyon evening paper speaks of "Hitler's generosity."

But some people have the feeling that a whole civilization is threatened with shipwreck. A professor in Lyon whose whole life was spent in the peace of archaeology and never had the slightest involvement in politics is wondering if he shouldn't think of leaving France and settle in North America with

---

[3] The "debacle": *la débâcle* was the word commonly used for the rapid defeat of May-June 1940.

[4] The exact quotation is: "I'll enter France as a liberator. We will present ourselves to the French petit bourgeois as the champions of an equitable social order and eternal peace." Hermann Rauschning broke with the Nazi Party, went into exile, and published *Gespräche mit Hitler* (*Conversations with Hitler*) in Switzerland; it was immediately translated into French.—J.-P. A.

his wife and children. He probably hasn't reserved cabins on the Compagnie Transatlantique. It was not a firm plan, it was only the last recourse of a worried thought, confided to a friend. But what a sign of the turmoil of these times!

"We don't even know," a peasant tells me, "what country we're in . . . We're like animals . . . We wake up in the morning without knowing anything about the world."

"Alas!" I said, "my lord, there are times when it is not easy to know what the nation wants . . ."
    "At these sorry signs, several foreigners thought we had fallen into a state similar to that of the late Roman Empire, and serious men wondered if the national character would not be lost forever."—Alfred de Vigny,* *Servitude et grandeur militaires* (*The Warrior's Life*)

I climbed through the woods to the top of the plateau. Before me, I have the panorama of the plain. But the slope of the meadows is gentle. So the plain doesn't seem to be down below, but begins where I stand. You'd think someone threw it out to the horizon the way you throw out a party streamer. It breaks the panoramic boredom, the "picturesque view."

SAINT-AMOUR (Jura). — Vue générale prise du Mont d'Amour.

A parish priest wanders outside Saint-Amour in the prewar years. Werth would have enjoyed this view of the town and surrounding countryside on his own walks. *Author's collection*

I stretch out on the grass. I have forgotten the war. But a plane passes overhead, German or Italian. Before the war, they didn't fly over me without permission. Now, they're watching me.

The peasants are immunized against the newspapers and the radio. They have the sense of doubt and build their passions slowly. As for the news, sometimes they catch it in the air like signs of rain or fine weather. They know the fate of France is being played out on the Thames.

News—true or false—comes into the town from Chalon or Besançon. The town is beginning to realize that German victory has more effects than soldiers passing through on military exercises. The town, now, is making a wish for England.

That's the way it is: France is making wishes. It expects nothing more of itself. It's choosing between England and Germany the way a bettor chooses a horse.

And me, what can I do but ruminate vaguely?

The press in Lyon comments docilely on the government's themes—that mix of Nazism and rustic romanticism.

A day laborer is sentenced to six months in prison for defeatist talk. I would like to know the legal definition of defeatism in this month of September 1940.

I get a letter "opened by the supervising authorities."[5]

A few Chateaubriants* write in the newspapers of the *Kommandatur*. I hope, since they're paid by our German masters, they show some indulgence for those French writers who are inspired by Stalin: at least he didn't have two-thirds of France under his boot.

We expected that whatever the government might be, above all it would declare itself provisional and continue in a reserved, modest way until peace came. But this one is imposing its partisan passions on us, dressing them with the rejects of fascism.

France is like a factory destroyed by fire. Everything has collapsed. Only the little janitor's apartment is intact. The concierge lives in it and watches over

---

[5] "Postal and telephonic supervision" was carried out beginning in the fall of 1940 by an official agency of the Vichy government. It was used for government surveillance of individuals and for checking on public opinion.

the ruins. But he has gone mad: he doesn't merely drive away looters and people stealing metal. He imagines he's the master of the factory. He pastes memos and pastoral letters to the workers on his windows, and keeps a careful watch over a time clock that no longer registers arrivals or departures. Such is the marshal.

Lucien Febvre* is my neighbor in the country. His two giant cedars now give him only a pleasure mixed with bitterness. Enclosed in a hollow of the undulations that lead gently up to sharper peaks, his house is no longer an inviolable refuge for him. It is invaded by history—and not through archives. He is accustomed to reconstituting history. But it's happening around him, all by itself. Perhaps he resents historical scholarship for not giving him a key to what is happening. In fact, he doesn't need a key. The righteous anger of the mountain peasant is enough for him. The anger of a historian too, for whom history was never a botanical classification, but the pursuit of a certain physiology, or you might say of poetry. I have seen him extract life out of old stones. And also from an old brochure. He was holding some local 1840 monograph or other in his hand. The author was studying the marble industry in the department of the Jura in a style that was academic but rang true. From this poor little text for a provincial academy, Febvre magically made a whole bourgeoisie appear, proud of itself, proud of having enough money and landed possessions to vote, rich in principles and rich in land.[6]

Old François[7] is perhaps the last of those craftsmen Vichy talks about so much. He makes chairs and armchairs and weaves the straw on their seats. His workshop, long and narrow, is in an alley. He uses a primitive lathe; his father used the same one. I can't describe this machine, halfway between a weaver's loom and a knife grinder's wheel. But it doesn't look anything like industrial machines.

No power on earth will reduce Old François to silence unless it kills him. Not that he talks a lot. He says what he has to say. Nothing more, nothing less. He's the one who measures the dosage and not the powers that be.

He learned to read at the Christian Brothers School (there was no other in the district at that time). I don't know what he learned since then. Less than Lucien Febvre, most certainly. They say he only reads last year's newspapers. That establishes a certain analogy between Lucien Febvre and Old François. For reading last year's papers is already the technique of a historian.

---

[6] Property and financial requirements to vote were gradually abolished in the course of the nineteenth century.

[7] A chair maker in Saint-Amour, "Old François" is a recurrent character in this journal.

Normal schools for schoolteachers abolished.[8] It's as clear as the nose on your face. It is true schoolteachers taught too many raw facts. But to consign them to the degenerate humanism of the Baccalauréat, to want them to be similar to those lawyers and doctors who think they're cultivated because they've brilliantined their mind the way women get their hair curled at the coiffeur's!

All *Le Progrès* talks about is family and country.[9] An amplification of the Bac, coating the fascist drug with traditional morality.

It's not surprising that a journalist should work on mass-produced, imitation ideas, interchangeable and reversible. But never have governments been philosophical to this degree, never, at least, have they used the dregs of philosophy so impudently.

No postal communication between the two zones. What do the Germans mean to do? Break us apart? Decompose the country? That and more. The time for wars of pure conquest has passed. Germany wants to convert other nations. To dominate the world is only the old dream of a pygmy. Germany wants to reduce the world to just one substance.

I'm told a civil servant in the Occupied Zone was dismissed for masonic Judeo-Catholico-Marxism. It's more than just a joke. It doesn't matter if the ideas are true or false, contradictory or not. To connect them, all you need is a hyphen.

If General de Gaulle ever landed in France, what a destiny! Storybook images: General de Gaulle lands in Cherbourg or lands in Calais. France awakes. The men of Vichy run away and hide in cellars. Or, hoping to stave off the victory of the people by doing this, they bring him the keys of France.

He's politically on the far right—a royalist, I've been told. So what? Everything has been turned inside out. He returns from London and brings France back to France. Whether he will or not, he is the man of a whole people, the man of history. He saved France and whatever remained of civilization and humanity

---

[8] The "Écoles normales primaires" were thought to be bastions of secular education that supported the republic Pétain had abolished. Henceforth, future schoolteachers would simply have to pass an exam, the Baccalauréat (the "Bac"), at the end of their years in lycée (secondary school). The Bac is the only degree French lawyers or doctors must earn before law or medical school.

[9] *Le Progrès* was, and still is, the major newspaper of Lyon and its region. It stopped publishing when the Germans occupied the "Free Zone" in November 1942 and resumed publication when France was liberated. Next sentence: "the Bac" is short for the Baccalauréat; see Translator's Introduction.

in Europe. What he wished for happened. And what happened is greater than he could have imagined. He had carried within himself a tough, secret will, conceived when the disaster was beginning.[10] It was only the will of a military man then. And then his victory would only have been a general's victory. But when the flight of soldiers on the roads ended, we saw France flee itself. We no longer knew where France was. He lands in Cherbourg, or he lands in Calais. Did one ever see such a contact between a man and a crowd?

But isn't this hoping for a miracle? What if England collapses tomorrow; if, tomorrow, Europe is Germanized for twenty, thirty, fifty years, or a century? And not even Germanized in the old sense that we could give this word twenty years ago. And not even militarized. For military discipline has its limits. Tomorrow, perhaps Europe will be nothing but a machine to make chemical products and synthetic men.

What is General de Gaulle hoping for? Looking at it coldly, does he think English planes will defeat Germany? Or is he persevering so as not to betray himself? Is he a prisoner of his own resistance, of his initial refusal? That is, of an attitude he decided on, but will now govern all his decisions whatever may happen? He did not want France to deny itself, but hasn't he been carried away since then by the sole obligation of not denying himself?

September 24

De Gaulle in Dakar.[11] Shelling of Dakar. The foreign minister declares: "General de Gaulle is a traitor."

Reading the paper is becoming intolerable. I get exhausted reading British and German communiqués. They work on me the way the announcement of a number in roulette works on a gambler. The number of German planes shot down always seems weak to me. I have the same impatience as when I'm vainly striving to destroy an ant's nest. And I whirl around in space on board every English plane that's shot down.

I'm disappointed. I was expecting the complete destruction of Berlin. So here I am, just like the café strategists and the gung-ho patriots of 1914? I won't dissimulate the analogy, I'll confront it: it's a false analogy. I only accuse myself for a moment in order to be scrupulous. If anyone accuses me, his sophism won't disturb me at all.

Sometimes I feel sorry for the Germans as much as for the peoples under their boot. But the Germans don't know they should be pitied.

---

[10] "The disaster" (*le désastre*) was another word in use for the defeat of May-June 1940, along with the still more common *débâcle*.

[11] Free French naval forces supported by a British squadron arrived off Dakar on September 23 to make sure French Equatorial Africa was won over to the Free French and obtain the backing of

What if Europe is Germanized? All would be lost, the main thing lost, but the main thing only makes a slight difference. When Hitler gives bread to the crowds, will they suffer a lot because they don't have the right to read Spinoza since he was Jewish? Between freedom and oppression, there is only the difference between pure air and polluted air. But the people Hitler drives out, strips of their belongings, or tortures? They'll just die, like others who are already dead and forgotten. Oppression will be stabilized. Over half of humanity won't even feel it.

They threshed corn last night. Threshing means freeing the *panouille*, as they say here, the ears of corn, and only leaving two or three husks in order to hang them up. Once the ear of corn is stripped, its grains look polished, like ivory.

After which, following the tradition, we ate a rustic cake at the farm, raised dough made of flour and eggs. But it wasn't merry like other years. We talk of restrictions, food rationing cards, and the price of butter: not one block of butter to be found in the market, but it's sold clandestinely in stables, under the sheds.

City people amuse me when they claim they know "the peasant." They think he's a naïve, sly animal. They judge him by his language. But they don't really understand that language. The ideas of city people slide one after the other, like marbles. The important thing is to keep them rolling. They wrap themselves in ideas like a smoker in his smoke. But a peasant's idea is one of those bridges made of logs thrown over a stream. The trunks aren't squared off. Your foot slips on them. You have to approach it carefully. Someone who builds those footbridges doesn't think about the beauty of viaducts and general ideas. It's made to walk over, and that's it. Someone who walks over it doesn't give a hoot about the gracefulness of acrobats. Hence the stubbornness of peasants and the difficulties of convincing them by using the methods of the city.

September 25

Sophisms against freedom. Freedom to starve, etc. We needed a proof of freedom. We were breathing, without thinking about it, an air with particles of freedom floating in it. Now we have a proof through asphyxiation.

"Today it is fashionable to claim that geometers and metaphysicians inspired the nation with a disgust for arms, and if we were beaten on land and sea, it is obviously the fault of philosophers or scientists" (Letter from Voltaire to the Maréchal de Richelieu, from Geneva, June 22, 1762).[12]

French West Africa, but the Vichy governor ordered troops to fire on the Gaullist plenipotentiaries, and the Anglo-Gaullist squadron had to leave without accomplishing its mission.—J.-P. A.

[12] Vichy propaganda claimed the fall of France was due to "decadence" and the national spirit had been sapped by intellectuals.

If Hitler weren't powerful, he'd be laughable. Hitler's ideas aren't even popu-
larized ideas, they're advertising slogans. It's like pharmaceutical advertising.
It couldn't care less about physiology or pathology, couldn't care less about
patients' health, and creates kingdoms of commerce and industry. The teaching
of medicine given over to poets selling Quintonine . . . The number of diagnostic
mistakes is decreasing. For they don't make diagnoses anymore. They're through
with the mistakes of freedom.

A Paris policemen is here on leave. "People are discontented." "With what?"
"With the government." "Who's complaining?" "We don't really know . . . the
Communists . . ." "What are they saying?" "We have no way of knowing."
    On one point, he was clear and precise: he recognized one of his comrades
in a German officer's uniform, a man who had served in the police for years in
the same arrondissement as he did, a policeman like him. He thinks he wasn't a
German spy but a French traitor. "Did he speak to you?" "No . . . He acted like he
didn't recognize us."

September 26

Solitude. In the mornings, the countryside is closed off by the fog. Solitude
without the diversions of the city. A prisoner's solitude, almost. A self shut
in a house. The non-self is the war and nothing but the war. I'm alone with
the war. What reaches me from the outside world is the war or depends on
the war. The farmers, at least, keep taking care of their animals and picking
potatoes.

Vichy wants to regenerate France. Back to the land, family, morality. Regenerate
France with Bac-level clichés. For they don't even know the fine language, the
impressive periods, the toga style of the bourgeoisie in 1840.

The burn of Pascal,* the tenderness of Corot, the sharpness and emotion of
Stendhal, relativity . . . are you really sure you would agree to die for that?

Dakar. Possibility of a civil war. De Gaulle or Vichy. But do the French want to
choose? And what if Germany occupies all of France?

If old women are less afraid under the bombs in London than in Berlin, that
would be enough, England would have won.
    The peasants say: "They don't tell us everything . . . If the English and de
Gaulle left like that from Dakar, if they went all the way over there and left like
that . . . it's because they're stupid bastards . . . I don't believe it."

"Why were so many people for the Germans in August? It's simple. When the French soldiers came through, what'd they look like? . . . A shoe on one foot, a slipper on the other. They came to my farm. They requisitioned straw and they spoiled the haystack. They were taking advantage of my wife being all alone, they didn't leave a requisition voucher . . . Besides, they took whatever they could, little things or whatever . . . Didn't really ask and didn't even say thanks. OK, I know . . . They weren't in their right minds . . . But the Germans came through two days later. Nicely dressed, nice and clean. And they didn't do anything wrong . . ."

"Why're they only fixing the prices for our butter and eggs? Do they set the price of plows? And the cloth merchant selling a meter of cloth for eighty-five francs and last month it was twenty-eight francs? Don't tell me he got new supplies . . . The cloth was moth-eaten. And the hardware dealer, who raised the price of his stoves? He had them in the store. He couldn't have got them from Chalon. Why only us?"

They've gotten rich since the last war. But we forget that thirty years ago, not one of them had enough to eat.

"We know less about the economy of the seventeenth century," Lucien Febvre tells me, "than that of any other era of French history."

If all historians revealed their ignorance, how much more we would know!

September 29

Sunday in Bourg-en-Bresse. Buildings of the military government. A soldier in front of a sentry box presents arms to an officer. With remarkable mechanical precision and an admirable, intimate knowledge of the handling of weapons. France only has a ghost army now, but they haven't forgotten to teach this ghost to honor the hierarchy.

Newspapers are posted in a shop window. French culture won't die of starvation: it has at its disposal the *Journal de la Femme*, *L'Alerte*, *Candide*, and *Gringoire*.[13]

People who used to be called the conservatives in times past at least had a positive plan: to conserve good guaranteed incomes and good morals. But in between the two wars, they felt these possessions were already slipping out of their hands. They were led to a kind of revolution, which is only permanent

[13] Heavily ironic. First, *The Woman's Journal*; next, *The Alert* (or *The Warning*) was a magazine founded by Vichy to spread its propaganda; *Candide* was an anti-Semitic, far-right weekly with articles on culture and politics, often by well-known intellectuals; *Gringoire*, which had been a pacifist weekly of some quality, turned anti-Semitic before the war and pro-Vichy during the Occupation.

repression. And so the world war veterans confused the doctrinaires, whose knowledge consists only in turning textbook history upside down, with people who were barking vulgar patriotism or purity. As if the war, unfortunately, bestowed veterans with any other distinction than having fought or claiming to have fought. The doctrinaires and the barkers were led to Hitlerism and regeneration by the police. The brutality of events threw the scholastics off their syllogistic perches. Out of sadism or masochism, they gave in a little more every day. Maurras* called Mussolini a man of genius shortly he entered the war.

At the beginning of the Popular Front,[14] the crowd was just waiting to be catalyzed. The Stalinists decomposed it. The tactical politicians of temperate socialism put in place their lackeys and those strange hybrids who were both Radical-Socialist and Stalinists. The occupations of factories had the same effect as they did in Italy before the march on Rome.[15] Those occupations frightened and simultaneously reassured the forces of money. They showed that the crowd was only the chorus in an opera and all the best scholars and laborers can do when they unite is pray together.

September 29

For once, a rather amusing bit of news. R—— has just been dismissed. Before the war, he worked in the cabinet of a moderate minister, and then in the cabinet in a ministry of the Popular Front. Then became a hardline Stalinist. The debacle . . . He gets Vichy to give him a sinecure. But in this month of September, Vichy finally finds out about his past and dismisses him. This dismissal is a break in the line of his career and his character. I'm disappointed. I thought he'd have the gift of erasing his successive political pasts all his life. I thought he was a more skillful Proteus.

From the town, this piece of news: "The people are saying there'll be a revolution."

They don't say: "We'll make a revolution" but "There will be a revolution."

Hitler, a monster of insensibility. Insensible like those hysterics who can imitate all the emotions but feel none. That frigidity facilitates both pride and

---

[14] The Socialist-Centrist-Communist coalition that governed France from 1936 to 1937 and introduced social security (general health insurance) and paid vacations. It was a time when workers occupied factories with sit-down strikes to demand reforms.

[15] The "Radical-Socialist Party" was neither, but centrist and moderate. Mussolini's march on Rome with his "blackshirts" brought him to power in October 1922.

action. You kill Röhm, you kill social democrats, communists, Jews. You torture in the prisons and the camps. Thus the march on Vienna, the conquest of Czechoslovakia, and the conquest of Poland were perhaps only Hitler's Don-Juanism, never satisfied.[16]

I am told that during the war of 1914, Hitler was examined for psychic blindness (that is, without lesions, hysterical blindness). And the doctors who examined him still wonder if Hitler was a hysteric or a malingerer or both at once.

In modern Western Europe before Mussolini and Hitler, people in power were intimidated by the scientist, the artist, or the writer. Think of the relative freedom France didn't dare refuse to give several unorthodox authors during the war of 1914. Power respected the mysteries of the intelligence. Around 1900, even if the re-enlisted non-com bullied the "smart guy," the student, he feared he could cast some spell.

Hitler is not intimidated by speculative intelligence. You can't even say he scorns it. He nullifies it, he transcends it, but the way a dog transcends Spinoza. Not only did he prove to Germany that it can live without Einstein because he was Jewish, Hitler showed the world that what must, after all, be called the higher values of civilization were actually superfluous.

When Hitler drove out Einstein, he only deprived a few Germans of having conversations with him about relativity. Burn all the Rembrandts in our museums and you'll change nothing in the life of Europe. No, you change everything. But what am I getting into here . . .

October 3

The stagnant Armistice has turned the Frenchman into a strange character. He depends on Germany, he depends on Japan, the United States, and Russia. Planes shot down and planes victorious, a house burning in London or a house burning in Berlin decide his fate. The whole universe is fighting for him or against him. But he's not participating in this fight. History is being made, for him as for others, but it's being made without him. Events come to the Frenchman, but he doesn't make those events. He has one power, one right left to him: he can make wishes. He can practice all the virtues of the inner man, to the extent that the inner man is motionless and mute. His condition is that of Simeon the Stylite.[17]

---

[16] Ernst Röhm, a leading Nazi who had been very close to Hitler and founded the Sturmabteilung (SA; the storm troopers), was murdered during the "Night of the Long Knives" when Hitler decided to eliminate the SA. Further on: Hitler annexed Austria in March 1938, invaded Czechoslovakia a year later, and Poland five months after that.

[17] Simeon the Stylite (ca. 388–459 BCE) was a saint who lived for thirty-seven years perched on top of a column near Aleppo.

Vichy is preparing a statute regulating Jews.[18]

A Polish Jew at least felt Jewish. People in the Nalewki neighborhood of Warsaw did not conceive of themselves as Polish.[19] But French Jews no longer felt Jewish. Those who felt most Jewish in their hearts were only Jewish through the memory of a few family traditions. If they were naïve, they didn't understand anti-Semitism because they knew nothing about the political technique of finding a focal point for grievances. That's how we can explain, if not justify, their cowardice or their reluctance to say they were Jewish.

So that some Jew might well ask: "Am I not as good a philosopher as the best of the Christians?" And another: "I was the only Jew on this board of directors; was I therefore the only crook?"

The Jew has faults: if he's rich, he has a rich man's faults; poor, a poor man's faults. If he's in a country where there are pogroms, he only has the choice between servility and revolution. Thus Protestant émigrés from France went to serve the king of Prussia at a time when, for well-born people, passing from the service of the king of France to the service of the king of Prussia was nothing more than a permutation, a change of arms or corps.

October 4

Key words: the words dictators and crowds volley back and forth with their rackets. The drunkard has stopped on the road. He bends toward the ground in a position both of vomiting and meditation: "They say they're going to take the whole country and organize it." And he repeats, sounding out the syllables as if he was spelling aloud: "Or-ga-nize it . . . Or-ga-nize it . . ."

When I was taking refuge in the Loiret[20] and learned, among a thousand contradictory rumors, that the Armistice had been signed, an upstanding French bourgeois developed the theme of the marshal's grief to me. He didn't realize the extent of the defeat. Neither did I, in fact. He anecdotally, sentimentally reduced the defeat to the emotion of a great leader, the artisan of an old victory, obliged to sign the abdication and throwing the weight of his fame onto the scale of nations. It was a fine monologue out of classical theater. And for an official painter of historical scenes, the tableau was finished. Tears come to the eyes of the great soldier who feigns impassibility and stiffens his torso. And in his noble

[18] This "Statut des Juifs" was the first of Vichy's anti-Semitic measures.
[19] Nalewki Street was the center of the Jewish quarter of Warsaw, which the Nazis transformed into the Warsaw ghetto.
[20] Le Loiret is a *département* about sixty miles south of Paris where the Werths stayed for a while in June 1940 during the month it took them to get from Paris to Saint-Amour: the roads were clogged with refugees. See Werth's *33 Days*, trans. Austin D. Johnston (Brooklyn, NY: Melville House, 2015). The Loiret is in a region called Le Gatinais.

grief, the vanquished warrior of 1940 impresses the victor as much as the hero of Verdun seemed formidable to him in 1918.

"You do know he's eighty-four and he's only a flag . . . Without him, we would've had a revolution . . ."

"You certainly decided very quickly you'd rather have a France transformed by Germany than a France transformed by revolution. And could you tell me what revolution means, in 1940?"

"What else could he do? He couldn't do anything."

"Yes he could."

"What?"

"Break his sword in half over his knee, make a historic pronouncement, and declare that he had agreed to be the liquidator of the defeat but not the accomplice of the enemy; call on the universal conscience, on his conscience as a soldier, on any of those countless consciences that have their tribunal between earth and heaven."

October 4

It's raining. The little leaves fallen from the bushes neither crack nor roll. Pasted to the ground, they cover the path with a mosaic. Beyond a vault of leaves, the meadow is so green you'd think it was a sheet of light of the same artificial shade as the liquids in jars you could see in the shop windows of pharmacies in bygone days. Today I have no other contact with the outside world, whether men or things.

It's not true that the men of Vichy are comparable to past revolutionaries who hoped to extract revolutions from a war or a defeat. For those revolutionaries did not claim to subjugate their country to another: their dogma was the equality of countries or their negation.

"I'm playing the German card," says a neighborhood squire to whoever will listen to him. An odd confession: he's playing cards with his country.

"I don't understand," says Major F——, whom I met at the fair. "He went through the whole war of 1914 and his five sons were called up in this one."

An old opposition between aristocrats and patriots. But the doctrine of today's squire is: order. Crude? No matter. The men pushing that doctrine present it as the very expression of national continuity. There is no country without order. There's the sleight-of-hand: Hitler is bringing us order, and order contains the country.

Vichy shows us that a dictatorship can be as vacillating as a parliament. You can't make a dictatorship with an old marshal. In the legendary pre-1900 Balkans, they mass-produced dictators from generals.

Hitler used to go into trances, and Germany with him. Mussolini would howl out Latinity by bellowing. The western dictator must have the eloquence of a street peddler and a disreputable look about him that he corrects by watching himself in the movies. There's nothing he can do if his people haggle with him about providing informers. But a masochistic dictatorship . . . !

In a scrap torn out of an old newspaper, I read this morning that those responsible for the war and the defeat are workers who were saboteurs and shouted in the street or at rallies "Free Thaelmann!"[21] That's history, nations and men locked into a passionate logic on the level of a barroom argument. That kind of logic heats up, the way we say a motor heats up. But when he blows a rod in his car, the man locked into his system doesn't notice it, and his idea keeps turning over in his head. Does this gazetteer really think men live in their country like cows in a pasture?

I heard Lucien Febvre deploring the weakening of France after the debacle. As a historian, he is careful not to bind the present to the past with fragile threads. He doesn't claim to apply to the present the impassibility that the historian applies, with some difficulty, to the past. And Febvre proceeds by soundings and thrusts. We react to what's happening now. And if he said to me "France is done for," he didn't claim to make the final judgment or even a historian's judgment. It was a way of expressing sadness, our common sadness.

If France is done for, I'm not resigned to it. I had gotten used to France.

October 8

In Alsace in the middle of the nineteenth century, there was a certain Jewish purity, as there was a Protestant purity. Those austere religions offered only demanding things to lean on. Those who practiced them were in a suspect group, in the opposition. That led to pride more than to facility. Catholic souls are gentler and suppler than Jewish and Protestant souls. Sometimes they are even court souls, so strongly do they have a perfect ceremonial at their disposition.

But I know Jews who have decomposed into shreds. Among the rich. They've lost—and they're proud of it—all contact with Judaism, not to say with anything resembling religion. They didn't feel Jewish, they felt rich. Their ancestors

---

[21] Ernst Thaelmann, or Thälmann, head of the German Communist Party from 1925 on, was arrested on March 3, 1933. Rather than try him publicly, the Nazis preferred to transfer him to various concentration camps. Large-scale campaigns were launched to free him. Thaelmann was executed at Buchenwald August 18, 1944.—J.-P. A.

shut themselves away in their faith, not in their money. Here we don't have the revolutionary Jew who decomposes society, as the anti-Semites would have it. It's society that decomposes him: we can see a similar decline in Christian families of the bourgeoisie. They became regular churchgoers in order not to think of faith or anything else. Man has become an automobile accessory. He is not from a particular country or religion. He's a brand of car. Those Jews would also like to go to Mass, without believing a word of it. But Mass, since Hitler came to power, does not de-Jew you.

Prisoners escape from the Occupied Zone, or civilians cross its border. They come from Chalon or Dole. They're taken to a wood or a place where you can ford a river. Sometimes the German sentinels are accomplices, sometimes not. But in all those stories, there's a common point: you "slip a coin" to the guide. I thought it was one of those favors you can't pay for. That coin (it seems the tariff is fifty francs) would make me truly believe that "France is done for."

October 9

In its press and radio, Vichy draws from Fontenoy[22] and Waterloo and paints naïve illuminations. Vichy smiles at the universe, at France, and at itself. The most astonishing thing in the people of Vichy is their beatitude. They reign over a principality of Andorra or Monaco and talk as if they reigned over France. Thus paupers struck by delusions of grandeur think they're Christ or Napoleon and boast of their golden palaces.

October 10

I am alone. I have a house and a self. This solitude is not as good a condition as one might think for feeling one's self. The self goes to sleep or rolls out its memory.

I don't feel like reading. But I remember. Pascal or La Bruyère . . .[23] the words leave me, but the author takes his place inside me. I apply to books what Hokusai said when he was almost a hundred: "Ah, to live long enough to make the geometric point expressive!"[24] My old reading has become expressive. Beyond words. Between the lines. Something like the memory of a face. I also have nature at my disposal (as they said in the Romantic era). I take pleasure in looking at these

[22] The battle of Fontenoy (1745): a French victory over British, Dutch, and Hanoverian troops. (The latter would now be called German.)

[23] Jean de La Bruyère was a seventeenth-century "moralist" famous for one work—his *Caractères*: short, generally satiric portraits of different types of people.

[24] Hokusai (1760–1849) is the foremost master of Japanese brush painting and woodblock prints.

grassy slopes, these hillsides with their steep paths. But this region isn't mine. My region is Brittany.[25]

If Germany wins the war, Pétain remains in power or is replaced by any old local policeman. If England wins, the German troops will evacuate France, Belgium, and Holland. Hitlerism breaks down. An idyllic, blissful time for England and France? Unfortunately, whether victors or vanquished, the people of these countries will have gone through postoperative shock. And not only through the dislocation of families and friendships. But the familiarity with death that goes along with war, as well as continual risk, doesn't lead to lofty meditations and great plans but to fatalistic acceptance. How many French citizens, after the 1940 Armistice, simply said: "Whew!" In the same way, as early as the second year of the 1914 war, when the soldiers in every army saw enemy prisoners going by, they said, "The war's over for them . . ." Those thousands of aviators who flew out every day, who were no longer extraordinary envoys to death but took off the way infantrymen start out on the wrong foot—who can think that their kind of heroism will turn into the subtle heroism without which any peace turns rotten?

October 11

A "message" from Pétain. It does not begin "We, Philippe . . ."[26] They must have told him it made a bad impression. He hails the regimes of Germany and Italy. They have "their meaning and their beauty." But "the new order cannot be a servile imitation of foreign experiments." So: servile, no, but imitation, yes.

Bland Nazism. Only one conclusion can be drawn from this jumble: the fate of our Caudillo here depends on his police.[27] Will he find militiamen and informers in France as he has found scribes?

If you look for a meaning in his emotionalism, it is full of threats for the French and full of promises to the Germans. We shall see.

A walk through the meadows, the thickets, and the paths. A stick in my hand, not a cane. The car had gotten me off the habit. It gives me a change of era. I return to the time of the solitary walker.[28]

---

[25] Werth apparently appreciated its rocky coasts. A crucial incident in his first novel takes place in Brittany.

[26] None of Pétain's other speeches begin "We, Philippe . . ." either. Only the Constitutional Act of July 11, 1940, begins "We, marshal of France, head of the French State" (*chef de l'État français*). The "Message to the French" of October 10 is a speech laying out the program of Pétain's "National Revolution" or "new order."—J.-P. A.

[27] "El Caudillo" was one of the titles of the fascist ruler of Spain, Generalissimo Francisco Franco.*

[28] The "time of the solitary walker" is an allusion to an unfinished self-reflective, philosophical essay by Jean-Jacques Rousseau, *Rêveries du promeneur solitaire* (1776–78): *Reveries of the Solitary Walker*.

I go to the market for some outside-world therapy.

Pétain's message did not convince M——, a mechanic and fire captain . . . (I saw him a few years ago in a burning barn, standing on a beam. It was nighttime. Lit by a car's headlights, he was aiming the jet of water.) "I have great hopes," he says, "That one fine day you'll see de Gaulle landing in France. If he needs a rifle, I'll be there."

Two young airplane mechanics. Stocky and muscular. Leather overcoats. "If the English wanted, we could've stopped the Germans at the Somme. But the English left in their boats . . . The workers were saying 'We don't have enough raw materials . . .' and the bosses, 'The workers aren't working . . .' As far as sabotage, no doubt about it . . . Communists or fifth column? Can't believe workers did that . . ."

This stagnant Armistice gnaws at you as much as the war. The war was a roll of the dice, with the emotion of gambling. The soldier's fate and the fate of the country were being decided. A roll of the dice, a tragic heads or tails. This one's killed, that one isn't. But the Armistice war operates by little touches.

The world outside. Rather Japanese, but a bit long for a haiku: from my window, I see a path through the bush. A young peasant woman walks into it. She's no more than a dark spot among the shrubs. And suddenly a burst of light, a quicksilver streak vacillates and floats, without a support, lighter than air. I can see only a mirror and the back of a bent neck.

"De Gaulle," says N——, whom I met in Bourg, "could have been a 'great man.' But he's just a little staff officer and a little man with great pride . . . True, he predicted motorized war. A proof of tactical sense. But he's drunk with himself. He's nothing but himself. He won't go beyond himself."

"Watch out . . . Aren't you just nonchalantly transmitting propaganda? Three months ago, when the town was all Germanophile, an old lady who'd had a steady diet of German radio was saying to me: 'De Gaulle's just pretentious.'"

Politics are complicated on a number of levels. I can understand how you can very quickly become a scoundrel. I won't record a conversation with M——, who said to me yesterday: "If de Gaulle lands in France, I get out my gun."

The world outside. The reds of the Virginia creeper aren't vegetable but coral or old leather.

I don't know what it's like for prisoners. But free solitude—I can even say it changed the taste of time in me. It erased time. Time is absorbed in me without my being aware of it. And I don't know if it's long or short. It has lost its mobility. Slack water. It doesn't move and neither do I. But my son, Claude, arrived last night and leaves this afternoon. As soon as he was here, there was an unbelievable gallop of time. As if the minute of his arrival and the minute of leaving attracted each other. As if time was carrying us away with him. I can understand the resignation of certain old people. They have settled into time. They fear the smallest possible event, even visits that shake up their time.

October 14

"We, Philippe . . ." The heralds strike the ground with the staff of their halberds to announce the arrival of the marshal. And that plan to make stamps and coins with his effigy!

This trembling dictatorship is merely a dictatorship of political grudges. Right-wing clowns are throwing left-wing clowns into prison.

Meanwhile, they're lopping off one of our freedoms every day. We hardly notice it, because freedom has become a luxury item. And our way of life contains such a reserve of it that there is no law or decree that can exhaust it in one stroke.

At first the crowd accepted Pétain as a military man who's outside of politics, a military man soaring above it. He covers for the nastiest of politicians. Laval* is regenerating France. Laval is working for eternity . . . Nah—Laval doesn't have a mug for eternity.

October 15

Saint-Exupéry* spent two days with me. Friendship, "exercise of souls, with no other fruit."[29] Friendship has hardly ever been an inspiration for literature. There is more friendship in those words of Montaigne than in centuries of books. Why the extraordinary privilege given to love? Perhaps because it is almost universal, and there are few men who have not known something of it.

Friendship is as mysterious as love; more, perhaps. For many men can define the qualities or shapes that stir desire in them. In the houses of love they ask the customers what their preferences are. There are no houses of friendship.

There is no friendship if the friend doesn't accept the friend as he is. There is no friendship without the acceptance of oneself.

Tonio read me a few passages from his next book. It's a block of crystal. All he wants to see in it is a gangue. In that case, the gangue is made of crystal.

I remember a flight from Ambérieu to Paris. Tonio was piloting a Simoun. He flew very low for a long time, and when he nosed up the plane to go over a wood, I could feel all the power of the acceleration in my body.

[29] Werth is quoting Montaigne's *Essais*, Book 3, chapter 3.

If I ever wanted to surprise him by my fine acquaintances and thought of organizing a philosophical evening, I would invite Vigny along with him. They would agree about "servitude and grandeur." But Tonio wouldn't accept the "cold silence," which is Vigny's recourse.[30] He thinks the resistance of the universe and the constraints man imposes on himself are occasions for his deliverance. I'll invite Vigny anyway. He'll thank me.

That restaurant in the Bois de Boulogne where we had dinner together last year. How did we come to judge some of the men who were then leading France—in other words, ministers? We ascribed projects to them, a grand plan. And suddenly Tonio murmured: "I think we're indulging in anthropomorphism."

October 15

I'm looking at one of those postcards the Germans allow us to send between this zone and the Occupied Zone.[31] You have to cross out or fill in the printed formulas the way you fill out a tax form. You have the privilege of writing that you're in good health, you need money, or you're deceased.

In town, in the hotel dining room. Two shopkeepers sitting at a table in front of a bottle of red. They talk travel permits, gas distribution. Then they go back over history to the debacle. And one of them repeats tirelessly: "Betrayed—sold out—sold out—paid off."

Dictators' faces. Without prejudice: they're not handsome. At the beginning of his career, Mussolini looked like a plump little tenor touring the provinces. But he worked on his mask. He made himself the square jaw of a leader. Films show the steps of that transformation. But it's all too easy to see he's overacting with his torso. And he's "dynamic" the way smooth-talking stallholders are dynamic at fairs, selling their wares in packs and giving housewives the illusion of buying a whole souk.

Hitler's face is so poor it's pathetic. It's made with a shrunken line. Its vulgarity is haunting. And his gaze is dirty. That's the way it is.

The "Occupation authorities" destroyed the matrixes of Wanda Landowska's records, because Wanda Landowska is Jewish.[32]

---

[30] It is the "recourse" the poet advises as a response to the silence of God in the last line of his poem "The Mount of Olives."

[31] At that time, mail regulations between the two zones allowed people to send only postcards called "familial," with thirteen lines of prepared formulas. Rules specify that "every card whose wording is not limited to family matters will not be sent and will probably be destroyed."—J.-P. A.

[32] Wanda Landowska was a leading harpsichordist in the early twentieth century, particularly renowned for her performances of Bach and Scarlatti.

It's a strong government that can smash ebonite and make musical judgments based on chromosomes.

October 17

Young people are being asked to pick chestnuts. The regeneration of France through the recipes of Aunt Annette.[33]

Pastoral advice: young typists, the typists from offices and films, should give up their Remington typewriters, arm themselves with shepherd's crooks, and milk cows!

Agricultural technique: it is forbidden to kill a pig weighing less than one hundred kilos.[34] Forbidden to feed potatoes to pigs. "We'll fatten them up on clear water," the peasants say.

D——, here from Paris, spends a few hours with me.

The Chateaubriants and Drieu La Rochelles* are working with the Germans. In their heart of hearts, their sympathy for fascism, for Nazism, is stronger than any feeling for the nation, whether impulsive or with a base in history.

Her husband's a prisoner of war. She planted the crops with her father. "What's going to become of us? . . . The English, the Boches . . . What if all the prices went up again? . . . Counting everything . . . Threshing was sixty-five francs an hour . . . My bread costs me as much as bread I buy at the baker's . . . After all, there have to be people who sow."

That's what they're all thinking. They feed the world, they feed the bourgeois, and they feed the workers, whose paid vacations they cannot forgive.

October 21

I care about a civilization, about France. I have no other way of dressing. I can't go out completely naked.

The peasants are on strike. They used to sell their slaughtered poultry in the Louhans market at thirty francs a kilo. The Prefecture or the Bureau of Supplies slapped a fifteen-franc tax on it. The next week, there was no poultry in the market. The peasants stayed home.

---

[33] "Regeneration" (*redressement*) was one of Pétain's favorite words to describe the goals of his "National Revolution." Next paragraph: the supposed virtues of rural life in contrast to the "decadent" city was another favorite theme of the Vichy government.

[34] One hundred kilos is roughly 220 pounds.

To hang on to France—what a strange obsession! "France cannot disappear," they say. It's not true. It hasn't even existed for twenty full centuries. And the Savoyards have only been French since 1866. Like all figures on the earth, France changes and can die. As for Greece, you know very well. . . The monks transmitted Greece to the West, but not to Greece. In how many centuries will a Germanized France be resuscitated? And who says it will be? Perhaps, however, in ten centuries, a Chinese bonze will reveal France to China—that is, reveal it to a handful of Chinese professors, a French poet or philosopher whose very name is unknown to 38 million Frenchmen in 1940.

When I saw a German regiment marching over French soil for the first time in Montargis, that regiment insulted both my feeling for the nation and my internationalism. Both equally wounded. But I didn't know yet that under German occupation and Pétain's occupation, France would become a myth more distant and more elusive than internationalism.

The paper's full of exercises in good humor and optimism. France will recover, France is recovering. This rhetoric on command is disconcerting in its foolishness—I was going to say, in its boorishness: you don't dance in the bedroom of someone who's seriously ill.

October 22

Le Progrès: "The Israelite Herschel Grynszpan, who assassinated Monsieur vom Rath, an adviser at the German embassy, on November 8, 1938, has just been transferred to Berlin, where he will be tried."[35]

When the anarchists of the 1890s killed people, they were tried, they weren't delivered up to a foreign power. Caserio, who killed Judge Carnot; Luccheni, who killed the empress of Austria. "Poor little Caserio," wrote Charles-Louis Philippe.[36]

Grynszpan will be tried by Hitler. How far he's come since the Reichstag fire! Such was still the prestige of France that French lawyers could watch the trial and Moro-Giafferi could defend Dimitrov.[37] And yet Hitler was well aware that France wouldn't declare war if he expelled the French lawyers.

[35] Grynszpan was a seventeen-year-old German Jew who killed vom Rath in Paris to draw attention to the fate of his parents, deported from Germany to Poland without any luggage, like fifteen thousand other German Jews at the time. The assassination was the pretext for Kristallnacht: on the night of November 10–11, 1938, 367 synagogues were burned, ninety-one Jews killed, and thirty thousand rounded up and imprisoned. The French police delivered Grynszpan to the Germans in July 1940, although he had not been tried.—J.-P. A.

[36] Charles-Louis Philippe was a writer of "populist" novels in the late nineteenth and early twentieth century. He wrote about the lives of working-class people.

[37] The Reichstag (the German parliament building) burned down February 27, 1933. Claiming the Communists were responsible, Hitler used the Reichstag fire to obtain emergency measures to

Poor little Herschel Grynszpan. You saw your people incarcerated, massacred, and humiliated. You weren't a great politician. But you had some of the courage of those anarchists who were criminals only because they wouldn't accept crime: they weren't the kind of domestic animals who can't recognize the taste of what is intolerable.

Poor little Grynszpan. At least you proved to your tormentors that a Jew can kill. Christians have heaped enough blame on Jews for being cowards, for turning the other cheek. The other cheek to pogroms, the other cheek to Hitler.

Vom Rath may have been a courteous diplomat. And his mother came to Paris to keep a vigil over his body. Did she think for one second about what happened to Jewish children under Hitler? And no doubt this diplomat believed neither the legend of Hitler nor the legend of the Jews. But he accepted them for the sake of his career. And because a subtle complicity in crime does not frighten well-brought-up people.

Solitary leisure. I'm reading the Bible. If Abraham had refused to cut Isaac's throat, God would have had more respect for humanity and sent it fewer catastrophes.

October 23

"The Day in Vichy.[38] At last schools will take an interest in the private life of the elementary school teacher. Monsieur Ripert has judged that it is no longer tolerable for opinions expressed outside school by the teacher to be in conflict with his teaching in school.[39] Entirely devoted to a task given to him by the state, henceforth the schoolteacher will—just like an officer in the army—no longer be an ordinary citizen . . ."

Met the schoolteacher:

"They want to make spies and stool pigeons out of us . . ."

"Will you react?"

"We can only remain passive . . . Most people won't budge; they'll just think about getting their grub . . . Unless something changes, unless England . . ."

Strange times. France waiting for England to settle its fate like a sick person waiting in bed for the doctor, like the way it would wait for the sun to return after the rain or for a certain conjunction of the stars.

---

fight Communist terrorism. This led to his assumption of total power. Georgi Dimitrov, a Bulgarian Communist sent to Berlin, was one of the defendants in the Reichstag trial. He was defended by a French criminal lawyer. As there was no evidence against him, he was released in 1934 after an international campaign for his liberation.

[38] A daily report in *Le Progrès*.

[39] Georges Ripert, a notorious reactionary, was appointed secretary of Public Instruction and Youth in 1940.

October 24

The little lawyer from Auvergne had his eye on politics.[40] The broad smile of a fat woman and the mustache of a cop in the old days. At that time, his shoes curled up and the soles gaped. Now one of the greats of the world. The greats of the world, you say, used to look better than that. Aren't you duped by ceremonial costumes and fine disguises? In the Berlin Museum, you can see a Charles V who's just a poor moron, a vacillating fool.[41]

In his nightmares, does he sometimes see his head on the end of a pike? No . . . that little lawyer plays chess on the land registry of France. He would work just as impassibly on the land registry of the world. And nothing will stop him from losing unless, as sometimes happens, the pieces in the game awake from their wooden sleep and jump at the players' throats.

If the old military man and the little lawyer had met by chance in the time of their youth, they wouldn't have sensed the other's existence or even guessed at it. The origin and likely ending of each man had no relationship to the other's. If Pétain hadn't been a marshal, he would have been a gendarme. If Laval hadn't been a minister, he would have run a brothel.

If Laval had served his time in Captain Pétain's company, the only political future he would have predicted for Pétain would have been mayor of a village, where he would retire. And Pétain would have thought Laval a man one could only promote to supplies sergeant or, better, quartermaster (because of the till). But fortune has brought them together and made them a team.

The junior minister of finance: "The regime that is being created only wishes to be inspired by these great ideas: work, family, country . . ." So now we are delivered from democratic mistakes.[42] But we still have the style ministers always used in their Sunday speeches. Hitler and Mussolini are better molders of human clay. Hitler barks out ideas in his speeches. Mussolini uses a shinier rhetoric and the kind of eloquence a moron would call "Mediterranean."

Hitler-Laval meeting. The former house painter and the little lawyer from Clermont come together in a historic tableau.[43] Those two swindlers, standing eye to eye, are going to manufacture history.

[40] Werth is talking about Pierre Laval.

[41] Charles V ruled the Spanish Empire and the Holy Roman Empire in the sixteenth century.

[42] The French Republic's motto was (and is) *Liberté, Égalité, Fraternité*. Vichy replaced it with *Travail, Famille, Patrie* (Work, family, country). *Patrie* has overtones of "motherland" or "homeland."

[43] In Montoire on October 22, Pierre Laval met Hitler, who was going down to Hendaye to talk with Franco for the first time. It was Hitler himself who claimed he had to work as a housepainter to earn his living in Vienna. Whether this is true is far from certain. It is certain, on the other hand, that he sold watercolors and paintings. As for Laval, he was first a tutor, then a lawyer. He came from the village of Châteldon in Auvergne, but set up his office in Paris.—J.-P. A.

One facing the other: they have the same vulgarity, the same commoner's soul. But Laval is more coarsely vulgar, more patently vulgar. He doesn't feel equal to the other man. There was no junction between the crowd and him. Germany stamped its feet for Hitler. German soldiers died (you could read that in the newspapers of the Reich): "für Führer und Vaterland." Hitler before homeland.

A solitary walk. Fairly high up in the mountain. I sat down on the grass. I was happy. A state of great perfection, which must be the way animals are, when they're not suffering. A state one could also call meditation. It seemed to me I could live there for years, a venerated hermit. Provided that the people in the village consented to walk six kilometers every day to bring me an offering of bread and milk.

Or simply anesthetize myself, like so many other people. Drive the future away from me the way you drive away an unwelcome guest. But I can't. Someone who has no children can tell himself: "What do I care about tomorrow, or about France in ten years, in centuries and centuries? What do I care about the wounds of the world? If I wish, I am invulnerable."

Whoever has a son is vulnerable.

October 25

A paradox. The peasant is a useless, anachronistic luxury maintained by old countries. Without protective tariffs, there would be no more farmers in Western Europe. Their wheat is more expensive than Canadian wheat and the meat from their cattle more expensive than beef from Argentine cattle. If the distribution of wealth were well regulated and transportation increased and improved, the French peasant would place ahead of the most hermetic poet in the category of unnecessary luxuries.

October 28

The talks between Laval and Hitler, Pétain and Hitler, are preparing France's "integration" into the Germanic bloc. Laval and Hitler are trying to drown the French people's feeling for the nation in a peace offensive. I learn that Laval is indulging in historical passions. As two German reporters were saying goodbye to him before leaving Vichy for Paris, "I hope you'll send me a postcard from London soon," he said, "when those English pigs are beaten."

Le Progrès has published a photograph of the cabinet: the marshal and Laval reporting on their negotiations with Hitler. Ten men are grouped around a green carpet. This photo is strangely shameless. Except for two ministers who only show the back of their necks and Pétain, who seems worried and distracted, all the others are glowing with bliss and jubilation. You'd think they were guests at a lunch after the hunt, rejoicing with wine and bawdy stories. You'd think they were laughing at the latest Marseilles joke. Even if France had crushed Germany, this photo would not be entirely devoid of indecency for eyes of some slight refinement.

In the village, they're saying Laval sold out to Germany. But the marshal supposedly doesn't want to follow him. And they say several ministers—and perhaps the marshal himself—are in favor of playing a double game: signing on with Germany and, if England wins, welcoming de Gaulle and uniting with him.

For an aesthetics of the radio.

The announcer is developing the theme of Franco-German collaboration in a languorous tone. In this little jewelry workshop, no one is listening. They don't turn off the broadcast and don't even turn down the volume. It doesn't bother them when they speak and listen to me. I have some difficulty in not hearing it. Not them.

The radio teaches us not to listen. It is annulled, like the tick-tock of the clock. But the clock gives out two equal sounds. Sleight-of-hand artists say the difficulty of a trick increases if the props are of unequal weight. By using the radio, the ear magician gains astonishing mastery: he makes all noises, sounds, and words disappear.

October 29

Italy and Greece at war.[44]

Laval's press releases to the Foreign Ministry, grain, fuel, the authority and responsibility of the prefects, Franco-German cooperation, the idyllic promise by Italy of a "peace with no losers"—all that is just padding, hypnotic potions to soothe the crowds. But a new sign: a ban on listening to English radio in public places.

They don't strike homes yet. It's only in "public places" that listening is forbidden. But they'll get to it, if they're not swept away. And in 1940, is French morality strong enough for us not to soon have the spectacle you can see in Germany and Italy: neighbors informing on neighbors?

At B——'s, a local shopkeeper, the radio's on all day, but he never listens to it. "They're brainwashing us," he says. "We're in a hell of a mess."

Germany or England, it's all the same for him. He thinks the English are going to bomb Paris.

---

[44] Mussolini's hopes of gaining prestige by invading Greece failed. Germany was forced to invade six months later.

Laurent has ten head of cattle in his barn.[45] Two months ago, when he learned how a former gendarme who came from Bresse but owned a little farm in Alsace had been driven from his home and only allowed to take the contents of a little suitcase with him, Laurent had a brief fit of Anglophilia. Today he feels solid on his land. They're not talking about the transfer of populations anymore.

Laurent was also afraid of mass requisitions of cattle, pigs, wheat, and oats. Then I felt in him the anger of the peasant who picks up his pitchfork. "You don't know what can happen," he told me. "Things might get hot in the country-side. When a man is hungry . . ." He then thought the Germans meant to starve France and distrusted the government in German hands.

Today, he's waiting, without fear. He's convinced neither Hitler nor Pétain will be clever enough to take his farm away from him with all his cattle and crops. London and Vichy seem much further away than they were three months ago.

October 30

I was a soldier in the other war, mixed in with millions of men who lived between life and death. But as they had gone from a civilization that was still warm into a cataclysm, they thought very little about death and life. I had sunk into the earth. If I raised my eyes, I could only see the earth swollen by the anthills of the men on the other side. I was part of those millions of men who thought the air would have the same taste as before: a taste of slippers and civilization. But I'm living through the stagnant Armistice of 1940 alone; I brood over it.

Went down to the town.

I go see G——, the watchmaker, who's ingenious at solving the problems of min-iature mechanics. No sooner does he glance at my winding stem than he finds four tricks to make sure it does what it has to do.

He talks about the war dispassionately. As if it didn't touch him. He puts English victory and German victory on two pans of the scale. He doesn't try to tip the scales through prayers or wishes. "You can't see," he says, "what England will do with its victory if it topples Germany . . ." Is Germany capable of erasing borders and unifying Europe through persuasion and the force of arms, assas-sination, and its police? Will it fulfill the old pacifist dream through crime?

This isn't some unhinged intellectual talking, but a craftsman. I'm surprised at this lofty philosophy, seeing things as if he were standing on Mount Everest. Zigzagging and badly informed, G——'s thought, craftsman though he may be,

---

[45] "Laurent" is Werth's pseudonym for the tenant farmer living next door, a recurrent character in *Deposition*.

On a prewar day in Saint-Amour, villagers go about their business in the Place des Quatre-Vents. *Author's collection*

resembles the dialectic that D—— attributed to the Drieus* and Montherlants* of this world: "Germany is vacant, Nazism is vacant. They're all empty constructions. We can put whatever we want into them, we can put their opposites into them. The framework doesn't matter, the hive doesn't matter: an intelligent bee may be able to produce its honey. Perhaps the honey of the future will be anti-Nazism, inside Nazism itself."

October 31

I read in the paper they've dismissed all "Marxist" mailmen. So all opponents of the government are "Marxists." It would be extremely amusing for someone who imagined the marshal's face, or Laval's, reacting to three lines of Marx chosen at random.

In town, they're not talking about peace anymore, nor about England or Greece or Italy. They're not even talking about the restrictions. A few days ago, the town was terribly worried about whether it would be able to eat next winter. Now it isn't even thinking about next winter anymore. It lives from day to day, it's asleep.

November 1

Laval's statement to the press. A hilarious sentence: "When I saw Marshal Pétain face to face with the Führer, Adolph Hitler, I understood that there were other ways of settling the fate of our two nations than through battles." Indeed.

Pétain and Hitler face to face. We learn that Hitler didn't bully the marshal. The marshal testified to that. "No pressure, no *Diktat*," he's been made to say on the radio. Swollen as he is with history, he's satisfied. Didn't they grant him military honors?[46]

November 2

Old François: "I hear they announced on the radio peace was signed . . . It's going to turn nasty . . . All the young men I know, not one would fight against England . . ."

A gendarme: "We're waiting, we're waiting . . . But for what?"

The woman who sells notions: "Families are cut apart. The mother in the Forbidden Zone,[47] the father here, and the children God knows where . . ."

An old peasant woman: "Some people say that's going to work out all right . . . If only it was true . . ."

The nationalists betrayed the nation. The revolutionaries betrayed the revolution. The nationalists are saying they're revolutionaries (from the top down). No doubt that's due to the criminal use politicians make of words. It also proves these words should be redefined.

November 3

The first German regiment I saw parading down a French road brought tears to my eyes. I don't like military parades. But this German regiment was intolerable to me. It was a banal feeling, conformist, if you like. It has become unorthodox. It's one of those feelings that is censored now. It has become "defeatist."

At the end of June, when for the first time I met two French women who were completely open to Hitler, thighs and head, I was stupefied; to me they seemed two monsters. I thought I was observing two cases and I didn't see the epidemic. I was persuaded that if an informer had denounced them, they would have endured the rigors of military justice.

---

[46] Arriving in Montoire on October 24, 1940, Philippe Pétain was greeted by top Nazi officials, while the Führer's personal guard hailed him with military honors to the sound of the Marseillaise; Hitler was particularly deferential to him. Pétain's important radio address of October 30, strongly encouraging the French to collaborate with the Reich, specifies that he, Pétain, had received no "*Diktat.*"—J.-P. A.

[47] Theoretically, the French couldn't go into the "forbidden zones." The woman may be talking about the Occupied Zone, as communication between the two main zones, Occupied and "Free," was strictly limited.

Historic handshakes. The photos in the paper showed us the Hitler-Laval hand-shake. Two broad smiles, two beaming faces. "It's a deal!" The Pétain-Hitler handshake. Hitler, strong and kindly, seems to be cheering up the marshal. The last handshake the newspapers showed us was Stalin-Ribbentrop, in August 1939.[48]

November 5

In the town, they're living a reduced life, like the animals in zoos.

The S——s in Paris stuffed their cupboards with provisions. Since the month of June, they've had provisions sent in from the country and the towns. They used to keep open house before their apartment resembled a grocery chain store. Now they don't invite anyone over anymore. Some of their pro-visions are spoiling. But they've made a kind of "transfer." Their food has taken on a special character, the sacred character that money acquires for a miser. A day will come when they'll let themselves die of hunger in front of a full cupboard.

Napoleon is supposed to have said that between two forces, the sword and the mind, the mind would always have the last word. Napoleon was a timid dictator.

November 6

Today the paper has only one important piece of news for me: "The marshal brought the people of Toulouse the comfort of his solicitude."[49]

I walked over a carpet of leaves. I met three hunters. I forgot Europe; I lived in the fall.

November 7

When freedom is suppressed, a few dozen people suffer from it: for them, it's the salt of the earth. But in town and on the farms, they haven't felt the dictatorship yet. It's true that it proceeds by stages, and, as they say, we're waiting.

---

[48] In Moscow, August 23, 1939, the signing of the first German-Soviet pact was followed by champagne toasts and handshakes.—J.-P. A. Joachim von Ribbentrop was Hitler's foreign minister from 1938 on. After the war, he was sentenced to death at the Nuremberg Trials for "crimes against peace" (starting World War II), "war crimes" (killing civilians), and "crimes against humanity" (facili-tating the Holocaust).

[49] In the fall of 1940, Philippe Pétain made a series of tours to consolidate his regime. They brought him to the main cities of the Southern Zone; he received a particularly warm welcome in Toulouse on November 5.—J.-P. A.

A free people soon becomes like rich men who no longer feel the luxury they live in.

November 8

The government is getting ready to "reconstitute the elites." And the marshal goes through the barracks shouting: "Get up, in there! . . . The élites down here, in dress whites."

This government is all "dressed in candid probity and white linen." It is swathed in a white cloud. It is devoted to white the way a little girl is devoted to pink.

The people in town couldn't care less. They don't read the pastoral messages anymore. But they're in a bad mood and close to anger because of the latest taxes. The butcher says he's losing two francs a kilo on beef. Customers aren't happy to pay five francs a kilo for beef bones and eight francs for a pound of cow's liver. The men of Vichy are handling their fileted ideal better than butcher's meat.

November 9

Walked down to the town. Open-air market.

The fields are frosted over, beneath a sun that has the quality of a dry white wine with a flinty taste. Cloudless.

In P—— the blacksmith's workshop. A peasant drops a sack in a corner. "Contraband," says P——. I don't know what's in the sack. I don't ask. He would gladly have told me. But I don't like to reply to a confidence by an indiscretion.

Before the last war, the match smugglers who went to get phosphorus in Switzerland used to deposit their bags in the smithy. The tradition went back to P——'s father, to his grandfather. Did they have a resister's affection for smugglers, or even simply the sympathy of a rebellious spirit? No, you have to look deeper. The old people wanted to decide for themselves what is honest and dishonest. Their morality went beyond the morality of a gendarme. It wasn't obedience, but a commandment they gave to themselves.

"It's amazing," a peasant tells me, "Amazing, this . . ." (He gropes for the word.) " . . . this turnaround: in June and July after the Germans went through, everybody in town swore by them. There was a shopkeeper saying, 'They're the only ones you can do business with.' Now, they're all for the English, and the ones who shout the loudest are the same ones who were waiting for Hitler to 'take care of everything' . . ."

The newspaper. Marshal Pétain will have his oak. The Druids.[50] We learn, with emotion, that the marshal had lunch in Cérilly in the house where Monsieur Jacques Chevalier, general secretary for Public Education, was born. But Monsieur Jacques Chevalier is deluding himself and will fool no one: Cérilly is not his birthplace, it's the birthplace of Charles-Louis Philippe.*

November 9

I've often jotted down the name of Pascal in these notes. How did I get to know Pascal? Our teacher of "rhetoric" gave us a few lines of "The Mystery of Jesus" to learn by heart. The power of form. I was gripped by a painting and ignored its subject. My emotion was musical. The mystery of form, the benefits and dangers of culture, which gives us beautiful paintings, stripped of their original meaning. But that sensation of burning inside? Why was it burning? What was it burning from? I didn't care. But whatever didn't burn like that had lost the power to move me.

The four butchers in town will be closed for two weeks. The butchers were selling above the taxed fixed price. The shops will alternate in shutting down, so the town won't be deprived of meat.

November 11

In the morning, the clouds are low. The landscape is pallid, wrinkled. You'd think it spent the whole night in a railway car.

As I lack information, I'm reduced to putting the present and future into syllogisms. But the unexpected wins out. The total debacle was not expected; the most pessimistic only predicted a defeat. At the beginning of 1940, who would have predicted a dictatorship in the pay of a foreign power and a miniature White Terror eager to expand?[51]

If the conflict goes on for a long time, accumulating its destructions but ending in nothing, for how much longer will the crowds tolerate this temporary state, this parenthesis of war or Armistice? In some country or other, will a man

---

[50] The ceremony of "the Marshal's oak" took place November 8 in the forest of Tronçais. After lunch, before a sizeable crowd, Philippe Pétain watched his initials being hammered into the trunk of an oak following the ritual of the Forest Service (Eaux et Forêts), apparently recalling a ritual of the Druids. Further on, Jacques Chevalier, Pétain's godson and a future junior minister of education, was born in Cérilly; so was Charles-Louis Philippe.—J.-P. A.

[51] The "White Terror": in 1795, taking their revenge for the Jacobin Reign of Terror, royalists and right-wing Catholics massacred suspected Jacobins in the south of France. A similar episode occurred in 1815 after Napoleon's defeat: the victims were suspected Bonapartists and republicans.

appear who doesn't bark like Hitler, who's not a wheeler-dealer like Laval, not
a cunning politician, but a *man*, liberator or despot, of the kind that one could
call "a great man," as Stendhal called Napoleon? Will the people in countries
everywhere subjugated by dictatorships turn toward a future of comfortable
brutishness?

November 12

All night the wind blew stormily, in two registers. The noise of a wave breaking
and sweeping in with a long whistle, a moaning voice, the entreaty of a ghost.
The wooden shutters creaked the way boats creak. Sometimes I expected a visit
from the ghost, sometimes I was at sea, swaying in my cabin.

Mistinguett is giving a few shows in Lyon, I see in the paper.[52] Mistinguett
will have lasted longer than Napoleon. I saw her when she was twenty, in the
Eldorado in Lyon. She was very good at somersaults and the high jump.

The newspapers are posted on the glass door of the tobacconist's. I almost
bought *Action Française*. Well, no . . . I know their plays with formal logic, their
mixture of hatred and intellectual silliness.[53]

Maurras is the real assassin of Jaurès.[54] He accused him of being paid with
German gold. Here hatred turned into infamy. It's a hatred that gave Maurras
and his disciples in syllogistics some appearance of solidity. They harbored every
kind of fascism within them, and they weren't even really royalists.

Under the entrance to the cathedral of Clermont-Ferrand, marshal Pétain is
received by Msgr Piguet. An exchange of great politeness between great powers.
Perhaps the bishop can see beyond the ritual. But perhaps the marshal doesn't
know what he's transmitting. The marshal is like an unlucky traveler transporting a trunk where a criminal has hidden his burglar tools. The marshal is like
those carriers who spread a disease they don't know they have. The marshal may
think he's renewing the alliance of the throne and the altar. He's unaware of the
properties of the Hitlerian toxins Laval is hiding in his trunk.[55]

[52] Mistinguett was the stage name of a music-hall singer and dancer.

[53] *Action Française* was the daily newspaper of the monarchist, nationalist movement of that
name, part of the far right since 1898 and a strong supporter of Vichy, particularly its anti-Semitic
measures. Charles Maurras was its intellectual leader.

[54] Jean Jaurès (1859–1914) was an extremely important socialist leader and a philosopher and
historian. He was assassinated on the eve of World War I because of his pacifist views. Streets in
many French towns and cities (including Paris) bear his name.

[55] A few months later, Msgr Piguet was saving children and hiding English aviators; he was
arrested by the Gestapo as he came out of High Mass. He was deported to Germany on May 28,
1944.—Léon Werth.

However little real Christianity there may be in both Catholicism and Protestantism, that dose is intolerable to Hitler. Hitler can't bear any sharing of power or prestige. If the German people get distracted for a moment, he can no longer hypnotize them. He threw a few Catholic priests and pastors in jail. He couldn't strike all of them as he did the Communists and Social Democrats, because religion is more strongly tied to custom than revolution. Hitler agreed to compromises, and so did the churches. At the beginning of Nazism, Protestant theologians questioned if religion and Nazism were reconcilable. The few pastors who failed to find a theological foundation in Nazism meditated on the contradictions of the century and their faith—in prison.

The old marshal walks up the steps of the cathedral. He thinks his uniform and the bishop's robe are the definitive image of the world he had dreamed of. Catholic order and military order are saving France.

But Laval knows where he's going. At least, he knows there are several paths to the crossroads. Laval gambled on his own fate. It's not just a question of getting rich or keeping his millions. He's playing another game. He performed, in his own way, an act of faith. He gambled on Hitler. He only holds on through Hitler, and Hitler's demands will depend on whether England wins or loses, according to the degree of his victory or defeat. If there's a shaky peace, if it doesn't completely give France over to Germany, Hitler will demand nothing more of Pétain's order; he will leave France to its domestic quarrels. But if England loses, Hitler won't be satisfied with the marshal's order. For a victorious Hitler won't restrain the march of Hitlerism. He'll be pushed to destroy not only all that opposes him but also all that doesn't culminate in him.

Laval knows this. Cynically, he contemplates the bishop, who may be persecuted by Hitler tomorrow, and the marshal, who prepares the way for that persecution. He tells himself: "The marshal can't know that, the bishop may."

The newspaper: "The Comité des Forges no longer exists."[56] A historic tableau: marshal Pétain and Laval driving out the Schneider family, which flees, begging along the roadsides.

Marie-Claire has reappeared.[57] Will France die of Germany, alcohol, or *Marie-Claire*? I don't have the heart to go on. But it's a fine subject for the essay on the Baccalauréat.

---

[56] Eugène Schneider and Charles Wendel founded the Comité des Forges in 1864 to organize the French steel industry and control its markets.

[57] *Marie-Claire*, founded in France in 1937, is now an international fashion magazine for women.

November 13

Like everyone else, I confess, I've used those revolting postcards for correspondence between the two zones. All our effusions and all circumstances in time of war as in time of peace go into prepared boxes on the cards. Even if peace is signed, a strong government has a duty to authorize only this sort of correspondence. In that way, it would spare its people the dangerous aberrations of intimate feelings, and this people would constantly be warned that all feelings and all thoughts are under state control.

November 14

The simplifications today's politicians give out. Horse medicine, and only one, for all illnesses. Like the infirmaries when I was in the army, where there was only one medication: ipecac.

November 15

An official communiqué from the Vichy government: "The German authorities in Lorraine have just invited" (*invited* is remarkably gallant) "French-speaking Lorrainians to choose between their transfer to Poland or their departure for non-occupied France. . . . Since Monday November 11, their expulsion" (a strange effect, for an invitation) "has been taking place at a rhythm of five to seven trains a day."[58]

For a French peasant, this transfer of populations does not evoke pleasant images. You leave the land, you leave your animals, and you take what you can put into a suitcase. And as a farmer was saying to me: "It's not just the animals, it's not just the furniture, it's the little things you own or whatever . . ."

Interview with the marshal. The author of this interview, Henri Béraud, wrote one day, when he was young, that I was his conscience.[59] Since then, I've felt like asking him if he really thought my conscience was so flexible. But already I had no more appetite for what the newspapers call "polemics." I will always be grateful to Valery Larbaud* for writing that even if he detested some of

---

[58] From November 11 to 21, some sixty thousand supposedly Francophile Lorrainians would be expelled from Lorraine, which was now part of Germany. Whole trainloads of them kept arriving in Lyon. In a radio message, Pétain said he was "quite saddened" by this, while emphasizing that the measure was taken by Germany alone.

[59] Henri Béraud was a writer (he won the Prix Goncourt in 1922 for his novel *Martyr de l'Obèse*) and above all a journalist for the big Paris dailies *Le Petit Parisien* and *Paris-Soir*. He put his polemical talents to use for the far right. He was an Anglophobe (the unusually violent articles he wrote in October 1935 were collected in a pamphlet: *Should England Be Reduced to Slavery?*) and an admirer of Mussolini and Franco. His interview with "the Marshal," which appeared in the November 15 issue of *Gringoire*, is extremely platitudinous and boundlessly sycophantic.—J.-P. A.

my fits of anger, reducing them to the level of "polemics" would never occur to him.

I can see Béraud again, arriving in Paris and ringing at Vildrac's* door and knocking on mine, thinking he would find in us chroniclers in the style of the Second Empire, masters of the boulevard.[60] And asking us for advice: he wanted to live as a writer, to bring his work to fruition. I remember preaching to him: "Since you earn your living in the provinces, shun Paris, shun the newspapers. I know what it costs when you can't do without them. If you're resigned to being no more than a journalist, come to Paris. Otherwise, go back to Lyon, give yourself the luxury of five, ten years of silence, of work . . ."

He thanked me effusively. But that evening I met him in the antechamber of *Gil Blas*.

November 16

On the farmhouse table, an issue of *Paris-Soir*: Sunday October 2, 1938. "At 2:00 PM, the Germans began the occupation of the Sudetenland. . . . Gifts are pouring in to give Monsieur Neville Chamberlain a 'house of peace' and grateful recognition from Messieurs Daladier and Georges Bonnet."[61]

And in an article by Saint-Exupéry that will be part of the material for his memoir *Wind, Sand and Stars*: "When peace seemed threatened, we discovered the shame of war. When war seemed avoided, we felt the shame of peace."

I don't have the heart to argue with Saint-Ex. I'm defeated. I owe him too much: he gave my youth back to me; I had lost my youth and he made me the gift of another one.

When he's there, we look as if we're arguing. It's an illusion. Seeking the best hold on things isn't arguing. One wants to move the other so he can see something on the horizon. The other one resists. He thinks his position is solid. But sometimes, when I talked with Saint-Ex late at night, I realized a few days later that I had moved.

---

[60] The legendary power—and sleaze—of the late-nineteenth-century Paris press is depicted in Maupassant's 1885 novel *Bel-Ami*, which, ironically enough, was first serialized in *Gil Blas*, an arts and literary weekly that lasted until 1938.

[61] Hitler had demanded that this part of Czechoslovakia be annexed to Germany, claiming German-speaking people there were being mistreated. On September 30, 1938, English prime minister Neville Chamberlain and French prime minister Edouard Daladier signed a treaty in Munich that Georges Bonnet, the French foreign minister, had helped prepare; it allowed Germany to annex the Sudetenland. Chamberlain returned to England predicting, "This means peace in our time." He and Daladier were both greeted by cheering crowds. The day after Munich, *Paris-Soir* and *l'Œuvre*, a pro-German daily, set up a subscription to give Chamberlain a "House of Peace on a plot of French soil," but the project went nowhere. A visitors' book signed by more than a million "grateful French" was, however, given to Daladier and Bonnet.

And he wrote me a few days ago: "I remember long discussions with you. And I'm not biased; I almost always think you're right."

But our friendship is so much more than a banal harmony of ideas!

November 17

Fixing the price of foodstuffs and slapping fines on shopkeepers on the one hand and the transfer of the Lorrainians (those mysterious Lorrainians, those Lorrainians of the communiqués, foreign to all arithmetic and geography) are waking the town out of its lethargy. The town is wondering "where we're headed."

We may be defenseless against Germany; at least we're defended against our own mistakes. Surgeon Laval and his anesthetist Pétain are strange practitioners. They bring them someone with serious trauma, fallen from the sixth floor. Fractured skull. And they lean over his bedside and recommend a diet, a few principles of hygiene, and physical education.

Claude brought me the *Paris-Soir* of the thirteenth and fifteenth from Bourg. I hadn't seen *Paris-Soir* for months . . .

"150,000 kilos of bombs on London in one night." But those bombs are in big heavy font, much bigger and more murderous than the four wretched lowercase shells that shot down four German bombers.

Medium lowercase informs me that in Lyon, at the opening ceremony for the universities' academic year, Msgr Gerlier exalted the work of marshal Pétain, "an admirable leader, venerated by a people to whom he gave back hope and the secret of its greatness." A few days ago, Msgr Piguet greeted the marshal under the great entrance to the cathedral. Nothing to shock tradition in this. In the seventeenth century, Bossuet* was able both to give homage to the great of the earth in his century and to belittle them in eternity. But I ask myself the question again: Are these prelates giving the old warrior an academic homage? A powerful Church, a marshal by divine right, Church morals, military discipline, France with those morals and that discipline? Are they fooled by this idealized imagery? Don't they see that the poor marshal is a vehicle for the Nazism and fascism condemned in the court of Rome?[62] Don't they see that the stage of clerical conservatism will be brief? Don't they see that even if France accepted dictatorship for years, the dictator would not be Laval but someone they didn't

---

[62] In an encyclical written in German, *Mit brennender Sorge* (With Burning Care), promulgated March 14, 1937, Pope Pius XI does not explicitly condemn "fascism" but unreservedly rejects Nazism, its totalitarianism, and its racism. He urges the German clergy not to compromise themselves with a reprehensible system of thought.—J.-P. A.

plan on, who would at least galvanize the mass of morons and propose something to them besides monarchism and defeat? And don't they see this would mean the reign of absolute violence and in France it would not be used in favor of the Church?

If Germany wins, we will have one compensation. Despairing of all civilization for years and perhaps centuries, curators of a pillaged, deserted museum, at least we'll be delivered from all spiritual unease. The reign of the brute will have arrived. If Germany wins, not only will the past be dead, but the future will be blocked. As we wait for death, all we'll have to do is give ourselves up to total, monstrous egoism.

I hear some people say France has a strength of its own, which would prevent it from ever descending to the level of Hitlerian Germany. The finest organisms are not immune from the most serious illnesses and they don't start with a great orchestral introduction. It's as if you said a complete athlete can't get syphilis. Look at the insidious beginnings of Nazism in France.

November 18

News from town: they say the Germans have restricted the length of conversations between family members at the barrier that separates the two zones if some live in the Free Zone and others in the Occupied. They say the Germans are sending men under thirty to Germany.

The paper: Laval is back from Paris. He didn't speak. But "it was noticed that he looked particularly pleased with the results of his trip." This reporter is evidently a great reader of faces.

It seems the marshal has a clear gaze. An empty blue gaze is the rule with old military men and old family servants.

November 19

In a letter from Paris, smuggled of course, I learn that Langevin* has been arrested. The raw fact is given without comment or details.[63]

Thus Langevin joins Einstein, so to speak, in the pantheon of Nazi victims. Here is proof that French Nazism exists, and strikes the same targets as the other one. Vichy's conservative, "family," "right-thinking" stage has been left behind.

---

[63] The first internationally known French scientist to suffer from repression under Vichy, Langevin was arrested October 30, 1940; incarcerated in Fresnes along with common criminals, despite his age; and put in solitary confinement. After a protest campaign succeeded in freeing him, he was placed under house arrest in Troyes.—J.-P. A.

Are the professors going to remain silent? If they want to run a risk, they don't risk much today. If they don't run a risk, tomorrow they'll all be in danger. Do they realize that?

There was a time when we were skeptical enough to be amused, perhaps, watching the villainous ascension of a Laval. I've seen a few characters in the papers up close who were made of the same stuff. And when I looked at them, I felt the same satisfaction as when I was a child coming back from the zoo.

Who's jailing science? Who's jailing Langevin? The corrupt politician and the stupid soldier. Thus we have the image of the France of the future.

November 21

From M. Scapini's declaration in Berlin about our 2 million prisoners of war: "I appealed to Chancellor Hitler's generosity."[64]

In 1871, the Alsatians could choose their nationality.[65] Those who wished to remain French left freely. The Germany of Kaiser Wilhelm and Bismarck did not drive out the Alsatians and replace them with Wurtemburgians. Wilhelm and Bismarck wouldn't have dared. And they were not stopped by any physical constraint, by any real impossibility. Wilhelm and Bismarck only gave in to a moral constraint. They didn't drive out the Alsatians for the same reason that they didn't follow the example of the king in the Bible and order all male children to be put to death. It was, at that time, in the realm of the inconceivable.

Hitler is expelling the Lorrainians from Lorraine. While the marshal watches a parade in Lyon, holds out a flag to the crowd, and lays the cornerstone of the Philippe Pétain Bridge. To great cheering from the crowd, the marshal goes through thirty-five columns of newsprint in two days.

Hitler is driving out the Lorrainians. From Bismarck to Hitler and from Marshal MacMahon[66] to marshal Pétain, anyone can see there has been a great simplification in politics. Peoples have become cattle. The state mass-produces them in a standard model. Even if they're not as good at it as Hitler, there is absolutely no reason why a Laval or a Pétain shouldn't manufacture "French" as Hitler has manufactured "German."

[64] The former far-right deputy Georges Scapini was authorized to move to Berlin to see to the protection of French prisoners, thus indirectly giving Vichy control over 1,650,000 men in prison camps.

[65] After France lost the Franco-Prussian War in 1871, Prussia annexed Alsace and Lorraine. So did Germany in the Armistice signed by Pétain in June 1940.

[66] Patrice de MacMahon was head of the French army defeated by Prussia in January 1871 and of forces that crushed the Paris Commune that May. He was president of the Third Republic from 1873 to 1879.

I'm ashamed of these banalities, of these bird's-eye views, these wretched generalities. But it's not my fault if something glaringly obvious surges out of the chaos.

The newspaper talks about prisoners and the inhabitants of Lorraine. All I know comes through the paper. Political reality is enveloped in the paper, as the Lord was enveloped in a column of smoke.

November 22

It's raining. You can't see the trees or the village perched on the mountain. It's covered by a tarp.

They bring me the paper at least every other day. I have home delivery of current events. I glean clues from the paper as my cats glean meager little scraps of meat from their cat food.

The Greek-Italian front. Anxiety in Turkey.

The propaganda for collaboration continues. More than a column on "the efforts made by the German military administration in occupied France to make sure supplies of food get to the people, to collaborate with French authorities and reorganize production." You no longer know where to set your foot: all France is completely covered by the tons of potatoes imported from Germany. Figures, idyllic figures. Coal, milk. If we are to believe Vichy, Germany is France's wet nurse. Conclusion: "These comments prove that the policy of collaboration followed from the nature of things."

The nature of things is the finest talisman for politicians and political journalists. The nature of things *is* their policy.

I don't think the editors of our newspapers realize the power of their comic genius. Any page of the paper is full of the finest contrasts of high farce. The minister of finance gives the French wise advice about their available capital.

That might displease a few Frenchmen who happen to have very little money available in their wallet or drawer. The editors have thought of them. In a neighboring column, we read this fetching headline: "The bliss of being poor." Thus the rich can depend on the solidity of Vichy's financial policies. And as for the poor, they need nothing, since they're happy. "Poverty may be the sole form of happiness that we are given on this earth. Even when one wants for nothing, one does not always like one's work. Whereas liking one's work is what truly matters."

Why read these things, you say? And what sadistic impulse makes you so attentive to them? I read these things because a sign is a sign. Because in these times the news is managed, like everything else, and amplified in a definite direction. Because pathology is a fine science. Because never was there such close collaboration between M. de la Palisse, M. Prudhomme, and King Ubu.[67]

My Siamese cats have found a beam of sunlight. They don't let it go to waste. They settle into it and let it be known that they are not to be disturbed.

November 23

At the market. "The Italians got a real shellacking . . ." says an old woman, one of those who still wears the traditional Bresse bonnet. She doesn't expand on this, and I ask her no questions. I haven't read the paper today. Neither has she, no doubt. But it's a piece of news that's making the rounds, and it left her in a state of political beatitude.

This idea is flying around all over: the marshal is playing against the men of Vichy, he's not their accomplice, and on the contrary, he's waiting for his chance to give them their just deserts.

Old François, the chair mender, is not far from believing this fable. I ask him what he's basing this on. "I don't know," he answers, "Little things here and there . . ."

Vichy, neglecting the regeneration of our souls for the day, turns its attention to our bellies and advises us to pick acorns. "They can be used either to feed hogs or as a substitute for coffee . . ."

November 24

I waited for Claude at the station. From the station to our house you have to allow over half an hour. Hardly had we left the town and entered the uphill path than Claude was expounding the operations of the Greek and Italian armies to me. Claude is fifteen and a half, and one of the effects of the war is that he is, unfortunately, a boarding student at the lycée in Bourg. Another effect of the war: lycée students have an astonishing knowledge of the geography of the Near East. The lycée is divided into two groups: a Pétain group and a de Gaulle group (sometimes you can hear "God Save the King" being hummed in the halls). But Laval is never brought up. Laval is out of the question.

White frost on the fields. Down below, a landscape framed by pines: the sloping path, the gate to the yard, a tree with yellow leaves gleaming like metal. Nothing

---

[67] The sixteenth-century Seigneur de la Palice unwittingly gave his name to the *lapalissade*, a stupid tautological truism; M. Prudhomme is a caricatured personification of the average bourgeois, and Ubu is the grotesque, comic anti-hero of Alfred Jarry's proto-Dadaist play *Ubu the King* (1896).

mingles with anything, nothing goes into anything, and nothing floats or sways as in a summer landscape. All the pieces are cemented. Everything is assembled, tightened, frozen. It's astonishingly solid.

Laurent was driving his oxcart, and on the way he killed a hare with his goad. I am invited over to eat hare. I had dinner at the farm.

"Whatever happens," Laurent tells me, "It'll take years for us to get back the freedom we used to have . . . It'll be a long time before I go back to the fair to sell or buy cattle, like it's in my interest and I like to do . . ."

"If England won," Laurent says, "Pétain wouldn't run away . . . They wouldn't do anything to him. But Laval—Laval would've already vanished."

November 25

Some Parisians have a country home in a nearby hamlet. They drive back and forth between their house in the fields and their Paris apartment. They have as much gas as they want and cross the Demarcation Line with no difficulty. We know through their maid that in Paris they entertain German officers. "In Paris," they say, "People have enough to eat, there are no lines in front of the shops, and life goes on as it did before." Have they been given a propaganda mission, or are they abominably honest, like people stuffed with food who can't see the poor at all?

It's whispered about the countryside that these optimistic tourists who cross the zones with such ease are German agents. I'm not so sure. As far as I can see, these people are the kind who would have been hawkish hardliners from 1914 to 1918. They would have believed whole German divisions gave themselves up if you held out some bread and jam to them, Germans who cut off the hands of little children in Lille and Lens. They would have classified the Boches as unclean beasts and informed on a neighbor who played Wagner. That was what conformism meant then. Now they're boasting of their fine German connections.

November 27

The papers are full of "the indignation aroused in France" by the bombing of Marseilles by English planes.[68] A farmer is laying manure on his field. Hardly have we exchanged a few words about the wind and weather: "The planes in Marseilles," he tells me, "were Italian planes disguised as English. That's what they're saying in town, and it wouldn't surprise me a bit."

[68] November 25, 1940, bombs from supposedly English planes left four dead and five injured.—J.-P. A.

An effect of dictatorship: the press counts for nothing. The town invents its own symbols.

The paper: the prefect of Saône-et-Loire has forbidden "listening to British radio in public and, in general, all radios diffusing anti-national propaganda." Tomorrow, they'll ban listening at home. The day after tomorrow, neighbor will inform on neighbor.

"We learn from German sources" (where are the others?) "that only fifty thousand Lorrainians" (the *only* is admirable) "have been transferred to the Unoccupied Zone."

White frost has covered the fields. In the path, it draws the veins of leaves on the ground and covers their hollow with an implacable sieve. Each leaf is a fairy's masterpiece. I walk through a landscape of lace.

November 28

Drive the war away from oneself. No longer think of France, England, Germany, civilization, of an unstable way of life, no longer suffer inside oneself for the suffering of 2 million prisoners and fifty thousand Lorrainians driven from their homes.

The time we're living in touches me, goes through me, invades me, attacks my flesh. But it operates with such figures, in such dimensions that I don't have enough points in my body to receive the stimuli. Two million prisoners, fifty thousand Lorrainians, and the dissolution of this civilization have become nothing more than historical abstractions and now only touch me in the cold regions of my being where I contemplate the exodus in the Bible, the great classical massacres, the conquest of Greece by Rome, and the defeat of Vercingetorix.*

The conciliation of the temporal and spiritual in Catholicism seems to me an admirable construction. Bossuet has an answer for everything. Revolutions and wars are God's means of serving his designs. Bossuet knows how to praise the great in this century and lower them in eternity. But the century has become too troublesome, and nobody's on a crusade except Hitler. What God is moving something to throw the world out of order?

And money poses blunt questions that require a personal answer. I don't know if the war made money sick. But it didn't do away with it. Don't tell me "Today even the richest people aren't sure of the future." If there's a famine, the rich will be the last to die of hunger. If I didn't have money worries, I'd make my niche in the disaster much more easily, and I'd polish up spiritual ornaments at my ease.

Or I'd live the life of a domestic animal. I would live, like so many others, with no other reason for living than to be alive.

November 29

All I have to imagine Paris with is a few dispersed signs. Lines in front of the shops. A friend asks me to send him a bag of cabbages and leeks. Student demonstrations.[69] I don't know if the university is really shut down. The students in the all-female Sèvres School have to sign a register every morning at the police station. The night and the street are without light, and there's a curfew at midnight. But I don't know if Paris is suffocating, growing angry, or asleep.

An astonishing diptych. On the one hand, the papers are full of Vichy's plans: "Remake the race, remake education." On the other hand, the whole country's hanging on the words of English radio. The government is operating in isolation. If it thinks about the crowd, the crowd doesn't think about it. A strange parallel: When and where will those two lines stop being parallel, when and where will they meet?

"I don't buy the paper anymore," the young railroad worker Aimé François tells me.[70] "I listen to English radio."

I ask him about the city and his friends. "We're only interested in the restrictions," he says, "and for the rest, we're waiting. We hope England's going to win. That's all. We don't talk about politics." "How about Laval?" "Very unpopular." "And Pétain?" "A lot of people think without him the Germans would do worse."

1.9 million francs have been voted for the construction of stadiums, playing fields, pools . . . A replay of ten years of movies: the parades of Hitler Youth, all the blessings of closed ranks. Major de Maisonneuve reveals to the press that "physical development will be the cornerstone of general education." They have to develop men of character . . . "Intelligence gets nowhere if it is not based on character . . ."

For this category of simpleminded men in secondary education, intelligence is either a mechanism that turns without gripping anything or an arsenal of subversive devices. They're not completely wrong. Indeed, in a world organized by them, the intelligence will always be subversive.

I think of Stendhal and his "two pet aversions, hypocrisy and stupidity."

---

[69] On November 11, more than three thousand students from Parisian lycées and the university demonstrated, particularly along the Champs-Élysées, to protest the arrest of Paul Langevin and above all to express their patriotism; some were seriously injured, and German and French police made two hundred arrests. The occupying authorities closed the university and authorized it to reopen only after Christmas vacation.

[70] Aimé is the son of "Old François."—J.-P. A.

November 30

Unity of the snow, dry trees. The landscape is unrecognizable. The snow reveals unknown planes. It doesn't embellish the hedges or hollows. It separates and defines what was not defined before. A landscape with no agitation or metamorphoses of colors, a landscape into which doubt does not enter.

A young peasant woman writes the marshal: "I am so happy to see our dear country starting over on new bases to remake France as we always would have wished her to be . . . I wanted the marshal to know (they say he is so good that I'm sure he'll listen to me) all the merit of our dear parents in bringing us all up . . ."

The scribes in Vichy—or from elsewhere—should strive for more verisimilitude.

The prestige of France in times gone by: classical France, land of liberty. Legend or not, that's how France was imagined, despite its diplomats, despite the Foreign Office. As a French traveler, I was intimidated by it. I hadn't thought I was carrying so much liberty around in me and, from the mere fact that I was French, liberty was radiating from me without my even noticing it.

Big words. So France was the country of big words. And I wonder why one category of big words makes people smile and not the other, and why the only words in honor should be the big words of religions and dictatorships. For "order" is not a smaller word than liberty, nor is it less metaphysical.

November 30

An order by the prefect: "The discovery of extremist leaflets on the territory of the commune will lead to the administrative confinement of known Communist activists, unless they are already being prosecuted by the courts . . ."

This goes beyond prosecution for the offence of expressing one's opinions. Not only is the author of the offence prosecuted, but so is whoever can be suspected of agreeing with it.

The town cares about the economic restrictions, but not about freedom. It's waiting for the final score of the England-Germany game. I don't know if it has forgotten freedom or if it thinks a victorious England will give freedom back to it.

Four fraud inspectors were at the market yesterday. The look of income-tax assistants, of cellar rats, but shadier.

As for the peasants, they think that whatever happens, they'll never die of hunger. They think it with no special pride, but it's natural they should think so. They go to the town hall to declare their animals and the milk they get from them. Their declarations defy the administrative forms. They're studied by civil servants who don't know if a cow yields two or twenty liters of milk a day and who have no idea that it yields less in winter than in summer.

I'll eat boudin tomorrow. Laurent's going to slaughter a pig he didn't declare, a pig that weighs around 130 kilos.

Pleasures of the undergrowth. For a few days, my feet had been sinking into a layer of leaves spread over heavy compost—two carpets. That walk is a sweet luxury. Today, the hollows were filled with ice, and the slightest wrinkle in the earth set me bouncing. I was walking from springboard to springboard.

Chiappe is dead. Poor Guillaumet.[71]
The pages Saint-Ex wrote about him in *Wind, Sand and Stars*.[72]
Guillaumet so calm. Guillaumet lost in the Andes, alone, near the wreck of his plane. They fly out, they look for him, and they don't find him.
"I could see your plane," Guillaumet said to him. "How did you know it was me?" "Nobody else would have dared fly so low."

December 2

The marshal is not allowed (I mean that entity for crowds that they've manufactured from the marshal) to speak the blunt language that was Hitler's. He would have to add a few assassinations to his administrative confinements, and it seems the country isn't quite ripe for them yet. Above all, the men who pull the marshal's strings would have to invent a new advertising campaign. The character of the marshal is like an old song.

December 3

I remember Professor Polanyi, who taught physical chemistry at the University of Berlin, saying to me in 1932: "The authorities are asking us—not to say

[71] Jean Chiappe, former prefect of police, was one of the protagonists of the events of February 6, 1934, when right-wing organizations demonstrated violently on Place de la Concorde across from the Chamber of Deputies in an attempt to bring down the republic, many felt. Sixteen people died, with hundreds injured. Chiappe had just been named high commissioner in Syria and Lebanon; as he flew to his new post, his plane, piloted by Henri Guillaumet, was accidentally shot down on November 27, 1940, in a dogfight between Italian and English planes over the Mediterranean.—J.-P. A.

[72] In that 1939 work (*Terre des hommes*), Antoine de Saint-Exupéry has a particularly glowing chapter on Henri Guillaumet, one of the great figures in the pioneering airline Aéropostale. (Saint-Exupéry was one of its pilots.) It delivered airmail at a time when flying was extremely dangerous. In June 1930, Guillaumet barely survived an accident while crossing the Andes. Saint-Exupéry's *Night Flight* describes a postal flight across South America.—J.-P. A.

more—to increase our practical research to the detriment of speculative research." I don't know if he saw a sign of rising Nazism in this. But assuredly a sign of German decline in those months when Germany, he said, was wavering between Nazism and Communism.

I may have lavished too much admiration on the peasants. I was dazzled, because they didn't talk in abstractions. Land and animals. They sow the land and lead the animals with their goad. But I'm beginning to wonder if they aren't a bit too concrete. Sometimes I find their concreteness a little tight on my foot. Sometimes I can't walk in those shoes. You don't move forward.

And they're so tight-lipped, so diplomatic. So many precautions and circum-locutions, such reticence! When Laurent tells me a good story from the town— one of those stories he probably wouldn't have told me ten or fifteen years ago because he wouldn't have trusted me enough—sometimes he gives it to me in one go. But he's so used to taking verbal precautions that he can't do without them, and instead of putting them before or during, he puts them in afterwards. When he's told me everything and I know everything, he starts over, using a thousand detours and hesitations. As if like that, he was attenuating the audac-ity of his first version.

They're proud of their freedom, I mean the freedom of a job that only takes orders from the earth, the sun, or the rain. But they don't show any surprise when one of their own becomes a cop in Paris.

They work hard, but the only ones who get rich are the ones who have a flair for shady dealing, and shady dealing soon becomes an artistic pleasure for them.

During the exodus of June-July, I lived in a hamlet in the Gâtinais for two weeks.[73]

In Abel Delaveau's place, at the gleam of twilight or an old oil lamp with an onyx base (the electric wires had been cut), those peasants didn't limit events to the hamlet, nor did they dully accept fate. They had dreamed of justice and peace (don't try to tell them those are metaphysical clouds, they'll laugh in your face). They had dreamed of socialism and disarmament; they had dreamed of a world ruled by reason. Reason may no longer be fashionable with intellectuals; it still is, among the old peasants of Chapelon. I don't know if they sense there is something beyond, but I know they hate what they see on this side: that is, war

---

[73] Le Gâtinais is a region not far from Paris. Werth relates this in *33 Days*, the account of his trek across France along with tens of thousands of fleeing refugees. He and his wife, Suzanne, were taken in by Abel Delaveau, a farmer in the village of Chapelon.

Panicked refugees leave Paris in June 1940. Léon and Suzanne Werth were caught in this exodus as they tried to drive the 220 miles to Saint-Amour—a journey that would take them thirty-three days. *Library of Congress, LC-USZ62-128308*

and oppression. Such were these Cartesian peasants, and it's not my fault if this peasant wisdom is not exactly the one attributed to them by academic novelists. "What we were missing," said one of these old men, "was Jaurès."

The socialism of these farmers is not a doctrine. It's a response to two problems: to live from the land and not live like animals. The answers of the past don't satisfy them. They know something about the past. Something of the past is preserved in these farmhouses, where their parents lived. The old people have the time to tell children how they ate and how people used to think in their day. The young farmhand knows his father slept in the stable. Now where could workers, in the flux of the poor outlying quarters of the city, learn about their recent past? Their visions of history come from school and political meetings.

How they ate, how they thought . . . How vulgar that sounds to our mystics of "order" and "action." How vulgar it sounds to the delicate spirits who, in a decomposing world, fabricate a religious mystique for themselves on the level of readers of *Marie-Claire*! No doubt they're shocked by the association of those two words—"ate" and "thought." But to them the second seems as crude as the first. To them, thinking seems as disgusting as eating.

Reason is an instrument for callused brains.

That's the way it is. The Gâtinais peasants believe in the philosophy of the Enlightenment. Their thought can be translated into the language of the men of the eighteenth century. My naïveté will be scoffed at, my historical connections will be laughed at. But if I had written that those old peasants were all just like the parents of Joan of Arc, our present "philosophers" would have admired my good sense and my perspicacity.

Five months have gone by, and we know what has happened in these months. We measured the violence of the disaster but not how long it would last. What are they saying, this month of December, in the living room of Abel Delaveau's farmhouse? And no doubt a German field kitchen is still set up in his yard.

December 4

The sun has hardly slipped an eye over the mountain. The clouds have no light. The brown trees and bottle-green fields where the snow has melted, the amber snow—that amber, that glaze—it's very precisely an old Dutch painting.

The marshal in Marseilles. Twelve columns of newsprint. Yesterday, they compared him to Napoleon, pinching the ears of his old guard; today, we see a "girl who absolutely wanted to kiss him, couldn't succeed and bursts into tears." So the newspapers have instructions to fabricate a legend for the marshal. But the presses are not as effective as one might think in this regard. The people don't accept the verities they churn out as true. I say: the presses. For the government commands the printing presses, and journalists are no more than an organ of transmission between the presses and the government. Tomorrow, a clever engineer will replace them by a machine, as you replace a team of porters by an inclined plane or a dump truck.

We no longer see Laval's name at all. The press works at transferring the passions of the crowd onto the marshal. Its hatreds are discharged on Laval, and its available loyalism is directed toward the marshal. The crowd no longer has a government before it but an old soldier who pinches the ears of the old guard and kisses little girls who bring him bouquets. As for the ministers and state secretaries, you can hardly retain their names. They're staff sergeants, the marshal's watchdogs.

We don't know if the marshal is led by his watchdogs or if other puppeteers, backstage and invisible, are pulling the strings. And then there's the hypothesis that the marshal is leading himself. At the beginning of the dictatorship, he was thought of as a protective idol, forever wedged in his niche. But since his trip to Lyon and his trip to Marseilles, the marshal has proved he's perfectly transportable.

I can't resist an intolerable feeling of disgust when the marshal invokes "the human person." For a few days now, the newspaper has been putting "the human person" in the spotlight. The marshal has been talking about it or is being made to talk about it.

I only have a wood-burning stove, and I dream of a fireplace where you can throw in tree trunks. I give myself a miniature fireplace. I open the stove door, go down on all fours, and watch the flames licking the wood and the resin seething near a knot.

Last night, a clear night, in the frozen sky with a few unmysterious stars clearly showing in it, planes flew by right near the house. They say they're English, going to bomb Italy. Those young men up there flying at three hundred miles an hour are not, like the infantrymen of the other war, closed in, sleeping in the war. Death doesn't come for them where they live; they go toward it, circle around it.

But after the war, what about the survivors? I can already hear the fine academic discourse (we heard it during the preceding war): "Here are the men who were able to win and conquer themselves. We will reconstruct a world in the image of their heroism." Unfortunately, as rotten as the virtues of war may be, the virtues of peace have nothing in common with them. These men will return as agitated or weary children. They'll look for a good hot meal and bedroom slippers.

All through the war, Antoine de Saint-Exupéry flew long reconnaissance flights. Day after day. I can see him between two flights. He took his place among us again as if the day before or that very day he had no relation with death, as if he weren't going to have a relation with it the following day. Sometimes I couldn't help imagining his plane shot down, the cabin smashed and him, motionless forever, in that cabin. And immediately I would say to myself: he is invulnerable. Not to think him invulnerable seemed to me a betrayal.

He wanted that risk. How many times did we tell him, again and again, that he could serve better through his example than through his death.

When it's not a matter of restrictions or requisitions, the peasants around here are absolutely indifferent to everything the Vichy government says and does. They don't even read "The Day in Vichy." They're interested in the duel between England and Germany, and now especially in the Italian-Greek war. They've discovered Albania, and every Italian setback is cause for jubilation.

So all the acts, measures, and reforms or plans of Vichy go unnoticed. As if the wave of a magic wand had rendered the men of Vichy invisible and impalpable. The peasants and townspeople are neither overjoyed nor frightened by that Hitlero-fascism. Either they don't identify it or they think Vichy's out of it and the game is being played out elsewhere.

December 7

The peasants or the townspeople greet me like this:

"What do you think of it?"

"Of what?"

"The situation . . ."

I make a vague gesture with my arms that means: "What do I know? I don't know any more than you do . . . It's too complicated for all of us . . ."

Then they say: "We're waiting." If I ask, "For what?" they answer: "England . . ." Never a word about Vichy.

"What do you think of the situation?" I don't think much of it, but all I do is think about it. Perhaps I'd think about it less if I weren't isolated from my family. From my friends. I'd be sharing the situation with them. But I'm alone with it.

During the other war, how often did I say and write that the dimension of events was not something you could consider and that man could take refuge in himself. And now, deep down, I bump up against Hitler and Laval. I had never been inhabited by such filth. My guests were of another quality.

Deep down, I have a certain coarseness. It is coarse to stick to the news like a leech. What is elegant is to filter it, to treat it only by allusions, to strip it of that vulgarity which is not separable from current events, to give it a historical flavor while it's still warm, make a well-chiseled concept out of it, a delicate crystal block.

To master time, to master oneself, not to lose one's inner freedom, I find this theme even in the newspaper. Thus do noble popularizers escape both Germany and Vichy. They sometimes suggest being a thinking reed, sometimes the flexible reed that resists the storm.[74] I detect the scent of hypocrisy in these words. They're not removing themselves from events, but from risks.

December 8

The snow is intact, except for perfectly drawn lines of arrows of equal length. Those arrow signs, that high-precision work, are the traces printed by the claws of the hens.

The tenant farmer bought an issue of *Paris-Soir* in town. I learn that "the amateur spirit must be revived in boxing." And with a forty-five-yard-wide garden you can live in autarchy, if you raise a goat, chickens, and rabbits. In Merovitza, Serbia,[75]

---

[74] "Man is only a reed, but he is a thinking reed" is Pascal's definition in his *Pensées*. The "flexible reed" would make French readers think of La Fontaine's fable "The Oak and the Reed"; only the latter resists the storm.

[75] Probably Mitrovica, now in Kosovo.

husbands buy their wives by the kilo, and a future father-in-law had tried to cheat on the weight. They're going to restore a fresco in the Lyon city hall.

I also learn that Maurice Chevalier represented France before 1,500 Zurichers. "This first reappearance of a French singer goes beyond the limits of an ordinary artistic performance . . ." Maurice Chevalier "bows with reserved dignity . . . and gives an example of tact and nobility."

And people are surprised at the debacle.

Ten centuries from now, a historian compiling texts will show that Maurice Chevalier incarnated the France of 1940.[76] Indeed, marshal Pétain's learned articles in the *Revue des Deux Mondes* and the Vichy government's preaching in the press urge us to develop our character and warn us against the bad effects of intelligence. Thus Maurice Chevalier sings, in Zurich, the "regeneration" of a France whose values are not intellectual:

> She wasn't very bright
> But in bed that's quite all right.

December 9

Vichy's policy means integrating France with Germany. The country is rejecting it half-heartedly and disapproves of it. But that's an intimate impulse, an inner disapproval. The country doesn't resist and no doubt cannot resist. And I've resisted it for six months by facing my paper. But isn't it high time I got away from those thoughts and passions so narrowly attached to the present?

I'm a Jew, but am I going to reduce the world to the comforts Jews will have in the Europe of tomorrow? Will my judgment depend on the fact that for a few weeks now I've no longer had the right to be a marshal of France?[77]

Could I be one of those idealists with empty eyes who slip their hand into the gears of the machine that makes history and get it crushed? Could I be fooled by old words (not so old as all that, actually) in yesterday's papers and the Sunday speeches of politicians? Could I still not have learned that the crowd doesn't think? It's true that scientists don't think much more either, when they're not thinking about the things in their laboratory. Don't I know history can't be enclosed in a logical system? To make that France I care so much about, hanged

---

[76] That is exactly how he is shown in Marcel Ophuls's 1969 documentary *The Sorrow and the Pity.* It is not a favorable depiction.

[77] It was actually October 4, 1940, that Vichy promulgated, on its own initiative, its first Statute Regulating Jews, which excluded them from the professions, the civil service, and the military.

men had to swing on the Breton roads near the Marquise de Sévigné?[78] The
Lorrainians and the Jews make history the way those hanged Bretons did.

A little wisdom now, a bit of an overview. If France died, who would notice it?
Certainly not those patriots who so lightheartedly accepted the risk of it dying.
Who would notice it in a good Germanic peace? Old Cournot perhaps, in his
grave,[79] who said the French genius was inseparable from a "habit of opposition." Einstein, Eddington, and Langevin are not indispensable for the functioning of electric power plants.

I don't have so many years left to live. What better can I do than to fix them up
comfortably? And I don't mean the years of history, but mine. I've lived enough
for my past to be a very long novel. And for my present, why should I try anything else but to protect it, to isolate myself with the people I have chosen, to
deny myself the great conflagrations and only observe as a bystander those huge
conflicts of forces that stir up childish thoughts? Thinking against a Hitler or a
Laval—isn't that as low as limiting your thinking about the world to a Hitler or
a Laval?

What would stop me from staying in bed today?

I was going to detach myself from the world. But Andrée François is back
from town:[80] "General de Gaulle spoke on the radio yesterday . . . He said the
Italians were done for and the Germans would be done for soon . . ."

December 10

Sometimes this lethargic France dreams and, like an opium smoker, sees no
obstacle to its drifting desires. It must be the tenth time I've heard the tale of
the escaped prisoner: "The Germans told me," says the prisoner, "This year we're
guarding you, but next year, you're the ones who'll be guarding us."

After all, it's possible that a German said it, and this word-flake snowballed
into a legend. Words have their fate, too. And perhaps there are words in which
the people's instinct recognizes a premonitory virtue. But the last of those
escaped prisoners (this one's allegedly not a myth; he supposedly was seen in
town) is going a bit too far when he claims to have gotten this confession of
discouragement and a fatalistic announcement of a reversal of fortune from a
German officer. I can't see a stiff *Oberleutnant* breaking down like that before a

---

[78] In 1675, Brittany revolted against a new tax. The king's soldiers repressed the revolt by hanging dozens of Breton peasants at a time. The Marquise de Sévigné, whose correspondence is trea-
sured for its literary quality, describes the repression dispassionately in one of her letters.

[79] Antoine Cournot, a nineteenth-century French mathematician, economist, and philosopher,
developed a relativistic, probabilistic conception of knowledge; he can easily be thought of as a
nonconformist.—J.-P. A.

[80] The daughter of "Old François" and the brother of Aimé, Andrée François was employed by
Werth's wife, Suzanne, since 1922 and was considered part of the family.—J.-P. A.

French soldier, his prisoner. But who would have predicted that in June French officers would abandon their units and try to pass caravans of refugees on the roads, transforming the left side into a track for car races?

The newspaper quotes the Italian publication *Regime Fascista*. Thus I learn that Switzerland, just like England, is "masonic and Judaic." The silliest texts or the ones most like advertisements have a meaning, if they converge. The Mason, the Jew, the Judeo-Marxist are not there by chance in dictators' polemics. You'd even think they have their own virtue, independent of place and climate. If anti-Semitism was traditional in Germany, it seems it was unknown in Italy and Mussolini was late in borrowing it from Hitler, like a magic wand, like a talisman, as if it had incantatory properties.

December 12

Monsieur de Gaulle (that's what the paper calls him) and General Catroux have been stripped of their French nationality.

So has France.

The snow, the thick sky, and the thin trees, drawn as if on the whiteness of a sheet of paper. As soon as the landscape gets covered with snow, I think of my childhood. Because in less than one night the snow turns the habitual landscape into "a surprise," because it has worked a miracle, the way a magician does, because it all happened as in a fairytale? No, not only that. The world of the snow is the world of childhood. Everything in it is limited. I can count the pickets of a fence; I follow its direction like vertical strokes on a page of writing. Everything is closed, locked inside the box of mist. Everything is motionless. It really is a child's world.

Vichy is not neglecting economic problems: new coins of five, ten, and twenty francs will be minted bearing the marshal's effigy.

A member of the Academy,[81] this old marshal is giving us the very finest example of the way words shift in meaning: he borrows the language of speakers at socialist rallies and the people's universities of 1900 to attack capitalism and suddenly wants money to be "the reward for work." Tomorrow we'll see him debating the question of surplus value and denouncing "the exploitation of man by man." If need be, he'll shout, "Long live the socialist republic!" and "Long live the socialist republic" will have acquired a comfortable resonance, a fascistic-academic resonance.

---

[81] The Académie Française. The forty members of this venerable institution, founded by Cardinal Richelieu in 1635, are supposed to watch over the purity of the French language.

According to the undersecretary of colonies, "Communist elements, who have long been subject to propaganda, committed certain excesses . . . especially in the provinces of Tay-Vinh, Mytho, Vinh-Long, Tra-Vinh . . ." The white light over there, the delicate nights; an ancient people, childish and refined, where men have finely chiseled faces.[82] Perhaps if France had sent poets there . . . Or even good ordinary people. But for administrators, residents, and governors, France chose the worst specimens you could find in France, with no exceptions. The engineers and officers knew this very well. But they kept quiet, or weren't listened to. It was these administrators who introduced Communism to Cochin-China. It was totally unknown between 1920 and 1925. But if an Annamite showed not even some resistance but a bit of dignity, he was incarcerated as a Communist. So that Communism became, for a part of Annamite youth, the very figure of justice and dignity. The propaganda of Moscow followed that of the administrators.

Anyone who has lived there a little can guess, through this communiqué, that the prisons are full, our troops have massacred generously, and our police have tortured abundantly.

I meet Riffault on the path. He stops his oxen. "You don't really feel like working," he says; "when will it end? When will we have some peace and quiet again?"

But from whom, from what, does he expect peace?

He also says: "I never got involved in politics . . ."

It's not hard for me to show him he's wrong:

"Don't tell that to me . . . I saw you in politics up to your neck, thrown into politics, giving away everything to politics. Yes . . . on this same path, in September of last year. You weren't very happy . . . you were on your way to the draft center. That wasn't politics?"

"Well yes . . . that's true," he says, "I didn't think of it."

"The government," Laurent says as he loads manure onto a wheelbarrow, "maybe the government agrees with de Gaulle. It's trying to fool Germany."

I express a few doubts about that. He resists:

"Not Laval, of course, but the others . . ."

The government is revamping municipal government. In principle, all governmental "reforms" seem shameless to me, since two-thirds of France is occupied.

I'm incapable of judging this reform. In the sense that Riffault understood politics, I'm less involved than he is. I have never voted. Not out of principle or laziness. Nor, as one might think, because of my police record. But every time

[82] In 1925, Werth spent time in what is now Vietnam and Laos and was then Cochin-China, Indochina, and Annam. A year later, he published a blistering 120-page account of French colonial rule there, entitled *Cochinchine*.

I thought of registering, I was stopped by my horror of the corridors in barracks, prisons, and administrative office buildings. Those Parisian buildings are just too depressing. If I'm not a registered voter, it's the architects' fault.

December 15

I spent yesterday evening at the farmhouse. For a moment, I began living in society again. We spoke about Laval's dismissal by Pétain.

Alone in my room again, I was ill at ease, like a marmot pulled out of hibernation. In Paris, the many sources of excitement cancel each other out. I was no longer used to playing the racket game of conversation. I couldn't sleep.

Laval dismissed. Flandin is replacing him.[83] When we were in Chapelon in July, there was already a premonitory piece of news going around: the Constitution of 1875 was abrogated, and Flandin was now dictator. We said to each other, Abel Delaveau and I, that he hadn't made a legend. But at least he had his Hitlerian legend, which could still be used. Then that was too soon. Now it's done.

Hitler has announced to Pétain, in terms marked by the highest nobility, "the return to France of the ashes of the Duc de Reichstadt . . ." France had been waiting for this restitution with feverish impatience.[84]

December 22

Tomorrow it will be a week since I left my nest and my snow. I spent those days in Lyon at my old friend Latarjet's place.[85] For three months, I'd been living alone, confronting the war, not even confronting myself.

My solitude melted away. It seems quite simple. You sit down around a table. And you find a family and a civilization again.

From my bed, I could hear the wheels of the tram creaking as they rubbed against the rails making a turn. That song of the tram is as lovely as the silence of the countryside.

In the country, the marshal wasn't an obsession. We only saw his picture in the paper. Sellers of postcards didn't go all the way to isolated farms. In Lyon, the

[83] Pierre-Étienne Flandin was foreign minister when Hitler invaded the Rhineland in 1936; France did not budge (nor did England). He would be Pétain's vice–prime minister for only two months.

[84] The ashes of Napoleon's son the Duke of Reichstadt were first taken to Les Invalides (which houses Napoleon's tomb) and later sent back to Vienna. His coffin arrived in Paris on December 15, 1940; a ceremony was organized by the Germans. Werth's irony is in tune with the many who said, "They're taking our coal and giving us back ashes."

[85] André Latarjet, a professor of anatomy at the Medical School of Lyon, had been a fellow student of Werth's in Lycée Ampère in Lyon.—J-P A.

marshal is everywhere. His portraits, his speeches, and his radio addresses are pasted on the mirrors of the stores. A sign of undeniable enthusiasm. I learn that before his visit to Lyon the prefecture had distributed these posters, and no shopkeeper would have taken the risk of not putting them up. Publicity for the marshal was organized like the publicity for a big circus. On the trees of the quays, the prefecture had put up long paper strips with the inscription "Vive Pétain!"

I read a few lines of an article signed by Henri Béraud on display in a bookstore. Chiappe is a great Frenchman. England hates us. You understand nothing about what is happening if you don't begin with this historical principle: England hates us. I couldn't read any further. I found the dregs of historical conversations. As I've seen that journalist's face once or twice, I refused to let myself be drawn into making a total judgment. If you've seen somebody in the flesh, you give him the nuances and complications of a man. And you're afraid of attributing to servility what is merely vulgarity. That scruple, that odd psychological habit, fooled me. There is only servility here. Those few lines are enough to reconstruct the whole thing. Whoever could write them is mean and servile. He is a disgrace.

Latarjet shows me an issue of a new weekly: *Valiance*. He just read a few lines, no more. He shrugs. He erases these small symptoms. I don't have that wisdom. That weekly is unbearably childish: anyone with the slightest nobility would be disgusted forever by the family, any discipline and any nation.[86] That orthodox childishness is worse than any kind of rottenness. It disgusts me as much as pornography, and I have a hard time distinguishing between them. Both of them soil anyone they touch and turn them into morons.

N—— hopes for an English victory and desires it; at the same time, he believes in Pétain. I already saw that some farmers separated Pétain from the men of Vichy. But for them, Pétain is a sort of good old man. Whereas N—— gives him firm plans. He saved all that could be saved in France after the debacle. While waiting for England to win, Pétain is sitting in for de Gaulle in the interim. To resolve this contradiction, N—— has no lack of logical arguments. All the more so as ever since he was young, he's lived without caring about politics and is naïvely "a good Frenchman." He was hardly troubled by the right-wing propaganda about "healthy politics." As for Marxism, he never brought his nose anywhere near it, even to sniff. All the doctrines and passions of politics have been foreign to him for thirty-odd years. He believes in the holy duplicity of Pétain. The marshal is above Vichy, a picture postcard in colors, an image of piety, an

---

[86] Werth is alluding to the motto of Pétain's French State.

icon in a niche. N—— constructs a France without the Saint Bartholomew's Day massacre,[87] a France where Henri IV was never assassinated, a France without a rebellious nature, a France of craftsmen and good laborers with the photograph of the good marshal hanging on their wall.

We go by the "Centre de Propagande Individuelle des Français" on the rue de la République. Gendarmes or riot police walking around in front. There are little stickers on the windows: maxims drawn from the marshal's speeches or testimonials of fidelity. I read on one of these stickers: "You were forced into the war by five thousand Masons and Jews in the pay of foreign powers." Such is the marshal's philosophy of history.

I have a date with some friends at the Lion d'Or brasserie. That big room with dark wooden walls makes me think of some pub or other in London. But how strongly do you feel you're in Lyon! A Lyon that has its real Lyon weight! Far from the agitation of the world and the rue de la Ré, the tavern of the Lion d'Or is a silent retreat at five in the afternoon . . .

"The mass of Lyonnais," my friend Faure tells me, "isn't consistent enough so you can simply divide them into people who support de Gaulle and people who support Pétain. There are a few Lyonnais who wish for German victory, out of a desire to get it over with. But there are a few of them who firmly believe in an English victory."

Mermillon[88] describes a bizarre little group of Lyonnais for whom defeat and the debacle are null and void. It doesn't count. In a world exhausted by the war, France will be the arbiter.

December 23–25

Two hours of train. And there's the town, then the path uphill, then my refuge. The snow has changed everything. Before I left, it had only proceeded through allusions; it set down touches of white and made chopped-up landscapes for haiku. Now it's thick and covers everything. You don't dirty it when you walk on it anymore. I'm in the high snow, like being on the high seas.

I'm waiting for Suzanne. I don't give a damn about the war, I don't give a damn about civilization. I'm waiting. Millions of men are like that, sometimes moving away from the course of history, sometimes moving toward it.

---

[87] On the night of August 24, 1572, Saint Bartholomew's Day, thousands of Protestants were murdered by Catholics led by the Holy League; it is the prime example of murderous fanaticism during France's Wars of Religion. King Henri IV, who ended these wars, was assassinated by a Catholic fanatic.

[88] Marius Mermillon was an art critic (and a Lyonnais wine merchant) who contributed to one of the cultural and political journals for which Werth wrote in the 1920s.

December 26

"Suppertime" at the farmhouse. They turned on the radio. Nobody listens or even vaguely lends an ear. If it were suddenly cut off and they were asked, "Was that music or words?" no one could answer without thinking a bit.

I listen to it for a moment. It's a talk for the peasants. They are the class cherished by the government. They are the salt of the earth. They must not migrate into the cities. The economy and morality of the country depend on them. In the newspapers and the radio, the tone of the homily is reinforced. France is becoming more and more beautiful, more and more cleansed of the stains it had before the marshal. France is becoming more and more France. To the point where it really would have been a pity if the debacle hadn't occurred.

December 28

Frozen inside by cold, frozen by solitude. I wake up in the morning wondering what the far-off catastrophe that keeps me here is. Oh, yes . . .! The war. What war? I put my nose to the window. A snowy slope and the horizon two hundred yards away. The landscape is more enclosed than my room. I'm really locked in. Outside that snow and haze, I vaguely remember England is fighting with Germany and Italy, the Germans occupy France, and I'm living in a privileged principality, governed by marshal Pétain. But I don't get into that easily. I've been waiting for Suzanne since Christmas Eve, and I haven't heard from her.

Water freezes in the pipes and sinks. The snow is hard, rough to the eyes: it doesn't cushion the landscape anymore.

For weeks, I hadn't read. I had half-opened some old musical scores. But Claude brought *The Charterhouse of Parma*:[89] "The Paris Directoire, giving itself the airs of a well-established sovereign, showed its mortal hatred for everything that was not mediocre. The inept generals . . ."

December 29

The head of the army has become the head of a factory. He works in an office. He doesn't run any physical risks. You can no longer imagine him sitting straight in the stirrups with his saber showing. But Stendhal doesn't even leave that legendary image of Napoleon intact. I quote from memory: "But what prudence on the battlefield and what concern for decorations."

---

[89] Stendhal's classic historical novel (1839) goes from Napoleon's early years to the post-Napoleonic era. A brilliant general under the Directory, Napoleon overthrew it in 1799.

And this, from *The Charterhouse*: "And there's the source of your danger, dear Fabrice! It's those moronic fools who are going to decide my fate and yours!" I'm hardly extending the sense of Stendhal's text by applying it to the present. He contrasts the despot, the courtiers, and the valets to sublime souls, to men of character. In that sense, it's still moronic fools who are deciding our fate.

The day in Vichy: "The visit of Monsieur Jacques Doriot,* who recently arrived from Paris, was all that broke the monotony of the day in the halls of the Hôtel du Parc."[90]

One of the arguments they'd given me in Lyon in favor of the marshal was this: "So would you rather have Doriot instead?" People are indeed saying Pétain's government isn't docile enough and the Germans are preparing a Doriot administration backstage.

The classifieds in *Le Progrès*. Interesting use of the adverb: "Seeking young woman to keep house and cook, even refugee."

---

[90] Pétain's government set up its offices in this hotel in Vichy.

1941

January 2

The snow melted away in one night. The fields are moss-green, like freshwater algae.

Hitler's speech to the German army. He promises the army that "God will not abandon it."

Letters to the marshal from the little children of France: "Monsieur Marshal, I felt like hitting my little sister, and I didn't do it, to make you happy . . ."

"Dear marshal Pétain, all day I was obedient so your ministers will obey you nicely too."

"We don't like being treated like retards . . . ," Laurent said as he prepared the litter for his cows.

January 3

My wife has arrived. Not by official means, not with the stamps of the *Kommandatur* on her papers. She crossed the Line through the fields at night, between Montceau and Mont Saint-Vincent.[1] An ingeniously networked organization gets you across the Line illegally, for a set price. The customers first contact someone in the back room of a café near Place des Ternes. At the Gare de Lyon, they're greeted by a certain Roger, wearing a cap and a red scarf. With Roger is a young woman. He makes the trip with his customers. They get off the train at Montceau. They stop in a café. Roger shows the greatest affection for his young friend. At night, they take to the road, they leave it, they cross fields. They have to walk six miles to reach the Line of Demarcation. That night, the road and paths were covered with ice. Men and women kept slipping. One of the men fell seventeen times.

The group, led by Roger and a local man, was composed of three escaped prisoners, Suzanne, and a lady who was going to meet her husband and sons in

[1] "The Line" is the Line of Demarcation, the boundary between the Occupied and Unoccupied Zones.

Suzanne Werth, ca. 1940. *Centre de la
Mémoire, Médiathèque Albert-Camus,
Issoudun*

Marseilles. Roger's girlfriend was wearing a hooded rubber raincoat, and the
wind swept into it with a flapping noise. "Take that off," the guide said, "We're
not going to a dance . . ."

"We'll see all that later in the movies," Roger said, "but don't worry about it
too much . . . The sentry's hard of hearing."

They don't know if Roger's discovered the sentry's deafness through experience, or if he bought it.

They get to Saint-Vincent. They're in the Free Zone.

I feel violently indignant at this story. Getting paid for this kind of service is
so abject! My whole sense of morality bristles at it. But morality is an imperfect
framework in which to insert the actions of men. "It's not so simple," Suzanne
says. "In the first place, they didn't ask the escaped prisoners to pay." Their
milieu is hard to define! Milieu or mob, perhaps. They remind me of the habitués
of Montmartre nightclubs who deal coke.

Since they're the only ones who have safe conducts in order, they carry their
customers' money, jewels, and letters on them. The customers get them back
once the Line has been crossed.

In the café in Montceau, one of them laid a bag on the table and displayed,
with even more vanity than pleasure, what he earned in his week or his month: a
hundred and fifty thousand-franc bills. Someone said: "You'll be sorry when the
war is over . . ." He stood up, indignant. "I'd give all of it for the war to be over
right now. And not just because we have a heart, but because we don't give a
damn, we'll always know how to make money . . ."

It is true that Langevin* was imprisoned for a few days by the Occupation
authorities. They stole his watch. He's now under house arrest in Troyes. I ask

what form the protests took in the Collège de France and the Sorbonne. It seems they didn't budge, or if they showed their sympathy to Langevin, it was so discreetly that nobody noticed. I think with some sadness of a commentary I wrote a few years ago on a photograph showing German professors listening docilely to a speech Goebbels* was making to them. I showed that such consent was not absolutely impossible in France, and academic careers can easily lead to cowardice.

The Germans informed Langevin they were imprisoning him as a "warmonger," but they hadn't asked for him to be dismissed. Only Vichy was responsible for that. So it really was the marshal who dismissed Langevin, for the health of his little principality.

The marshal's France cannot tolerate a Langevin. The marshal is locking up Langevin and physics as Hitler would have locked up Einstein and relativity if Einstein hadn't gone into exile first. I'm talking broadly, I know. Academism demands more nuances—and also more lies. I can hear the objection already: Einstein was only expelled by Hitler because he was Jewish, and Langevin was only dismissed by the marshal because he attended Communist rallies.

"France doesn't need intelligence. France has all too many intelligent men." I heard that at the beginning of the war from the mouth of a staff officer. That's the way many of those clever philosophers talk: the ones who learned philosophy in their Bac textbooks.[2] Stendhal already answered "philosophers" like this and denounced their "vulgarity."

It seems the Paris newspapers attacked Langevin and Perrin in a despicable way.[3] It is comical to see the editors of these papers placing the debate in the scientific sphere and denouncing them as poor scientists. It is vile to see those "physicists" for political rags hiding behind the Occupation authorities to insult French scientists.

France is cut into slices: occupied France, the marshal's France, the peasants' France, the workers' France, bourgeois France, and right- and left-wing France, one intending to smother the other and solve everything through fascism— fascism, which may decompose tomorrow in Italy itself. Working France, scientific and thinking France, the France of the marshal's postcards—will all the slices of France come together again? Under the German boot, through the brutality of fascism and the party of order at any price? Or will France reinvent

---

[2] Philosophy is still a required subject in the last year before the Baccalauréat in most tracks in all French lycées.

[3] The Paris press was directly controlled by the Nazis.—D.B. Jean Perrin, a renowned nuclear physicist (winner of the Nobel Prize in 1926), succeeded in getting to the United States.—J.-P. A.

itself? Will the people reinvent it? The bourgeoisie is no longer capable of conceiving of France. The idea of France has become a difficult idea. Will the people clarify it? But does the people exist anymore?

Whatever France may become, whether it is lost forever or reinvents itself, France is hoping. I now know that Paris is hoping and resisting. The town is hoping. It's no longer the town after the debacle anymore, the town that was giving up, contaminated by a whiff of Hitlerism. I don't know if it's weighing the English victories in Libya correctly.[4] But it is hoping, and in defeat is taking on a winner's attitude little by little: "They're done for," the doctor tells me when I meet him in the snow-covered street. "They're done for." And he said that as he would have said "It's cold out," with the same certainty.

An elderly lady who only knows about politics through the rumors circulating through the air of a little provincial town, calling a friend, asks her for news of her children's health and suddenly asks this question, quite simply: "Is it true marshal Pétain got together with de Gaulle?"

"I'm not rich," Laurent told me. "But I'd give one of my cows for England to win."

January 6

I've changed solitudes. A hotel room in Bourg. The décor is not very appealing. But man is a funny animal. In two days, I already have my habits here, my attachments. I won't leave it without a touch of melancholy.

The paper: Monsieur Jacques Chevalier[5] has decided "to give everyone the sense of spiritual values, of the divine norm that measures them and the faith that adheres to it, without which nothing here below can be done that is great and durable."

I would be quite incapable of saying how the Pétain-Laval*-Abetz* scenario formed inside me: Laval opening to Germany the railroad lines of the Free Zone that lead to Italy, Laval dismissed and under surveillance by the marshal's guards, Abetz demanding Laval's return, Hitler's ultimatum, the marshal's refusal.[6] How much of this is oral tradition, how much my interpretation of Vichy's brief communiqués, I no longer know. But the scenario is firm and well

---

[4] On December 9, General Wavell's forces launched a counterattack against Marshal Graziani's forces in Libya. Three days later, the Italians were beaten at Sidi-Barrani and would lose Tobruk January 23. In this lightning offensive, the English lost 476 men and took 130,000 prisoners.—J.-P. A.

[5] Jacques Chevalier was Pétain's godson and a future junior minister of education.

[6] Laval was dismissed by Pétain in mid-December.

established. And not only in my mind but in everyone's mind. In the Free Zone as well as the Occupied Zone. And this unanimous agreement is free of any divergence in detail. Everybody has his own scenario, and that scenario coincides with all the others. Millions of people, of which not one could give the same version as another of a brief movie sequence or a bicycle accident, have an identical scenario in their minds. And if you look for sources that can be checked, you can hardly find half a newspaper column, reduced to this: Laval was dismissed, Pétain had lunch with Abetz, and at the end of the afternoon he received Laval.

January 13

I rented this hotel room in Bourg so Claude wouldn't be a boarder at school anymore. It is large, but it's aired by a little courtyard, and its window gives onto a wall. But there is a radiator. We live in a radiator.

On the difficulty of interpreting texts, the precision of language, and the art of reading between the lines. In *Le Progrès* of January 13, I read: "The members of the Conseil de l'Ordre des Médecins[7] of the Department of Ain adopted the following: 'The Conseil de l'Ordre sends Marshal Pétain its homage and gratitude for his confidence. It assures him of its most devoted support for the work of regeneration based on the traditional notion of "value," replacing the cult of irresponsibility and the sovereignty of "number" and, consequently, on the reconstitution of elites whose main role is to close ranks around the Head of State, to help to promote the dignity and liberty of the human person.'"

I hadn't paid much attention to this flabby text. I had only noticed that the doctors of Ain had no hesitation in considering themselves an elite. But I learned through Dr. D—— that they were intending to show there was a limit to how far they would go, both demonstrating their loyalism and showing they weren't "totalitarians" and they didn't want anyone—even the marshal—to touch "the dignity and liberty of the human person."

But why didn't they speak a less flabby language? Because they don't know any other? Because their tranquility might have been disturbed?

Strange times, when the word "human person" serves both the totalitarian marshal and those who claim they disapprove of totalitarian regimes. Strange times, when the Conseil de l'Ordre des Médecins is obliged to appear

[7] As part of its program to reorganize France, the Vichy government created the Council of the Order of Doctors on October 20, 1940. The rough US equivalent would be the American Medical Association (AMA) and, in the United Kingdom, the General Medical Council (GMC). It instituted departmental councils and a Conseil Supérieur, whose members were appointed by the government. The Conseil de l'Ordre still exists.

totalitarian to say that it isn't, and appear to approve unreservedly in order to express reservations. Such is freedom under a dictatorship. Anything can be said as long as no one understands it, not even the person to whom it is addressed.

January 14

London bombed; Brest, Lorient, and Le Havre bombed; operations in Albania and Libya. The war, day by day. Each day has its dose of war filtered through the provinces, deadened by the cold (the thermometer went down to −16°),[8] reduced to God knows what in this hotel, which is nowhere. Outside of Dr. D——, who is immersed in Greece and India, I know no one in Bourg. I don't know how Bourg is taking the war. I could only observe one sign: the optician put up a chromo of the marshal on the wall of his waiting room. The girl who does my room talks about the temperature and not about the war.

We've seen that the crowd—a part of the crowd at least, and the practitioners of Ain—separate the marshal from his ministers and cancel out his own words. They construct a marshal who resembles the marshal they desire, a good tyrant. As for the acts of his ministers and his own words, they repress them according to a Freudian process or out of mental laziness. And it is not impossible that the marshal could become something like the person they have imagined. He gave rise to his legend when he used his ministers like a puppeteer, when we saw Laval trace a semicircle as he fell quietly, like a Guignol puppet thrown backstage.

On the first page of *Candide*, an article by Charles Maurras.* Its polemical puerility is such that one might only see the sign of an individual pathology in it. But when this interpretative delirium appears as a thought to some Frenchmen who have been to lycée, the sign is serious. Mind you, all the points of departure aren't false, nor is every point in his delirium. "But he's not mad; he reasons perfectly," the parents of the sick man say to the doctor.

This article expresses total jubilation. The marshal saved France to the extent that he is a disciple of Maurras. The ideas of Maurras are in power. Since the marshal came, France is no longer the slave of Jews and wogs, "who made men blow innocent prisoners' brains out on the roads." Louis XIV has triumphed over Blum* and Mandel.[9] No argumentative madman thinks more strongly that the world is contained in his system. Maurras explains the defeat down to its

---

[8] Celsius; roughly 3°F.

[9] "Wogs": Maurras uses the derogatory slang word for foreigner: *métèque*. Léon Blum and Georges Mandel were both Jewish. As minister of the interior, Mandel had some editors of the pro-Nazi journal *Je Suis Partout* arrested in June 1940.

smallest details. He would not have had more problems in explaining victory. The debacle came from Blum and Mandel. Victory would have been explained by the persistent presence of the Ancien Regime.

Maurrases pullulate in political clubs and little cafés. But the doctors and lawyers who think he's a great man show the extraordinary decline of one part of the middle class. Sharing Maurras's passions is not what is disturbing. But accepting Maurras's theories and his simplistic vision of history to justify those passions, thinking themselves historians and great political thinkers when they turn elementary school textbooks upside down—that is more serious. They admire themselves in that pathetic scholastic reasoning. You can see the path that leads them from narcissism to Hitlerism.

Maurras the megalomaniac: "June 10, 1940, a young astrologist, skilled at deciphering our future in the sky, declared that the stars were favorable only on one point: once disaster and collapse are confirmed, my ideas were found extremely close to acceding to power."

The stars weigh the June debacle and the ideas of Maurras equally. The triumph of these ideas is no less important than the defeat of France, since there is no France without those ideas.

Bergson is dead. *Candide* has two articles on Bergson, two good journalistic articles that don't hold back their admiration for the philosopher. But the authors of these articles don't say that if the marshal had been reigning at that time, Bergson would not have had the right to teach in Clermont-Ferrand, nor in Lycée Henri-IV, nor in the Collège de France.[10]

Bourg at six in the evening, in the snow. Passive defense lighting. The sounds of passersby muffled. I brush by two young women who have stopped, leaning toward one another, no doubt confiding the depths of their souls. And in fact, I hear words of hope and deliverance: "*Marie-Claire*," says one of these young women to the other, "*Marie-Claire* has arrived."

And *Paris-Soir* too. Some poor devil is melancholically crying out *Paris-Soir*. Above the debacle, above catastrophes and revolutions, *Paris-Soir* floats above the surface and will always float above it. *Paris-Soir* is the essence of man. There will always be *Paris-Soirs* and writers to write it and typographers to print it and readers to read it.

[10] Henri-IV is an elite Parisian secondary school, the Collège de France perhaps the nation's most prestigious academic institution. Vichy excluded Jews from professions like teaching, and the philosopher Henri Bergson was born Jewish. (He had become a faithful Catholic but delayed his conversion because of the discrimination against Jews.)

The marshal has opened one of my letters again. This indiscretion annoys me. Even when I was in the army, the colonel didn't open my letters.[11]

January 20

Claude's schoolbooks include selected poems of Victor Hugo. I think I haven't dived into that ocean since I was an adolescent. Now I understand why mediocre men of letters say it's an ocean of words.[12]

For the last few days, the war and all thoughts about the war have seemed to me far off. Like millions of other people, I've reduced the war to its effects on me. Let it be over, so I can get back my own life.

A letter from Serge.[13] How brave he is and how cowardly I am! How revolutionary he is, in the great sense of the word! . . . This old world is falling apart, as he says. But where does Serge get his certainty that life will revive again?

The paper: Meeting between the marshal and Laval. "The misunderstandings that had caused the events of December 13 have been dissipated." Is the marshal abandoning his legend?

How can one be a Christian and not understand what being revolutionary means? Do Christians think they can get off by giving a few coins to a poor man? Being revolutionary doesn't just mean putting a tiny part of your savings, and not a counterfeit coin, into the begging bowl of the multitude.

January 21

In the lycée of Bourg, a leaflet was pasted on the bulletin board.
"If you want freedom: PÉTAIN.
If you want to be slaves of the Jews and Freemasons: DE GAULLE."
What's most depressing here is that you can't stop stupidity any more than you can madness. I know: the bighearted bursts of energy of the crowd—and the mind, which always has the last word. But if wise men aren't wise with rage, Europe will be governed by madmen leading idiots for the next twenty years.

---

[11] Mail was routinely opened under Vichy. Prefects used it to identify possible sources of resistance and to report on public opinion. Historians have found the prefects' reports to Vichy a mine of information.

[12] Werth goes on to quote a bitterly satiric poem by Hugo mocking Napoleon III, who "saved family, church and society."

[13] Born in Brussels to Russian parents, Victor Serge (Victor Lvovich Kibalchich) was a Marxist but anti-Stalinist writer and activist who was twice imprisoned in France. Of his twenty-odd books available in English—all translated from the French—his *Memoirs of a Revolutionary* is probably the best known.

Antonescu,[14] Hitler, and Pétain will be able to reach out and hug each other across Europe.

I found my room quite dirty. The maid has seventeen rooms to do per day. But soon she will be rich. The marshal said that from now on "money would be the reward for work."

In a review of the press, Monsieur Fernand-Laurent (*Jour-Écho de Paris*): "The new regime is striving to reintroduce what is actually the old notion of our peasants and craftsmen, the notion of work well done . . ."[15]

Stupid people cling to that poetry of the past, that poetry for gossip columnists, that vague moralism. I heard two guys in the street with fine alcoholic faces, two little shopkeepers or salesmen: "We're just getting what we deserved . . . Nobody wanted to do their duty anymore."[16]

As proof of our decadence, I've only been given the forty-hour work week, paid vacations, and sabotage. Holier-than-thous talking. But not the impurity of lawyers, judges, doctors, and the lust for money of the professions. And those officers in June 1940 who fled in vehicles, passing their soldiers on the road. And just today someone read me the letter of a doctor denouncing another who allegedly abandoned his unit in June (these two doctors are in bitter competition, practicing in the same village). The abandon of all decency, and stupidity in fear—and this well before the war—there's the explanation of the debacle.

We can't escape from the categories of right and left. All political thought fits into them. And the left, in its vague hope for a humane civilization, tries to embrace an elusive future. And the right, in its desire for a hierarchical, well-controlled world, tries to embrace a past which is no less unknown than the future.

We're registered at the hotel.

Sometimes I exchange a few words with the maid or the men who work here. Never a word about the war. Life goes on in the hotel, life in Bourg goes on in slow motion.

---

[14] Ion Victor Antonescu, the ruler of Romania from 1940 to 1944, participated in Hitler's war effort and his mass murder of European Jews. He was executed by a People's Tribunal for war crimes, crimes against the peace, and treason in 1946.

[15] Camille Fernand-Laurent was a conservative member of the Chamber of Deputies.

[16] Knowingly or not, they're in line with Pétain's radio address of June 25, 1940: "Our defeat came from our laxity. The spirit of pleasure destroys what the spirit of sacrifice has built."

January 25

I have no more ideas about the war.

Maybe Bourg and the hotel kill ideas. In this hotel room, every object, every piece of furniture seems to me soiled, dishonored. They all give me the same nervous jolt as if I were constantly meeting the gaze of a motionless rat.

The experience of Hitlerism shows that 10 million workers can be immobilized from one day to the next, hypnotized by the gaze of a dictator. Is the fate of Europe going to be decided as if the masses did not exist? Is what Kropotkin called "spontaneous rising of the working masses" just a joke or the most real, most mysterious force in history?[17]

The newspaper is announcing the creation of a National Council and gives the names of its 128 members.[18] This is beyond Ubu. We see the names of the men of February 6 and the ones they accused of being their assassins. We see Prince de Broglie and Doriot.* Does de Broglie approve of Langevin's dismissal? I can imagine Prince de Broglie and Doriot exchanging a few elevated thoughts about astrophysics and the fate of nations.[19]

January 27

When I left Paris in June of last year, I told myself: "Perhaps everything will be looted in my apartment and I'll find none of the things I love, nor the things I value without loving them." I accepted this inside myself (those general acceptances are easy). To what we conceive of as definitive and total, we oppose a geometry of resignation. "They'll loot everything," I would say to myself, "And afterwards we'll begin all over again." I almost imagined a new youth of things and myself. When the Germans were at our heels, we thought: "There will be a front along the Loire." To some dramatic event, we opposed an event, a succession, a visible development of facts. When the Germans occupied the village in the Gâtinais where we were immobilized, we could already see their regiments leaving France. The word "armistice" itself had something provisional about it. You'd think it was a brief parenthesis between war and peace. You lay down your arms, you lay your cards on the table.

---

[17] Prince Peter Kropotkin (1842–1921), a professional revolutionary, is one of the major theoreticians of revolutionary anarchism.

[18] The law of January 22, 1941, created the Conseil National, which was supposed to be a consultative, intermediary body in the authoritarian regime of Vichy. All its members were appointed. They were former deputies, union leaders, Vichy activists (such as Doriot), and representatives of the economic, social, and cultural elites.

[19] Prince Louis de Broglie won the Nobel Prize for Physics in 1929.

We couldn't imagine—nor did the peasants and bourgeois with whom I had a few conversations—the immobility of the Armistice and how it would settle in over time.

Through the effect of habituation and distance, the events of the war our fate will eventually depend on (bombing of England or Germany, war in Libya, war in Albania) are merely a daily abstraction, inert matter in a newspaper. People unfold their paper and say: "Nothing's happening."

I slandered the city of Bourg. Bourg is more involved in events than I thought. There's this family of shopkeepers. They lead me into the back of the shop.

They're resisting, but inside themselves, without wondering how their resistance could be effective. They judge harshly those who welcome the Germans with open arms. That customer who agreed to lead the German soldiers from shop to shop. "But it only lasted a little while," they say. "Aside from people in a certain clan, everybody wants the English to win, and everybody believes they will." They miss the Sundays from before the war, the little trips in their car. They're afraid the currency will collapse. They'd like the economic disorder of the world to be sorted out, for people not to throw coffee into the sea anymore, not to throw out cargoes of sardines. All that is clear and not connected very well. But is the world connected very well?

As I was walking back to the hotel, I passed by two women dressed in black, skinny and ascetic. And one of them was prophesying in this way: "I say it's going to end in a revolution."

At the news dealer's, the newspapers and magazines are grouped in racks. The marshal's press—the official press—is abundant. If there's a change in the men in power and a political upheaval, you would see the same press, the same newspapers serving the new policies as long as those policies were equally authoritarian. So many magazines! I leaf through them. What an outpouring of virtue! But you still see the adventures of movie stars and mechanical fairytales. And photographs give you raw reality, captured in the five parts of the world and giving the emptiest of idiots the illusion that he's a Buddha in the midst of appearances.

The world of 1941 can only be roughly explained by the opposition between fascisms and democracies. This explanation is not at all to the taste of delicate minds. They find it too easily understood by the common herd. One must recognize that it doesn't allow us to judge what will happen in the near future. No doubt if fascism wins, it will hold out for a while, because it can do what it wants as long as the people accept it. But if the democracies win, they must define themselves, invent themselves on the ruins of the world.

January 31

Andrée François, who goes down into town every day, told me: "The people here expect a Trafalgar thing." "That is?" "A Trafalgar thing . . ." "What do they mean by that?" "*You* know, they're waiting for a revolution." "They're against Pétain?" "No, but the shopkeepers are sick of gluing on ration tickets, and the peasants aren't happy with the requisitions . . ."

January 31

Hitler's speech. "I came up against Jewish internationalism." This explanation for the disorder of the world satisfies both our Maurrases and the thugs they hire for street demonstrations. So it is not ineffective. "In 1941, there will be no more privileges, no more tyranny, no more great financial powers. . . . Our movement does not come from one man; it will last a thousand years . . ." Now I'm reassured. That leap into the clouds of the future reassures me. With my eyes closed, I can tell National Socialism won't last a thousand years. If Hitler believes this, he's mad and he's lost. To believe National Socialism will last a thousand years is a greater illusion than to believe in immanent justice. And now, through Hitler, immanent justice has become a creature of flesh and blood.

"You're wrong," says D——, "to try to understand the thinking of the people in Bourg. They think with their bellies." That's too simple. If I said the people of Bourg think only of the immortality of the soul and the destiny of France, it wouldn't be much less true. What D—— says only expresses his own suffering. It doesn't date from the war. D—— is sensitive to the impurity of the world, as others are sensitive to cold. He shuts himself away from the outside. I don't know what his attempts at contact were with men and women when he was young. But today he flees from everything, like a doe. Or he shrinks back. He has a gray beard. But he's a wounded adolescent.

In 1914, I left for the war because I wanted to. I volunteered before I was called up to the front. We had to give a lesson to the aggressive Germans. We were a little detachment commanded by a private first class. We were giving up our lives, or rather we took that risk for peace. We were volunteers. They didn't load us into the train like military cattle. And when we got to the front lines, PFC Fabre, who was killed later on, came over to me and hummed into my ear: "And tomorrow / The Internationale / Will be the human race."[20]

Today it would make people smile. That's the way it was.

[20] Communists opposed the war, but the private is singing the last lines of the chorus of the Internationale, the Communist anthem written by a Frenchman in 1871. Although the Communist Party has all but disappeared in France, the song is still sung today by people on the left at political anniversaries and demonstrations.

Before 1916, we realized the lie of the war, its absence of meaning or its despicable meaning. All we had to do now was to free the world from it and free ourselves from it, as from a venereal disease.

February 3

The paper is announcing thirteen new people stripped of their French nationality, among whom we find an admiral, a navy lieutenant, a former governor of the colonies, a civil engineer in Indochina, and a professor in the medical school in Hanoi. But a decree of October 1940 on the loss of French nationality has been revoked. French nationality has become a gift of the marshal—one of those gifts that little children play at giving or taking back on a whim.

February 5

The marshal is popular. Yesterday, in a tobacconist's, a child whose head didn't reach the counter and was sent to do an errand on his own, asked for "the card with the marshal on it." This morning, a peasant woman (it's a market day) buys a journal at the newsstand and unhesitatingly asks for *France Nouvelle*, a propaganda pamphlet with a portrait of the marshal. A pamphlet, almost a book. I had never seen a peasant woman buying a book.

February 7

A policeman told the manager of the hotel there was a Laval administration in Paris.

February 8

I learn that strictly speaking there is no Laval administration in Paris but a "national popular gathering" that is opposed to the national revolution (how does it oppose it, how can it oppose nothing?).[21] Who can say exactly what the relationship of this group of politicians from all over the map is with Germany? Tolerated by Germany, it's as if it were inspired by Germany.

The newspaper. An appeal from Monsieur Jacques Chevalier to young people. "Let them be patient, like the peasant who knows how to wait for autumn to harvest the promise of spring flowers." What a strange idea he has of work in the

---

[21] The Rassemblement National Populaire (RNP) was officially born on February 1, 1941, with the blessings of the German embassy. It grouped former neo-socialists and pacifist union leaders around Marcel Déat* and far-right activists. Its objective was less to form a party than to set up a pool of pro-collaboration activists. For the moment, it supported Pierre Laval.—J.-P. A.

fields, this minister![22] His whole text is worth quoting. He has a genius for commonplaces to a degree unheard of even in Vichy. In the load of politicians before and after the marshal, he stands out as a picturesque old fool, an old "spiritualist" idiot. This auxiliary of fascism comes from another era.

A Bourg Sunday. Bourg has its fair share of Sunday boredom. The passersby are disguised as people in retirement and people with a small private income from former times. There's a dense crowd in front of the cinema. You no longer see the Sunday soldiers, stiff and pulled down by their combat boots. They've been replaced by the "youth campers," enveloped in long capes that make them look like seminarians in khaki.[23] Others wear leather jackets with wide facings: you'd think they were boys from a dissolved jazz band. A few skiers back from the mountain. With two hands in front of her belly, an old ataxic woman is holding her bag—the bag of a refugee, a wanderer, an exhausted nomad; every ten yards, she lays it down on the sidewalk. You feel ashamed, you turn away your eyes. This street is a dismal, reduced image of France.

February 11

In a letter from Paris. "I saw the R——s. Nice, but so vague." If you look beyond appearances, that's war, any war, does to people; it makes them vague. And from 1914 to 1918, above this vagueness rose the song of hero-worshipping writers and today, the weaker song of Vichy writers. One difference, however: today other people can't boo them.

February 13

France, England, Germany, the English successes in Libya—we reason about those vast entities. We deal in thoughts that cover a vast expanse and have little depth. In truth, we're entirely in a world of abstractions. We're doing algebra.

England + United States > Germany + Italy

England + France = liberty + dignity

There are other equations: Germany + France = new order.[24]

---

[22] This product of the elite École Normale Supérieure with an advanced degree in philosophy, a conservative Catholic in favor with Pétain, reorganized education in fascist Franco Spain. He was briefly at the head of public education in France: December 1940–February 1941.—J.-P. A.

[23] The "Youth Work-Sites" (Chantiers de jeunesse) dreamed up by General La Porte du Theil were first improvised structures to take in 100,000 recruits born in 1920 who could not be integrated into the army. For young men from the years after that, the law of January 18, 1941, set eight months as the time to be spent in what were called "youth camps."—J.-P. A.

[24] The "new order" (*ordre nouveau*) was a term Pétain used to describe his program. In his speech of June 25, 1940, Pétain announced that "a new order is beginning." Philippe Pétain, *Discours*

Forerunners: in the French literature textbook the lycée prescribes for Claude, Maurras is presented as a thinker.

February 14

Meeting in Montpellier between marshal Pétain and General Franco.*[25] Admiral Darlan* accompanied the marshal. Nothing but civilians here.

The chambermaid: "There are eight thousand refugees in Bourg." There are no more tourists or people passing through, "Because of the events, which are bothering us."

Bourg at eight-thirty at night, Bourg totally dark, docilely complying with the rules of civil defense. Sometimes the headlights of a car or the lamp of a bicycle light up the street. Shadows slip along and follow each other—a file of ants. They gather together, they stop. What unexpected obstacle immobilizes them? A movie theater.

February 17

Admiral Darlan, minister of the interior.[26] There's a shortage of everything, but we have sabers.

The members of the "native consultative assembly" of Laos are eager to solemnly proclaim the unanimous will of the Laotian people to remain united under French protection. Four lines in this tone, and: "The motion received the spontaneous adhesion of the population . . ."

This dispatch recalls another, during the war of 1914–18; the natives of some Cameroon or other display their enthusiasm as they learn they've been delivered from German oppression and from now on would taste the joys of French or British freedom.

Here we can see one of the propaganda methods all governments use. For you can't even say this news is based on lies. A lie still supposes changing a fact, the opposite of a truth. By reversing it, you can make a kind of truth. But these

aux Français: 17 juin 1940–20 août 1944, ed. Jean-Claude Barbas (Paris: Albin Michel, 1989), 66 (my translation). In April 1941, four members of Pétain's government sent Hitler a "Plan for a New Order in France," ending, "We beg the Führer to trust us." Henry Rousso, *Un Château en Allemagne: Siegmaringen, 1944–1945* (1980, rpt. Paris: Fayard/Pluriel, 2012), 70–71). In August 1941, Pétain deplored the slow pace of "building, or more exactly imposing, a new order"— Pétain, *Discours*, 166.

[25] After a conversation at Bordighera with Mussolini, Franco met with Pétain at his request on February 13. After courteous greetings, they sought to establish a relatively common position toward the Third Reich.—J.-P. A.

[26] Head of the national police force, the minister of the interior is responsible for maintaining order in France.

dispatches are based on nothing at all, fed by the impossible. Whether fabricated by Vichy or anyone else, they're annoying and make anyone who's traveled beyond Port-Said laugh out loud.

February 19

The fair. I go see the oxen and cows to give me the feeling of the country. But it's a stock market. The oxen and cows are surrounded by cattle traders. I feel like buying a goat. I would go to a mountaintop with it and live off its milk. What nonsense! On that mountaintop, I'd miss everything I truly value.

The woman who sells good-luck charms is there. So she comes once a week. She also tells fortunes a bit. Her system is cryptographic: she asks her client what day she was born, then she slides a grid over a few lines of her writing. A client consults her about her daughter: "Very nervous," says the magician, "And she's too kind-hearted." The client, leaning over the flimsy trestle table, nods and murmurs: "That's exactly right . . ." And, turning to the closest onlookers: "She told me everything, all my joys and all my troubles . . ." "Oh yes," says the magician, "people don't realize what influence the planets have on all of us . . ." I affirm that peasant woman was not in cahoots with the sibyl of the fair. And today I have no desire to laugh at her credulity. That sibyl was probably telling the truth. She encompassed the life of that peasant woman in a far larger view than the peasant herself. She evaluated a set of simple probabilities. She interpreted a few clues and a few signs. That's how great leaders operate on gullible peoples.

I loathe the war. I'm sick of thinking France, England, Germany. For months, wasn't I that gullible peasant? Didn't I believe in the crudest symbols? Strategies disgust me, whether they're military, literary, or political. I have never lived in that filth, in base schemes and exaltations. Leave me to a few wonderful memories of paintings or books.

The Guild of the Daily Press of Paris, presided by Monsieur Jean Luchaire,* gave a dinner for foreign correspondents in a restaurant on the Champs-Élysées. Among the guests: Messieurs de Brinon;* Scapini; Achenbach, an adviser to the German Embassy; Schleier, consul general of Germany; officers of the Propaganda-Abteilung, the prefect of the Seine . . .[27]

We can see that communication between Messieurs de Brinon, Scapini, Luchaire, and the Germans is much easier than between the French in the Occupied Zone and the French in the Free Zone.

---

[27] Jean Luchaire, a journalist close to the German ambassador Otto Abetz, headed the two controlled press "guilds" put in place by Vichy in 1941–42 in its effort to consolidate power. Georges Scapini, a former far-right deputy, was a prominent member of the Vichy government.

A battalion parades by, preceded by a band. The drums are covered with green velvet decorated by gold crosses. This velvet woven with sparklers has the same shade as the one foot-jugglers in the circus use to adorn their accessories. It's a listless parade. But the soldier on guard before the offices of the army staff presents arms with mechanical precision to a general getting out of a magnificent automobile. D—— and I watch this with some stupefaction. The spectacle seems to us almost shameless . . . The army of police is playing soldier. And seeing this general sprightly as a conquering general, it occurs to us that if the marshal saved France, what he saved above all was the chiefs of staff. Never has the marshal's press, which denounced all of France's failures, made the slightest allusion to this high command, which in June so unanimously stopped commanding.

In the street, you meet countless hybrid or "disused" people. Youth camps, neither soldiers nor civilians, "Companions," neither unemployed nor workers, recalled from Switzerland, wearing clothes of civilian design cut from military cloth.[28] Young people in blue wander around, hired into some team or other. Perhaps they don't know either. But they define themselves and recognize one another by the insignias sewn on their sleeves or chest. A few years ago, I knew a young Swiss who no doubt felt at a loss, with no connection to French society; he put the diamond-shaped Renault trademark in his buttonhole.

February 24

Speech by Hitler. "Our enemies still don't understand. They don't understand that when I consider a man as a friend, my friendship is faithful, and this position has no commercial machinations in it."

If there is an infinitesimal scrap of immanent justice in this world, this is what will destroy him: having invoked the notion of friendship.

"We don't construct our economy according to the desires of New York or London bankers, but exclusively in the interest of the German people. In this domain, I am a fanatical socialist who never sees anything but the general interest of his people."

If that infinitesimal scrap of justice exists, he'll be destroyed for having invoked socialism. I don't know if it exists, but he affirms that it does: "We

---

[28] Indeed, Vichy meant to have an active youth policy. The "Compagnons de France" were the first official Vichy youth movement; as early as the summer of 1940, Henri Dhavernas gathered unemployed youths in camps in the Southern Zone; they could be obliged to perform useful public works, for which they were paid.—J.-P. A.

believe in immanent justice. . . . Providence will bless those who deserved its blessing . . . just as Providence has protected us from 1931 to the present, in the same way it will support us in the future."

Will he be destroyed for having invoked Providence? It's not certain that Providence is so finicky.

February 26

The paper: "The new organization of the administration." No one had said anything to me about it in the town or on the farm. If I had asked them a question about it, they would have wondered if I'd come from Mars. They hold the government's policies for a negligible quantity. They think about getting food supplies, they think about requisitions. And they take the postcard of the marshal for a fetish that temporarily maintains a third of an undefined France.

Mayors dismissed by the dozen "for having adopted a hostile attitude to the task of national regeneration undertaken by the government."

February 27

"The announcement has been made that marshal Pétain will be in Saint-Étienne Saturday, March 1."

Eloquent syntax. The accredited correspondent of the *Progrès* in Vichy gives us backstage information about premeditated enthusiasm. "The Postal Administration will provide the shopkeepers in Saint-Étienne with little posters reproducing the speeches and messages of the marshal: shopkeepers will post these in highly visible places. . . . All the inhabitants of Saint-Etienne will give the industrial city a festive air by putting up flags at their windows, large or modest, rich or poor . . ." It's not always easy to distinguish the future from the imperative.

"The marshal will make a pilgrimage to the cathedral of Le Puy, to revive a tradition established by ten kings of France."

The marshal in Saint-Étienne: "Give up hatred . . . we can build only with love and joy."

Meanwhile Germany is governing France, the Luftwaffe's bombs are bursting on England, bombs of the RAF on Germany, German troops are entering Bulgaria, the English are beating the Italians in Somalia,[29] twenty thousand soldiers of Chiang Kai-shek are entering Burma, Europe doesn't know how it will eat tomorrow, or if,

[29] Led by the Germanophile Bogadan Filov, Bulgaria joined the anti-Comintern pact on March 1, 1941, and authorized German troops to enter its territory. British and Free French forces had been on the attack in Italian East Africa since mid-January 1941; Mogadishu fell on February 26.—J.-P. A.

in ten years, ten men capable of understanding a thought—even a poor one—will be left. But in the middle of this cataclysm, the marshal is playing the pipe.

March 3

Le Progrès. The marshal in Le Puy. "He visited the basilica where fifteen kings of France *also* came to affirm their faith." There were only ten of these kings counted by the same paper on February 27.

March 4

Dole, in the Forbidden Zone.[30] A man speaking perfect French comes to see the priest: "I'm an escaped prisoner. How can I get into the Free Zone?" The priest indulgently tells the escapee how. The escapee was an informer from the *Kommandatur.* The priest is in prison.

Mademoiselle R——'s nephew, who has a notions shop in Saint-Amour, received a letter from a friend discharged from the army. "You'll see, we'll get back into it . . . They'll see if we're soldiers." During the 1914 war, I learned what those affirmations of patriotic decency, and that capitulation to conformism was worth. But that's just it: the young soldier is not a conformist. The marshal never asked him to get back into it. He even explained in one of his messages why we shouldn't "get back into it."

Is there still, in the people, a national feeling against Vichy? And will its time come? In a massive uprising that sweeps all before it? In a civil war? For in manufacturing his national revolution on a crumb of territory, the marshal has prepared fairly good conditions for civil war, if Germany were conquered or abandoned him and couldn't ratify his messages.

I wander through the streets of Bourg. I know all the shop windows by heart. I know all the faces by heart. I hit up against them like prison walls. My life is floating away and I can't catch it.

Claude took Flaubert's *Sentimental Education* out of the library. Now I'm under the influence of reading. I'm not used to it. I let myself go.

March 8

"They only think of their bellies . . ." And I'm beginning to think of it too. The opposition between the belly and the ideal, between patriots and "sellouts" isn't new. In *Sentimental Education* (Flaubert is describing a soirée shortly before the

---

[30] The city of Dole, about seventy-five miles from Saint-Amour, was actually in the Occupied Zone, not the smaller "Forbidden Zone" the Nazis had created, where the French were not allowed to go.

revolutions of 1848), I read: "Most of the men there had served at least four administrations; and they would have sold out France or the human race to secure their fortune, to spare themselves from discomfort, embarrassment, or even out of simple servility, the instinctive adoration of power." You'd think Flaubert had a few Frenchmen of 1941 in mind.

March 11

Claude gives me this approximate statistic: out of forty students in his eleventh-grade class, 20 are Anglophiles, whether Pétainist or Gaullist; 14, Pétainists for Vichy, of whom 2 are Hitlerian, 3 for Action Française,[31] 3 for Collaboration; and 6 indifferent.

Is this a picture of unoccupied France?

Claude has to prepare the first twenty lines of Virgil's First Eclogue. He is unenthusiastic. I try to encourage him. "Sure, it's not a barrel of laughs. But follow the words to the end—the syntax—and try to find equivalents. It's at least as amusing as a crossword puzzle, and it's not as dumb." . . . But he has already picked up the newspaper, and he's dissecting it. "The events are weighing on my brain," he says.

March 12

Open-air market. Under a parasol, the accordionist and his wife are selling old sentimental songs. You see strange trades. How can people make a living from them? An old man sells a few verbena leaves every Wednesday. Another offers a few pairs of glasses against the sun. Not smoked glasses. They must have tough eyes in the province of Bresse.

March 13

The paper: "Something new for boules players! The season is going to begin; competitions have already been announced. But the 1941 season will open under the sign of a new line of conduct which shows the strong desire of the National Federation to participate in the work of National Revolution." The regeneration of France through the players of boules.

In elementary school every morning, they have to write "Work, Family, Country" on the blackboard. Three inventions of the marshal. Three discoveries of Vichy. They invented work, family, and country. These words will have to be vigorously scrubbed off. Thus did Mirbeau, dedicating one of his books for a fundraising lottery to benefit some Russians persecuted by tsarism, write on the

[31] Action Française was a monarchist, nationalist movement and a strong supporter of Vichy, particularly its anti-Semitic measures. Charles Maurras was its intellectual leader.

title page (they were playing *Michael Strogoff* at the Châtelet Theater): "Against God, against the tsar, against the country."

March 14

I'm getting nails hammered into my shoes. The shoemaker has a mobile face with wandering, roaming eyes. This trade is supposed to encourage "advanced ideas" and even "anarchism." This one isn't anarchistic in the slightest. He is—like his wife—of average opinion, but average in a sleepy, unoccupied provincial town. "No leather. No eggs, no milk in the market. Fixed prices. You have to sell for less than what you produce. The guys who set your prices work on paper . . . Old Pétain does what he can, he's a good Frenchman. Still—whether you're left or right—your hopes are all with England. Me, I'd rather have the Bank of England than the socialism of Hitler." He says these last words in a burst of laughter, as if to apologize for being too obvious.

"Oppositional mania" is inseparable from the particular genius of France, according to Cournot.[32] A professor at the Normal School for Elementary School Teachers said to his students: "The government's circulars define the spirit in which I must teach history to you. I'm warning you, and I think you're old enough to make the necessary corrections." Claude got that from one of the students.

March 16

In a magazine devoted to mountain climbing: "For the homeland, through the mountain." The mountain doesn't cure you of idiocy.

March 17

Jérôme Carcopino's* program for the regeneration of the university . . . No, we're not going to comment on that.[33] And yet, if you have a taste for the lower depths, Chevalier and Carcopino give you a royal treat. Chevalier was an old spiritualist harlot. Carcopino garbs himself in university dress, works in a high-necked robe in salons, and knows how to make conversation. Chevalier had reintroduced God into the schools. Carcopino says that's no place for God. They're playing now-you-see-me, now-you-don't with God.

[32] Antoine Augustin Cournot, the nineteenth-century mathematician and philosopher who made major contributions to economic theory, also contributed to the development of psychology.

[33] Jérôme Carcopino had been the new minister of national education for almost a month. The need for the moral "regeneration" (*redressement*) of France was one of Vichy's propaganda themes.

A premonitory piece of news and the future imperative. The newspapers, March 19: "Grenoble will give a warm welcome to marshal Pétain today."

March 20

Nothing seems to chip away at the legend of the marshal who is distinct from his ministers, pure, aseptic, sterilized in an autoclave. That legendary marshal is not only the one who's remaking France but the one who's defending it against Germany.

Bulletin no. 25, dated March 15, of the Association of France, Center for Studies and Professional and Social Support. Direction of propaganda, 11 rue Alquié, Vichy. "We know who's behind this (social) struggle: the capitalists. We know their accomplices in profit: the socialists. The marshal recently expressed himself very clearly about their shady alliance, and we are indicating their unfortunate victims: the workers."

Our presidents of the republic unfailingly spoke gelatin. But at least they didn't try to perform exercises of prestidigitation and magical disappearance with the hands of a paralytic.

March 21

The boarders in the hotel have made themselves a temporary country.

My neighbor is the amuser and animator. He's rich in table talk and bawdy jokes and tells them from table to table.

I'm not saying this young man killed his father and mother. But he is stupid. An obvious, palpable stupidity that is part of his being. This man "knows what's what," but he's stupid. He reads *Candide, Gringoire*, and *Action Française*; so does the group of boarders. For he lends them his newspapers. But the political position of the French doesn't really depend on the newspapers they read. These people are all anti-German and Anglophiles. I sensed that they're hostile to General de Gaulle. In a word, they're waiting, with their noses in the air, for a victorious England to lay 2 million prisoners and occupied France at the marshal's feet. The same class of Germans would be grosser, and have gravelly laughs deep in their throats. These people are annoying like wasps.

It seems to me the Anglophiles against General de Gaulle are rather cowardly bettors. They're making an inner choice, with no risks. De Gaulle has risked everything. And if England wins, do they hope to place de Gaulle under house arrest or give him a position as secretary in the offices of good old Papa Pétain?

Claude is reading *Les Châtiments*:[34] "Times like ours are the sewers of history." We know the grimace of disgust "distinguished" men of letters will make at this kind of poetic eloquence. They're delicate, but in the sense that we say a stomach is delicate. They claim they only love the most subtle elixirs, but in reality, they can only digest noodles.

March 26

The war goes on, and Yugoslavia has adhered to the Tripartite Pact.[35] The fate of France is being played out in England, in the East, and in America. France is not participating in the chess moves, nor the rolls of the dice, nor the new deals of the cards. France is like those gamblers around the table waiting for a bit of charity from the winner. A few Frenchmen aren't even hoping for anything except for tomorrow to replace today and for meat and bread to miraculously return to their tables in abundance. France doesn't even know if the marshal is playing the collaborationist policy of his meeting with Hitler at Montoire or is only pretending to play it. But France is asked to believe in the marshal as one believes in a holy relic. France's salvation will come through radiations, effluvia, and fluids from the person of the marshal.

March 27

War is born from the stupidity of human beings. But every state of war increases that stupidity. We may expect to see the day when there will only be war and stupidity on earth, each engendering the other.

When I walk by the newsstand, I step away from it, as if I had to fear some stain, some toxic emanation. Sometimes I feel this when I go into a newspaper office or hall. Perhaps it's only the persistence of an old memory I haven't repressed. At the beginning of the century, when I did some job or other in a newspaper for the first time, I was in a wonderful state of innocence: one day, I brought in a snake, coiled around my wrist. It was an object of horror and disgust. People moved away from it and from me. And yet I am attracted by linocut landscapes and by those machines in motion. But I also feel a sensation of "a place of ill repute." This is where money goes to bed with ideas. As soon as the money arrives, all the ideas line up to be selected. The money selects the one it

---

[34] *The Chastisements* (1853) was Victor Hugo's collection of poems violently attacking Napoleon III, the dictator whose coup d'état was the cause of his long exile.

[35] The Tripartite Pact, signed in September 1940, defined the military alliance between Germany, Italy, and Japan. Japan recognized the leadership of Germany and Italy in "establishing a new order in Europe," and the European countries did the same for Japan's "new order" in Asia.

wants. All the smells of all the moneys mingle: money from secret funds, money from embassies, money from industry, money from finance, money from stores, dressed-up money, naked money.

March 28

Monsieur Matsuoka visits Hitler. Coup d'état in Yugoslavia. Keren has surrendered. And in France? In France, "The bust of the marshal will replace the bust of Marianne in city halls, schools, and courts."[36]

March 30

State of siege in Yugoslavia, protest from the German minister in Belgrade. Meanwhile, the Vichy government adopts a law on divorce and to soothe all social conflicts decides to celebrate May 1 as both Labor Day and Saint Philippe's Day. Perhaps it is even suggesting that the prince of Monaco modify the rules of roulette.

"I'm not for England and I'm not for Germany either; I'm neutral . . ." That's what a sixth-grader was saying in the Bourg Lycée.

April 3

The masses' hope, and my hope: Yugoslavia and America. Tomorrow, we'll expect our salvation from the planet Mars.

The rottenness of the democracies. . .[37] Yes, no doubt. But the decomposition happened in the open. Whereas with Hitler, Mussolini, or the pallid Pétain, there is rot, the same rot, locked in a closet. One hole in the armor, and even the coarsest nose will smell the stench.

The proprietress of the hotel took pity on a wretched German Jewish woman and gave her a room for three months without asking anything from her. She seems to apologize for that, afraid I might judge her harshly for it: "It was a little room, a very modest room . . ."

---

[36] Yosuke Matsuoka was Japan's foreign minister; in Yugoslavia, pro-democracy officers forced the pro-German government to resign as Peter II acceded to the throne; British forces took Keren, a city in Eritrea, on March 26 after fifty-three days of fighting. "Marianne" is the symbol of the French Republic abolished by Pétain. There are busts of Marianne in town halls today, and postage stamps bear her image.

[37] The "rottenness" (*pourriture*) of the French Republic was a theme of right-wing propaganda between the wars. The occupied press magnified it, throwing in the anti-Axis democracies for good measure.

April 5

I've left Bourg, a nowhere city, not even really in Bresse.

As two inspectors wanted to get into the "laboratory" of a pastry maker in Saint-Amour, he threw his white jacket over them and knocked their two heads together.

I learn from the parish bulletin that God has granted France a miracle in the person of the marshal.

From Paris. The historian Lucien Febvre* and the librarian of the École Normale Supérieure loaded a handcart with the papers and work notes of the historian Marc Bloch* and conveyed them to safety; he is a refugee in the Free Zone.

A few scientists and men of letters who can in no way be suspected of treason like Chateaubriant* have agreed to enter into contact with the delegates of German propaganda. Delegates of high culture, without any bestial Nazism. They may not even have a definite mission, except to create an atmosphere, save face, and disguise or blur the image of Hitlerism. Unnecessary, of course, to point out their extreme courtesy. But I'm too simple not to be bothered by the courtesy of the French. That courtesy means giving in to Hitler.

April 9

Hope in Yugoslavia. Our passions play with far-off death, abstract death. We wish for thousands of German corpses.

What happened to the time when Shoum, the Siamese cat, fed on fish and rice? He's taken to soup. He's lost half his weight. A little while ago, I saw him devour, like a prey, a piece of paper that had wrapped some boudin.

April 10

Vichy radio: the Gaullists are nothing but Jews, Freemasons, and Communists, all warmongers responsible for our defeat. Their warmongering stands in stark contrast to Hitler's reorganizational pacifism.

Contrasts. A village a few miles from Chalon. A few girls are joking with German soldiers. A few young men are wearing the Cross of Lorraine.[38]

---

[38] The Cross of Lorraine was the emblem of de Gaulle's Free French, based in England—a "center of dissidence," as Vichy called it.

From the Occupied Zone. The Germans sometimes ostentatiously polite, sometimes using little doses of the methods of humiliation—the methods of Nazism at its beginnings. Thus, in Chalon they arrest some fifteen people who were trying to cross the Demarcation Line, men with one woman. They lock them into a room with no furniture and make them stand up all night. They place a little tub in the middle of the room. The woman asks permission to go out for a few minutes. They refuse and point to the tub.

A circular from French authorities asks Parisian reporters to inform on those of their colleagues who show pro-English feelings.

P . . . , who's hiding out in Paris, thinks Stalin is waiting for the moment when he can save an exhausted Europe and force or convert it to the mystical economy of Communism and work for the revolution and not for Russia.

An isolated farm. Old Mireau goes down to the cellar and brings back a bottle of four-year-old wine. On the table, the newspaper is open. The headlines are powerfully orchestrated: "The government has decided to take strong measures to end the emigration of Frenchmen to centers of dissidence. . . . In the Orhid sector, the forces of the Reich have joined the Italians. . . . The Hungarian army has entered Yugoslavia. Monastir and Ochrida taken by the Germans . . ." How can anyone resist these blunt headlines? How can the reader not believe that Gaullism is error or treason and the only France is the one the marshal and Germany are spreading over the world like an invincible force? Who could resist these obsessive headlines, the repetition, the continuous advertising? The newspaper is laid out on the table. It's impossible for it not to be the truth of the household.

But Old Mireau said: "They want to sell us farmers rotten corn at three francs a kilo. And the price of our wheat is set at two francs fifteen . . . They tell us to raise chickens, but we don't have the right to give them any grain . . . Are the Yugoslavians going to hold out? Tonight we'll get Swiss radio or English radio. Vichy radio's more Boche than the Boches . . ."

The mad bourgeois says furiously: "I'm neither German nor English. I'm French."
Hypocrisy or stupidity?

The legend of the good old man is disappearing. I see the legend of the right-wing conspirator being born. "Sold out, betrayed . . . ," we were betrayed and sold out before the war. The plot started in Spain: Hitler, Mussolini, Franco, and Pétain were in cahoots. The war was only play-acting, with walk-on parts intended both to hide the plot and make it work—an episode added to the main plot. They don't have any proof yet. The legend is still in limbo.

"Number 31 of the Bulletin de France, Organ of the Association for France and Social Propaganda of the Marshal, April 1941." This leaflet is mailed to the homes of doctors, lawyers and merchants. "What we need is to act for our prisoners above all. Slip a little phrase into your letters that mentions the marshal's solicitude for the prisoner, the pity he feels for his fate . . ."

Are the people of the cities and working-class outskirts, the people of the "red belt" around Paris, resigned, revolutionary, Communist? The wisdom of the peasants is beginning to weary me. It is too lacking in the wrath of ideas. I'm not cured of my addiction to ideas and crowds. I feel the anger of the worker rising in me.

A bit after the debacle, the miners of Sens went on strike because the coal they were mining was being sent to Germany.[39] The Germans shot a few miners. Suzanne has this fact from the wife of a mining engineer. She disapproved of the miners and not the repression.

April 28

A week in Lyon. The buildings lined up like double-six dominoes and the hanging gardens, Babylonian gardens in the hills. A week of friendship at the Latarjets'. They're worried about the crushing defeat of the Yugoslav troops, the German advance in Greece, and the occupation of the islands. We try to warm ourselves with English radio.

Catherine is three. I wrestle with her. "Who's stronger?" She answers: "You are." And adds: "Me too."

Going back to the country house. April has done its job very well. The buttercups are playing at Claude Monet.

The Lyon-Perrache station. An old man wearing a rosette and a Military Cross gets into my compartment; two sleeping soldiers are there already. He looks very much the public figure from the provinces. Hardly has he sat down than he points to a young woman on the platform and says: "You see strange things happening . . . That lady did three months of preventive detention on the pretext that she made some pro-Communist remarks . . ." I start. If it weren't for the rustic, trusty look of this old man, I'd think he was an agent provocateur. The young woman gets into our compartment. She's wearing a big, floppy, felt hat. She is lively, one of those women that gush up like springs. The old man completely forgets my presence and resumes his conversation

---

[39] Sporadic strikes broke out here and there, particularly October 9 and 11, 1940, but nothing comparable to the big strike—with very patriotic accents—that would shake up the whole coal basin from May 27 to June 9, 1941.—J.-P. A.

with her. I gather she was involved in a trial for Communist acts against the mayor of Oyonnax and a few members of the ex–Communist Party.[40] The man with the rosette is a retired colonel in the gendarmerie. He was called as a defense witness. I learn that the trial had been set up by the denunciation of nasty, small-town people. I learn that this colonel and the mayor make no distinction between their political supporters and opponents. Rather solemnly, he repeats: "Charity is neither politically left nor right; it is one." He also says and repeats: "You either have a conscience or you don't." I understood that he was asked to give false testimony or at least altered testimony, and the judges thought, like Monsieur Charles Maurras, that false testimony is not reprehensible when it fortifies a good cause. The colonel and the young woman got off at Bourges.

Another passenger got on. One of the soldiers woke up. The civilian spoke loudly and very familiarly to the soldier. At first I took him for a horse dealer or a carnie. He was a merchant from Belfort who trafficked in potatoes. The soldier had been in the battle of the Somme and was stationed in Périgueux. As his parents lived in the Forbidden Zone, he was going to friends on furlough in a village in the Jura. First, they talked about the restrictions. Then they rose to the summits of high-level politics. The merchant seemed quite satisfied: in Lorraine, everything's been fine ever since Austrian soldiers occupied the region.[41] "At the beginning, everything was all screwed up . . . but now things are OK." He's not worried about the future: "They really maneuvered well in high places . . . Hitler? He'll wear himself out in his own victory . . . History proves it . . . Look at Caesar, look at Nero . . ." He repeats "Look at Caesar, look at Nero . . ."

As for the soldier, he hopes to start fighting again one day. However, he likes the Germans as much as the English. "Nobody wanted to work anymore . . . The workers got their forty-hour week . . . They would've demanded thirty hours, then no hours at all . . . Hitler's a man of genius, he's not ambitious for himself but for the good of the Germans . . ." I'm quoting as exactly as I can without stenographic notes. They have clear ideas, but with no connection between them. They repeat phrases from the newspapers. Their ideas slide around inside them and follow each other like hallucinations.

"German forces are continuing their occupation of the Peloponnesus." The town sags under the news, and worries. The former rural watchman who was trepanned says: "I like the Germans better than the English. The Germans are workers, the English are capitalists."

---

[40] The Communist Party had been illegal since August 1939, well before Pétain took power.
[41] Under the terms of the Armistice, Alsace and Lorraine were annexed to Germany.

April 30

Laurent killed a pig. He gave me a roast of pork. I think too much about this roast.

"What's happening in the world?" the gendarme G—— asks me. What can I answer? I know no more than he does about the industrial power of the United States. But he leans over to me and says: "I have high hopes . . ." You can't quite despair, if gendarmes no longer believe in the marshal.

May 10

The old Parisian lady who preferred the Germans to the English last August has no preference today. She even admits that "with the English, we'd be freer . . ." But she "hates them as much as the Germans, because they take everything and never give you anything back."

Why am I not in London or America? It seems you can find France again by leaving its land. The way you leave a sick person's bedroom for a moment to get a whiff of fresh air.

How beautiful France is, seen from America!

May 12

Vichy declares "We are in the midst of a period of difficulty in satisfying demand, due to the sudden increase in the scarcity of pasturage, which has been struck by the recent frosts. The government, therefore, had to requisition incompletely fattened animals."

"The guy who wrote that," Laurent says as he grooms his cows, "either he was never in the country or he thinks we're dumber than the animals."

Six people sentenced by the court in Chalon for "remarks liable to exercise a bad influence on the spirit of the population."

May 16

Meeting between Darlan and Hitler.[42] "This new conversation," declares the marshal, "Enables us to light the way to the future." It will enable France to "overcome her defeat."

---

[42] Darlan met with Hitler in his Berchtesgaden mountain retreat on May 11 and 12 in a relaxed atmosphere. Darlan, who wanted to show that collaboration would continue despite Laval's eviction from the government, said over and over that the French government would develop the policies outlined in the Hitler-Pétain meeting in Montoire. He asked Germany to make some political concessions in return.—J.-P. A.

Rudolf Hess parachutes into Scotland.[43] Confused notes from the DNB.[44]

General de Gaulle, England wins and you land in France. All we ask of you is a little genius.

Paris. Inauguration of an Institute for the Study of Jewish Questions.[45]

If you want to judge anti-Semitism, it is absurd and contemptible to take it where it hits: you must take it from its starting point. For the Jews are indefensible. Just as much as the Auvergnats, those public poisoners, as much as the Corsicans, those lousy customs officers and sergeants. Moreover, one can see that the crowd almost always gives negative attributes to ethnological denominations. The Norman is litigious, the Breton is crude, and people from the Midi are cowardly and talkative. To each human group, the crowd man immediately gives a defensive, disapproving judgment. It flatters his narcissism. But when it's a question of the Jews, the word sweeps everything before it. It is heavy with stains from twenty centuries of persecution. The abstraction of "Jewish" is one of the least reversible. It is easier to go from perfidious Albion to trusty England. It is easier to go from the gluttonous, looting German to the well-ordered, organizing German. So is there nothing specific about Jews? Yes there is . . . And about the Marseillais from the Midi, too. There's nothing to prevent you from explaining Cézanne by Marius.[46]

May 17

Market day. A dead market, a useless market. Just one merchant set up his stand, the ghost of a merchant under a light gray rain. Not a soul in front of his suspenders and garters.

"Darlan," a farmer says to me, "Sold out our colonies to Germany. He wants us to fight against England . . . Roosevelt told him where to get off." And, in a tighter voice, "We're going to have a revolution . . ." "Because of empty bellies, or the government's German policy?" "Both."

I heard that word—revolution—three times this morning. A fearsome thing, which doesn't know how to act with moderation, smashes everything,

[43] To everyone's surprise, Rudolf Hess, who had been considered Hitler's heir apparent, had himself parachuted into Scotland, saying he was bearing a peace plan. After a few days of hesitations, the British authorities treated him as a prisoner of war, while Hitler called him "mentally ill."—J.-P. A.

[44] DNB: Deutsches Nachtrichtenbüro, the German press agency the Nazis established in 1934.

[45] In May, the Nazis sponsored the Institut d'études des Questions Juives, a French propaganda agency headed by Captain Sézille, a violent anti-Semite in the pay of the Occupation authorities.—J.-P. A.

[46] Werth invokes traditional French stereotypes for people from various regions of the country, and for the English and Germans. "Marius" is a "typically Marseilles" character in Marcel Pagnol's folksy films. Cézanne was born in Aix-en-Provence, not far from Marseilles.

often does more harm than good, and no one knows how it will come or from where, but it will come to punish that criminal of darkness called treason. That revolution is not desirable. It is justice through catastrophe. It's a catastrophe for justice.

May 19

Tongues are wagging in town about the schoolteachers who took their pupils to the Mass for Joan of Arc. So is the town anti-clerical? It sticks to its customs. It can't imagine being without baptism, wedding, and burial in church. The peasants are pleased to welcome visits from the priest, as long as he doesn't talk to them about God. If a fireman dies, a delegation of firemen accompanies his coffin to the doors of the church but doesn't go in. If a fireman feels like following the service, he leaves the group. And none of the others approve him or blame him. That's the custom. And it is vain that in a neighboring town, the mayor—a country squire—tried to change it. The church is one of the points where the peasant tests his freedom.

"I myself," says the marshal to the representatives of National Assistance, "have had the occasion to bring you certain resources, which have just been specified to me, particularly through the sale of my portraits. That sale alone brought in 150 million . . . So I helped you as best I could."

May 20

A long communiqué defines "the role of the Legion in the nation."[47] It's an invitation to become an informer. However, the "spokesman" of the Legion's leadership declared that "it's not a question of organizing informers, but more exactly of supporting a government overtaken by events . . ." That "more exactly" is admirable. Where do they find these spokesmen? In this way, the head of a gang of thieves could say it's not a question of organizing theft, but "more exactly" of waiting for isolated passersby in the street at night in order to rob them.

May 21

"Say what you will," an old gardener told me, his teeth clamped on his pipe; "democracy's really something . . ."

---

[47] The Légion Française des Combattants was created on August 29, 1940, in the Free Zone, grouping some 1.6 million veterans. Its officials had just held a press conference with the theme "The Marshal sets out and reinforces the important attributions of the Legion in the state." In reality, the Legion had difficulty finding its bearings in the Vichy State.—J.-P. A.

A sentence like that makes merchants and refined people smile.

The regulation of foodstuffs changes from week to week. Egg sellers receive ten typewritten pages every week or even twice a week.

André Mandouze,* who teaches the senior classes in the Bourg Lycée, sells *Temps Nouveau* at the doors of the church.[48] His Catholicism is not the paunchy Catholicism of so many bad writers. In the marshal's last message, he asks the French not to "calculate" the chances of an English victory. Mandouze believes in these chances and doesn't hide it from his students. And no teacher tries harder to lead his students to the stupid Bac without cramming.

A few years back, Paul Nizan was teaching philosophy in the same school.[49] He was one of those young academics who used Marxism to wash themselves clean of the grime of the old conceptual games. To them, Marxism was a religion.

In those two young men, two certainties of equal strength. And I wonder if the contradictions between their two doctrines aren't easier to reconcile than the inner contradictions of each of them.

Two lycée students suspected of Gaullism were summoned to the offices of the police. Who had informed on them? Must we really suspect classmates of theirs who are in contact with the propaganda center of the National Revolution?

Threats of requisitioning potatoes, a ban on digging up new potatoes. "What are we going to eat?" They speak of taking up their pitchforks. Even if they took up arms like that, Germany is there, with its machine guns to oppose their pitchforks. Meanwhile, Darlan is negotiating.

They have committed France. All of them hoped to be Goebbels or Goering.* Goering's splendor, palaces in marble and gold . . . They'll pass the army, the navy, the air force, and the people in review. The people will march in lockstep. But if England holds out and wins, will they hide in the cellars, will they end up in Germany, will they form a circle of émigrés, or will they try civil war?

[48] *Temps Nouveau* (New times) was a Christian journal with a democratic, anti-Nazi orientation; it was soon banned by Vichy.

[49] Paul Nizan, a Communist intellectual and writer, left the Party at the Stalin-Hitler pact. He taught at the Bourg lycée from 1931 to 1932. He was a friend of Sartre and Beauvoir. *Aden Arabie* (1931; English translation, *Aden Arabia*, 1968) is still read today. Its opening is well known in France and elsewhere: "I was twenty. I won't let anyone say that's the best time of your life."

France—or what I can see and presume of France from here—lets itself be muzzled by Vichy, like a docile dog. It can't escape, it must consent to the muzzle. But at least it might growl.

May 28

War makes you indifferent. In peacetime, when a barn burns down, the whole village is moved by the fire. In wartime, when a city is destroyed, it's only a fact, a fact of war. On land, on sea, and in the air, death is no more than a figure. War leads people to a coarse acceptance of fate.

Solitude is drying me out. The paper brings me the outside world: outside France, the battle of Crete, the sinking of the *Bismarck*;[50] in France, the reorganization of the police, who "will be given technical means equal or superior to material used by foreign police forces . . . fast, small vans, teargas . . ." (That will take care of order in the streets.) But the surveillance of every French citizen is no less well taken care of: "Extremely modern machines will enable the police to print a large number of identification sheets very quickly."

May 30

After the 1914–18 war, Germany was sick. It consulted a few physicians and brought the Weimar Republic to its bedside. It did not make the right diagnosis. Then it did what many sick people do when they're weary of it all. It called in a quack "bonesetter." Sometimes bonesetters put muscles back in place or act through persuasion. German thought Hitler had saved it. But bonesetters don't know how to cure diabetes or syphilis.

It was after the 1914–18 war that music-hall patriotism died:

Who can beat the Boches out there?
My man can, my dear old Pierre.

The virulent forms of patriotism and the diverse categories of nationalism tended to be resorbed into fascism.

As early as the end of the nineteenth century, patriotism had become a kind of narcissism, a frenzy of hatred, or an attribute of small savings accounts. The press directed it at will, against Germany or England, whichever. The word was colored by electoral vulgarity, by the baseness of the dancehall or the academy.

---

[50] German paratroopers landed on Crete on May 20, 1941, as this English base had to be neutralized before the invasion of Russia. The Wehrmacht took the island after twelve days of heavy fighting. The *Bismarck* was one of the flagships of the German navy, a thirty-five-thousand-ton battleship. It was finally sunk 380 miles from Brest after a veritable hunt organized by a whole British squadron.—J.-P. A.

It no longer gave out the same sound it did in the middle of the nineteenth century. In *The Country Doctor*, Balzac shows the human and social virtues of Catholicism and royalty in long essays. But suddenly he uses the word "patriotism." And now he's on another level. What he calls patriotism is an austere passion for the good; it is almost charity.

An official lecturer goes from county seat to county seat and from town to town. She talks to children in their schools. Her name is Dorvyl, a good stage name for an extra or a second-rate singer. She entertains them with Saint Louis, Montaigne, Corneille, Péguy, and the marshal.[51] These lofty flights through the centuries have always figured prominently in official speeches. And they're given as essay topics to lycée students taking the Bac. But in France, clichés—the engines of those little games—are not the residue of ordinary truths, the results of a tradition: they are free-floating words. For while France is full of its history, it is only in its unconscious. France does not have a passion for its historical heroes. They are only school memories and museum glories. It's the twentieth century that discovered Joan of Arc. We know what kind of entertainment Voltaire used her for, without being scandalous. Then she became a pretext for parades, the patroness of right-wing parties.[52] If Hitler gets France, he'll make her his saint. You'd think the French only like history when it's not history, when it's current events or politics. Vercingetorix does not move them. The men of '89 hardly more. They feel passionately about the Revolution—for or against—but they know nothing about Robespierre or Danton. History is only a memory of childhood picture albums, fairy tales, a few images: Clovis and the vase of Soissons, Saint Louis under his oak, Louis XIV in Versailles.[53] National heroes do not haunt the soul of the people. And they're in fashion—for a season or so—only if bad writers and pop historians get into the act.

Claude tells me the students in the lycée get together only according to their ideas, depending on whether they're "collaborationists" or not. The collaborationists go looking for fights. They have nothing to fear. They have connections in the propaganda club. Schoolteachers' sons must be prudent. If they spoke up too loudly, their fathers would be dismissed.

---

[51] Historic names famous in France: Saint Louis (Louis IX) from the thirteenth century, Montaigne from the sixteenth, the classic playwright Pierre Corneille from the seventeenth, and the nationalist writer and poet Charles Péguy from the early twentieth.

[52] The far-right Front National still celebrates Joan of Arc Day.

[53] The story of the fifth-century Frankish king Clovis I and the Soissons vase was traditionally taught in primary school, and the image of Saint Louis dispensing justice under his oak was displayed in children's textbooks.

When we were sixteen, we used to argue about poets. What kind of generation will it be when they're arguing about France and Germany, England and liberty?

Student refugees from Besançon and Alsatians resist any idea of collaboration with all their might. Among the students whose families live in Bourg, most are inert. For them, the Germans are far away, and there's still butter in the farmhouses.

June 1

Once more, the portraits of Pétain and Darlan are the same size in every paper and symmetrically placed in the layout. France has even lost her typographic liberty.

June 5

A farmhouse room. Two glasses of marc on the table. I'm with the rural policeman of a neighboring town.

"Of course," he says, "I wouldn't say this in the café, you'd go to jail. But we're alone. Maybe you know more than me. I think the debacle was being prepared for years. There was an agreement between the fat cats of the two countries. They wanted the debacle to take power. And Vichy's doing more than Germany's even asking . . . I mean in the Free Zone . . . Do you think they can drag us into a war with England?"

I try to be optimistic: "You can't imagine a government more artificial than Vichy."

But he shakes his head:

"No, France is 'faltering.' Look at my commune of six hundred people. The schoolteacher—he's been there for ten years, he was a good socialist— well . . . He's dancing faster than the music. He's afraid of being dismissed. One day it's two people the government gets, the next day three. It's working on us . . ."

And this line: "I don't even know what day we'll be *exactly* French."

He speaks calmly—I was going to say: serenely. The French have adopted a lofty point of view.

June 9

In 1918, I reduced a girl to tears by showing her the absurd uselessness of the slaughter. She cried because I had shaken up her comfortable orthodoxy; she cried because I was taking away the consoling thought that her dead were cozily ensconced in heroism for all eternity, and because I was making her think millions of men had gone into nothingness for nothing.

What illusion, what passion would be strong enough today to make a girl cry—if she were shaken up, if she were deported? Our era is listless. But before the storm, the weather is listless too.

The paper: "The English and Gaullists have attacked Syria."[54]

Will the town wake up? Andrée François, who has returned from town, says: "People are gathered in little groups, and they're talking . . ."

June 11

Speech by Darlan. If you're not nice to the Germans, they won't be nice to you . . . Communism and Gaullism, same thing.

June 12

From the *Pester Lloyd*:[55] ". . . Admiral Darlan's speech proves, once again, that he recognizes that the full, rapid integration of France into the new Europe is the only way to preserve French unity and save the nation." There is something lively and perky about "full, rapid integration." One thinks of Alsace and Czechoslovakia.

June 14

The "Statute Regulating Jews."[56] Declaring Judaism is obligatory, like declaring a contagious disease. Jews can no longer be croupiers. The profession of croupier will find its grandeur again and the tradition of Joan of Arc.

The vilest part of it is the exceptions. Will Jews who are authorized to exercise their profession have to choose between dying of hunger and accepting the favor that Vichy's Vallat,* Darlan, and Pétain deign to grant them?

[54] Syria was a French mandate and thus under Vichy control. On June 8, English and Free French troops entered the country, where Vichy had granted transit facilities to the Luftwaffe a month earlier. Gaullist French soldiers fought French soldiers who had remained faithful to Vichy.

[55] An old German-language newspaper published in Budapest. Before the war, it had criticized Hitler's racist 1935 Nuremberg Laws and compared Jews in Germany to the helots, slaves in Sparta. Clearly things have changed.

[56] The second Statut des Juifs was published on June 2, 1941. It modified the statute of October 3, 1941, clarifying the definition of "Jew" and multiplying the number of professions forbidden to French Jews. The same day, a law required that a census be taken of Jews in the Southern Zone. It obliged Jews to give the prefecture "a declaration indicating they are Jewish in the terms of the law and stating their civil status, family situation, profession, and assets."—J.-P. A.

Young Clerc, whose truck no longer works, is pulling, by himself, a cart loaded with barrels. He believes in the collapse of Germany and Vichy. "But we don't have real leaders," he tells me. "We need men, like the old republicans."[57] Now there's something that would make a young fascist laugh.

Clerc harnesses himself up to his wagon again, leans toward me, and says in a low voice: "We'll get our freedom back."

June 20

Yesterday, a message from Darlan to the dissidents. Today, most of the newspaper is nothing more than propaganda for "the new order." The iconic marshal is paraded through Limoges and Saint-Léonard. The bishop of Limoges receives the marshal. The factory that manufactures historic phrases is never idle. "You have three prisoners," they have the marshal say. "I have a million and a half, for, you know, all the prisoners are my children."

The teacher of senior year history André Mandouze; the philosophy teacher; ten teachers from the Lycée Lalande, both men and women; teachers from the girls' lycée; and a Dominican (Father Chéry) demonstrated in Bourg yesterday with a few high school students against the screening of the anti-Semitic German film *Jud Süß*.[58] Father Chéry had wondered if he should hide his clerical robe out of decency. He finally decided to cover it with Mandouze's raincoat.
The teachers, students, and Father Chéry shouted: "Down with Hitler . . ." A few adversaries called Mandouze and the philosophy teacher "dirty Jews" and "sold out to the Jews."

A few moviegoers with bourgeois souls protested: they paid for their seat and they'd come to see the show.

The cry of "Down with Hitler" disconcerted the marshal's supporters. They didn't dare answer with a "Long live Hitler," after all.

A little old man who remained calmly seated in his chair kept murmuring "Heil Hitler," softly, nicely, without anger.

The gendarmes took André Mandouze and the philosophy teacher to the police station. Mandouze was merely surrounded, but they put the philosophy teacher in handcuffs. Around forty young people followed them in the street and were able to get the cuffs removed.

The two teachers were released after an identity check.

[57] That is, the revolutionary leaders who fought against the monarchy and for the republic from 1789 through the first half of the nineteenth century.

[58] Xavier Vallat decided to give his patronage to the screening of this notorious film by Veit Harlan in the Southern Zone, dubbed in French. In May, students demonstrated against its screening at the Scala, in downtown Lyon; in Bourg, it was indeed André Mandouze who organized the demonstration with C. Devivaize, a teacher of philosophy.—J.-P. A.

This is the story according to Claude, who acted as a citizen last night for the first time.

June 21

At the mill. I'm in the living room, plunged into peasant civilization. Not with the peasant on the calendars, who's been made into a fetish by a few bad writers in order to reassure the ruling classes.[59] Not with one of those peasants who has his head filled only with keeping the books on his fodder and cattle. I feel a certain bliss at being in this civilization. I experienced it with peasants in the Far East.

Michel, his wife, and I talk . . . Everything is said by them nobly, without a nasty comment, wisely. Michel does not have those circumlocutions, precautions, and discretions so common among men of the land. Yet he says: "Me, I'm only a simple peasant, I'm not an educated man." We compare the men of the fields and the men of cities who have more words at their command. We talk of the war and of freedom. Here, freedom is not applied to skimming milk or declaring your cattle.

Michel is convinced that the high command betrayed us last June: frightened by the fear of revolution, it ordered the debacle in collaboration with the German high command. He thinks the high command had been preparing a coup d'état for a long time. "And how strange it was," he says, "that in the midst of the debacle the rumor spread even into the smallest hamlets in France that 'the schoolteachers were to blame.'" Indeed, who has not heard that infamous "explanation"?[60]

June 23

Germany has declared war on Russia. First image: Cossacks and Tartars sweeping through the steppes. We see Germany sinking into the plains.

Hitler sends out a call to the German people. "In the past, England ruined Spain with many wars. In 1815, it attacked Holland." The tone of a review textbook for the Bac. We're surprised Hitler doesn't go back to Joan of Arc. All the politicians in the world excel at these soaring textbook surveys of history. At the end, Hitler invokes the Lord in heaven.

Is Hitler acting out of despair? Is he throwing himself at Russia as he would throw himself into the water, or does he think he'll win? Will the world be freed from Hitler, or will that crafty lunatic dominate the world?

---

[59] In speeches and articles, on calendars, posters, and even in appointment books, Vichy propaganda glorified "the Land" and the Noble Peasant, happily and submissively tilling the soil.

[60] Elementary school teachers were notoriously left-wing and anti-clerical. To some extent, they still are.

The paper—that is, Vichy—declares this war "is less an offensive against Russia than a reaction of the European spirit against Bolshevism." It is no longer the Polish soldier standing guard at the gates of civilization; it's the German soldier.

An appeal to Russian troops invites them to fraternize with the German soldiers. "The German army is essentially revolutionary: it seeks to establish social justice throughout the world." Like his French partisans, Hitler even tries to annex words. The transfers of meaning are the complements to the transfers of populations.

June 24

One of the faces of France under the marshal's Napoleonic Consulate: the prefect of the Jura announces he won't take any account of anonymous letters. The prefect of the Jura himself feels the people he's administrating are going too far.

Laurent remains faithful to the marshal. "He's not happy with what they're doing . . . But what can you expect him to do at eight-four? They lead him around like I lead my oxen with the goad."

The Parisian cop on vacation helps hoe and make hay. Not like an amateur. He knows farming and the peasants respect his work and his zeal for work. . . . I ask him: "Would the Paris police fight against the English?" He answers sharply: "No."

June 25

"When there's a funeral," Laurent says, "Sometimes I go into the church and sometimes I go to the café with friends during Mass. It depends on a lot of things. Depends on who I meet. With this one, I go to the café, with that one, no. But above all it depends on who died. If he went to Mass when he was alive, I go into the church. If he didn't go to Mass, I go to the café."

The truck driver and his son, back from Besançon, told people in the café the Germans were behaving very well, people weren't unhappy in the Occupied Zone. But the son admitted he'd got some kicks in the ass. He said, "Well of course, you have to obey them, you have to obey." Old François interrupted him: "What about freedom? A slap, a kick in the ass . . . They could've killed me, I would've hit back till they killed me."

June 30

Vichy is orchestrating Syria. "The defenders of Syria are motivated by the spirit of Verdun," says General Huntziger.

Laurent is a tenant farmer. He started out with no other fortune but two cows bought on credit. He works hard. He knows how to take care of animals, and he's a skillful horse trader. He's done all right for himself. I knew him when he was shy. I can see a kind of pride growing in him. The currency can collapse. He has his cows and oxen in the stable and pork in the salting tub. He glides over the war. But I'm not planning on writing a peasant novel.

The background: Syria, Russia. The foreground: belly and tobacco.

In the cities, in the towns, in the villages, everyone says: "The papers are lying." Nobody gets indignant or angry about it. They don't resent them for it. As if it were in the nature of the newspaper to lie, as if the lie was the very essence of the paper. We're far from living in a civilization where the only crime punishable by death would be the lie.

July 8

Moune (seventeen) and Poulette (fourteen)[61] have arrived from Paris. They slipped across the Line illegally (through Buxy and Ouroux) and walked for thirty kilometers. All adolescence and light dresses. They get off the train like two exotic birds flying into a dark cage.

According to them, Paris is not asleep, like the Unoccupied Zone. Two girls speak, and I can see thousands of German corpses on the steppes, fine historic corpses from historical paintings. The world is delivered. Two girls from Paris have come to bear witness to its deliverance.

July 9

I'm going to Lons. As I stand on the station platform, it seems to me the world has had a relapse. A gendarme asks the newsagent if she has a *Paris-Soir*. "For the serial," he says. And he wants to know if *Gringoire* has come out.[62] Last night's world, lightened by Moune and Poulette, has disappeared.

I'm going to Lons to declare that according to the terms of the Law of June 2, 1941, I am Jewish. I feel humiliated. It's the first time society has humiliated me. I feel humiliated, not because I'm Jewish but because I am presumed to be of inferior quality because I'm Jewish. It's absurd; it may be the fault of my pride, but that's the way it is.

Thus the marshal and M. Xavier Vallat[63] have forced me to claim I'm from a Jewish nation to which I felt no connection. Just one nation can be cumbersome

[61] The respective nicknames of Lucien Febvre's two daughters, Lucile and Paulette.—J.-P. A.

[62] Like all the Paris dailies during the Occupation, *Paris-Soir* was violently anti-Semitic and pro-German. *Gringoire* had been a right-wing, xenophobic weekly in the 1930s and naturally became pro-Vichy and pro-Nazi later.

[63] A well-known anti-Semitic politician, Xavier Vallat had headed Vichy's High Commission on Jewish Questions since March.

enough already. You don't think about it, you don't think it's particularly important. But if a foreigner means to humiliate me through this nation, I am hurt,
and I don't know if it's that nation or myself I must defend. But simple dignity
obliges me to identify with it.

Just after the First World War, I took the train from Budapest to Paris.
My third-class car was full. A Hungarian began to exalt Germany: soon, he
said, it would take its revenge. At that time, I still thought you could save
the world by showing the stupidity of war, and the people could triumph
over the arms merchants. Meanwhile, all the passengers in the compartment were looking ironically at this Frenchman that someone was trying to
humiliate. It seemed to me it would have been cowardly to evoke my pacifism, my internationalism. Perhaps I was wrong, perhaps that would have
been wiser. I laboriously prepared my response. I mobilized my German
vocabulary (which I owe entirely to M. Célis, my language teacher in fifth
grade), and I answered like this, more or less: "I have some German friends,
but none of them would be boorish enough to talk like that to a Frenchman
he doesn't know." My aggressive Hungarian fell silent. The car was on my
side. I had won.

So now they're trying to impose another country on me, another group. It would
be just too cowardly to deliberate about whether or not I feel Jewish! If you insult
the name of Jew in me, then I am Jewish, totally Jewish, Jewish to the tips of my
toes, Jewish to my very guts. After that, we'll see.

Thus I decided to give the prefect of the Jura the declaration I was obliged
to make according to the law of June 2. I walked down the path leading to the
town, where goats were grazing, standing up straight on their hind legs like
goats in fables. I took the train to Lons-le-Saunier. As others go to declare their
cattle and the weight of their pigs, I went to the prefecture to declare I was
Jewish.

I remember a session in the criminal court where affairs of adultery were tried.
The judge asked a young man who was approaching the bar: "Who are you?" "I
have come," announced the young man, "to say that I went to bed with Madame
Gorenflot."

I made my declaration at the prefecture. I threw out the word "Jew" as if I was
about to sing the Marseillaise.

I wander around at lunchtime under the sun, in a city with no passersby. You'd think
it was a city forgotten in an isolated cove of time, where time has stopped flowing.

The paper informs us that "marshal Pétain has established the principles of the
future constitution of France." France couldn't care less about his plan for a constitution: it knows it will only take effect if the nation is annihilated.

July 11

Hardly did General Dentz ask for a ceasefire in Syria than Vichy began to multiply anecdotes of the kind that circulated during the First World War, about "heroes of the empire."[64] It's brainwashing through historic words. The general visits the wounded in the hospital. The dying man stops groaning and, in fine Roman style, condenses his hatred for the Gaullists and the deep satisfaction he feels in dying for the empire. Blind propaganda. They've got the wrong era.

The *Völkischer Beobachter*[65] has again denounced the collusion between plutocracy and Bolshevism. Hitler wants neither Bolshevism nor plutocracy. Just as yesterday's petit bourgeois wanted neither reaction nor revolution. Here we see the formal logic of the stupid petit bourgeois heated up by Hitler until it boils. Hitlerism is the rage for the happy medium, an insane transposition of the passions of shopkeepers.

July 19

I feel like the insects that play dead when they can no longer run away.

The peasants and the townspeople used to be characters in our vacations, vacation extras. I can't manage to turn them into resources of my daily life.

Claude received a circular from the colonel of the Fifth Infantry Regiment, garrisoned in Saint-Étienne. (They must have taken down the names of the boys who just passed the Baccalauréat.) This colonel invites him to enlist in his regiment, which "was the regiment of Navarre and has remained full of chic and get-up-and-go."[66]

"Criminal Court of Saint-Claude. Pierre M., seventeen, a student, was sentenced to three months in prison and a ten-franc fine for shouts liable to encourage the schemes of a foreign power." A few days ago, I forget where, one year in prison for offenses to the person of the marshal.

The Free Zone is waiting for the results from Russia, but with slightly less impatience than it waited for the results from the Tour de France in other days.

July 23

The paper: "Enlistments in the Legion of Volunteers against Bolshevism."[67]

[64] General Dentz, the commander of Vichy's forces in the Middle East, was recalled to France three days later.

[65] The newspaper of the Nazi Party.—J.-P. A.

[66] Formed in 1588, the regiment had lasted under this name through the revolutionary and Napoleonic Wars.

[67] Parisian collaborationists created the Légion des volontaires français contre le bolchévisme (LVF) on July 18 with the approval of the Occupation authorities. Some seven thousand French volunteers would eventually join a regiment of the Wehrmacht to fight on the Eastern Front.—J.-P. A.

July 25

Under the Vichy government or under the Third Republic, the colonial lie is the same. I read in the paper: "The week of overseas France was a new occasion for Indochina to show its deep attachment to the mother country."

So where have I already heard of collaboration? It was in Indochina, in 1923. A few Annamites, in the pay of the colonial government, accepted unconditional collaboration, a few emoluments for them and oppression for everyone. Nguyen-An-Ninh was sentenced to three years in prison for having said: "We don't mind collaboration, but not the collaboration of the water buffalo and the plowman."[68]

The pied pipers of Hitlerism. The paper is announcing a new magazine: *Homeland.*[69] A message from the marshal. An article by Giraudoux, who talks about the regional development of our country in the scintillating style we know well . . .[70] So Giraudoux is going over the marshal's head to court Hitler. Nothing surprising about that. It never occurred to Giraudoux that words could have the least significance. I could never read more than six lines of Giraudoux, a sparkling pedant.

The paper has published Carcopino's plans for the educational system. I heard a peasant's voice about that: "We sent our kids to school so they could learn a little more than we did. But it's not worth making them do eight kilometers a day." (His farm is two kilometers from town.) "All they teach them now is to sing one or two verses of the Marseillaise and march in line."

Present times: food-ration coupons, Japan, Indochina, America, death of freedom.

Oh! Let there be a great transfiguring event, an event that transcends current events. Let us see an archangel appearing in a cloud! Or let men somewhere not even revolt but awaken; let their gaze be enough to annihilate the old diplomats and the great political parvenus and the stinking armies and their tanks.

---

[68] Opposition to foreign rule in Indochina (Vietnam) did not begin in the 1960s.

[69] *Patrie* in French, the same word used in the first line of the Marseillaise: "Allons, enfants de la Patrie . . ."

[70] Jean Giraudoux was a novelist and dramatist whose plays were applauded in many countries, including the United States—on Broadway, for example, as late as the end of the1960s.

July 30

The paper: "Saint-Claude. Severe sentences for seditious songs. The gendarmes caught five individuals on the road to La Mouille as they were singing a song *having no connection whatsoever* to the program of the national revolution . . . They were sentenced to six months in jail and a five-franc fine."

Dialogue. The English teacher in the Bourg lycée stops in front of a farmer who's working at the edge of his field.

The farmer: "So . . . it's happened!"

"What?"

"The miracle."

"What miracle?"

"The Russians . . ."

But an old lady in Saint-Amour whose table is decorated with a bouquet of paper flowers:

"Communism better not come here . . ."

August 1

The paper: "The Annamite people's attachment to France . . . The ministers of the Annamite government sent the French governor general a message of unfailing attachment, etc."

The ministers of the Annamite government!

France cannot die, said Prime Minister Reynaud a year ago. If I look at the big retailers in town, I see quite clearly that France can die. They would gladly relinquish France, as long as they could keep some hope in their business. France is threatened with death by their acceptance of Germany and by the patriotism they're holding in reserve in case Germany is defeated.

August 2

The Smolensk sector: Soviet losses, German losses. France will do the statistics on the corpses. While history is manufacturing millions of corpses, Barthélemy,[71] the minister of justice, defines the future constitution: "The marshal wants it to be permeated by a great, noble, humane vibration." He also wants to "restore the mystique and the chivalry of labor." Yesterday or the day before, Carcopino was announcing his intention of abolishing "the

[71] Joseph Barthélemy was an early supporter of Pétain and a strong backer of Vichy's increasingly authoritarian and repressive measures; he also signed the Statut des Juifs and held Jews responsible for the decline of France.

borders between the school and life." This world of clichés and corpses—what a stench!

I learn Paul Nizan was killed in May 1940 in the Somme.

August 5

Solitude is like hunger. Someone who hasn't eaten for a few days can't digest food that is too coarse. I ran into C——, who's just gone on vacation a few kilometers from here. Everything in his mind is translated into algebraic formulas. Current events slip over him as if on an oilcloth. Getting fresh supplies of food is his one anxiety, and the only threat he sees in the future is that of famine.

He can do nothing for my solitude. I can't appease my hunger with clay.

August 6

They're saying around town that there have been disturbances in Saint-Étienne. Miners have reportedly been killed.[72]

I chat with laborers working on broadening the road. A group of five. One of them (a flabby face, you'd think it had no bony framework) takes me aside and tells me he's not a road worker by profession; he's anti-union and reads *Action Française* every day. If I reasoned like Maurras, I would conclude that one French worker out of five reads *Action Française*.

August 9

I'm waiting for the train to Bourg. On the station platform, a gendarme announces to me that Germany has asked for peace. The news, he says, was given by English radio. I doubt this with all my critical spirit. I get on the train with the gendarme, his wife, and their little girl. But the news has invaded me. I wouldn't be surprised if all the passengers in the car started kissing each other. The little stations and their skimpy gardens are bursting with joy. The little stations are singing victory. But the passengers do not kiss each other.

August 11

The young barrel maker tells me, as he pushes his cart: "There's a change, even with the peasants. The time of fear is over. They're *feeling their way . . .*"

I had given Old François a copy of the leaflet *Liberté*.[73] He wanted to distribute it. He copied it out by hand; he stayed at his table from 9:00 p.m. to 2:00 a.m. And

---

[72] This was merely a rumor.—J.-P. A.

[73] One of the very first resistance movements with political goals, Liberté was created in the fall of 1940. Its leaders were law professors and Christian Democrats, including François de Menthon, Pierre-Henri Teitgen, and René Courtin. The activists put out a "newspaper" (a sheet of paper

another one of the old craftsmen did the same. They applied themselves; they copied as best they could: say, if you will, that they copied like saints. Let little writers of "fine literature" smile as much as they like. I say those manuscript copies are at the heart of history. I say France is there.

The government is requisitioning "nonferrous metals." It wants this requisition to be "a good deal for good Frenchmen."

The government is not saying what our pots and pans will be used for. But all the peasants think they'll be transformed into German cartridges. Laurent says, as he pumps liquid manure in the stable: "Even if they gave me a cow, I'd rather bury everything under my manure . . . They're not telling us what they want to do with our copper. They're right . . . that makes one lie the less . . . Of course I wouldn't say that to them, but I'm saying it to you."

August 20

I tell a charming old lady whose rooms are all fluff and fringes that the capture of Odessa would not be a catastrophe. But she read the paper and, as if she had a map of every seam of metal in the world inside her heart, she counters: "But what about manganese?"

English radio is quoting Msgr Baudrillard,[74] who heralds Hitler as the great peace-maker. A new Christendom of free nations will be born, a new Middle Ages . . .— What about the left-wing Catholics? Where is the unity of Catholicism? But where is there unity?

August 26

They threshed yesterday. At nine in the evening there was a big supper at the farm, according to custom. I was invited. They had killed two rabbits and two hens. The café was not "national." And the marc was distilled by the farmer himself. I remembered the supper of August 1939, when they young men were saying, "We'd like to leave . . . We're sick of never being sure you'll have a harvest."

We joked around like in peacetime until midnight. A few people who had come to help out left. Around two in the morning, there were only five or six

printed on both sides) and leaflets against the occupiers. So the first resistance movements appeared relatively early.—J.-P. A.

[74] Msgr. Baudrillard, the rector of the Catholic University of Paris, who went to the École Normale Supérieure, was anointed cardinal by Pius XI in 1935. A declared German hater until 1940, he clearly took the collaborationist side, especially its crusade against Bolshevism: "I affirm that the tomb of Christ will be delivered," he said as he blessed the weapons of the LVF [which became a collaborationist militia], "by a new chivalry."—J.-P. A.

young people left, grouped at the end of the table. And they distrusted every-thing, from England to Germany to Communism to the government. But they all seemed to have one hatred in common, a hatred of workers: "They envy us, but they don't envy our work. If there was a revolution, they'd come here, they'd take their revenge on us . . ."

I told them that the image of a crowd of rioting workers pillaging their farms seemed unreasonable to me. But a young peasant: "If there was a famine, they'd come here. They tell us 'You're rich, you have milk, you have butter, you have eggs' . . . They'd come here . . . They'd rob us . . ."

Then there was the comparison of the hard labor of the fields and the easy work of the factory. A young peasant blamed them for working only eight hours, when he worked from dawn to dusk, and he blamed them for their excessive wages. You would have thought international high finance was working-class finance.

I came back home sickened, discouraged.

August 29

When the people spoke of treason, I wouldn't let myself go and construct some facile scenario. I would say to myself: "It's more complicated than that . . ." I would try to construct a plausible marshal, not too much of one piece. To avoid the simplifications of melodrama, I would lose myself in the kind of psychologi-cal complications you find in novels. I threw around ideas too much. An engi-neer at the little station café yesterday was telling the real truth: "A bunch of bastards, all of 'em."

In the Occupied Zone, Jews no longer have the right to own a radio.[75] That's not such a bad idea. Repugnant or grotesque measures are the most satisfying for devotees of pure obedience. The more odious or unreasonable the authorities become, the more obedience becomes a gratuitous pleasure, the pleasure of art.

The attempt to assassinate Laval and Déat is elating the villages.[76]

September 4

A day in Bourg. Countless portraits of Pétain in the shops. In the bookstores, *Gringoire* and *Action Française*. Maurras is the philosopher for readers of quotable

---

[75] The German edict of August 13, 1941, forbade Jews in the Northern Zone to own wire-less receivers and ordered them to drop them off at the city hall of their town or at the police station.—J.-P. A.

[76] Paul Collette tried to assassinate Déat and Laval, wounded them, and was immediately arrested and sentenced to death (later commuted).

sayings and books of historical anecdotes. Maurras is only a slight symptom. But the important sign is that part of the French bourgeoisie takes this polemicist seriously. The symptom isn't that part of the bourgeoisie shares the passions of Maurras but that it accepts and even admires the justification Maurras gives for them.

September 6

The newspaper carries news of Déat and Laval. But not a word about Paul Collette. Vichy is afraid of providing material for the legend of a martyr. Déat and Laval are no longer the victims of a terrorist act, but simply ailing.

Laurent has stopped his oxen. We talk about current events and the wishy-washy politics of the town. "Yes," he says, "I think about it a hundred times a day . . . But some of them only think about it when you bring it up."

"What a life," the wheelwright says to me. "It's all just lies and smuggling now. We live in lies through the papers. We're reduced to smuggling so we can eat."

Met the retired major. We go back over the debacle, to the "connivances" without which it is inconceivable. "I don't believe," he says, "that there was one French general who wished for the total victory of Germany." I take this in. I show him the involuntary admission contained in his "total."

On the train, a well-dressed moron in new gloves was saying: "I am neither an Anglophile nor a Germanophile; I am French." It's actually the tenth time I've heard that.

The Germans, the courts-martial, and a few magistrates of the Court of Appeals have handed out death sentences in Paris.[77] Reaction of the old Parisian lady who's taken refuge here: "People in Paris aren't reasonable . . . That complicates things."

September 17

Ten hostages shot by Occupation troops in Paris. The possessions of the queen of Holland have been seized because she's involved in the Bolshevik-capitalist front. General Dentz has been received by the marshal. General Dentz is already a phantom.

September 21

Either the Church is divided or it is strangely conciliatory. The archbishop of Toulouse, the archbishop of Montauban, and other prelates have denounced the

---

[77] Two young Communists were sentenced by a German court martial and executed on August 19. Two days later, a German officer was killed in the Barbès-Rochechouart metro station. On August 24, Vichy set up "special sections" of the courts to judge such cases quickly. Three Communist activists were guillotined on August 28.

persecutions. The Church will be able to say: "We excoriated the crime and the criminals."

But here's another sound. "Message from the clergy of the southeast to the head of state. Monsignor the Archbishop of Aix, the bishops of Fréjus, Nice, Monaco, the most reverend priests of Leytins, Frigolet, etc., address to the head of state, the savior and rebuilder of the country, the respectful assurance of their loyal veneration and their full collaboration with his work of religious, moral, and material regeneration of the new France."

September 20

Communiqué from General von Stülpnagel, head of the German administration in occupied territories: "Raymond C—— and Louis T—— from Argenteuil were sentenced to death by the military tribunal for helping the enemy. They were shot today."

General von Stülpnagel is asking the Paris population to become informers. "In all cases, the population did not sufficiently support the investigations undertaken to identify and arrest the guilty parties."

I go looking for horn-of-plenty mushrooms in the woods with Claude. We run into Riffault, whose farm is about a hundred meters from there. He tells me two farmers of a neighboring hamlet were sentenced to eight years hard labor for "Communist talk." . . . "You can't talk too loud," he tells me. And we look right and left, as if, in these woods, someone could spy on us.

Riffault also tells me the gendarmerie received two letters—anonymous, needless to say—whose authors accused him of not selling all his milk to the official dairy "collector."

September 22

The marshal is asking the French people to inform on the authors of violent acts against the occupying forces.

Three Communists sentenced to death in Paris.

In town, a guest of the hotel reads the paper and comments on this piece of news: "Communists—you can't kill enough of 'em."

The Saint-Amour parish bulletin: "The disappearance of Bolshevism would undeniably be a blessing for the universe. Its fearsome, sneaky hand has appeared everywhere. France was not spared, and our Popular Front was merely, for many, an attempt to Bolshevize the nation . . ."

What are the Russians up to? Will the English try to land in France? But it's already a miracle that we can conceive of an English landing. A year ago, the most tenacious optimists were imagining the failure of a German landing as a supreme bit of luck.

September 24

Semi-dream: The people's tribunal is going to deliberate. A tumultuous audience is demanding blood. The collaborationist writer who is being judged has no chance of escaping the death penalty. He is pale in the dock between civil guards. His overripe face is decomposed. Then I intervene with eloquence, the eloquence of disgust: "Do not profane the majesty of death. Let your generosity outstrip his ignominy. Do not make a corpse out of this rotting carcass."[78]

They're executing men by firing squad in Paris. Madame L——, who, the farmers say, gets on fine with the Germans, has returned from Paris. She says the provocations of the Parisians are silly and the Germans are being admirably patient.

At the beginning of the war, Madeleine B—— would go into trances of joy when the radio announced German planes had been shot down. You would have said that, in a state of bliss and jubilation, she was trying to see planes descending in flames in the radio. Today, she admires Hitler's "holiness," a pure man, who taught sacrifice to his people.

I passed a leaflet to Old François. He passed it on to a worker in the Bourg wireworks, who circulated it in the shop. The police intercepted the worker, who had the tract in his hands, and he gave them inept replies that enabled them to trace it to Saint-Amour.

As I tell Old François I intend to relieve him of all responsibility (I'm the one who gave him the leaflet), he answers that he absolutely refuses. He'll say he found the tract on the floor of his workshop and someone must have slipped it under the door. "Even if you told them you're the one who gave it to me, I'd say it's not true. They'd be much happier to get you than me."

A policeman arrived and tried intimidation: "Don't you know something's changed in France? Don't you know there are camps surrounded by barbed wire?"

There was no follow-up.

October 4

A speech by Hitler. Churchill alone is responsible for the war—Churchill, the agent of Judeo-masonism.

---

[78] Werth's dream is premonitory, though not for him: after the war, there were pleas from writers to spare the lives of well-known collaborators who were tried for treason, especially when they were writers or journalists. The pleas were not always successful.

Hitler, you say, can't really be taken in by this stupid theme. Don't be too quick to attribute to Hitler the cynical slyness and absolute bad faith of a political libertine. A Hitler doesn't believe, a Hitler doesn't think, a Hitler has no experience of the anxiety of those intimate deliberations through which a man tries to rise to the truth as if he were trying to cling to a wall. Hitler doesn't break his fingernails at that game. Hitlers believe in their ideas the way a fortune teller believes in her cards. And the crowd believes Hitler the way people who consult a fortune teller believe in her cards.

Suzanne crossed the Line of Demarcation hidden in the tender of a locomotive. "I lived for an hour," she writes, "like a rat in a sewer half filled with water."

Febvre will go by road, dressed in blue to look like a worker who crosses the border every day.

October 7

"Two French steamships were sunk by the English, one in the Aegean Sea, the other in the Tyrrhenian Sea. Both were transporting a load of tobacco to Marseilles."

Laurent moves his lips as he reads the paper. "The guy who wrote that report is no fool," he says, "But he's taking us for fools."

October 13

In a sense, the Lavals and the Darlans are traitors of melodrama. They wear a Nazi uniform. Their roles are cut from one piece. The people who support them openly are easy to enumerate: raging bourgeois, perverted semi-intellectuals, hired thugs, and failures in all categories who find "positions" in youth camps, the bureaucracy, and parts of the police. But there is a class that is no less repugnant: the category of writers, teachers, and journalists who rub elbows with people in power—no matter what power—and who support the regime, whatever the regime may be. Shady characters from the right or the left. Before they offered themselves to Vichy, they were devotees of "eternal France" or the Stalinist revolution.

Whatever may happen, even if France were rid of Germany and Vichy, the people won't call its press to account. The civilization in which ordinary morality judges lying the way it judges murder has still to be created.

I'm thinking of Fernand Braudel, a prisoner of war.[79] I think of him with all my strength. Other people's misfortunes give me a feeling of guilt if I've been protected from them. I feel responsible.

---

[79] Fernand Braudel was, with Lucien Febvre and Marc Bloch, a founder of the Annales school of history and one of the leading historians of the twentieth century.

I paste a stamp on an envelope. It bears the image of the marshal. A few months ago, when the newspapers announced that stamps were going to come out with the image of "We, Philippe . . . ," I remember it seemed funny to us, ridiculous. We imagined a puerile old man pasting stamps with his effigy into an album. But this stamp isn't funny anymore. With this stamp, we can take the measure of the steps in the Nazification of France. The marshal merely used to be a philatelist. Now, he kills men and sentences them to hard labor. He's as good as the murderers of Bohemia-Moravia and Serbia. He kills in the service of Germany.

Letters of denunciation have been proliferating. Yesterday, the inspectors made another good catch at the railroad station: a woman who was transporting six eggs. One half of France informs on the other. But the most surprising thing is not that half of France is informing on the other; it's that the part that is informed on seems to feel neither anger, nor disgust, nor indignation at the part that informs on them.

Claude crossed the Line of Demarcation. I have a message from him that the driver brought into the Free Zone. The "lady of the little café" is the one who arranged everything.[80]

I knew the smugglers' trade had become a kind of licensed profession. Men walk through the corridors of the train cars without making any pretense of hiding and offer their services as if they were travel agents.

That was my excuse. But the money I offered was refused, simply and with dignity. It was impossible to insist.

It was during the debacle and the huge traffic jam on the roads, the mix of soldiers and civilians who were going down "toward the Loire." Suzanne asks an officer in a shiny uniform: "But what's happening? It's incomprehensible . . ." And the officer answers: "You shouldn't have voted that way . . ." In his political fury, the officer was forgetting that women in France didn't vote and not all men voted "red."[81] But one could already see that Vichy's scenario was ready. Yesterday, General Dentz was addressing the soldiers in Syria

---

[80] "Madame Marie" ran the café stand at the Saint-Amour station. She acted as an intermediary between the railroad workers and the candidates for clandestine crossings of the Line of Demarcation. Léon Werth often went to this café, as the railroad workers also transported mail, which enabled Suzanne and Léon Werth to correspond fairly freely.—J.-P. A.

Legal correspondence between the two zones was severely limited.—D. B.

[81] A 1944 edict by de Gaulle's provisional government gave women the right to vote, and they first voted in 1945.

and echoed that soldierless officer a year later: "The British violated their signature because they were under the domination of the politicians of the Popular Front."

October 17

The train to Lyon. "Oh, if only you'd heard English radio last night . . . !" said the woman who sells newspapers on the station platform. In a concentrated voice, as if she were praying, as if she were thanking a god. If I had listened to English radio, she would not have made me happier than by this sudden, discreet effusion.

At Paufique's.[82] I overhear a few words of the people next to me: "Rights . . . we don't have rights anymore . . ." Then they go over prewar cinema; they miss the time when there were great variety shows at the Casino.

A Vichy poster. "The *Times* admits the Anglo-Saxons and Russians divided up the world between them on the *Potomac*.[83] They gave Europe to the Soviets and their agents, the Communists." Who said that the weight of stupidity would make the world capsize? The world does not capsize. It is no longer even capable of capsizing.

Assassinations in Nantes and Bordeaux.[84] "If the cowardly assassins in the pay of England and Moscow are not captured by midnight October 26, fifty hostages will be executed. Consequently, I am offering the total sum of 15 million francs to the inhabitants of France who might contribute to discovering the guilty parties."

Latarjet is back from Paris.[85] It was rumored there that Lapicque, Borel, and Wallon had been arrested.[86] He tells me this news in a room of the medical

---

[82] Paufique was an ophthalmologist in Lyon.—J.-P. A.

[83] In August 1941, Roosevelt and Churchill signed an agreement on the USS *Potomac* that soon became the Atlantic Charter. The signatories pledged a joint effort to disarm aggressor nations, to support the self-determination of peoples and their freedoms, and not to use war to expand their own territory.

[84] In Nantes, the lieutenant colonel and *Feldkommandant* Karl Hotz was killed by Gilbert Brustein, a young Communist, on October 20, 1941. The next day, the "adviser to the military administration" [Hans] Reimers was killed in Bordeaux by another member of the Communist youth organization. Groups of the clandestine Communist Party performed individual assassinations to force the Wehrmacht to maintain the maximum number of troops in France and relieve the Soviet Union.—J.-P. A.

[85] Werth was staying with his friends the Latarjets in Lyon.

[86] This information is partly inaccurate. Louis Lapicque was a professor of physiology at the Museum of Natural History; Henri Wallon, a well-known child psychologist who taught at the Sorbonne, was to join the Communist Party in 1942.—J.-P. A.

school, in front of a professor, an *agrégé* and a department head.[87] No one comments, gets angry, or seems moved. A second of silence. And their professional conversation starts again. Indifference, or scorn for useless words?

October 31

A Vichy decree forbids us to listen to radio stations, whether foreign or not, that "indulge in anti-national propaganda." I can see the big, white notice again, signed by the general commanding the troops of the Occupation, posted on the wall of the Chapelon town hall in June of last year, when we were refugees in the Gâtinais. That poster seemed monstrous, apocalyptic. But it was signed by a conquering German general. We took it as the sign of provisional oppression that was naturally resulting from the defeat. We didn't imagine that a French signature could ever authenticate a document like that, we couldn't imagine that a ban like that could ever be formulated by a French government talking to French citizens.

Nobody talks to me about the decree in town. They're afraid. A year ago, Vichy wouldn't have dared sign this decree. It's new proof of its initial hesitations and its progression. New proof that the slightest resistance would have been effective and Vichy was afraid of resistance. This is the measure of the cowardice of the French in the Free Zone. But it may be said in their defense that they didn't believe in the occupation of their freedoms by the Pétains and Darlans and of two-thirds of France by the Germans.

November 5

The countryside brings me back to my solitude. The trees are dead wood. The grass is blackened green. The shade of an old wooden secretary in the depths of an antique store.

To bear this weather you'd need blazing fires in a hearth, red meat, long hikes.

Who is right? Old François, who wants to be free, or the concierge who said to me in Paris: "German or French, I'll always be working the bell pull to let people in"?

If I were born a peasant, I would have tried relentlessly to be hired by the railroad or for day labor in the city. I would have gone toward the city, toward knowledge, toward science, toward life.

P—— used to love the peasant, "the breast of France,"[88] wise as the land, who nourishes us, who is economical, respectful of order, and is not tempted

---

[87] An *agrégé* is someone who has passed the *agrégation*, a competitive nationwide examination leading to a good teaching position and/or the doctorate.

[88] Werth is alluding to a saying attributed to a minister of Henri IV: "Plowing and pasturing are the two breasts of France."

by the turbulence of city workers. The peasant—the foundation of a strong France and a stable currency. But ever since his tenant farmer has refused to sell him milk and butter, he never stops denouncing the peasant's lust for lucre and his cupidity, his lack of feeling for any ideal; he takes advantage of our general misfortune—the peasant, a parasite of the land who lives off the sweat of city dwellers.

A Nazified world . . . What would be changed? Nothing, except for the essential, the invisible essential. Engineers would build bridges, doctors would make diagnoses, and active painters paintings. I saw this quite clearly in Lyon. People who have an absorbing profession haven't yet realized that they're living in the middle of Nazism. And how many times a year do they, and others, think about thought?

December 2

The meeting of Goering and Pétain. Monsieur de Brinon declares: "The lunch was very cordial and the two marshals quite merry."[89]

December 7

Hitler has twenty-five days left to annihilate the Russians, according to his promise.

Conversation on the farm. "There're a lot of people," Laurent tells me, "who'd rather see Germany win than Russia . . . because of Communism." I ask: "Bourgeois or peasants?" "Specially bourgeois, but some peasants too . . ."

He's making swill for the pigs and feels like chatting. "If Germany evacuates from France, there'll be a civil war. The peasants hate the workers and even city people. Not all of them, but a lot. Not so long ago, we were jealous of people in the cities. Now, they're the ones jealous of us. All they do is tell us: 'You have eggs, milk . . .' But not so long ago we were hardly getting by . . . In my father's day, there was no question of wine. Coffee? My father had some coffee for the first time the day he drew lots.[90] We didn't eat white bread, we sold all the wheat . . . We only ate cornbread and buckwheat—waffles. Old M—you knew him—still used to tell me: 'White bread's too good for us . . .' Once I even

[89] At Pétain's request, Goering met him in December in Saint-Florentin (in the *département* of the Yonne, not too far from Paris) to go over the situation. The conversations were disappointing, for Pétain had to realize that the Reich was not at all inclined to make the concessions imposed by collaboration at the state level.—J.-P. A.

[90] Military service from 1872 to 1889 had two tracks: one fraction of the army did a year of military service, and the other, five: this was decided by drawing lots.—J.-P. A.

answered him: 'If you think it's too good, put some shit on it . . .' Yeah, in my father's day, if a tenant farmer ate white bread, I think his boss would've thrown him out."

I ask him how the boss would have been hurt if his farmer had eaten white bread. "It wasn't a question of self-interest," he answered; "it was the big guy wanting to keep the little guy under control, bring him down."

I recall that when I was a child, bourgeois ladies would get indignant when their maids didn't want to go out without a hat, like ladies.

You have to have the strength to wait, scornfully, and take what pleasures you have left on the way. Wasn't I happy yesterday biking on the road, when the rain was throwing its needles in my face? And this morning, can't I content myself with the simple thought that I'll eat duck liver for lunch? And can't I content myself with that walk over the mass grave of fallen leaves in the fog, where the curtains of trees are ghost ships?

December 10

I listened to English radio at the farm. A commentary on America's entry into the war, and on Japan. Montage of a few excerpts from President Roosevelt's speech and the applause of Congress. Defeat of the Germans in Russia. Reminder of Hitler's promises, announcing the end of the war this year. "Only twenty-two days left." Each evening, English radio counts the decreasing number of days Hitler has left to keep his promise. Georgette, a girl of seventeen, takes care of some of the housework and walks through the room without making more noise than a cat.[91] She smiles at the count of days. I thought she wasn't listening. The father is nailing rubber soles onto his clogs. The sound of the hammer is a rhythmic accompaniment to the broadcast. The son, a guy of twenty, seems foreign to all politics and strategy. He's leaning over one of those songs that wandering singers sell at the fair. He studies the words and tries to remember the tune. The farmer's wife is doing her knitting. They're not gathered around the radio. Not at all the painting *Radio on the Farm* composed by an anecdotal painter of the Society of French Artists for the Salon, supposing that there still are anecdotal painters. They're not grouped around the radio with their ears perked up. They have their own way of listening: they receive the words by absorbing them through their pores.

At the station café, an engineer was saying: "Getting Frenchmen across the Line on the train is my way of showing I'm French."

---

[91] Georgette is Laurent's daughter.

December 12

Speech by Hitler. America's entry into the war is due to the international Jew and the Freemason. Hitler is smashing the myth by using it so much. Pétain and Darlan pick up the pieces. Hitler brings up Greece and the barbarians. History doesn't suit him very well. Proclamation of Mussolini, oratorically rotund like a nymph in academic sculpture.

December 15

I learn that a hundred or so Frenchmen will be executed by firing squad in Paris. At the same time, I learn that Derain, Vlaminck, Segonzac, and other painters, musicians, and writers have accepted Hitler's invitation to take a lovely trip to Germany.

A lovely trip . . . Perhaps through their train window they will wave their handkerchiefs to gallantly salute a few Frenchmen that another train was bringing to the camp of Auschwitz, who were going to die in the camp of Auschwitz.[92]

What a fine documentary they could have made! A banquet presided by the sculptor Breker.[93] "Montage audio": the clink of champagne glasses, the popping of corks, the crack-crack of machine guns. Visual analogies: a waiter lines up the empty bottles on the floor; German soldiers line up a few corpses of executed French hostages on the ground.

In 1871, a few girls who had partied with German officers were whipped and dunked in the basin of the fountain on Place de la Concorde by the crowd.

The forest floor is covered with leaves covered with frost that draws their finest veins. You walk over a lace rug. A winter sun varnishes the countryside.

December 25

The village of Le Villars. The warm hospitality of the Nicot cousins. House from 1840. Chardonnay in its plenitude. Ageless marc, with a walnut aroma.

I learn that the faces of the ladies in Tournus grow longer every time the German retreat becomes more certain, every time one may reasonably hope that it's taking the form of a debacle. Thus, in Lyon, a chambermaid told me: "All the same, the Russians better not win completely, because Bolshevism . . ." She pronounced the word with a grimace of disgust. The mystery of ideas in the air and injected passions.

---

[92] Auschwitz had functioned since June 1940. Deportation of French Jews began in the spring of 1942: could this mention have been added later? As Werth's later entries indicate, however, Auschwitz was not a secret. The French artists' trip to Berlin would take place in January 1942. Of those who went, Derain (who hesitated at first), Vlaminck, Segonzac, and Van Dongen were the best known.

[93] Arno Breker, the Führer's favorite sculptor, would be treated to a deluge of congratulations and homages from élite French artists and writers at the inauguration of his show in Paris on May 15, 1942.—J.-P. A.

1942

January 3

The penetration of Hitlerism. "Hitler is a saint," Madeleine B—— told me a few weeks ago. In October '39, she was eating the Boches alive à la 1914. Now, while she was introducing a new saint into her hagiography, her husband was earning a few millions by dealing in metallurgy with the Germans. Madeleine B—— can't perform the most grossly self-interested act without making it sublime. But would she have been a Hitlerian even if her self-interest weren't driving her? The biggest ideas circulating in the current climate enter her by osmosis.

In 1837, Stendhal wrote, in his *Life of Napoleon*:[1] "The art of lying has developed radically over the past few years. The lie is no longer expressed in clear terms as in our fathers' day, but is produced by vague, general forms of language. It would be hard to blame the liar for using them and especially hard to refute them in a few words." I opened the book by chance and found this sentence. Like readers of the Bible who slip a pin between the pages and seek their inspiration in the verse where the point of the pin has stopped.

January 4

It's Sunday. No newspaper. It's as if the war were taking a rest. The papers should only come out once a month. That way, we'd have a chunk of frozen events every month.

The frost has covered the pine needles with identical crystals so minutely sculpted that the trees seem artificial, dolled up, sprinkled with tassels.

---

[1] Stendhal (Henri Beyle, 1783–1842) is better known for his novels *The Red and the Black* and *The Charterhouse of Parma*.

"A magnificent old man is saving us, and many people refuse to understand this." That's what a provincial bourgeois lady wrote to Suzanne. A whole bourgeoisie is still living in its shell. Who will break it open?

January 9

Montage: The Japanese advance in Malaysia is intensifying. "The German nation now represents," says Dr. Goebbels,* "the last defense against the assaults of the Mongols." Assassination of a policeman in Paris. German troops taking heavy losses on the Eastern Front. Counterfeiters of ration coupons to get life sentences at hard labor. Communists sentenced in Saint-Étienne. Soccer: Lugny vs. Tournus. The locals must work hard to try to match the other team in the first group. In Tournus: Branges A.C., leader of Group E for the second division championship, will face the reserves of Étoile, reinforced by a few stars from the first division. Financial incentives to encourage families to have more children.

The retired sergeant turned-grocer is one of the heads of the Legion.[2] "They saw him," a farmer tells me, "in the back of the shop, putting his wife and daughter through drills—about-faces, at his orders . . ." I have my doubts, and smile. "No, no—they were doing it to be nice to him . . . He likes it so much."

Deprived of tobacco. Say what you will, the pipe was a fine thing. The first puff was the beginning of bliss. And in its own milieu, the pipe gave one the same calm as an ocean voyage, when it seems the boat has come from nowhere and has no destination but the horizon.

January 16

It's cold out and the snow is monotonous. I go out over the steppes. I walk, I walk myself the way you walk a horse so he doesn't spend whole days without leaving the stable. My reasonable self walks my horse self.

I saw the conductor who smuggled my wife and son across the Line: "When I got the lady and the young man out of the freight car, I was happier than they were."

---

[2] The "patriotic" veterans' organization Vichy created, not to be confused with the Légion des Volontaires Français, a fascistic militia.

January 17

At the same time Vlaminck, Segonzac, Derain, Florent Schmitt, and company were banqueting in Berlin, in Paris the Germans were torturing the physicist Holweck to death.[3]

I'd met him during the "Phony War" near Saint-Dizier at the mess hall of Saint-Exupéry's* squadron. Together, we'd listened to songs of liturgical obscenity—an inverted form of modesty in a barracks and a war.

I saw him again in his laboratory, another time. I was with Saint-Ex, who was consulting him about an "invention": locating places through photoelectric cells. Everything about it was a mystery to me.

February 7

Chat with Laurent while he's making mash for the pigs. Yesterday, a market day, he spent part of the time in the café. He deposed the farmers about their opinions on current events. He reports their testimony. He follows his usual rule: not saying what he thinks. It's a rule of prudence he formulated to me several times. "You can be sure I didn't say a thing . . . I'm not that dumb . . . I let them talk . . ."

"Some of them were saying five years like this would be a good thing for factory workers, it wouldn't hurt them. They said before the war the workers broke the windows of the factories, they can't forgive them for that . . . Me, I don't know exactly what happened . . . The workers, at five they're through with their job, they're sitting in front of their doors on a bench, on chairs or whatever. All they have to do is turn with the sun. Us, we go by with our carts. They watch us go by. We bring in one cart and we go back to load another one." (Like all peasants, he forgets it's not harvest time every day.) "They don't like us . . . When I went to Lyon with the firemen, the workers insulted us." They were kidding around, I tell him. "No, they were insulting us . . . Oh! We weren't scared, we were in groups."

He's unhappy with the requisitions. "There are things that shouldn't be. They requisitioned wheat at 2.90 francs a kilo. But they sell us flour for sows at 3.20 francs a kilo. And it's nothing at all, that flour. (He picks up a fistful from a box for me to smell.) An animal would die if that's all you gave it . . . Yesterday, some of the guys in the café were saying, 'We'd rather see the Soviets than see what we're seeing' . . ."

But it wasn't deep anger. It was a figure of speech.

[3] Fernand Hollweck, a distinguished scientist known for his work on wireless radio, was a member of a resistance network. He was arrested on December 11, 1941, and died of cardiac arrest, according to a German report. In fact, he was horribly tortured and transported, dying, to La Pitié Hospital on December 21.

February 9

That petit bourgeois woman from Paris, vulgar and fat like blubber, deplores the fact that there's no movie theater in town. Riffault's wife never went to the movies. That peasant woman doesn't read the paper, and she never saw a town bigger than Dole. There are few images in her head. But at least her head isn't a trash can.

February 20

The Riom trial.[4] The timidity of budding dictatorships. They simulate the forms of justice.

A peasant aphorism. "On the Lyon train," says young Jeanne Riffault,[5] "they were all boasting about what they'd found: a chicken for some, flour for others . . ." "These days," her mother said, "It's not enough to keep quiet; you should complain."

February 24

The wars between Germany and Russia and between the United States and Japan have become part of the times. The details don't much interest the French. They receive the strategic news of the day as they would take in a history of the War of the Spanish Succession. If the Russians beat the Germans and Germany collapses, they think the Krauts will go away.[6] It's all a game of heads or tails for them. Same for the fate of France. It's heads or tails. And they're not even the ones who are tossing the coin. And they don't see that even with Germany beaten, peace won't just settle in.

Laurent bought two oxen for 17,500 francs. For twenty years now, he's been dealing and trading. He speculates on livestock the way others speculate on stocks or paintings. Money, nothing but money. And yet that's not it. "I wouldn't have wanted a pair of black oxen," he says. "There was a nice pair there, as nice as these. But these go with my cows." And in fact the brown or tawny spots go well with the hides of his cows. You might say the contrast wouldn't have been any less pretty. That doesn't matter; he's influenced by art, whether he knows it or not.

---

[4] Vichy used the Cour Suprême de Justice (High court of justice) in the town of Riom on August 8, 1940, to try the men it claimed were responsible for France's defeat. On February 19, 1942, Léon Blum,* Édouard Daladier,* General Maurice Gamelin, and others appeared before the court. Pétain had already sentenced those three to detention in the fort of Portalet on October 15, 1941.—J.-P. A.

[5] The daughter of "Riffault" (a pseudonym for the neighboring farmer's real name).

[6] "Krauts": Werth writes "Fridolins," a slang word for Germans that became more common than "Boche" during the Occupation.

He brought back his oxen from the market at Saint-Julien, on the mountain eleven miles from here. He sank into the snow, the animals were tired. But that's not the trip he's full of, it's not that trip or that fatigue he tells me about, it's the excitement of the marketplace, the bargaining, that play with words that aren't quite lies nor quite truths either, that game where the cleverest wins and not always the most deceitful.

The god Mercury lives in him.

"We'd like it to be over with," says a shopkeeper in the town, "So no more people are killed and business starts up like before."

I smoked my pack of shag tobacco in one day. And then a week without smoking. But I'm waiting for a miracle to make a few packs fall from heaven for me. I smoke my last pipe of this decade. It's not true that it's only the pleasure of habit, an obsession. Each puff feels like it gets me back on my feet again. Each puff leaves a taste of sea spray and chocolate on the palate.

March 7

In Paris, seven Communists sentenced to death by a German tribunal.

March 8

It snowed again last night. I'm sick of nature turned into an operating room. Sick of white daintiness and trees like Santa Claus beards. We're sick of it; we already gave.

"In Mâcon, two religious ceremonies will be celebrated in memory of the French victims of British bombings: in Saint-Vincent Cathedral and in the Protestant church." God in Mâcon is no more than a sycophant. He commemorates the victims of English bombings, but he couldn't care less about the victims of German or even French executions in Paris.

A fearful, narrow-minded, illiterate bourgeoisie. Barbarian technicians of medicine or law. The manufacturers are revolting, with their philanthropy that comes from being scared stiff. They no longer make perfunctory judgments about books. They have transferred their culture. Their culture is now painting. A painting can be seen more quickly than a book can be read. And there is a scale of prices. Art is a superstructure of market quotations.

In Lyon, behind the vaults of the Perrache railroad station, there is a sign on the wall of a brothel. It reads: "Genuine French."

March 16

From the newspaper: "Statues taken down in Poligny. A team of specialists took down the statue of General Travot . . . Everybody was consoled by the thought

that this metal could supply copper sulfate for our winegrowers." This correspondent in Poligny really has a naïvely bucolic soul.[7]

In Bourg, I saw the empty pedestal of the statue of Bichat.[8] Statues of great men
or local heroes, statues in little cities and towns, so ugly they're touching, ugly
with an ugliness that the wind and rain diminish little by little. Statues that were
so many crimes against art, but as they went through the bad weather, they
took on the graces of Little Sisters of the Poor and almost an air of antiquity.
Village statues, we miss you: you had a way of being ugly and ridiculous that was
yours alone.

In a magazine devoted to mountaineering: "For the motherland, through the
mountain." The mountain doesn't cure you of idiocy.

March 22

A railroad worker from Dijon confirms that four high school students were executed in Dijon. And he adds: "As the noncommissioned officer ordered to command the firing squad refused, he was immediately shot." Is this true? Is it a
legend? Doesn't this NCO personify the pity of the people?[9]

In 1831, a Lyon manufacturer named Olivier said he would welcome the Canuts
with pistol fire.[10] Another: "If the workers don't have bread in their bellies, we'll
fill them with bayonets." And in fact the bosses, who formed the first legion,
fired on a peaceful demonstration. Eight dead. The marshal-type bosses' style is
more veiled. They're all about love, they're more socialist than Lenin. In reality,
for a certain type of bourgeois, the worker appears as a necessary serf who tends
to turn into someone who upsets civilization. I am stupefied by the anger I provoke in N—— when I quote him a sentence pronounced by Jean Perrin at the
inauguration of the bust of Curie:[11] "The day will come when one will no longer

[7] The Germans were melting statues down for their metal, in short supply as the war went on. Vichy
was cooperating. Poligny is a nearby village; Jean-Pierre Travot, one of Napoleon's generals, was born there.

[8] Marie François Xavier Bichat was an eighteenth-century physiologist. A Paris hospital bears
his name.

[9] Four students in the teacher training school, Communists, were shot as an example on March 7:
René Laforge, René Romenteau, Jean-Jacques Schnellnenberger, and Pierre Vieillard, as well
as a young cabinetmaker, Robert Creux. The German NCO did not refuse to command the firing
squad.—J.-P. A.

[10] The Canuts were the silk workers in Lyon. Their revolts in 1831, 1834, and 1848 were the first
working-class uprisings in Europe.

[11] Jean Perrin won the Nobel Prize for physics in 1926, as did Pierre and Marie Curie in 1903 for
their pioneering work on radioactivity. Werth is probably referring to Pierre, or else he would have
said "Madame."

dare call degrading tasks 'work'—tasks to which two-thirds of humanity is condemned." "That's the way you weaken a people," he tells me. And he starts talking
about the forty-hour work week and Blum, the causes of the defeat.

March 27

Germany, Russia, England, America, Japan. The trial in Riom. To get enough to
eat, you must be a farmer, or rich. Vichy bustles about with words and decrees.
The peasants have to bring all their wheat to the mill. They have to supply six
eggs per month per hen. Passengers transporting five, ten, or twenty kilos of
bacon into the cities are arrested in the railway stations.

I'm waiting for Suzanne and Claude. I push the time forward.

German firing squads are at work in Paris, Lyon, Besançon.

Why this memory of a dinner in "good society" in Paris, a bit before the debacle? A dinner of philistines. They exchange dead opinions. The way pigeons fly
around when their brain has been removed. They would make me hate Bonnard
and Debussy. Why should I attach so much importance to comments about art?
The fact is, they're Pharisees. They're really saying: "Look how subtle, delicate,
knowledgeable we are. If anyone interferes with us, he's destroying civilization."

Suzanne has come.

She gave up going through Chalon and tried it by way of Tours. One of our
friends had sent her to people who were supposed to get her through in a small
boat. But they were away, on vacation somewhere. For ten days, she roamed
from village to village. No path possible. Germans everywhere.

The buses were full of wretched people the police were arresting at the last
stops. They got off encumbered by children, suitcases, and bundles.

In the evening, she finds a bed in a boarding house. The boarders and a few
wanderers are gathered in the kitchen. They get English radio. An argument
begins between a young man and a vague man, an inspector for the gas company.
The vague man has an outburst: "During the other war, I was an officer . . . I killed
more than one of them, I used to shoot them between the eyes. I'm ready to
begin again. If I had a rifle . . ." The young man doesn't answer. The vague man
continues: "You insulted the marshal. I'm going to go the prefecture, denounce
all of you, and get you arrested." He leaves. They don't know if he's going to the
prefecture. But there's a panic. A few boarders, the maid, and the Parisians who
were hoping to get through the Line come out of the kitchen and scatter into
the streets. Suzanne and a young schoolteacher from Avranches pushing a baby
in a carriage decide to join forces. They find a place to sleep in a "reception center." A room with fifty empty beds, while at the station, refugees pile up—men,
women, and children. They say the lady from the Red Cross who's the head of

the center organizes passages with a nurse—if you pay up. The truth, or a vile calumny?

The next day, Suzanne tries to get through the Line alone, at night. She hears steps, and a shout: "Halt!" She lies down in a thicket. German soldiers flash their lights around. They walk by. She remains prostrate. For a few minutes or half an hour. She doesn't know.

She goes from village to village, on foot, by bus, by train. She finds the schoolteacher and her baby again. They're driven from the farms: "We don't want to go to jail for you."

A farm: an old woman and two peasants are digging their spoons into the same bowl. The room is sordid, badly lit. "You're not really going to let us sleep out in the open . . ." "We'll give you a bale of straw." A bale of straw is thrown into the middle of the cowshed between the hindquarters of the cows. The animals pull at their chains. Sounds of chains and the plopping of cow dung.

The next day they leave. On the train, a priest who knew Félix le Dantec[12] tells Suzanne that personal memory is abolished in eternal life and *Mein Kampf* was not written by Hitler but by a Benedictine monk. This priest was probably mad.

At night, they get to Liguiel. No rooms. They ring at the door of a convent. The portress opens the door: "This isn't a hotel." Suzanne forces open the door. "We'll sleep in the garden, but we're not going to stay out in the street." "You won't sleep in the garden." A sister comes over and argues with them. "What about Christ and Saint Vincent de Paul?" says Suzanne, invoking Christian charity with violence, if one may say so. Beds are prepared for them. The next day the sister shows Suzanne the pyrography done by the pupils. The tops of boxes decorated with doves gently pecking at each other and Bretons in big hats. "Bretons are nice on box tops . . .".

No more smugglers. Some were arrested or shot. The others are afraid.

Meeting in a church with an old lady smuggler. She has nothing to suggest for the moment. Maybe it's better that way. She's accused of delivering her customers to the Germans.

Fifteen miles in a peasant's cart. "I'll take you to the Line. But nothing more." A farm. The farm lady shouts, "Go away . . . If you gave me fifty thousand francs it wouldn't change my mind. Get out of here . . . The patrol's going to go by." "When?" "In five minutes, maybe . . ." "Tell us where the Line is." The farmer's wife holds out her arm: "There's the Line. Between two guard posts." Five hundred yards of fields, bushes and a little station at the end. The station is in the Unoccupied Zone. Suzanne pushes the baby carriage with one hand and drags along the schoolteacher with the other.

---

[12] A distinguished biologist and philosopher of science.

They get to the track at the station. The stationmaster raises his arms to heaven: a few days earlier, the Germans had fired and killed someone.

In the waiting room, the young schoolteacher (I haven't said she was a Gaullist yet) sees a big picture of Pétain. Exhausted, freed, and happy, she raises her arms to the picture and shouts. "Marshal, here we are . . ."[13]

April 1

Riom trial. The trial has become the trial of Pétain.[14]

At the beginning of the war, quite by chance, I met one of the generals who's a witness for the prosecution. He asserted at the time that we were ready as could be and the Maginot Line was impregnable. True, he was only a colonel at that point, and he has risen in rank quickly since then—after the debacle.

April 2

The force and precision of thought of some members of the military. The causes of the debacle, according to General Langlois: "The League of Nations poisoned the public's mind."

April 3

Met the sergeant of the gendarmerie, the "sergeant major." Not like a gendarme at all. Half schoolteacher and half soldier. Speaks bluntly. Hardly lowers his voice when someone walks near us. Against the Germans, against Vichy. Speaks with holy wrath of that suspect Parisian couple who lives not far from the town. (They cross the Line of Demarcation freely and entertain German officers in Paris.)

He doesn't like the Communists. He was in Paris when the workers occupied the factories.[15] "I talked with the workers . . . I do my job, but I try to understand . . . The workers weren't demanding a salary increase. When I asked them what was driving them, they answered 'I don't know.'" I would like to be able to explain to him that there are times when crowds obey other motives than the motives of the belly and pure reason.

---

[13] "Maréchal, nous voilà" (Marshal, here we are), written in 1941, unofficially replaced the Marseillaise, which was banned in the Occupied Zone, as the national anthem.

[14] In Riom, Léon Blum and Édouard Daladier did more than defend themselves; taking advantage of the relative liberality of the court and using evidence to support their case, they put the military high command on trial—particularly Philippe Pétain, the true head of the French army during the whole period between the two wars.—J.-P. A.

[15] Massive sit-down strikes played a role in the general push for social justice in the mid-1930s when the Popular Front governed France.

He tells me that during the debacle, a French officer stopped at the house of the schoolteacher in Nanc. On a map the teacher had kept in his house, this officer, giving in to some impulsion to boast, drew the course of the future Demarcation Line—an exact, prophetic line. Impossible not to see in this the proof of premeditated, organized treason.

In the concentration camps, the young prisoners (Spaniards, Jews),[16] in good health when they were arrested, are in such a state of physiological degeneration after a few weeks that they no longer have the strength to pick up their straw mattresses and let their excrement escape onto them, under their bodies.

From a medical student in Paris. Consultations at Hôtel-Dieu[17] are being given by the head of Dr. Fiessinger's clinic. (I don't remember his name.) About fifteen students look on.

A very old woman, bent, wrinkled, scarred, complains of stomach pains. On her admission slip, the doctor sees she's from central Europe and she's Jewish. The old lady is stretched out on a bed. She relates her illness as well as she can. From time to time she sits up, as if she wanted to talk nearer to the doctor, to be understood better and make the words of her jargon reach him better. Each time, the doctor pushes her down and lays her out on the mattress. You'd think it was a sinister, grotesque sketch. The doctor turns away from the patient and, addressing the students as if the sick woman did not exist, launches into a long monologue about the ignominy and omnipotence of the Jews. Two students approve. The others are full of shame and disgust, but of that shame and disgust, they give no visible sign.

April 10

Trees blooming in the countryside. But the sky is gloomy and the light is poor. Like women in ballroom dresses on the sidewalk at dawn when there's not a taxi to be found.

"America," the trucker–café owner said, "announced on the radio it would declare war against France if France kept on delivering most of its wheat and wine to Germany."

I must confess something in me believed him at that moment. The trucker's testimony was an organic whole, one flesh; it had in it the image of a far-off and all-powerful America that felt the same anger he did: "If you keep supplying the Germans, I'll give you a punch in the nose . . ." All that was fleshy, fiery, and indivisible.

---

[16] Spanish refugees from the civil war were detained in French camps before the war. Many were later deported to German camps as "Red Spaniards."

[17] The oldest hospital in Paris, with a tradition of treating the poorest patients.

A railroad worker tells me the Germans shot ten hostages in Dijon yesterday and the day before.

In a narrow street, children are playing at shooting arrows (their bow is made of a piece of string and a curved branch.) They're aiming at an image of the Legion pasted on an old gate. The ripped picture is coming off in shreds. But they have no ulterior motive. They're not aiming at the marshal but at an abstract target. They're obeying old images of war and adventure. And one of them, the youngest, says to us: "We're good *arches*."

The Riom trial. "Meanwhile everything was dying little by little, or rather before our very eyes: the Kingdom entirely exhausted, the troops disheartened from always being badly led and consequently always unhappy; the treasury without resources; no (resource) in the capacity of the generals or ministers; no choice made except through taste or intrigue; nothing punished, nothing examined or weighed; equally powerless to sustain war and to reach peace; all in silence, in suffering. Anyone might dare raise his hand against that tottering arch, ready to fall" (Saint-Simon,* *Memoirs*).

April 12

It was November of last year when I first heard, from Gilbert, the discourse of collaboration. Gilbert didn't give me his opinion; he wasn't "joining" but analyzing a state of mind, that of some Frenchmen who believed German victory was a fact and it was impossible for England to win—and thus thought wisdom consisted in contacting the Germans and giving up a patriotism that had become as empty as metaphysical pacifism. Gilbert glided above all this and created a historical hypothesis, without adopting it as his own. His logical dream picked up fragments of facts and mountains of mistakes as it went along. "The German is empty," he was saying. "Who knows if we won't fill that vacuum? Who knows if servitude won't free up higher virtues, more delicate powers? As he is driven out of politics, perhaps man will find himself again in poetry." I hardly dared allude to the concentration camps and the executions. I felt a kind of shame in bringing up something so obvious it seemed vulgar.

It seemed to me Gilbert was merely seeking a solution through the absurd, if needed, simply feeling out possibilities, and he didn't know that his dream was fed by propaganda. The psychoanalytic hypothesis would apply pretty well. Gilbert had repressed the concentration camps, Einstein's exile, the suppression of Heinrich Heine.[18] But the dream censorship let one memory through: three years before the war, a bookseller in Berlin had told him that never had so many poets been published in Germany.

---

[18] The works of the great nineteenth-century German poet Heinrich Heine were banned in Nazi Germany because he was Jewish.

The cherry trees are squeezing out full tubes of their white.

A prisoner who returned to France said he saw Russian prisoners looking for earthworms in order to eat them.

On the path, old Mother Paré, who always has an angry look on her face, is bringing back her cows. She asks me for news of Suzanne and Claude. Through the thousand voices of the virgin forest, she already knows they're in Paris. "Sure," she says, "*them*, they got work and you don't."

April 15

Met the local schoolteacher. He's going to dig in his garden. He sees no light at the end of the tunnel. He's afraid. He only listens to English radio from time to time, so afraid is he of being denounced.

"The situation is ripe . . . ," says the shoemaker. And this rumor going around everywhere: "We're going to be called up . . . The Germans asked for 100,000 men." Others say a hundred and twenty thousand, others a hundred and thirty thousand. "They'll refuse to go along with it . . ." "The Germans will surround them with troops or make them work behind the front lines."

I used to imagine Pétain, within the limit of his intellectual means, obsessed by the highest problems. It was only my theatrical imagination. He spends hours on end comparing his postage stamp with a kepi and his stamp without a kepi.

April 19

The town has been silent for three days now. Nobody tells me a big piece of news a neighbor heard on English radio or Swiss radio.

Three railroad workers inside the café bar at the station. They're not even drinking; they're refugees, taking shelter. Bent over, with their heads leaning down and their eyes looking at the floor, hands hanging between their thighs. What is weighing on them so heavily? Sunday? Their momentary idleness? Fatigue? Insufficient food and no wine? The feeling of defeat? One of them begins to speak—to prophesy, rather. He utters incomprehensible words about North Africa and "throwing them the hell out."

April 20

"Lebrun," a farmer tells me, "looked like a good guy, but not guy who could be in command." [19]

---

[19] Albert Lebrun, the last president of the republic, was in fact utterly unable to cope with the military-political crisis of May-June 1940.—J.-P. A.

"Laval's* going to get bumped off," Old François says.

"The Germans are there, and he must be well guarded." "That doesn't matter," Old François answers; "there are still Frenchmen around." He means that being Laval's assassin is a complement to being French.

She looks like old ladies in the theater: her whole body leans on a stick. The atmosphere of her room is heavy, heavy with a moldy past. It goes without saying that she doesn't read the paper. News comes to her through other old ladies. She is old and whiny. But here are her words: "We learned yesterday Laval passed away . . . That made us very sad. They drove out the marshal who meant the world to us."

Laval on the radio this evening. I go listen to him at the farm. First the news: "The Wehrmacht is preparing a tremendous offensive. Germany will have its hands on all the oil in Russia." My knowledge of economic geography is so weak I can't judge this piece of propaganda. But I refuse to let Germany take possession of this oil in some vague Caucasus, some vague Urals. My heart knows that this oil will not belong to Germany.

Laval spoke. The timbre of his voice is brassy, but the metal softens over certain consonants. It's imperceptible, it's as if the consonants were growing too hard for him. A sign of fatigue or the sign of a flabby soul. Girls sometimes drop their consonants like that. The voice is, like his face—exactly like his face—greasy and tight, vulgar and hooked, like his nose.

I remember a few months ago I met an important civil servant in Lyon who was courageously Gaullist. To define the scorn he had for Laval, he compared him to Julien Sorel.[20] To Julien Sorel, that character out of a Corneille tragedy![21] We're living in terribly uncultured times when an enemy of Laval can have a brain as greasy as Laval's. But I think this important person hadn't read *The Red and the Black*; for him, Julien was ambition personified and he just wanted to decorate the conversation.

For years now, I've been meeting Old Messal on the road, a former hired hand, half farmer, who tends his garden with the meticulous care of a bureaucrat or a collector. He cultivates a bit of vine, some corn, potatoes, and some lovely dahlias. This old man doesn't like to talk. He is quiet and melancholy. You'd think he's dragging some old sorrow along the roads. But today he is loquacious. An ill-humored prophet, senile and not without pride, he doesn't talk to me of current

[20] The likeable young hero on the make of Stendhal's masterpiece *The Red and the Black*, who is beheaded at the end.

[21] Corneille and Racine are the classic French tragic playwrights of the seventeenth century; Corneille's heroes are known for their dramatic moral dilemmas.

events—which he probably doesn't even know—he doesn't talk about Laval, but judges the world definitively and fixedly.

"Soon we won't have anything to eat. We'll have a revolution. Hunger drives the wolf from the woods. It had to happen. Me, I never trusted the government" (he's talking about the 1939 government).

"They declared war. They're the ones who declared war. We didn't have a thing. They didn't give a damn. What they wanted was money. The debacle—that didn't surprise me at all. I predicted it. At the beginning of the month of May, the bailiff said to me: 'They're not here yet.' I told him 'If they're not here in May, they'll be here in June.' Some got scared and they left. Not me. The Germans stayed three days. They did less damage than our soldiers. The French looted everything they could. We carried away lots of empty bottles near the fairgrounds. The Germans had discipline, they had good manners. If an officer called them, you should see how they snapped to attention. I know what that's like. I did four years of military service." He straightens up, stands to attention—a residue of standing to attention—and salutes before starting up again: "Yes . . . they had good manners . . . I didn't see a single one pissing against the walls. They pissed against the hedges."

April 21

During the last few weeks, the lethargic town was waiting for the Messiah, whether from Russia, England, or America. It seemed to it that time had stopped in order to give the Messiah time to come. But Laval was thrown across its road to the Messiah.

April 26

They used to ask me: "What do you think of the situation?" They don't ask anymore. Because, through I don't know which of their senses, they know something about the situation. They know it's no longer in balance and it's going to tip. "Soon," the station master tells me in the café bar at the station, "the Germans will leave our country, the way I saw them leave in 1918, ripping the epaulettes off their officers. Soon, I'm telling you. They're ripe for it. Soon, we will be delivered. That's when the traitors—our traitors—will have to pay."

The words come to him like the words of a prayer. He speaks, like blindfolded seers and like prophets. But a few days ago, the prophecies were somber. The groaning prophets have turned into wrathful prophets.

April 27

Speech by the Führer. "The global Judeo-Bolshevik plague." Churchill is a drunkard.

The shoemaker and his wife and children with their heads lowered in the position of the peasants in Millet's "Angelus," listening to the radio.

"In Foissia," Riffault tells me, "the peasants wouldn't like the Russians to win. They're afraid of the Russians. They heard if the Russians came, they'd be 'mechanized' and lose their lands . . . Me, I told them if the regime was so bad, they wouldn't be defending themselves so well against the Germans."

My passions haven't stripped me of all honesty. I point out that his argument is more logical than correct. For it would also be applicable to the Germans.

It's not just some of the peasants who're afraid of the Russians. In Bourg, I met an old courtesan from 1900. She doesn't dye her hair anymore, it's white, and she has the distinguished look of American women in the great luxury hotels of yesteryear. She would like the Russians and the Germans to "squash each other." She doesn't like Hitler, but she "likes him more than Stalin." She fears the barbarian hordes. As for Pétain, she knows him, she saw him at work. "I was at Verdun during the other war." I show my astonishment: I didn't know she'd defended Verdun. "Yes, I was with the chiefs of staff, I had a boyfriend on the chiefs of staff." I walk away. It was high time. I was going to tell her I was well aware they had added whorehouses for the troops to certain formations, but I had no idea they'd created luxury bordellos for commissioned officers.

I spent the afternoon in Coligny with Madame M—— and her cousin. In a milieu of the very Catholic bourgeoisie, they are both Gaullists. We spoke of the escape of General Giraud. We imagined him going to join de Gaulle and modestly taking up his rank at de Gaulle's side.[22]

In came Madame M——'s son, on furlough from a youth camp. Contrasts and divisions in families, like during the Dreyfus affair: this young man, fresh and empty, speaks harshly of de Gaulle, who did not obey the orders of his superiors. "Youth had lost all discipline before the war . . . The debacle was caused by the occupation of factories, the strikes, the combined action of the Communists and the schoolteachers." He "hates Germans," looks down on the military successes of the Russians, and counts England's defeats with a strange jubilation. I ask him if all his friends have the same feelings he does. "Many do," he answers, "but not all. A few of them are Gaullists."

---

[22] General Henri Giraud,* who had the reputation of being one of the most capable higher officers in the French army, managed to escape, spectacularly, from the fortress of Königstein in Saxony on April 17 and reach Lyon. Despite Hitler's rage, he refused to go back to Germany. We know he did anything but put himself modestly at General de Gaulle's disposition.—J.-P. A.

There is a thread that links the Foissia peasant fearful of the Russians, the old courtesan, and this young man doped up on arguments. There is also a thread that links all those who love—provisionally—everyone who strikes back at Germany. Will it end in a civil war, or not?

May 6

Politics, for the peasants, is a man's thing, not a woman's. Yesterday evening, Laurent knew the English had landed in Madagascar. But today, at 6:00 p.m., his wife didn't know this. He hadn't told her about it. But Jeanne Riffault, who's only sixteen, perks up her ears when people talk about the war. And she knows more than what is said in front of her.[23] The news comes to her through the air while she's looking after the cows. Joan of Arc.

May 7

A shopkeeper in the town. She's young, plump, has a nice body, appetizing. She gently bemoans the miseries of the times: "I can't stand the bread they give us anymore. It makes me sick. We have almost no meat. Butter, you can't find it anymore . . . It just has to end soon."

She attributes the cause of her misfortunes to "the blockade," a mysterious divinity that has the name of blockade. For her, the miseries of war and the Occupation are merely the bad quality of the bread and being deprived of meat and butter. If these misfortunes are righted—no matter how—for her, the world would be righted.

Barely a month after enlistment, the "youth camps" had thirteen days of furlough. This unexpected furlough worried people. They said "they're going to send them to Germany."[24]

Father and son are digging on a sloping vineyard, their bodies bent forward over the hinge of the waist. Is it good, is it bad, that men should work like that?

May 9

The paper. On the occasion of Joan of Arc's Day, a call to us from the head of the Legion. "Frenchmen will find the timeless traditions of their national life in the story of Joan of Arc."

---

[23] Women only got the right to vote in France after the war, partly, it is thought, because of their courageous role in the Resistance. Jeanne Riffault is Riffault's daughter.

[24] Germany badly needed workers, as all its men were in the armed forces; Vichy tried to get volunteers to work in Germany. Since it was unable to get enough to satisfy the Germans, the government would eventually decree a compulsory work service for every male over the age of eighteen (February 1943), drafting them for work in Germany. This would swell the ranks of the maquis—the guerrilla groups in the countryside—and the Resistance generally.

May 10

"Before the war," Laurent tells me, "The tax collector used to sing the Communist Internationale in cafés. Now he's a member of the Legion and never misses a mass."

Are the traitors and the polemicists for treason supremely cynical and above vulgar morality? They're not so philosophical as that. They're moving slowly toward an end they did not foresee. One fine day they'll be astonished to bump their noses on it.

All they grasp of reality is whatever they need to act, for the time being. Thus, someone who's half blind will go from the Madeleine to the Bastille faster than a walker whose eyes are fine but dawdles in front of the shop-windows. I remember a dinner the editor in chief of a magazine threw for his staff before the other war. At dessert, the conversations were all among little groups and discreet. But Henri Béraud[25] went on talking in a booming voice without realizing nobody was listening to him except the waiters. One can see how that thickness, that distraction, that perseverance in oneself create a kind of somnambulistic state, and how it can lead to the most absurd theories and even to treason.

Febvre* was told ten thousand workers had gathered in front of the statue of the republic in Lyon and shouted: "Long live the republic! Long live de Gaulle! Down with Laval . . ." False news, perhaps—but perhaps a premonitory symptom. If there weren't ten thousand workers in front of the statue of the republic, somewhere there was someone who wanted there to be ten thousand workers and who would have liked to shout along with them.

May 11

Three columns in the paper on the celebration of Joan of Arc's Day. The marshal speaks. Abel Bonnard* speaks.[26] Why do I force myself to make this report of nothingness? Because in this nothingness there is something monstrous and something comical, because in this nothingness there is still man—the vileness and stupidity of man. Yes, that has a meaning, everything has a meaning.

May 12

The paper: "Yesterday, in over thirty cities of the Free Zone, there were demonstrations of protest in which tens of thousands of people railed against the English aggression against Madagascar."

---

[25] Henri Béraud was a successful novelist and journalist. During the war, his vitriolic attacks on England and the Free French led to his being sentenced to death when France was freed (the sentence was later commuted).

[26] Abel Bonnard was minister of education under Vichy. He was sentenced to death in absentia for collaboration with the enemy in 1945 and died in Franco's Spain.

That same day, Laurent, as he changed his horse's bedding—Laurent, who knows every peasant and every farm for miles around and excels in prudent investigations where he expresses his views as little as he can and gathers other people's views as much as he can, Laurent says: "In town, I dunno; but the farmers—I can tell you 95 percent are against the government. They realized being against England is being for the Boches. You're for the Boches if you're for the ones who're fighting along with them."

May 16

With a nod of his head, Riffault leads me into his cellar storeroom. I walk out of it with a piece of the meat from a pig, confidentially killed—a piece of the liver and heart. His wife wraps the whole thing in a towel. To go back home I don't take the road but paths through the woods, where I won't meet anyone. I press the package against my hip, held in place by my buttoned-up jacket. But the blood seeps through the towel, and when I get to the house, there's a wide bloodstain on my thigh. I'm surprised and worried, like a murderer who left an unforeseen trace of his crime.

Idiots: "We mustn't forget we were beaten . . ." "They can say what they like, but I still think the marshal . . ."

May 22

Communications with Paris have become difficult. The conductor of the train who used to get my letters in Dijon no longer crosses the Demarcation Line. Suzanne's letters used to reach me in two or three days. Now it takes at least a week. When I get a letter, it already smells of the past, it's cold, it's a faded sign of the past. That week-long interval is a black hole, and some misfortune may have slipped into it, a closed space I can't explore, and I can only fill it with my worry.

The town makes me sick, and so—almost—does the countryside. It's no more than a series of patterns for me. I have a forced familiarity with it, as you have with a traveler on a train or someone at your table in a guest house.

I ate pig's liver; I "cashed in" on a packet of tobacco. These events have dominated my life these past days. I've come to the point of trying to attenuate the images in me of Suzanne, Claude, and my sister. If I let them have their full force, they increase my feeling of privation, of solitude. I slow myself down.

There is reading. My solitude has brought me to volume 25 of Saint-Simon's memoirs.

"Thirty-four thousand French Family Medals were to be distributed on May 31 for Mother's Day. But in this exceptional case, since the necessary material for their production is lacking, the medals will be replaced by ribbons."

Today, no public celebration of some day or other can take place that isn't the celebration of the marshal and Vichy too. Honoring the mothers of France means, in a certain sense, also honoring Laval and Darlan.*

May 23

I'm told that Madame de F——had a hundred cords of wood delivered to her for the winter: that's fifty thousand francs' worth of wood. A doctor, the bailiff, fifty cords. I'm prepared to be indignant. But what would *I* do to make sure I wouldn't be cold if I had fifty thousand francs at my disposal?

In the background: the battle of Kharkov. Against this background, declarations by Abel Bonnard: "What we need is the education of views, of life and general functions, which respond to the new regime of the new conception of man." Should one accuse the typographer or advise him to get treated for malaria?

They say a German officer has been killed in Paris. Ten hostages executed by firing squad.

On the mantelpiece of an upstairs bedroom in Riffault's house, at eye level, there are two framed religious engravings, a plaster Virgin and two grotesque little human figures, prizes in a lottery at the fair. I've seen similar domestic altars in all the farms around here. I'm used to that Roman welcome of diverse divinities. In Indochina, I saw Saint Josephs and Saint Anthonys next to Buddhas. But here I'm stupefied: a portrait of the marshal is there among the familiar gods. I'm astonished because Riffault has only spoken scornfully of the men of Vichy and "the old man." I conclude that the legend of the marshal is very strong. But Riffault intercepts my gaze and bursts out laughing. "It's my kid who put that there . . . They gave it to him in school."

The kid (around twelve) brings me the portrait. On the back, there's a reproduction of the marshal's handwritten message. It's the note of thanks he sent in 1940 to the schoolchildren who, ordered by the administration, had sent him a drawing as a spontaneous testimony of their veneration:

My child,

I liked your drawing. You made it with a care that shows you have a taste for this kind of work. Congratulations. Keep up the good work.

Ph. PÉTAIN.

I read it aloud. And while I read, the father, the mother, the kid, and his little sister laugh without stopping, laughing in four voices, and they don't stop laughing when I've finished reading.

I ask Riffault if he thinks this propaganda, the vast advertising campaign, and that postal play-acting are effective. The child answers himself: "We know we all got the same letter." And Riffault adds: "They don't believe any of it because of what they heard us say."

June 1

The paper. "The battle of Kharkov is over." But the style of the German communiqué does not have a triumphant tone.[27]

"In Lyon, 773 moms were celebrated and rewarded. But the most touching part of this solemn ceremony was the reading of the best letters the schoolchildren wrote their mothers. The letters that were most appreciated were the ones that seemed most spontaneous." Indeed, they deserve credit for being spontaneous. We're entering a civilization in which there is no sense of decency. We teach children to invent tender letters to their mother on order—administrative order.

New RAF raid on the Paris region (in big type). British air raid on Cologne (in very small type).

A grocery store in Paris on the rue de Seine looted. Two policemen killed. "The identity of the arrested individuals conclusively shows the Bolshevik source of this affair." Bolshevik . . . They recognized Stalin's fingerprints.

"This Sunday is not only Mother's Day, it is also a great day for the Legion."[28] In the café at the station, people talk about it, but without passion. "A bus came to get them to take them to Lons. S—— (he's the grocer-sergeant) was bawling like a calf to get them into ranks . . ."

A man in blue work clothes, sagging, half-asleep, declares: "Me, I don't care about that; I care about trying to put something on my table."

June 2

Behind the bar at the station, a sad little space between barriers. Railroad employees are drinking saccharine lemonade or lukewarm beer. Two gendarmes order a sweet wine. Nobody speaks. The silence is heavy.

The railroad employees and the two gendarmes have left, leaving behind them a hopeless world. Then an engineer and his buddy come in and sit down at one of the tables. I was on a desert island. Two men appeared—real men. Before the war, the engineer drove long fast trains; now he does "easy jobs," sometimes freight trains, sometimes passengers, sometimes the "crawlers," the slowest

[27] In actual fact the Soviet attempt to retake Kharkov in May 1942 was a disaster: Stalin's overestimation of his raw, poorly trained troops and his underestimation of German forces led to terrible losses for the Red Army compared to those of the Wehrmacht.

[28] On May 31, Mother's Day [in France], activists in the underground French Communist Party attacked a grocery on the rue de Buci in Paris. The police intervened, and the protection group of the FTP [a large, left-wing resistance organization] fired.—J.-P. A.

freights. "The Germans are very low," he says; "I saw some in Dijon, kids of eighteen, who were crying as they left for the Russian front . . . We're the ones who equip them, we supply them with materiel, automobiles, and rifles." He gives the number of tons of coal that go to Italy, the tons of wheat that go to Spain, the tons of oranges that go from Spain to Germany.

"Pétain," he says, "Is the worst of all—after Laval."

June 3

The paper. While the engineer was talking like that in the bar, the minister of agriculture was speaking in Lyon to "the rural people of the Rhône": "Pierre Laval, son of the soil of the Auvergne, is fighting for us, faithful and silent like that soil, passionately attached to his land, a patriot in every fiber of his being . . ."

A last touch in this synchronic tableau: "In Paris, Monsieur Albert Clément, the editor in chief of the *Cri du Peuple*, was assassinated. It seems to be a terrorist attack by the Communists." The "it seems to be" is a pretty touch, in its elevated, restrained, critical impartiality.[29]

June 5

Jeanne T——has come from Paris to spend a few days with her parents, who are farmers. Her husband is a policeman, and they live in the 18th arrondissement. I expect a tableau of Montmartre under the Occupation, a revelation through the people. But I only get this: "In the lines in front of the shops, some people are for the English, other people for the Germans."

I never imagined those two pans of the scale, loaded with equal weight, the supporters of Germany and the others in equal number, looking at each other face to face until one vote creates a majority. But I'm a fool. I should have asked Jeanne T——a question that called for a global, historical answer. Or she imagined I was expecting a response like hers. So we have no common language. She's afraid of tattling, being a gossip, and she clumsily takes refuge in the serene regions of improvised statistics.

June 6

What remains of the rumors and news of the last few days is the bombing of Cologne. "Twenty thousand dead, fifty thousand wounded," Laurent tells me, "and they're on the roads, like us during the debacle."[30]

[29] On June 2, 1942, a commando of the underground Communist Party's "Special Organization" killed a former union activist, Albert Clément, on rue Vivienne in Paris. Until 1939, he was editor in chief of *La Vie Ouvrière* (Working-class life) and became the editor of Doriot's* fascist paper *Le Cri du Peuple* (The cry of the people).—J.-P. A.

[30] On May 30, 1,043 bombers dropped 1,500 tons of bombs on Cologne. The raid was more impressive than bloody.—J.-P. A.

The old Parisian lady who's taken refuge in the town wants Hitler to go away, but she doesn't want Stalin to come in.

June 10

Alsatian Jews, refugees. They're not bourgeois yet. Craftsmen or shopkeepers. They hardly have the southern type. Except for two, with tight profiles, hooked noses. They're in the same category as those sellers of old metal and rabbit hides, the kind I saw in the army, the kind you see in the town and even in some villages, who are perfectly Christian. In what way are they different? This way: their vulgarity doesn't tend to be the hearty cordiality of the salesman, but something sharp. People don't like the way they insistently prospect the farmhouses. But I see Christians who could give them back some points on that.

> *Those two Jewish second-hand goods dealers:*   Spinoza.[31]
> *Corsican sergeants:*   Napoleon.
> *Auvergnat café owners:*   Pascal.*
> *Marseillais chatterboxes:*   Cézanne.
> *Stubborn Bretons:*   Renan.

It's only a game. Anyone can play it. You can call it the game of the abstract and the concrete, the individual and the group, a game of tag for general ideas.

The paper. "Jews residing in the Occupied Zone are obliged from now on, by an edict of the Occupation authorities, to wear a six-pointed yellow star sewn on the left-hand side of the chest bearing, in black letters, the inscription: *Jew*."[32]

---

[31] Werth's list—his "game"—parodies Vichy's ethnic and "racial" stereotyping, using French geographical clichés: the seventeenth-century Jewish philosopher Spinoza came from a merchant family; Napoleon from Corsica, which has provided many sergeants in the Paris police; the philosopher, mathematician, and physicist Pascal was born in the Auvergne, the former region of many café owners in Paris; Cézanne was born near Marseilles, whose inhabitants are supposed to be voluble; and the nineteenth-century philosopher and historian Ernest Renan was from Brittany, whose natives are supposed to be stubborn and alcoholic.

[32] The eighth German edict "concerning measures against the Jews" appeared on May 29; it ordered Jews to wear the yellow star in the Northern Zone: "Jews over six years old are forbidden to appear in public without wearing the yellow star. The Jewish star is a six-pointed star as big as the palm of a hand, and black contours. It is in yellow cloth and bears the inscription JEW [*JUIF*] in black letters. It must be worn very visibly on the left side of the chest, solidly sewn onto the piece of clothing."—J.-P. A. The collaborationist Paris press insistently tried to persuade Parisians that this was a necessary measure—a sign most Parisians were deeply shocked. Admiral Darlan had actually expressed his shock at measures like this when they were in the planning stage, as Werth reports in the next entry.—D. B.

The bell that lepers carried was merely sanitary, not humiliating. No one claimed they were imposing an official humiliation on lepers.

Whether out of modesty or pride, I've always found all insignias intolerable or silly. I always felt ill at ease when they put a flower in my buttonhole, or a wild rose or the Legion of Honor.

The plain of Bresse is whitish, panoramic. The meadows are hardly green, like a sheet of liquid into which a few drops of absinthe have fallen.

June 11

Germany's done for: that's the unanimous opinion. By universal consent, Germany has become the conquered conqueror. The bearers of news transmit only omens of German defeat. We're quite ready to transfer our debacle of two years ago onto Germany. That certainty worries me sometimes. I fear émigré hysteria. Just after Mussolini's march on Rome in 1922, the Italian émigrés affirmed that Mussolini would only last a few weeks. Just after Hitler's elections, I heard German émigrés declare that based on the economy and especially the state of heavy industry, Hitler would be gone in a few months.

June 12

Vichy posters on the walls of the town: "France stabbed in the back by English bombing and Communist murders."

Every week, there's a meeting of the Legion in town. I know nothing of these meetings. The peasants don't go to them. Nothing gets back to me. I know nothing of that world of country squires, shopkeepers, and retired sergeants.

A three-column spread on the first page of the paper announces that the marshal and Prime Minister Laval "have affirmed their complete identity of views." The marshal and Laval hug each other. The time of the marshal of popular legend is already far away, when he was supposed to be fooling both Germany and Laval, defending France and its people against Germany and Vichy. "Upon his arrival, Monsieur Laval expressed his confidence in me. We shook hands and now we march hand in hand." A fine propaganda image: the marshal and Laval marching hand in hand.

If I didn't read the paper, I wouldn't have known that the marshal had adopted this new march. In town, they're talking only of Russia, England, and America.

The following document has reached me through channels I will not name:

CABINET OF THE VICE-PRIME MINISTER
No. 387 S.G.
Vichy, January 21, 1942
RE: Measures against the Jews

Reference: Note no. 678 of December 15, 1941, from the Commander in Chief of Military Forces in France

1. By the note cited in reference, the Commander in Chief of Military Forces in France is asking for the implementation, against the Jews in the Occupied Zone, of measures such as: obligation to wear a distinctive sign, being banned from public places with the exception of a few buildings particularly reserved for them, and the application of a special curfew.

2. I must respectfully inform you that I do not agree with these proposals.

I think the various rigorous measures taken against Israelites to date are sufficient to attain the desired goal, that is, to remove them from public functions and command posts of the industrial and commercial activity of the country.

There can be no question of going beyond this without profoundly shocking French public opinion, which would merely see harassment in these measures, without real efficacy as much for the future of the country as for the security of the occupying forces. The very excess of these decisions would certainly work against the desired goal and might well provoke a movement in favor of the Israelites, considered as martyrs.

Signed: F. DARLAN.

As he's doing badly on the Russian front, Hitler can no longer shape the world's fate and his own as he pleases. He has only one recourse: the old panacea, anti-Semitism. Thus, Maurras* in the tiny field of his literary politics: when he was blamed for the abstract, theological nature of his doctrine, he answered that it had an element of feeling and passion, fit to galvanize the masses—anti-Semitism.

With Hitler, anti-Semitism is a frenzy. Vichy's anti-Semitism is one of the points through which Vichy marches side by side with Hitler and makes contact with Germany. But Vichy knows that the reasoning Frenchman doesn't believe the destruction of the Jews will solve everything. At the same time, Vichy wants to give Hitler proof of its goodwill, but doesn't dare give its anti-Semitism the full Hitler touch. Vichy tries to measure out its anti-Semitism. But as they're hanging on to Hitler and see their salvation in him, they will simulate Hitler's anti-Semitic frenzy, and other frenzies, very well indeed.

The paper: "Admiral Darlan inspected the seventh military district. Continuing his detailed inspection of every unit of the new army . . ." Such is Vichy's communiqué. But, transmitted by the voice of the people, this piece of news takes on another face. "Darlan," Old Mireau told me, "visited the barracks in Lons-le-Saunier accompanied by German officers." The popular imagination can't conceive of Darlan going anywhere without being accompanied by German officers.

June 13

Jean Le Dantec was shot on Monday at 3:00 p.m. in the cemetery of Ivry.[33] His parents had been expecting his execution any day. The cemetery. Those last steps, between the graves. The soldiers pushing him along. The burst of fire. Alone in the house, I weep from pity, shame, and rage.

An administrative circular read aloud in the classrooms of Paris lycées: any student convicted of ripping off or tearing up a portrait of the marshal will be expelled and excluded from all the lycées of France.

A poster on a barn door. It invites French workers, men and women, to go work in Germany, "in full dignity and under the protection of the French government." A text signed by the marshal approves this invitation, a noble text, written by one of his official philosophers. The working men and women of France will thus be preparing "the vast perspectives of a reconciled continent."

That old man, who bowed before Hitler's "generosity" and sends hostages to Germany while the Germans execute young Frenchmen in Paris—that old man, a recruiter of French labor for Germany.

In the solitude of the village, the poster seems the only living thing. The walls, the roofs, everything has a gray patina. Only the poster pasted on the wall today is fresh. In blue letters, in red letters, shining brilliantly, pushing and shoving, it winks at us. It shows the extension of power into the smallest hamlets. I can see French workers leaving for Germany, joyfully waving their handkerchiefs from the doors of a train.

The paper. Headline across eight columns, right across the page. The marshal's trip to Narbonne, Carcassonne, Castelnaudary, Toulouse. Banquet at the Hotel Albert I in honor of the journalists who are going to leave soon to do a story on German centers where Frenchmen are working. Next to Prime Minister Laval, the consul general of Germany, Monsieur Krug von Nidda, and Professor Ritter, the representative of Gauleiter Sauckel . . .[34]

The mayor warns me I was denounced to the Sûreté for spreading Communist propaganda, particularly in the hamlet of Allonal. What's more, "You were seen with a professor at the Sorbonne named Lucien Febvre, who is also a Communist."[35]

---

[33] Born in 1903, he was the head of a resistance network in Paris that transmitted information to England.

[34] Fritz Sauckel was the head recruiter of labor in territories occupied by Nazi Germany. He was hanged at Nuremberg for crimes against humanity: the use of forced and slave labor, often under atrocious conditions. Gauleiter: head of a regional branch of the Nazi Party.

[35] The Sûreté Nationale is the French equivalent of the FBI. Neither Febvre nor Werth was a Communist.

Febvre is not a professor at the Sorbonne but in the Collège de France.[36] This confusion between the Sorbonne and the Collège de France does not come from a peasant. The peasants never heard of either of them. I couldn't have been denounced by a peasant. So a suspicion comes to me, unverifiable and perhaps unfounded.

They asked the mayor for information about my subversive activity. He answered that I couldn't be suspected of spreading propaganda for the simple reason that I lived in total isolation.

June 17

Two years ago, the marshal's government was being born. We were on the road. Paris was on the road. Half of France was on the road. Neither Paris nor France knew anything. The government was born from a vote of some bunch of deputies or other, born of fear—fear of the Germans and fear of "disorder." A few scraps of radio came to our ears from week to week. We imagined an interim government, an interim marshal, a state of siege, but provisional. We didn't imagine a marshal becoming symbol, sociologist, and legislator. We didn't know they'd slap a copy of the German and Italian regimes on France.

The Legion, empty of all Nazi frenzy and full of old military fools and honest idiots, does not satisfy the Germans. They informed Vichy of the fact. That's why Pétain-Laval are creating a kind of SS.[37] A section has been created in the town. Its head is a food-supply inspector, a former non-com from the Colonial Army (with the face of a thug). I don't know the others. This group is armed. In case of political unrest, either they'll fire or they'll be killed before they can move.

June 18

Variations of politics and propaganda.

A few weeks ago, trains full of food (vegetables, eggs, butter) were leaving Louhans for Paris. When they got to Dijon, they were directed to Germany. Today they no longer take these precautions or try to spare our feelings. They no longer hide the fact that the trains from Louhans are going to Germany.

Between the end of June and the first days of July '40, I found an issue of *Paris-Soir* in the Gâtinais.[38] In it, we read that if Parisians weren't getting their

---

[36] The Collège de France is an institution that invites highly distinguished intellectuals and scholars to give lecture courses to the general public.

[37] In reality, what is emerging from this creation is the Service d'Ordre Légionnaire (the SOL), which grouped together militants from the Légion des Combattants who were formerly active in the ranks of the far right. Contrary to what Werth states here, the SOL was created without any pressure from the occupying authorities.—J.-P. A.

[38] *Paris-Soir*, a daily with a large prewar circulation, was published in Paris during the Occupation and became pro-Nazi and anti-Semitic. (Another edition, published in the Free Zone, enjoyed slightly more freedom for a while.) *Le Petit Parisien* was another such paper.

usual ration of meat—for a few days only—they were receiving potatoes from Germany in abundance. So Parisians were not deprived of their national frites. The article was a lyrical oration about French fries. It gave off the smell of frites. Germany, leaning maternally over France, was sending her tons of pre-prepared frites.

June 21

During the lunch break at the farm between two cartloads of hay, they were saying that Granger—one of the four men I was with in the café yesterday, one of the four who don't want to give in to the Germans—informs on the inhabitants of the town and denounces people who listen to English radio. It's absurd, it's false. But what a sewer!

June 22

The town is more nervous than an isolated farm. This morning, the little shepherd's mother who came over to help bring in the hay told us, seriously and sadly: "The Germans took Tobruk, and Prime Minister Laval's going to speak this evening . . . We have to keep our hopes up anyway." She puts the capture of Tobruk and Laval's speech on the same level. The announcement of an unexpected speech by Laval, she feels, is as big a threat as a military victory by Germany. We're afraid that tonight Laval will announce something definitive and irreparable.

I decided to go hear Laval in the farmhouse this evening. I go to Laval with patience and disgust, as one goes to a place of ill repute. Laval speaks. He tries not to have a bombastic tone, not to vibrate, and to be simple. But his Rs are greasy. He holds in his vulgarity as you might hold in your belly. And that restraint, that decision to speak soberly and plainly, makes him "darken" his voice, like an old actor of melodrama.

His speech is clear. One theme: go work in Germany. Two arguments: that way, you'll prepare the pacified Europe of tomorrow, and Hitler will send thousands of prisoners back to France. Laval is proposing a sublime swap to the workers; Hitler's generosity will determine the conditions. He's trying to blackmail the workers with the liberation of the prisoners. The arguments are repeated insistently, like a speech for the defense in court. You can't deny the speech is clear—too clear to have the desired effect. For he's violating the feelings of a whole people.

Collaboration, the new order—they were only abstract terms, political vocabulary. But Laval intervenes in person, in flesh and blood. He says: "I want Germany to win the war, because otherwise tomorrow Bolshevism would move in everywhere." The argument, the "because"—even for those who are terrified of the Bolshevik specter—is too weak here to compensate for the "I want." That "I want Germany to win" dissolves any argument and gives us a shock. We don't hear anymore, we retain nothing else. We knew Laval wanted Germany to win. We did not think it possible that he would say it so baldly and publicly. Laval is lost,

Pierre Laval in 1935, when he was the right-wing anti-German prime minister—six years before he became the most hated man in France. *Bibliothèque nationale de France, Meurisse, 9684 B bis*

because of that cynical honesty. Even by most of his supporters, he is rejected, as a man would be rejected if, at the moment a woman is ready to give herself to him, he said, "And now we're going to make love."

"I want Germany to win." We had never heard that before. For the abstract anti-patriot of the past used to put himself above nations; he was neutral, he wanted nothing.

Laval's speech is too gross for the ordinary finesse of the French people.[39]

June 23

Laurent and Riffault are haying. Neither one of them has heard or read Laval's speech. Neither knows Tobruk has been taken.[40] Perhaps they heard the news. But it didn't penetrate.

---

[39] The offending sentence, in full, is: "I want Germany to win, because without German victory, Bolshevism would move in everywhere." The speech marked, in Laval's own way, the first anniversary of Hitler's invasion of the Soviet Union and announced what would be called "Prisoner Relief" (*la Relève*): French workers were to volunteer to work in German factories or farms in exchange for the release of some French POWs. When the government later established the Compulsory Work Service (in Germany), it kept Prisoner Relief as an excuse.

[40] The capture of this Libyan port on the Mediterranean led General Erwin Rommel to think he would go on to take the Suez Canal and cut off a lifeline for Great Britain.

In town, Laval's speech has the effect of a revelation. "I want Germany to win" gives out a stronger sound than the abstract expression of a policy, even a treasonous one. No one's talking of the capture of Tobruk and the battle of Sebastopol.[41] The town now takes Germany's coming defeat for an established fact. Germany has only held on to a few supporters: the dregs of the Legion and a few shopkeepers.

July 3

"People in Saint-Amour," says Andrée François, "are losing patience. They're waiting for an English or an American landing . . . They're losing patience . . ."

A young woman waiting in the station café and who'll try to cross the Line tells me that in Dijon many people support Germany.

Young Laurent is on a nine-day furlough from a youth camp. He lost twenty pounds. I ask him: "What do you talk about with your friends there?" "Nothing." "You don't talk about the war?" "Never."

The paper: "The military tribunal of the Fourteenth Region sentenced three French women and two men to death. They were involved in the same treasonous affair."

Those three Frenchwomen and those two Frenchmen, sentenced to death by a French tribunal, for having betrayed Hitler and Laval!

July 10

I don't know if there are as many volunteers to work in Germany as the Vichy papers say. But even if there were only a hundred, or ten . . . Are they leaving because they're forced to by hunger? Are they leaving out of flabby obedience? Are there some among them who're premeditating skillful, knowledgeable sabotage?

What would Lenin say—he of the union of proletariats over and above national borders—if he saw French workers going to Germany to make tanks against Russia?

Vichy is orchestrating the workers' departure with an idyllic feeling of pastoral and gastronomy. Vichy is proposing, to the sentimentality of the crowd, "blond German nurses."

"Standing or sitting on their suitcases, the volunteers chat. Their faces are grave. Indeed, all of them have taken the measure of the value of the act they are performing."

---

[41] After almost ten months of fighting, Sebastopol would fall to the Nazis on June 30; more than fifteen thousand Soviet troops were dead, and more than ninety thousand were prisoners. German losses were far smaller. The city itself was reduced to rubble.

"Frenchmen! Go work in Germany. German workers are inviting you." German workers were serving in the Wehrmacht, so Germany pressured Vichy for French volunteers to work in German factories. When it could not get enough of them, the government established the Compulsory Work Service. *Les Archives de la Vendée,* *(Fi) 1 W 52-7*

I generously shed Russian, German, English, American, and Japanese blood. The world is fighting by proxy for my civilization, for the civilization we all define so badly. And sometimes I wonder if, from this arithmetic of tanks, I'm waiting for something more than butter and tobacco.

July 13

Legionnaire days in Lyon. Speech of the "leader," Darnand.*[42] "I painfully felt the surprise of the German people before the reluctance of our people, who don't seem to realize the generous nature of Germany's gesture. . . . Then I saw Poland, with its population crushed in a defeat that its conqueror did not want to be a light one, for it did not have, for this people, the feeling it has for the people of France."

The marshal had already paid homage to Hitler's generosity. The firing squads in Nantes and Paris didn't bother him. They didn't bother the Segonzacs, Vlamincks, Derains, Friesz, Despiau, and other artists who took the trip to Berlin. This same day I learn that Fernand Braudel, a prisoner in Germany, is asking people to send him bread. And we don't know how to make sure the bread we send reaches him. A few weeks ago, these artists were breaking bread with Hitler.

In Dijon, the Germans sent a young man of seventeen to the firing squad and sentenced his brother to three years of military prison.

Three weeks ago, they executed three lycée students. (In the home of the presumed author of a bomb attack, they had discovered his chemistry textbooks. They concluded that these books contained the secrets of making explosives and the three youngsters were accomplices in the attack).

Madame Marie doesn't separate these killings in time. She gathers them together; she makes one whole killing out of them. The first time she told me of the lycée students who were shot, it was in a sorrowful tone. Today, she speaks in a tone of calm anger, so to speak—cold anger. Perhaps in their lethargy, the people are building up their anger.

July 17

Riffault has killed a calf. He told me to come over after nightfall, when the children were already in bed. "Kids can't hold their tongue." We go down into his cellar. He works at trimming the veal. If we had committed a crime, there would be the same scene. I carry out my portion in a bag. For a few days, I won't have that small sensation of permanent hunger.

---

[42] Joseph Darnand was the founder of the SOL. He inspected some 4,500 members of the SOL in Lyon on July 12. They swore allegiance, and he expounded the reasons for frank, active German-French collaboration. In 1943, the SOL would become the Milice Française—the Militia, a fascist paramilitary organization supporting Vichy.

The French fleet off Alexandria. Nobody's fooled by the "firm attitude of Vichy." Vichy barks at the enemies of Germany but can only bite France.[43]

July 18

Rumors. Old Cordet, who's a retired railroad worker, and the shoemaker have received letters their relatives sent them from Lyon. Thousands of people in Lyon demonstrated on July 14.[44] They shouted "Long live de Gaulle, long live the republic!" The cavalry (?) charged the crowd. In Marseilles, a huge demonstration. They say there were three dead: the Legion fired on the crowd.[45]

Febvre was in Lyon during the debacle in 1940. With anger and shame, he described an old woman who was singing the praises of the Germans—so polite— and a barber, and shopkeepers, praising their courtesy and how promptly they pay up. And I remember that pretty girl strolling along with German soldiers on July 13, 1940, with a flower in her mouth. And I saw small-town bourgeois open every pore in their bodies to the German. I saw France traumatized, hypnotized by the conqueror, bewitched by the boot.

Vichy preaches collaboration and Prisoner Relief, the Gestapo puts up posters warning Parisians that not only will anyone convicted of attacking the person of a soldier in the occupying army in any way be imprisoned or deported or shot, but so will his children, parents, grandparents, uncles, and aunts and cousins. A kind of original sin.

Febvre's son Henri, who arrived from Paris this morning (he crossed the Line inside a dog kennel in a freight car), tells me the repression there has gone beyond severity; it is now atrocious.

"A good sign," his father says, "the reactions of a cornered beast."

The progression, in two years, from the "nice" German to the German killer.

---

[43] The "X Force," under Admiral Godfroy, had been immobilized in the harbor of Alexandria since July 19, 1940. Because of the advance of the Germans' Afrika Korps, the United States wanted it to anchor in a safer port—a proposal that Laval rejected loud and clear.—J.-P. A.

[44] July 14 is what we call Bastille Day.

[45] There were in fact many demonstrations on that July 14, 1942, in Marseilles. It was the shock troops of the Sabiani PPF [the Marseilles branch of a far-right political party], sheltered in their party's offices, who fired on the demonstrators. Two women were killed, and several other demonstrators seriously wounded.—J.-P. A.

July 21

A letter from Marcel Martinet.[46] "Wherever you may be, I'm just about sure you haven't changed." These words worry me. I'm quite sure I haven't lived since September '39 without having changed. The war has transformed my experience of national feeling (at least I think it has), my revolutionary feeling, and even my religious feeling.

I understand that Martinet—who has tended toward a state of purity, of saintliness, all his life—isn't playing the monolith. After Lenin's death, he himself disavowed Bolshevik orthodoxy and answered those who accused him of having changed by saying they were the ones who'd changed and he had remained faithful to himself.

I ask myself once again what happened to the pure pacifists, the ones for whom pacifism was an essential source. Gliding over the massacres, do they make wishes for none of the warring parties? Do they respond to what is happening only with disgust and despair?

"Peace, nothing but peace," they say. They make me think of a doctor at the bedside of a patient who refuses to examine him or make a diagnosis or prognosis, but repeats tirelessly: "Health, nothing but health."

July 24

Claude says in the newsreels shown in Paris theaters they saw several actresses—Danielle Darrieux, Viviane Romance, and others too—chatting amiably with German movie stars in Berlin. In 1870, even the prostitutes had more sense of decency (see Maupassant).[47]

The papers in the Unoccupied Zone talk of Resistance attacks but never say a word about repression. Every piece of news that might show the occupiers as cruel or even harshly repressive is banned.

The townspeople are inert. They're waiting for the first American to parachute down in front of the obelisk.

---

[46] Marcel Martinet, a former Communist, was a revolutionary socialist writer and a pacifist. He was a close friend of Léon Werth.

[47] On the occasion of the Berlin premiere of Henri Decoin's film *Premier rendez-vous*, Danielle Darrieux (not without some hesitation), Junie Astor, Viviane Romance, Albert Préjean, and Suzy Delair went to the Reich and to Austria, where they were received royally.—J.-P. A.

In "Boule de Suif" (Ball of fat), a well-known short story by Maupassant, a girl who works in a bordello refuses to service German soldiers occupying France after the Franco-Prussian War.

Even though I know "general and particular orders," I am struck by these head-lines: "Hand-to-hand combats in the outskirts of Rostov." "German vanguards are now sixty kilometers from Stalingrad."[48]

July 25

"The paper," they say, "doesn't give you any information about anything." Yes it does: about Vichy.

July 28

I was expecting Suzanne at the beginning of August. We must find a new way of crossing the Line. "This morning," a conductor tells me, "the Germans searched everything."

A senior in philosophy in the Bourg lycée was interrogated by the police.[49] Last year, this kind of interrogation was handled in a friendly way. The police were courteous. Today, they proceed brutally and make threats.

July 30

Andrée François reports from town that thirty-five escaped prisoners were arrested in a freight car in the Dijon station and the conductor was shot. That's "Prisoner Relief."

The town is not particularly moved by this news. The town is weary. It turns away from the war and thinks of its vegetable gardens. "I didn't listen to the radio," Old François himself tells me, "And I didn't talk about anything with anybody."

His daughter, who looks on with terrible wisdom, the wisdom of a woman of the people, a wisdom that no comforting abstraction can penetrate, says again: "People have lost patience."

If the myth of an Allied landing doesn't come true or if some unexpected, great event doesn't occur, it will be like a second debacle for the people of the town—but a debacle in their sleep.

I learn from an engineer who slept over in Lons that a bomb was thrown into the office of the SOL last night. There were no victims, just material damage. The engineer and Madame Marie neither approve nor disapprove of the action. It's one more event, one of those events that come one after the other in these times, until the day when "it'll be over." Another event seems to touch them

---

[48] Less than forty miles away.

[49] Students in their last year of secondary school in France must take philosophy. For some, it is their main subject.

more: a wine merchant in Beaufort tried to sell wine to Madame Marie at fifty francs a liter.

The rarity of attacks against what is close to treason surprises me. Especially when compared to the relative abundance of attacks—whatever their origin may be—on the occupiers.

July 31

I think the attack in Lons was merely a nice little attack: the bomb only grazed a bit of woodwork and spoiled some piles of paper. But it's a warning, and some people in town are cheered by it. "It's a start," said Old François.

The paper. Vichy, the creator of myths and symbols: in the home country and in our overseas possessions, the chairman of the Legion in each community will gather a little bag of earth. All these bags will be "centralized" into an urn in each administrative region. "A magnificent ceremony will be celebrated on the plateau of Gergovie, where Vercingetorix achieved the unification of the Gallic tribes."[50]

August 1

I bike down a path lined with hedges. Suddenly a swarm of butterflies surrounds me and follows me. I don't know anything more like a fairy tale.

The paper. "*The Day in Vichy*. The death penalty for people owning explosives or stocks of weapons."

In Paris, at the beginning of the Occupation, Febvre tells me, the Booksellers' Bulletin published an incredibly ignoble note. They announced that before any intervention by German authorities, they had worked at sensibly eliminating certain books from their shelves and hoped this would conform to the intentions of the German authorities.[51]

Young Clerc says the Germans wanted to ship off three hundred women who work in a Besançon cotton mill to Germany. They refused. Their food ration cards were canceled. Now they're living on public charity, he told me.

---

[50] Vercingetorix (ca. 82–46 BCE) led the Gauls—Celts whom the French have traditionally thought of as their ancestors—in a revolt against the Roman Empire. He was eventually defeated, taken to Rome, and executed. Gergovie was the site of a battle in 52 BCE between the Gauls and the Roman legions of Julius Caesar.

[51] This is an exaggeration. It was the German authorities who imposed the lists of banned authors and books: first the "Liste Bernhard" and then, in September 1940, the "Liste Otto" [in honor of Otto Abetz*]. The Occupation authorities cleverly presented the bans as the work of French publishers. It is true that the publishers accepted the fraud when they were asked, above all, to practice self-censorship.—J.-P. A.

Departures for Germany celebrated by the paper. "In Bourg," Riffault says, "there was a departure: four ex-convicts and three Arabs."

Mademoiselle R—— has arrived from Algeria. "The Arabs," she says, "wear worn-out burnooses that rip like spiderwebs. They're afraid they won't be able to wrap their dead in woolen winding sheets as Mohammed prescribes. Afraid of being dispossessed, the French colonists are counting on Hitler. Military tribunals throw people into solitary confinement and randomly pass Europeans and natives in front of a firing squad on vague charges of Gaullism, Communism, or 'attempt to rebel against the mother country.'" Everything I saw twenty years ago in the French administration of Indochina applies to Algeria.

August 3

Vichy, using the highest strategical arguments, is teaching the French that an Allied landing is impossible. But if this impossible landing should succeed, it asks them to remain neutral and not create difficulties for the government and the Germans.

A few weeks after the debacle, someone or other was saying to me: "You'll see, you'll see the effect suppressing the right to vote has in the villages." That was merely imagining the logical consequences of one fact. Maybe the peasants wouldn't have tolerated being deprived of the right to vote alone. But they tolerate being deprived of all their rights—and all the French along with them.

I know Suzanne has left Paris; she'll try to cross the Line near Poligny, and she'll have to walk for miles. I'm living with her risk, with that risk I can't calculate exactly.

F——, an old drunk, asks me for a cigarette. I hold out my pouch, which has a little tobacco left over inside it. His fingers squeeze the bottom of the pouch. His fingers are strangling an animal at the bottom of the pouch. He pulls out enough to roll at least two normal cigarettes, of human dimension. Come on, he's not going to make himself a reserve! Squeezing, pressing, rolling, he manages to enclose the blunderbuss of tobacco in one cigarette paper.

August 6

The paper. The Legion is to "monitor the nominations of local political officials." A euphemism for ratting on people. Clearly translated, it means that nothing is to happen in the village without the "prior monitoring" of the retired sergeant and the pederast pastry cook. The way we live still contains a few particles of liberty, and our sense of the comic is not yet completely dead. The sergeant and the skull-faced invert still make people smile. But a few months of Nazism. . . and they'd be reigning over the village.

During the 1914–18 war, government propaganda invented hands cut off by the enemy. Today, the official lie takes the opposite form. It dissimulates or denies the most real atrocities. And the Pétain-Lavals are touched by Germany's benevolence.

August 9

An anonymous letter denouncing the words the mayor said on July 14 in front of the war memorial was sent to the prefecture. The same typing mistakes were found on it as on a bill from one of the village pharmacists. The pharmacist has no problem admitting his typewriter was used for the letter, but declares he has nothing to do with it. "I lent my typewriter," he says, "to V——, who runs the hardware store. I wash my hands of whatever someone might type with my machine." As for the hardware merchant, he readily admits he wrote and typed the letter. And they say he told the mayor, "We merely did our duty as Legionnaires."

August 11

P——, one of the shopkeepers in the town, doesn't hide his sympathy for totalitarian regimes. "France," he says, "Had become a country where no one respected anything anymore. A few years ago, I took a trip through the south of France and through Italy. Let me tell you, as insolent as the hotel staff was in Nice, they were obliging in Italy."

No news of Suzanne for a week. All I know is she tried to cross the Line. I wait, like a dog left alone in the house. A bicycle bell ringing on the path becomes a phone call. I imagine the worst. I see her in a cell, her little window, the truck taking her to prison camp, the transfer to Germany, even the firing squad. Then I make an effort to drive away the obsession. And that effort seems to me cowardly, a betrayal.
The voice of the village: "The Russians are retreating . . ."
The old watchmaker, for whom the world was never anything more than one more watch, this old watchmaker tells me: "If there's a shortage of everything, if we're victims of the black market, it's because the government doesn't have a strong grip on things."
No news of Suzanne. I'm worried sick. I go see R——, a specialist in clandestine crossings. I go to hear some reassuring words. And in fact he gives me a few good reasons not to worry. But waiting isn't intolerable for him as it is for me. That's all too natural. And he appeases me the way a minister appeases a supplicant, someone soliciting a favor. And indeed, I am a supplicant, a beggar. I'm begging for

appeasement. Let him build a world for me in which Suzanne isn't running any risk. I'm ready to accept the absurd, if the absurd is stated to me with authority. But all R——— does is weigh the chances. It's a fine scene in a comedy. I plead the worst in order for him to argue the most favorable. I persist, I insist, I come back to the worst, I demonstrate that only a miracle could have prevented the worst from happening. But he doesn't hear me anymore, he tells me his slightest problems, his radio's not working well, there's a pack of tobacco he hoped for and won't get.

August 12

The paper. A six-column spread: "The stirring arrival of the first train of repatriated prisoners in Compiegne. It passed a train of workers headed for Germany."[52] And everything is in this sentimental vein. So sentimental you could throw up.

It's almost as if the freed prisoners were weeping because they left Germany. But in those six columns of sermonizing text, there is no allusion to the number of repatriated prisoners. Laval is all heart; he doesn't give figures.

August 13

The paper. Marshal Pétain receives a group of schoolteachers. You've got to believe he writes his own speeches. "When I took power, I had a few ideas." (Who would have believed it?) "I expressed them in my messages. The future of the country lies in the association of good wills. Do what you must do and do it well. If everybody applied this formula, France would get back on its feet again all by itself." Senility? No, not just senility. That accent of pure imbecility can't be acquired: it's congenital.

August 17

The Vel' d'Hiv, the children penned in, torn away from their parents.[53] "For the parents," Laurent says, grooming his cows, "for the parents, you could die . . . Me, seems to me I could die . . . Me or anyone else."

---

[52] On August 11, Laval personally greeted the first train of prisoners repatriated in the name of "Prisoner Relief" (in principle, one prisoner exchanged for three workers leaving to work in Germany). The two trains passed each other in the Compiègne station. The first train held a little more than 1,000 repatriated prisoners; in all, some 90,000 prisoners would return in the name of "relief," and more than 750,000 French workers were to leave for the Reich.—J.-P. A.

[53] The news of the great roundup of Jews in Paris apparently reached the Southern Zone with some delay. On German orders, from July 16 to July 17, the French police arrested 12,884 foreign Jews, mostly women, among them 4,051 children, and bussed them to the Vel' d'Hiv (the Vélodrome d'Hiver, the winter velodrome). Parents and children were cooped up inside the stifling hot stadium for days, with no food and little water, before being deported. Not one child lived to return to France.

Suzanne is amazed at my impassibility. Indeed, you could die. And I try hard to dissimulate my feeling of pity, rage, and shame. It's all mixed up, and I feel guilty, as if I were one of the perpetrators myself. I probably have enough pride to think the depth of the gulf that separates a man of the Gestapo from me is infinite. But that depth can't be greater than the greatest possible difference between two men. This is frightening.

I'm also ashamed for the journalists of the German Paris press, who accept the screams and tears of those penned-in children.

I was also ashamed in Indochina (and I know colonial cruelty does not equal Hitlerian cruelty) when I witnessed the brutality of the Europeans and their desire to degrade and humiliate; I was ashamed of their senseless pride. There is a risk in compressing one's rage and pity to fit the crime into the framework of historical necessity: you can suffer as much by being deprived of butter or tobacco as by news of the children swarming and dying in the German trains and concentration camps.

August 18

In Germany, they're taking the names of Jews off the memorials to the First World War. It's an important symptom. Hitlerism is powerful through its negation, even of what is obvious. Through the confusion of the sign and the thing. No Jews died in the war if we decide there weren't any. There is no difference between the lie and the truth. Or rather, there is neither true nor false. Thus, Maurras was a precursor in his little sphere when he invented fake patriotism.

August 19

For a few days now, the press has been talking about Churchill's trip to Moscow and the eventuality of a second front. It's making a naïve attempt to empty the Churchill-Stalin meeting of anything harmful it may contain. The press is sterilizing it, in a sense, transposing it into a space of gray abstractions and intangible truisms.

The marshal speaks to a group of college students in the Occupied Zone: "Do you know at what age I made the decision to go into the army? At the age of twelve! In the little provincial town I was living in at the time, I could see a young, handsome regiment of chasseurs going by my windows. I resolved to become a lieutenant in the chasseurs myself."

Vichy is leaving the marshal to himself. They're not giving him well-educated young men to compose his speeches anymore. And so the voice of a child forgotten by his maid rises for a moment above the noise of conversations. The grownups aren't listening.

August 21

English landing in Dieppe.[54] "A political operation, an operation of dilettantes."

August 22

Old François is stuffed with leaflets. He takes them out of his pockets, out of his overalls, out of holes in the wall. He makes me think of the magicians who make cigarettes, pigeons, and an aquarium pop out of nowhere and then catch them in space.

On the path between two hedges, I meet a woman holding a child in her arms. I don't know her. With no forewarning, she launches into a litany, a cantilena on German oppression and cruelty. She tells me of her hatred of "the people who're for the Germans." She turns her thought over and over, as if she were doing a pastiche of Péguy. "The Germans don't like us, since they execute us by firing squad. If they liked us, they wouldn't shoot us." Something has changed. Hatred for the German is coming out of the stones and ruts on the path.

An old singer back from Paris. She tells anyone who'll listen that food is plentiful and refined there and life is quite pleasant under German rule.

Without Hitler's anti-Semitic policies, wouldn't you be a pacifist or for collaboration?

How vile, to isolate the persecution of the Jews and separate it from the system that set it off! The Declaration of the Rights of Man said that if just one limb is hurt, it affects the whole social body.[55] Marx said that if one nation is oppressed, there is no socialism on earth.

The peasants at nightfall, motionless in the fields they've hoed. The hard folds of their clothing and the impression they give of listening to the Angelus (Millet's) make a group composition in the noble style, very restful, very museum.

The children penned inside the Vel' d'Hiv'. Herod merely massacred them. But Hitler adds to the horror. He multiplies sorrow by anguish. The parents who don't know if their children are living or dead. Those orphans, whose parents are alive.

What kind of faces do they have, the men who push those children to their destination? What will they tell their wives and friends about what they did in the month of July 1942?

---

[54] Some 6,000 Anglo-Canadians attacked Dieppe on August 19 to test the German defenses. There were heavy losses: 3,670 of them were put out of action in a few hours.—J.-P. A.

[55] The Declaration of the Rights of Man (1789), partly inspired by the American Declaration of Independence, is the founding document of French democracy.

August 27

For six months now, I've heard some French people saying: "I'd gladly kill thousands of Germans; I'd kill them with no remorse at all." But I know very few who would risk being dismissed from their job, even if it were a temporary dismissal made by this ephemeral government.

August 31

In town, all they're talking about is Stalingrad.

The paper presents its readers with a beneficent Germany where French workers go to spend a few months of paid vacation, a ferocious England whose aviators watch for passenger trains to bomb, and a regenerated France where Vercingetorix and the marshal embrace across the centuries.

September 2

Laurent isn't disconcerted by the games of international politics. He confines himself to strict economic materialism; he thinks about clauses in a peace treaty like a horse-trader. Perhaps he's right. He goes from dealing in horned animals to high politics with no transition. "I paid seventeen thousand for this pair of oxen," he tells me. "I'm keeping them, because in the spring the price might go up." He talks about the war the same way: "The Americans don't want the Germans to win, but they wouldn't like the Russians to win too soon. They'd like the Russians and Germans to be exhausted, both of 'em."

In the station café, Suzanne asks Monot, the engineer, if he can take her across the Line. "Of course, Madame, I'll reserve an orchestra seat for you." Henri Febvre, whom he will hide in his tender tonight, brings him a little a bag of salt (it seems salt is in short supply in the Occupied Zone). But the man, black with soot, refuses: "Presents . . . you should give them to the wives of the political prisoners." And he says: "I'll bring French people across the Line until we're rid of Prussian militarism and our own despots." But I'm betraying his words even as I repeat them: they were said simply, with a veiled meaning. He translates Nazism into Prussian militarism. And "despots" comes from an old language. The literary aesthete can smile if he wants to: with my eyes shut, I know that with men like this you can remake the world.

September 3

There was a Mass in Notre Dame in memory of the Legionnaires who fell on the Russian front. "Cardinal Suhard leads the authorities present in a procession."

People say the pope sent two cardinals to intervene with Laval about the Jews. He allegedly answered: "That's my policy."

If the Russians don't create a sufficient quantity of German corpses fast enough, France will be Nazified.

September 9

André Mandouze* teaches the postgraduate class at the Toulon lycée that prepares students for the entrance exam to the Naval Academy. In every class, there's spying and informing—organized by a teacher. In each of his classes, there was at least one student who denounced Gaullist suspects to him.

As a topic for their French essay, Mandouze gave his students a text by Lamartine in which he contrasts the patriotism that is a love of one's country with the patriotism of expansion and conquest. [56] Over half the students said they were for warlike patriotism, whose conquests are only limited by military strength. The bourgeoisie is particularly hypnotized by victorious Nazism.

The lady who runs the notions store (Gaullist): "They're not advancing, your Germans."

The lady who runs the pastry shop (in love with Hitler and confuses Germany with paradise): "You're not going to teach *those gentlemen* how to wage war . . ."

The notions dealer: "No . . . I'll teach them not to wage it."

September 14

The marshal visited Bourg. "He walked forward with a lively step," says the paper, "without using his cane."

I went through Bourg yesterday at five o'clock. The heat of the Bresse region, a heavy sun. The marshal is gone. In front of the station the carpets laid out for "the steps of the illustrious soldier" are rolled up. I'm told they insured those carpets for 2 million. Flags out all over town. A monumental cardboard *francisque*[57] raised as high as the second floor. Portraits of the marshal, photos of the marshal, as big as life, retouched with paint. Pedestrians strolling slowly along like any other Sunday. Groups of scouts, of "companions" from the youth camps. Little girls from the youth centers, specially created and put into this world to hold out bouquets to kings, presidents of the republic and marshals who are heads of state. Agents of the Secret Police, having carried out their orders for surveillance and enthusiasm, gather near the station as a group of phony idlers. But here's something that's very New Regime: a column of cops marching forward on Avenue Alsace-Lorraine singing "Marshal, here we are . . ." Eight to a column, in a compact square. They sing without ferocity. I see many closed mouths.

[56] Alphonse de Lamartine was a French Romantic poet.

[57] The double-headed ax used by the ancient Gauls, taken by Vichy as the official emblem of the French State.

A new spectacle. The riot squads didn't used to move in closed ranks and didn't sing. When they clubbed demonstrators, it was silently.

Msgr Gerlier, Msgr Piguet, the archbishop of Toulouse, and the archbishop of Montauban in the Unoccupied Zone, along with other prelates in the Occupied Zone, have protested the persecution of the Jews. The Jesuits in Privas were hiding two hundred Jews and refused to deliver them to Pétain's police. Priests have hidden children. I believe in their charity, and I think it is totally disinterested.[58] But the Church is adroit in reconciling opposites and combining refusal and consent. I read in the paper: "On the steps of the cathedral, the head of state was received by Msgr Maisonobe, the bishop of Belley. In front of the cathedral, the Legionnaires were responsible for maintaining order." Thus, the Church both protests the crime and offers its ceremonies to those whose policy is the crime itself.

September 23

I'm more or less over that illness of laziness, that automatism that kills time: reading. But I do leaf through the Bible and find in the Gospel of John: "Ye shall know the truth, and the truth shall make ye free." The worst of it is, people put up pretty well with not knowing it.

"I'm for Pétain and against Germany . . ." says L——, an important person in town. Once Germany is beaten, all the French will be Gaullists. You won't be able to tell one from the other.

It would take a civil war to tell them apart.

Were 116 hostages executed in Paris by firing squad?[59] It seems true that the Germans have arrested thousands of people. Claude left the day before yesterday. I can't help imagining him caught in a roundup, sent to the salt mines, and fed on juice from potato peels or turnips. I can't get rid of this obsession.

September 24

Forget the idiot who says, "If the Germans and Russians kill each other off, I couldn't care less." But even the people who are passionately waiting, the most

---

[58] Six bishops in the Southern Zone protested from the pulpit against anti-Semitic persecutions (there were camps in their diocese) and roundups in the Southern Zone. . . . In his pastoral letter of September 6, read from his pulpit in Lyon, Cardinal Gerlier declared: "Our hearts are moved at the thought of the treatment to which thousands of human beings are being subjected, and still more as we think of the treatment we can foresee"; he recalled "the inalienable rights of the human person, the sacred character of family ties, the inviolability of the right of asylum, and the imperious demands of that fraternal charity that Christ made the distinctive mark of his disciples." With Msgr Gerlier's approval, RF Chaillet, a Jesuit, was able to hide a hundred Jewish children from the prefect.—J.-P. A.

[59] They were indeed, on September 20.—J.-P. A.

attentive people, the most scrupulous, must judge events whose dimension is too vast for them when they say: England, Russia, the United States. They can't measure the part of easy abstraction and the part of reality. They fill up the unknown as best they can. But there is so much unknown that their thought is like precious objects packed too well, lost in a mass of wood fiber and chips.

September 25

A poster on the walls of the town. Men leaning out the door of a train car. Their faces are bathed in jovial bliss. They're leaving for Germany.

September 26

Two headlines on the first page of the paper: "Relentless house-to-house fighting in Stalingrad." And: "Maurice Chevalier thinks the music hall is going back to a heartier kind of show."

I think death is death, and if by any chance it weren't death, I have no means of knowing what it is. If I believed in the beyond, it would seem to me absolutely incommensurate with the here and now. And yet I look down on people who have no sense of the religious. I'm curious about believers. And I see that in these times a few Catholics have shown a courage that could be an example to many nonbelievers. Could there be no real men alive besides a few Communists and a few Christians?

September 29

The paper: "After the capture of Tananarive, a handful of men have kept on fighting in the Madagascan savannah.[60] Their action goes beyond the boundaries of the great island. Thanks to that action, the voice of France can be raised more proudly in the world." There must be a shortage of scribes. The action thanks to which the voice of France . . .

The voice of France is silent when it comes to Indochina.

But the poorest laborer understands the situation. If I go down to the town, nobody talks to me about Madagascar. They say: "The Russians are hanging on."

The postmaster has been dismissed. His name was on the list of Freemasons in the *Journal Officiel*.[61]

---

[60] The British landed in the French colony of Madagascar on May 5; the conquest of the island had just ended.—J.-P. A.

[61] The *Journal Officiel* has recorded government actions (particularly parliamentary decisions, before Pétain got the power to govern by decree) since the nineteenth century—in fact, since the eighteenth under a different name.—D. B.

Vichy's law of August 11, 1941, excluded dignitaries in the Masons from the civil service; each month more names were added to the list.—J.-P. A.

October 3

The paper. "All our information," says Brévié, the governor of Madagascar, "confirms the feelings of suppressed anger of the native population against the English occupation, imposed by force." Anyone who has lived even a few months in a French colony will savor that "suppressed anger." A few years ago, a governor whose name I forget was running Madagascar. He was one of the cruelest and most corrupt of those administrators who made "French" an object of scorn throughout the world.

October 4

The Russians are hanging on. Stalingrad. Stalingrad is the center of the war. The feeling we have about everywhere else is "It can wait": it's from the Russian front that we'll see the first signs of German collapse.

Dialogue between two farm women. Speaking of a refugee, one of them says: "He's a Jew." The other: "No, no, he's not Jewish." "Then why does he say he's rich?"

A civil servant from Vichy came to ask questions at the mayor's office. He was received by one of the mayor's adjuncts. "Are people discontented?" "If I told you we're content, you wouldn't believe me." "Do they listen to English radio?" "Some don't listen to it. The ones who don't have a radio set."

"He didn't look like a bad guy," the adjunct confided, "but he wasn't very bright." They had a chat. "He told me the government didn't favor harsh repressive measures, except for anti-national activities. I asked him what he meant by anti-national. 'Saying bad things about the government.'"

On the walls of the urinal at the station, in big capital letters, in chalk: "Pétain sold out." I wouldn't write the history of the war through graffiti. But this is the first time I can see a sign of insult, a sign of hatred for the old man with his phony idealized image.[62] The sign may come from the lower depths. But hatreds of all kinds, justified or not, are picked up by the lower depths.

Msgr Saliège, the archbishop of Toulouse, is protesting "the use that has been made in France and especially abroad of his recent pastoral letter about the Jewish question." He affirms once again "his perfect loyalty to the marshal and to the government of the country. The affirmation of a Christian principle has never implied the negation of another Christian principle."[63]

---

[62] Werth writes *image d'Épinal*: simplistic nineteenth-century prints of traditional French life.

[63] On August 23, 1942, the archbishop of Toulouse denounced the roundup of foreign Jews in unusually violent terms. This indignant protest caused quite a stir, even if the press did not breathe

Clearly translated, this ecclesiastic language means that protesting in the religious sphere against a crime for which the marshal is responsible does not imply that one rejects obedience to the marshal in the temporal sphere. What is blamed *sub specie aeternitatis* can be temporally legitimate. In other words, the Church or a few prelates approve, through the obedience they owe to Caesar-Pétain or Caesar-Laval, what they disapprove of in the name of Christ.

They say English radio announced yesterday that seventeen young men under nineteen had gone before the firing squad in Angers. True or false, the fact was transmitted to me with apparent indifference. We're ready for great massacres. In their unconscious, the masses accept them and, perhaps, are calling for them.

October 7

In the gloom of these vague days, a few points of light. M——, the engineer, confides that he tried to set fire to a train full of ammunition headed for Germany by slamming on the brakes again and again. The train refused to burn.

A few pieces of news from the radio are transmitted to me. The French colony in Ankara allegedly protested the pro-German declarations of Bergery, that hideous little politician, spindly scum with no resonance whatsoever. Three-hour strike at the Renault factory: the Germans threaten to execute fifty workers. We sense a bit of wind rising in paralyzed France.

October 8

A certain Chasseigne, "director of worker propaganda," is asking for 150,000 skilled workers to go to Germany.[64] This trip will only be a return to the trade guilds. "In other times, craftsmen in the guilds went on the journeyman's tour of France. That yearly trip of masons from Savoy or from the center or west of France to Paris was longer than today's trip to Berlin."

Old François has passed on a few leaflets to me: *Libération, Franc-Tireur, Combat, 93.*[65] It takes such courage and faith to print and distribute these clandestine publications! I would like to be one of the most obscure writers of this underground press. But who could I contact?

---

a word about it. Msgr Saliège then decided to publish a clarification in *La Semaine religieuse*, the religious bulletin of his diocese, on September 27. Werth has retained the main point.—J.-P. A.

[64] François Chasseigne had a trajectory that was even more extreme than Bergery's: from Communist activist to recruiter of labor for Germany in the Vichy government.

[65] Hundreds of underground newspapers and periodicals appeared in France during the Occupation. *Libération* (no connection to the present daily of that name), *Franc-Tireur*, and *Combat* eventually

October 11

The stages of propaganda. Two years ago, it was the human person, order, hierarchy, and the virtue of Joan of Arc. Then it was the policy of Montoire and collaboration,[66] a collaboration that was still vague and idyllic—reconciliation. Vichy presented us with an evangelic Hitler. Germany became our ex-enemy. England, our ex-ally, became our enemy. Then it was the fight against Bolshevism. Then "I want Germany to win." Then the touching policy of "Prisoner Relief."

October 14

Louot, the gendarme, tells me: "I trust you. Today, you can't say what you think to everybody. I'd like someone to write a book after the war to explain how we were sold out." He's afraid Vichy's police will purposely provoke unrest.

I don't have the patience to write down the contradictory accounts I'm given about the draft of workers. And not about the draft all over both zones, but even about the town and the neighboring communes. Impossible to learn anything precise. Soft stories. The people who tell them don't seem to need hard news. They elaborate their opinions, their acts, and their obedience or refusal against that vague background.

October 17

Last night at the farm they were saying there had been strikes in Lyon and the railroad lines were guarded by French gendarmes supervised by German soldiers: three thousand German soldiers in Lyon, and "they didn't dare intervene." They said workers had hidden out in the countryside and taken to the maquis.

In fact, there were strikes of some importance, since this morning's paper announces "attempts at strikes in the Lyon region" and "work has started normally again." So the workers manufactured planes and tanks for Germany without protesting, and these first protests of "working-class consciousness" are provoked by the threat of being expatriated. The protests are a revolt to maintain the sedentary nature of their work. What is intolerable is not to make arms for the enemy but to make them on his soil.

This purely logical judgment doesn't take account of the circumstances. You can't evaluate the force of machine guns by taking account of machine guns alone.

enjoyed a circulation in the hundreds of thousands. They were published by the three large resistance movements in the Southern Zone bearing their names—movements solidly implanted by late 1942 and working to influence public opinion. *93* (which suggests 1793 to a French ear) was put out by a group that would later affiliate with Franc-Tireur, the movement closest to the Communist Party.

[66] A smiling Pétain shook hands with Hitler during their meeting at Montoire on October 24, 1940.

Machine guns are threatening the workers who don't want to leave as much as they threatened the workers who, from Villeurbanne to Billancourt, agreed to work for Germany provided they were left in Villeurbanne and Billancourt.[67]

October 19

The paper. "The Occupation authorities express their opinion about the problem of Prisoner Relief . . ." " . . . French workers must leave for Germany to avoid serious problems." The text prudently avoids saying who'll have them. The tone of a worn-out little lawyer arguing before a bad-tempered judge.

Febvre reads the fragment of a letter to me. "In Paris, N—— was picked up by chance and executed by chance. He was twenty-seven. We had loved him since he was a child, and you know what a noble mind and heart he had."

François, who teaches history at Henri-IV,[68] was arrested in Paris. They fear for his life. I had met him a few months ago in Lyon at the Latarjets. A tall boy, utterly candid and open, who resisted Germany as naturally as he breathed.

I don't know if de Gaulle's supporters are growing or diminishing in number. The English radio never names him. Is he preparing military action in silence?

October 21

The resistance to "Prisoner Relief" is the first collective fact since the debacle. And even then, since workers' organizations are banned, it's a disorganized action.

"The stubborn determination with which Great Britain has multiplied its attacks on our country," a Vichy communiqué says, "is inexplicable." The tone is maudlin.

Laval speaks. He says nothing. His speech is merely a barely transposed version of the timid German note the papers transmitted yesterday. The usual themes of collaboration, but watered down. No doubt there is one: "The government will not tolerate . . ." But the threat is vague, with no emphasis, a clause of style. Laval's speech is the empty chatter of a minister speaking in the provinces who knows his ministry will disappear the next day.

---

[67] Villeurbanne is an industrial suburb of Lyon. Strikes broke out spontaneously in the Lyon region, particularly in the railroad workshops at Oullins, above all to protest the requisitions of workers to Germany. The prefect, Angéli, decided to repress them but had to compromise to reestablish calm. Werth's opinion of these strikes is severe indeed. We note that they were supported by four resistance movements (Combat, Libération, Franc-Tireur, and Front National) as well as by a political party (the French Communist Party), which was something new.—J.-P. A.

[68] Louis François headed a resistance group at the Lycée Henri-IV (secondary school) in Paris. He was arrested in September 1942 and deported. He survived to have a distinguished career as a teacher and editor of classical literature.

I exchange a look of jubilation with Febvre. I can see the end of Laval in the future. Laval in prison, the Germans in flight, Japanese ships sent to the bottom of the sea.

He wants to speak drily, without pomposity. No shouting. But he speaks in a preachy tone. And he pauses, as if to meditate between two points, as if he were waiting for inspiration. There is one passage of high comedy: "France is an extremely cultured country." In Laval's mouth, that extreme culture makes us laugh.

I'm not choosing the contrast: it was given to me by chance. De Gaulle speaks. De Gaulle's voice enters the room. Perhaps a "collaborationist" would have said this was an empty speech. And truly it was not a commentary on facts, on the daily progress of the war. It was an act of faith. That's what it was, and it didn't try to be anything else.

I try to find de Gaulle in his voice. It seems a bit tight to me at first. If I hated de Gaulle, I might say his voice wears a monocle. That only moves me more. Thus, in the time of the Dreyfus affair, it is said that Lieutenant-Colonel Picquart was merely a cavalry officer whose mind was occupied with cavalry and salons.[69] What could be more moving than those pangs of conscience in a soldier? But the voice opens up and becomes freer. De Gaulle promises us victory and insurrection for the homeland. It will win, "I promise you." The "I promise you" was said in such a way that Febvre and I had the feeling he was talking to him and to me. And now de Gaulle's words are coming together as in a prayer, an authoritarian prayer. They come to us in one breath.

I must ask myself a question. Weren't my feelings influenced by my opinion? If I believed in resurrection through Pétain-Laval and thought de Gaulle a traitor, wouldn't I have recognized the simple common sense of a peasant from Auvergne in Laval's voice and the infamy of a rebel soldier in de Gaulle's? I answer: no. I'm sure of my no. But I probably would have said it is vain to seek the truth in the music of voices.

October 23

Febvre's gone. A new period of solitude is beginning. The two of us were here, taking in the news together. I'm alone.

He left me his radio. I can fill the silence of my room as I will.

---

[69] A graduate of Saint-Cyr (the French military academy), a member of the chiefs of staff and a declared anti-Semite, Lieutenant-Colonel Picquart was first convinced of the guilt of Captain Alfred Dreyfus—who was Jewish—after his trial. Then he headed an investigation and reached the opposite conclusion, denouncing the forgery that had led to Dreyfus's conviction for treason in 1894. Émile Zola and other writers, politicians, and activists led a campaign for a new trial. The Dreyfus affair divided France. Dreyfus was fully exonerated only in 1906.

The paper. "The funeral of the victims of the English aggression on Creusot."[70]
Speech by Brinon*: "Every day the martyrology of French families grows longer."
    But the hostages shot by Germany are excluded from martyrology.

The government and the whole French people have no point in common
anymore.
    "They think we're dumber than we are," Laurent says. "They may be pretty
clever. Of course, they're cleverer than me. But basically, they're not intelligent."

October 24

An issue of *Radio-Nationale*. I see the names of fifteen or so writers who
speak on state radio. For a few of them, I'm surprised to find them there. But
they'll say "One has to live" and "They don't talk politics." I'm not surprised
to see Giono's name there.[71] His rural anarchism always seemed repugnantly
facile to me.
    Radio-National does not hide the fact that its sources and references are
German.

October 25

The radio. Bombs, shells, bullets, cannons, planes, machine guns: Stalingrad, the
Indian Ocean, the Pacific, Libya; English planes over Italy and Germany. Real
men, not men made of communiqués and news flashes, kill and die. I'm alone in
my room in front of the big radio. The war comes to me stripped down, cleaned
up. The wounded don't bleed. The corpses are statistical. I'm above the war like
an old, tired god.

I remember that poster pasted on a garage door in the village of Aubépin.
A few months ago. It told you French workers could find well-paid work in
Germany. There was no question of obligation or constraint. An employer was
hiring. So Hitler and Vichy were feeling out public opinion. All Vichy's acts
were prepared like that, preceded by soundings to which the inert country
did not react.

October 27

Twenty hostages will be shot in Lille if the authors of an underground attack are
not discovered.

---

[70] On October 17, a hundred four-engine Lancaster bombers destroyed the electric power plant
in Creusot, killing forty people and wounding eighty.—J.-P. A.
    [71] Jean Giono was a writer whose work was rooted in his native Provence. Several of his novels
have been turned into films.

Impossible to get English radio. The scrambling is furious and covers everything. For the space of a few seconds, I can barely hear a voice in limbo and make out these words: "Japanese cruisers sunk . . ." So the world the radio is revealing to me this morning is composed of a far-off sea in which Japanese sailors drown.

The invention of scrambling is fairly candid. Scrambling a broadcast is an admission that it's transmitting irrefutable truths or an assumption that the listeners are too stupid to resist its lies. Scrambling an English broadcast is an homage to England and an insult to the French listener.

One of the butchers in town passed me two pamphlets around thirty pages long: *Cahiers du Témoignage Chrétien.*[72] These underground pamphlets are remarkable in their clarity. They contrast Hitlerism and racism not only with the principles of Christianity but with the facts of history and ethnology. All this is courageous, because their conclusions are compelling and leave no room for cowardice or vagueness. There is an evangelical inspiration in these journals. Tolerance shakes off its dust and acquires shock value. "What essentially makes Christianity intolerable to Hitler is its respect for man, its 'imbecilic' theory—'of Jewish origin'—that proclaims the equality of men."

Hitler's hysterical fanaticism becomes clear in these journals. The texts they quote are astonishing, almost unbelievable.

English radio. Workers are resisting in Lyon. Hitler supposedly gave Laval until the end of the year. Laval, they say, negotiated with worker representatives appointed by them and not with the "civil servants" of Vichy's "union." All this has developed over the past two weeks. Is it reported in its correct dimensions? If so, it's a symptom rich in meaning.

October 29

In *Cahiers du Témoignage Chrétien*, this quotation from Jacques Maritain:[73] "The hatred of Jews and the hatred of Christians have the same root . . ."

---

[72] Six *Cahiers du Témoignage Chrétien* (Journal of Christian witness) had been published by October 1942: they were intended to be an instrument of spiritual resistance. The program is summed up in the title of the first *Cahier* (November 1941): "France, take care not to lose your soul."—J.-P. A.

Témoignage Chrétien was the first underground publication in occupied France to denounce anti-Semitism.

[73] Jacques Maritain was a Catholic philosopher, an eminent specialist in the thought of Saint Thomas Aquinas.—D. B. Werth quotes at length from his 1937 article "L'Impossible Antisémitisme," which was reprinted in the fourth *Cahier du TC*, called "Anti-Semites"; it came out in June 1942.—J.-P. A.

November 1

Radio scrambled again. I turn the dial at random:

> Too bad, too bad,
> We don't give a damn about the Mississippi,
> Here it's the nice fragrance of France,
> Here the smell of a springtime dance.

A voice from an old garrison honky-tonk.

The day of the raid on Genoa, an English bomber went down in flames near a village named Montcony, I think. The nine aviators of the crew were burned to cinders. They were buried in Louhans. Two or three thousand people attended the funeral.

"They came from everywhere, even from Bourg. The coffins were covered with flowers. Never have I seen so many flowers. We sang the Marseillaise. On the graves, they wrote: 'Died for the freedom of the world' and 'You are far from your country, but you are near us.'"

Thus spoke a young woman, a friend of Madame Marie's I sometimes run into at the station café. She was quiet for a moment and simply added: "I cried."

"There was some fighting," her husband said. "We kind of messed up a few SOL."

That crowd, that ardent crowd, exists. That young woman and her husband were there. They're not repeating a story someone told them. Good witnesses. If you ask them a question, they answer it. That's not so common. Many tellers of news or gossipmongers seem insulted or uncomfortable if you ask them a question, don't answer the question, and repeat their story all in one piece.

The students in the girls' junior high school learned the English anthem and sang it. Some of them were denounced by informers and expelled.

November 3

The paper. Criminal court in Louhans. Half a column of prison sentences and fines for "illegal buying and transporting butter and eggs, or clandestine slaughter of a pig and complicity."

"Terrorist Activities in Unoccupied Zone." "Bombs went off in Vichy in a social propaganda office." The touch at the end is surprisingly candid: "The results of examinations performed on the debris show that the explosive devices were of English origin."

"The day before yesterday, we heard the English on the radio," says Mademoiselle Phine, the news dealer, "what they were saying for All Saint's Day . . . We cried . . ."

November 5

English radio is "good." The battle of the desert. The Germans and Italians retreating. I found this sentence very fine: "The French in France feel the same nostalgia for their country as the French who are abroad."

Headlines: "Many leaving for Prisoner Relief."—"Resistance in Madagascar." Prisoner Relief: the town waits. Madagascar: it laughs out loud.

News of the German defeat in Africa has spread through the town almost as quickly as a false rumor. "At least five or six of 'em who have a radio," Old François told me, "came to tell me the Germans got a licking. We were glad." And he adds, smiling: "They took me to the café to have a glass of white."

November 8

I was vaguely listening to the radio through the scrambling. I wasn't expecting anything. And I hear: "Landing . . . North Africa . . ." I'm alone with the universe and the radio waves in the center of an invisible world of sound. I have a childish image of this landing. I see boats, planes, oranges, Arabs, and blue-eyed Americans. This sudden piece of news comes to me like inspiration to the prophets. No one was there and yet someone spoke. I feel like calling, shouting, communicating this news to people. I'm surely the only one who knows it.

The Americans began landing during the night. But at this very moment, a quarter past nine in the morning, they're still landing. The English news bulletin isn't talking in the past tense but in the present. They're landing at this very minute. It's not a cold piece of news, it's not a piece of news that has slept, even for one night, even for a few hours. The Americans are landing in Algeria, so to speak, right before my eyes.

Nothing has been so rich in hope since the debacle. "A historic turning point," a new phase. Already it seems to me that between the debacle and this landing, time has contracted. These last two and a half years have lost something of their weight and dimension. They're going to join the war of 1914–18 and the war of 1870.

When the radio announced the defeat of Rommel's troops,[74] Old François drank a glass of white. I think today he'll drink two.

Lunch in Coligny, at Madame M——'s. We commune in the landing. We lean over the radio set. We try to get every station.

---

[74] At the battle of El Alamein, west of Alexandria, between October 23 and November 4, Montgomery's forces pierced the Italian-German lines and forced Rommel to retreat.—J.-P. A.

As soon as it gets a little cold, the station café turns into a refuge. People who know take shelter there. There is a café masonry. The little iron stove is lit. In this space, which doesn't even measure three square yards, six men, four standing and two sitting on boxes of beer bottles, are squeezed in, coagulated: two gendarmes, an engineer and his stoker, and two strangers wearing overalls and smocks. Madame Marie emerges from this solid block of humanity.

Hardly have I squeezed inside than I feel it isn't what it was on previous days. It's not dead, it's alive. I hardly had time to open the door when Madame Marie asks: "What do you think of the news?" She never asks me "political" questions and especially not in front of other people—especially gendarmes. And it's not just out of prudence. She takes in events like music in the air of the times, like sad or threatening music. She takes it in as if it were blown in with the wind. But today Madame Marie is looking for someone who'll tell her the news; Madame Marie is looking for a nail to hang the news on. Africa and America have entered the little café. "What do you think of the news?" I have to answer in front of two strangers and the gendarmes. I have to answer prudently and wisely. "I think it's satisfying." My "satisfying" strikes home. If I had said "great" or "incredible" it would have had less effect. They all understood the discreet concentration of my "satisfying." And one of the gendarmes adds immediately: "I haven't seen people look so happy for a long time." "It's because of the Germans," the other gendarme says. "The government has to pretend they're resisting."

The engineer and the stoker didn't say anything. Perhaps their thoughts were not something one could say in this kind of salon, with the gendarmes setting the tone.

November 10

The radio's pouring out news and emotions. Now I'm moved (a man of the eighteenth century would have said "I weep") if I hear: "The soil of the homeland . . . democratic freedoms." I'm surprised. It worries me. I'm well aware that neither England nor France cared about democratic freedom or things like that when they made colonies. I'm well aware that American judges convicted Sacco and Vanzetti and Tom Mooney.[75] I'm well aware that Stalin . . . So am I a little petit bourgeois logician hiding behind delicate skepticism, concluding that everything is a lie—emotional abstractions, weapons of governments like tanks and planes? Would I refuse to love women on the pretext that the word "love"

---

[75] Nicola Sacco and Bartolomeo Vanzetti, American anarchists of Italian origin, were convicted of murder in 1921 after a notoriously iniquitous trial, in a climate of extreme xenophobia and panic over the Russian Revolution. Despite a campaign of world opinion, they were executed in 1927.—J.-P. A.

Tom Mooney, an activist and labor leader, was convicted in 1916—wrongly, many felt—of setting off a bomb. He served twenty-two years in prison before being pardoned in 1939.

has countless meanings? Those who mock the great abstraction of justice are eunuchs of justice.

November 11

The German armies have invaded the Unoccupied Zone. I am incapable of measuring what the news means. It's probably the effect of the isolation I've been living in for two and a half years: the shock of every unexpected event tones up my body and gives me energy—which is, unfortunately, empty energy. The invasion regenerates me the way the landing in North Africa regenerated me. No longer a question of waiting inertly. I search through the future. I'd like to get rid of my immobility, volunteer in an army, volunteer for action. I look for ways to do so and find only absurd ones.

The marshal protests. "A decision incompatible with the terms of the Armistice." It is not impossible that the masses may be touched by the glorious old man's protestations. They've already forgotten his homage to Hitler's generosity.

November 12

Hitler's letter to Pétain. Hitler acts like a lamb. He was forced to make war. And when he won, all he did was give France proof of his friendship. He has tears in his voice: "I can understand, Monsieur, that your country has been struck by a hard fate." He gave his troops the order to occupy the Mediterranean coast only to confront American aggression and defend Corsica. "Side by side with French soldiers," he hopes to "defend the borders of France and, with them, the borders of European civilization and culture." But the lamb makes threats too: "I am expressing the hope that circumstances do not lead to new bloodshed between France and Germany." But suddenly, with no transition, he adds: "It is above all the conduct of a French general that led me to act in this way." So Hitler invaded the Unoccupied Zone to take revenge on General Giraud. If Giraud hadn't escaped, he wouldn't have defended Corsica. I'm not pushing the text in one direction; I didn't invent the "above all." Hitler hates Giraud as he hates Beneš.[76] He hates him with the hatred of a sergeant fooled by a tenderfoot. But whether it's Beneš, Churchill, or Giraud, Hitler lets himself fly into polemical insults. Not the invective of an orator but of a thug. Hitler is a megalomaniac thug whose delirium coincides with reality for a moment. The day when delirium and reality diverge completely—that's the day we're waiting for.

[76] As president of Czechoslovakia, Edward Beneš opposed Hitler's annexation of the German-speaking part of his country (the Sudetenland) in 1938. Abandoned by England and France when they signed the Munich agreement with Hitler, he was forced to resign.

Last night, despite Vichy's prohibition but responding to the appeal of the Free French in London, people marched by the war monument. In the night, in silence. "Three hundred people," says Old François, who was there. "Three thousand," says Laurent, who wasn't, but already got the news on the path. But something has changed since the American landing and the German troops crossing the Line. Laurent, the most prudent of peasants, Laurent, who's hardly inclined to "demonstrate," Laurent, who lives, as I do, fifteen hundred meters from town, told me: "I wasn't told about it, I didn't know. If I knew, I would've gone."

The sergeant in the gendarmerie reported a hairdresser in town who listened to English radio.

Germans are passing through the town. A detachment will sleep there tonight. I remembered the first German regiment I encountered on the road in the Gâtinais in June '40; I was expecting an emotion that didn't come. I have the same feeling as most of the townspeople. They say: "They're not showoffs." "We'll see them going back north soon." "Some of 'em won't be back." For the townspeople, these are defeated soldiers going by, living on borrowed time. That's the effect of the landing, and Stalingrad.

Met the old Parisian woman who took refuge here. She's angry as an old rooster, not against the foreign troops but against the town, which isn't doing them justice. When I tell her I saw a soldier, a child almost, who was going through the town as if he'd come to spend his vacation, she thinks I mean to denigrate the power of the German army and I'm claiming Germany has only children left to defend itself. And she throws out defiantly: "There are very handsome men among them."

November 14

Hitler and Laval meeting in Munich. What a scene, if you're curious about human monsters! The powerful Hitler and the horse-trader, both from the proles, not the people, both repugnantly vulgar. But Laval's vulgarity doesn't bother us; it is measurable. He's a hotel manager who wears big rings. Hitler's vulgarity is formless, without features; it's frightening because it's present everywhere in him, infinite and elusive. The fanatic and the crafty bastard side by side.

November 27

The Eighth Army in Libya, the Russian pincer movement, the Germans in flight in the desert and in Russia. Reasons for hope are increasing every day. And yet it seems to me that since the day of the landing our spirits are less high, our joy is more uncertain. At first the landing was like a tale in the *Arabian*

Nights. We thought it would all be over through enchantment, with the wave of a magic wand.

In the station café, too, the enthusiasm has dampened. Hope sprang up too high, too fast. Two old men are warming themselves around the iron stove, prostrate, as if they were waiting for the end of the world. I'm hardly less under the weather than they are. Yet the military news is good. But this strategic universe distresses me. These days, months and years of strategy are so many lost years. The Russians, says a communiqué, have killed 47,000 Germans. Too bad they can't kill 4.7 million in one blow! To get it over with. The head of the Gestapo in Poland has declared that from now to the end of the year, he will have exterminated all the Jews in Poland. Does this hemorrhaging world still have long to last, this world with its big ideas? It's all or nothing: you must digest lies wrapped in truths. Thus Hitler, Pétain, and the Anglo-Saxons themselves speak of the French Empire with identical respect that dissimulates colonial cruelty and coarseness in its geographic haziness. Does this world have long to last—this world that's bleeding all over, bleeding in Europe and bleeding in China? This world where all ideas are readymade or come from the secondhand clothes dealer?

The Germans have entered Toulon. "They took Toulon, they took the fleet, and the sailors have been discharged." That's all we know, all they're saying, even all we can even make up. Oh, yes: a trainload of French sailors was seen heading north. We don't know who saw the train go by, if it's a real train or a ghost train. When I ask questions, I can sense they're improvising answers: "German sailors went on board and made the French sailors get off the ships."

Hitler's letter to the marshal. Yes, he has resolved to give France back the colonies that the Judeo-Anglo-Saxons stole from us. Men in high places: a street peddler offering his transparencies to the old keeper of a little park.

November 28

Radio London. The fleet destroyed itself. Scuttled. Explosions—a naval graveyard of ships and men. In the past, I rejected that kind of historical glory, that kind of greatness. Now here I am accepting those deaths, those sacrifices.

General de Gaulle has spoken. Homage to the "instinctive feeling for the nation of the crew and commanding officers" off Toulon. A call for France to "come together." Not the tone of an oration—concentrated, simple.[77]

---

[77] In Toulon harbor on November 27, about fifty ships of the High Seas Fleet under the command of Admiral Laborde were scuttled when the Wehrmacht tried to seize them. In an extremely short speech [on] November 27, de Gaulle approved of their act, emphasizing the "national reflex" of sailors "deprived of any other option."—J.-P. A.

Astronomical figures. In Churchill's speech yesterday, he announced there were 300,000 Italian prisoners. In a few days, the Russians killed 60,000 Germans. Out of 400,000 Jews in Poland, 260,000 have been massacred, starved, electrocuted, or gassed.[78] You could abandon all political or moral reflection and simply interpret statistics to solve the problems of these times. The numbers that measure the war, cruelty, or death, like the numbers that measure the speed of light, are nothing more than mathematical abstractions.

The old lady who got rich in business and retired to the town takes in its scandalous pieces of gossip like a spider in the center of its web. But beyond gossip, she also thinks politically. Her politics were formed during the debacle and haven't budged since. "Oh, yes! It's terribly hard, what the Americans did—attacking a defenseless country, attacking Algeria. Why didn't they land in France? Huh? Huh?"

The "huh," repeated several times, means there's no answer to her argument and the Americans have been convicted of cowardice forever.

Radio-journal de France. "The English are increasingly hampered by their victory in Libya. Rommel's flight is increasingly becoming a triumphant flight, a strategic success." The *Radio-Journal de France* must be written by a Gaullist who infiltrated the radio.

I'm obsessed by the old lady who loves the government and hates the English. I may be more stupid than she is, since I try to convince her. Moreover, I've only found wretchedly bad arguments for her. I have an excuse: I gave up trying any argument she couldn't understand. So there weren't any left for me. But why am I obsessed by that old lady's words?

A German detachment must be sleeping in the town. I didn't see the detachment, I saw three soldiers, not in a group, each one wandering about alone. The first, gangling and heavy, dragging his boots along. The second, a tired peasant. The third was walking with his head down and seemed to be dreaming, a dark-haired young man, so much a dark-haired young man he didn't look like a soldier. I looked in vain for some sign of victory or defeat in them.

---

[78] Of the 3 million Jews in Poland before the war, 90 percent would be murdered by 1945.

December 7

The fog is spread out flat over Bresse and the town. Only the church steeple emerges: you'd think it was a sunken city. Perhaps an escaped prisoner will appear and hang on to the point of the steeple?

I ate at the farmhouse. Soup, a hotpot of cabbage, root vegetables with big chunks of bacon, head cheese, sautéed potatoes, peach jam, and white bread. I've lost the habit of these magnificent feasts. After the meal, the universe seems less intolerable. That's the way it goes. I don't push at history so hard, I have less impatience. I could almost settle for eight hundred Japanese corpses a day.

Image of the world. Mobilization and transfer of labor in Greece; eight thousand Poles killed for not obeying orders for requisitions. Thousands of Poles in concentration camps. Over a million Jews massacred in Poland.

Franco's* speech: "Old liberal prejudices are over and done with. Hitler's doctrine lights up the world."

Frost surrounds the leaves. All the tree branches and bushes look like funeral wreaths.

December 10

English bombers flew over the house last night. They were flying to Italy. From my bed, I can hear rumbling. The window panes shake. Imagining the inside of the fuselages and the crews with no other sign but those vibrations of air in the night. I can only see the dashboard and its magic gleams. The men's faces—what faces do theirs resemble?

December 11

The tobacconist only listens with one ear to the news coming into her shop. "I don't understand anything about it," she tells me, "except I wish it was all over."

A picture of France today: according to English radio, sixty thousand French citizens are in detention for political reasons, without counting those in concentration camps. Thousands of Frenchmen sentenced by the Germans are in prison under the surveillance of French authorities, who are now prison guards working for Germany.

December 13

A dozen German soldiers are living in the town. They stand guard in front of the slaughterhouse, where a stock of gasoline was discovered—some say forty thousand liters, others say four hundred liters. Impossible to have the shadow of a precise fact.

December 15

Suppose Germany wins and the food supply becomes normal again. How many lives, how many French lives would be the same! How many Frenchmen wouldn't know what assets they had lost, since they don't use them personally!

Censorship . . . The pamphlet and the witticism that thumb their noses at authority. Those days are over. Censorship is now totalitarian. It no longer distinguishes nuances. It offers no compromise between itself and freedom. And the taste for freedom is quickly lost. Between 1914 and 1918, censorship wasn't a blind, deaf monster yet. Censorship grows strong not only from what it takes from freedom but also from what freedom grants it.

Paralyzed spectators. We've been injected with curare. Everything has been left to us except movement.

December 21

According to the communiqués from Moscow, the Russians advanced 120 kilometers in five days, took thirteen thousand prisoners and killed twenty-five thousand Germans. I'm depressed. To me, these figures seem like something nice you say to believers. What poor creatures we are: I hadn't smoked for a week. I dig into my little package of tobacco and smoke a pipe. This figure of dead men comes alive.

How did the Germans learn there was a stock of gasoline in the slaughterhouse? Some say: "By looking through papers in an army office in Lyon." Others say: "Someone informed them." And Riffault, forgetting his peasant prudence, unhesitatingly, undisturbed by the enormity of a suspicion like this, points to two heads of the Legion, the grocer-sergeant and a merchant of the town. "Both are for the Germans," he tells me. Here we can see, at least, how passions and anger would be directed if there were political upheavals.

December 22

English planes over Munich. English and Swiss radio depict Russian armies sweeping through the land. The *Radio-journal de France* doesn't deny it, just eludes it altogether.

At the little café bar. A railroad engineer with violent, crude speech, of a kind I hadn't encountered since the debacle. "I'd rather eat shit with the English than brioche with the Germans . . . It's money, nothing but money.

For money, they're selling out France, for money women are making bastards with the Germans . . . They give bonuses to big families, they give the money to workers who make a lot of kids. Never mind if the kids get rickets or tuberculosis. A worker who makes six kids, he's a brute and a moron. You can sleep with a woman without swelling her belly . . . The Germans will be defeated. But they'll do like in '18. They won't touch capitalism, they won't touch Germany."

December 25

Darlan assassinated. For being in Vichy or for not being in it anymore?[79]

December 27

"In Allonal,"[80] Laurent says, "aside from one or two, they don't know what they want. But if the Germans won, they'd be for the Germans."

He asks me this question: "How come, with rich people, some are for Hitler and the others for the English? And yet both of them think about their money first."

A long walk with Riffault, who wants to buy some goats. At l'Aubépin, we meet one of the factory workers designated for Germany. He took to the maquis.[81]

December 29

Alone. It's not that there aren't some people in town with whom I could die—for France, for freedom, for the revolution, for whatever. But there's not one I could live with.

[79] A pertinent question after Darlan's assassination in Algiers on December 24, 1942. The men who ordered this murder armed young Bonnier de la Chapelle because Darlan symbolized Vichy.—J.-P. A.

[80] Allonal is a hamlet near Saint-Amour.—J.-P. A.

[81] L'Aubépin is a hill town a kilometer away from Paul B . . . 's farm. From September 4, 1942 on, French workers could be requisitioned, in the name of the French State, to go to Germany. So we see the first "evaders" appear.—J.-P. A.

‖ 1943 ‖

Suzanne came and cured me of my defeatism. I get back into the heart of current events. Velikiye Luki has been captured. I captured Velikiye Luki. Velikiye Luki is mine.[1]

The French bourgeoisie is afraid of de Gaulle. A bit of its post-debacle Pétain has been restored to it by Giraud,* rightly or wrongly.

De Gaulle, the only one who wasn't guided by fear or one of the thousand disguised forms of fear.

A farmer (from l'Aubépin) told me: "What I like about de Gaulle is, he doesn't shout." There's a lot in that.

On the slope of the hill, rectangles of snow and amber grass. The space is compartmentalized by curtains of trees or bushes. The empty décor of a Breughel.

The God & Co. department stores have all sizes: the highest in the sublime, the lowest in idiocy.

January 3

Suzanne names me some fervent Gaullists who forgot they were collaborators. An effect of the Anglo-Saxon landing in North Africa and the Russian advance.

There's a distinction to be made: some are guided by self-interest. Thus, among newspaper people, a few are already maneuvering to work for the papers that will replace today's German papers. Others (as unlikely as this many seem) believed in a philanthropic Hitler who would bring peace to Europe.

---

[1] The Red Army recaptured this important railroad center 280 miles west of Moscow on January 1, 1943. It had been bitterly defended by the Wehrmacht.—J.-P. A.

A gendarme who was on duty in Lyon the day German troops crossed the Demarcation Line, said to Laurent: "On the platform of the Perrache Station, I saw officers ripping off their stripes to blend in with the soldiers and not be arrested by the Germans. It was something like a second debacle. In the city, the German soldiers made the French soldiers give them their wide belts, and if a soldier or civilian was wearing leggings, they took them."

"Proves the Germans have a leather shortage," Laurent says. I can't draw such vast conclusions from the facts. I get lost in strategy. I can't discover the hidden meaning in Hitler's speeches. I've given up the easy job of knocking down Hitler as an ethnologist and philosopher. However, I can see that Hitler has lost the power to hypnotize the French. He can't create facts at will anymore; he has lost the providential virtue of manufacturing events.

January 5

French Radio News: The Anglo-Saxons are paving the way for Bolshevism (barbarian hordes, etc.), and at the same time, their policy is directed by capitalists and Jewish émigrés. —I'll gladly agree reason isn't everything, but I have a hard time accepting that madness is everything.

French Radio News: "De Gaulle is a foreign agent."

January 6

If you talk to L—— or J——, Suzanne tells me, about the hostages, Communists and Gaullists who were shot, the people who were deported, the concentration camps—they deny the facts, they maintain that they're "tall tales." They brush away those images, reject them. They don't want to be "disturbed."

January 7

A detachment of five thousand Senegalese troops has been sent to North Africa.[2] Amadou Lô and Mamady Koné, whom I knew in Saint-Tropez and Fréjus— friends of Lucie Cousturier, I ask your forgiveness.[3] A detachment of five thousand Senegalese . . . I know . . . it's history. But I'm not at ease with history. Someday we'll have to manufacture history differently.

---

[2] *Nos braves Sénégalais* was a common expression in World War I: roughly 200,000 men drafted from the French colony of Senegal fought for France. Some 80,000 Senegalese Fusiliers were taken prisoner by the Germans in 1940; 4,000 of them were massacred by the Wehrmacht. In 1944, well over 100,000 Senegalese participated in the liberation of France, particularly in the Allied landing in Provence.

[3] Lucie Cousturier was an artist whose paintings are in major museums. Her four books on African-European relations appeared in the 1920s; their sympathy for the Africans and their awareness of the elite position of the colonists made them ahead of their time.

January 8

Roosevelt declares that the Americans will land in Europe.

Does Hitler believe his own propaganda? Men of Hitler's type think and believe the way people get drunk. Their thoughts and beliefs are their cheap wine. But they're masters of their drunkenness. They guide their drunkenness cleverly. Drunks who walk straight. Until the day they stagger and fall. The uncultivated bourgeois drinks the same wine, but in weaker doses.

The bourgeois has become uneducated. He knows nothing of the physics that produced radium and element 85, baptized anglo-helvetium. As for the old education through Homer and Horace, he's equally ignorant of that and perhaps more so. He believes in a mechanical world, utterly dry. To oil the machinery, he throws in a bit of God—a bit of an indulgent, bourgeois God, an anti-Bolshevik God. And to assure himself that he's cultured, he buys paintings, in the hope that they'll "go up."

January 10

Jeanne Mireau, a maid for Parisians taking refuge in the Midi, is spending a few days with her parents. Her employers are bankers or brokers or something like that. "They're not for the French," she says, "Or the English, or the Germans. They're scared, that's all. They go from town to town and from hotel to hotel. They're afraid of being taken as hostages and shot." She also says, "Only the *people* are really against the Germans."

I'm quoting her words exactly. I do not think they contain the whole truth.

January 11

A sub-prefecture bourgeoisie. A bourgeoisie that has kept a few provincial qualities, closed on itself. A flabby Catholicism (to set a good example for the people). A "Catholicism of the wallet," says Colonel O——. They expect salvation from Germany. They expect from Germany what they expect from Catholicism. They hope Germany and the Church will preserve them from the Evil One, that is, from the Russian.

But Colonel O—— tells me: "There is no other law but the hatred of the Boche." A faithful Catholic. No fear of Communism whatsoever. "That's not the question." A tradition: the generals of the Revolution and the Commune, that Rossel, whose very name is concealed from pupils in the schools of France.[4]

---

[4] Colonel Louis Nathaniel Rossel took the side of the Paris Communards who revolted in May 1871 and became a war delegate in the Commune. He was executed by firing squad in November 1871.

January 15

Lyon. The city council has been dissolved, replaced by a special delegation headed by Dr. Bertrand, a surgeon and professor at the medical school. A Doriotiste.[5] The gendarmes pick up the workers drafted for Germany at their homes, at night.

Three German soldiers leave rue de la République, get to the Place des Jacobins, rue Mercière, and then the deserted rue de la Monnaie, where their boots make more noise, and go into a brothel.

January 16

The son of old Cordet, a worker in the Renault factory, has arrived from Paris. "Armed with machine guns," he says, "the Germans surround the factories and make the workers get into their trucks."

"When the Germans are driven out," Laurent tells me, "we'll have enough to eat, we'll be free." I try to show him that if victory comes too slowly, the seeds of Nazism that have been sown in France will sprout. "Yes," he says; "they want to bring us back a few centuries. But still, the children will know how to read." "Laurent, knowing how to read isn't everything . . ." "Yes, I understand, the children will know how to read, but there'll be nobody really educated anymore."

January 17

French Radio News: "The marshal has thought for all of us."

La Nouvelliste: "The Gaullist movement tags along with Communism."

Stalin has received the support of the metropolitan bishop of the Orthodox Church. Stalin, no doubt, has not stopped believing religion is the opium of the people. But for the moment, he's given up trying to detoxify the people.

De Gaulle is not terrified by Communism. De Gaulle won't have his legend like Pétain. But he'll be promoted to "great man."

The bourgeoisie is decomposing. The slightest shock would make it collapse. The only thing alive in it is its fear of Communism. So uncultured it no longer even aspires to culture. The engineer and the doctor have become semiskilled workers.

Marc U——, a factory truck driver, stops on the road to Bourg. Not in the middle of the road, but rather far from the shoulder. A car occupied by two German

[5] There were probably close to 300,000 followers of Jacques Doriot* in France and about 100,000 in his Parti Populaire Français (PPF), a pro-Nazi party that tried to attract former Communists with its "revolutionary" propaganda.

officers comes in behind it and stops. One of the officers gets out, walks over to
Marc U——, and slaps him.

January 21

German planes over London. Forty-four children dead. A third of the planes
destroyed. Should we find this arithmetic satisfying, or not?

"A propaganda bombing, petty terrorism," English radio says. I dislike this
kind of commentary. Where does grandiose terrorism begin? I can choose
between war goals. But I won't slide down the slope that leads us to idealize our
own means of waging war. "Everything about war is atrocious," wrote Madame
Jeanne Halbwachs during World War I.[6]

But there is an order in war, a convention in atrocity. It's not when a German
aviator kills forty-four English children that this order and this convention are
violated, but when the Nazis create extermination camps and perform acts
whose atrocity is not military.

January 25

"Our armies have successfully withdrawn from Voronezh," says the German
communiqué.

They say two women in town have slept with Germans. They say it was for
money: "Some women will do anything for money," says one gossip. "Some of
them will say anything at all out of malice," says another.

"Sports," Vichy says, "fortify one's courage, educate the will, and teach loyalty.
It goes without saying that anyone who has applied athletic virtues to sports
applies them quite naturally to life, on all fronts. The rapidity of one's glance,
the immediate muscular reaction, quick decision—all the qualities necessary
to be a good soccer player, skier, alpinist—whoever possesses these qualities
in soccer, skiing, or mountain climbing will quite naturally use them in spiritual and social life." The accomplished athlete will, by definition, be a perceptive
and decisive man. Flaubert thought he found the maximum amount of stupidity in a speech at the agricultural show.[7] But today sports are competing with
agriculture.

January 28

Goebbels* is reminding Germans of an edict a few centuries old: it authorizes
every person to kill, immediately and without going through the police or the

---

[6] Jeanne Halbwachs was an important figure in the pacifist movement of the 1930s.
[7] Werth is alluding to a satiric scene in *Madame Bovary*, the *comices agricoles*.

courts, anyone who performs his civic duty halfheartedly. In other words, it authorizes anyone to kill anyone. Will Germany go through a fit of mad rage or melancholy? There are other hypotheses. Indifference, frigidity from exhaustion, a taste for defeat, masochistic kneeling before the conqueror. We've already seen that elsewhere.

January 31

Goering* implores the German people to be strong. Goebbels swears Germany will never surrender. But swearing you'll never surrender is different from swearing you'll win. Ritual speeches, whose tone is dictated by the disaster that's in the air. I vainly make the effort to get interested in these speeches. And yet in the months that followed the debacle, I obstinately, childishly looked for indications of facts or intentions in the most mediocre words from Berlin or Vichy. But today's military events carry too heavy a weight. The speeches of the German leaders seem ritual chatter, outdated already.

Thomas Mann has spoken in America.[8] (He left Germany after Hitler took power.) What are the feelings of Germans who scorn and hate Nazism, Germans who're ashamed of Nazism? Are they hoping for the immediate victory of Germany and the abolition of Nazism in a thousand years, after the thousand years of peace Hitler promised to the world if he won?

February 1

Russian communiqué: Fourteen German generals and two Romanian generals have surrendered.[9] *French Radio News*: "The Bolsheviks have not succeeded at all." The whole program is devoted to the conference of the peasant guild presided by the marshal "in a blue-gray suit."[10] After which the journal returns to Russia: "Germany and France, yesterday's victor and vanquished, would have the same fate—a horrifying fate—if Stalin were victorious. That victory would result in Muscovite hordes flooding into our country."

These juxtaposed tidbits make a rather pretty montage, don't they?

A few trains have been derailed.

[8] At the height of his fame (he received the Nobel Prize in 1929), Thomas Mann left Germany in 1933 when it turned Nazi. He lived in Switzerland for five years before coming to the United States in 1938. Between 1941 and 1945, he gave fifty-five highly political speeches over the radio to incite his fellow countrymen to revolt against Hitler.—J.-P. A.

[9] The surrender of the Sixth Army at Stalingrad on February 2 was an extremely important event. Almost 100,000 Germans were taken prisoner, including twenty-four generals, among them the commander in chief Paulus.—J.-P. A.

[10] The Peasant Guild, established December 2, 1940, inspired by the agrarian movement, was supposed to modify the structures of French agriculture.—J.-P. A.

The French Militia has been created. Will these SS of Laval* be dangerous or not? And why the liquidation of the SOL? [11]

Military comedy: General Paulus is promoted to marshal by Hitler. He's taken prisoner a few hours later.

February 2

I have yesterday's paper before me, and Goering's speech. I read: " . . . In a thousand years, every German will still say the name Stalingrad with a sacred shudder. Every German must remember that it was there that Germany was victorious once and for all." This goes beyond the usual cynicism of political lies. It's the phantasmagoria of a world upside down. And, to conclude, Goering invokes the spirit of the Almighty, of the Nazi Jehovah. He would not be overly surprised, after all, if the Almighty transformed defeats into victories, knocked over the world, and kept it down with its head below its bottom.

Laval's lies are dryer and apparently more logical. He doesn't fly off into celestial space. He just agitates the specter of the revolutionary with a knife between his teeth. "If tomorrow," he says to the managers of the peasant guild, "Germany were beaten, Communism would take hold of our country. I'm telling you a certainty." Laval is a Cartesian.

February 3

M——arrives from Paris and thinks I can help him to get to Spain, in order to go to London. He wants to fight.

Jeanne Avril is dead at the age of seventy-two.[12] Lautrec. We came to Paris from our province. There was still a province then. And we didn't talk about painting. For us, Lautrec was the shock of the "modern." What does it mean to be modern? Perhaps nobody was modern except Lautrec. And yet he's hardly in the era of electricity. He's more in the age of gas jets. The taste for dance-hall girls and legendary figures in popular theater. And nothing anecdotal. A classic, aristocratic line. And no painting. Painting is too graphic, too much big machinery. He only wanted the lithographic line. He whispers his confidences through posters. His line catches the Arabian Nights of a Montmartre that has disappeared today, a taste for night and nighttime revels that have also disappeared.

---

[11] It became Darnand's* Milice Française, which eventually numbered thirty thousand armed, uniformed men with a homegrown program for the Nazification of France. While it was used mainly to fight the Resistance and root out Jews, the Militia also assassinated some well-known progressive figures of the Third Republic. Many Militiamen fled to Germany in August 1944, often with their families.

[12] Jeanne Avril was a cancan dancer at the Moulin Rouge. Toulouse-Lautrec's poster and painting of her made her famous.

Jeanne Avril, the survivor—what was her life like from the day when she no longer raised her legs?

German radio is admitting a defeat in Russia, playing funeral marches, and ordering three minutes of silence. Will Germany break down or fight desperately to the end?

Moroccan radio says forty thousand French workers have left for Germany. Laval is preparing a France emptied of workers, or more exactly of young men, since he's requisitioning engineers, office workers, and barbers. He's counting on the thirteen thousand mercenaries of his militia.

February 4

The *Nouvelliste*: "The battle of Stalingrad is over . . . The Sixth Army . . . succumbed to the numerical superiority of the enemy and the difficulties of the situation." (Special German communiqué.) Without having gone to the War College, we can easily understand that if an army was vanquished, it's because it was beaten, and if it was beaten, it's because the enemy was stronger, braver, or more skillful—that is, mastered "the difficulties of the situation" better.

February 5

De Gaulle spoke this morning. About Stalingrad, "The fury of despair," he said— a fine literary expression—"is not a reality in war." The time will come for a national uprising. "France will have the last word."

Why isn't the legend of de Gaulle flourishing? Does de Gaulle lack something that is common to Napoleon and General Boulanger? Or is de Gaulle's legend hidden in people's hearts and it will burst irresistibly into broad daylight only at the shock of a national uprising?

M——can't leave. He has to be called by London. London wants to be sure those who come over aren't Giraud supporters. So despite Giraud's declarations, there must still be a conflict between de Gaulle and him. Is Giraud an innocent soldier, and the Peyroutons are pulling his strings?[13] Or a patriot who wants Pétain's order in a France delivered from Germany? This general, made famous by two "spectacular" escapes—could he be nothing more than one of those acrobatic entertainers in public spaces who're tied up by an onlooker and get rid of their chains by stretching out their muscles?

---

[13] Giraud, who looked down on politicians, was a very poor statesman himself. He was often manipulated by dyed-in-the-wool supporters of Vichy and, among them, Marcel Peyrouton. He was formerly resident general in Morocco and Tunisia, Vichy's minister of the interior, and then its ambassador to Argentina before going back to Algeria after Darlan's death.—J.-P. A.

February 7

The radio gives us a few lines of an article by Chateaubriant.*[14] Capitalism is a kind of original sin. Stalin is something like the devil. No doubt about the diagnosis: this is an idiot inhabited by words. No other wrongdoing than that which always accompanies the sly innocence of this kind of idiot.

February 9

No letters from Suzanne. I tried to act like a marmot and live in half sleep, to sink into temporary nothingness, appropriately appointed. I didn't succeed very well. It's much easier to wake up deliberately than to go to sleep deliberately.

A walk in the woods. Grasses, moss, tufts of hellebore. But the trees are bare, unfinished.

I pick up a book, one of those books of the kind that were abundantly published after the war of 1914–18. It was a period when it was easier for a young man without any particular gifts to write and publish a novel than to pass the Bac with a French composition to which an honest teacher would have given a mediocre grade.

So it's been two days in which I find nothing to note except a yellow dog and a gray book.

February 11

A few days ago, German communiqués attributed the defeat at Stalingrad to the numerical superiority of the Russians and the difficulties of the situation. Today they're explaining the daily advance of the Soviet armies by Russian "fanaticism."

A year ago, the German press was affirming that Russian soldiers only held up under the threat of revolvers aimed at them by the commissars of the Jewish people.

The Russians are advancing. The French are waiting for the landing in Europe. Will the Vichy government vanish into thin air right after the landing? Will Laval try to repress the people like government forces from Versailles after the Commune of 1871?[15]

---

[14] Alphonse de Chateaubriant was a writer who constantly sang the praises of collaboration. After the war, he fled to Austria, where he died.

[15] After the defeat of the revolutionary Paris Commune in 1871, government troops executed more than fifteen thousand men and women, mostly workers. The temporary capital of the government was Versailles, and their loyal soldiers were called *les Versaillais*.

In the coming nine months, Roosevelt said, Europe will be invaded.

February 12

"Come on in and have a little glass of wine," says Debeau, half peasant, half shopkeeper. I resist just enough; I know these people. Debeau wants to get me to talk, and that's fine with me. And besides, if I want, I know how to talk peasant. "There is," I say, "what's finished and what hasn't begun yet." "What's finished?" "The German defeat in Russia." "But the Germans are still in Russia," he says. At bottom, he'd be rather pleased if the Russians were beaten. But don't think he's one of those collaborationists who trust Germany completely. Mistrust is the mother of safety. He distrusts everybody. "You heard what Roosevelt said?" he says. "What?" "Said at least this war had the advantage of ending unemployment." "So?" "So, maybe they're all in cahoots—Roosevelt, Churchill, Hitler . . ." "I don't get it." "Yes . . . they made the war to end unemployment and overproduction." We clink glasses and we have a glass of wine.

All the same, these days are offering a great promise of unconditional surrender.

There are four of them—the former sergeant, the pastry baker, the pharmacist, and the hardware dealer—that the town sometimes threatens in a muffled voice, like a dog growling but not barking. "We'll teach them a lesson," or "We'll send them to the Boches." "When will you teach them that lesson?" "When the Boches aren't here anymore."

It's not even certain that they've lost ten customers. And yet there are other grocers besides the former sergeant; there are several hardware stores, several pastry shops, and there's another pharmacist.

February 13

There was a denunciation, and tax collectors checked on Debeau. They went right to the cellar. He didn't have time to hide his demijohns. It happened just before the day he asked me in to "have a little glass." He didn't say anything about it.

He was selling his marc at a 150 francs a liter; his wine, 30 francs.

February 15

They took Rostov.

At the same time Vichy propaganda is brandishing the specter of Bolshevism, the feeling of Russian power is spontaneously entering the mass of people. They want to scare it with Bolshevism, but already it admires the military strength of the Russians. The mass isn't afraid of it; it admires it, it's hypnotized by it.

How much truth is there and how much myth in the news going around showing German soldiers in Lyon terrified at the thought of joining the Russian front? One of them is supposed to have said: "Instead of going to die over there, I'd rather they executed me right away."

February 16

Laval has issued a decree of industrial mobilization. (Men from twenty-one to twenty-three.)[16] A new census, designed, according to Vichy, to flush out "idlers" and "shirkers" between twenty-three and twenty-one years of age. Every Frenchman has his card, a few cards, which complete each other and can be cross-checked. The police card and the ration card can be cross-checked. Whoever escapes the gendarme or policeman is taken by his belly. All France is turning into a concentration camp. Anyone who changes residence must notify city hall within a week. And the rumor is even spreading that no one will be able to go out of the *département* or travel more than forty miles without the authorization of the mayor's office.

February 17

The Russians have taken Kharkov. The town doesn't much care what the government is doing. The suppression of its most material, palpable freedoms doesn't seem to touch it. What counts is Rostov and Kharkov, recaptured by the Russians. In November, it delegated everything to the English and Americans. For the past few days, it has delegated everything to the Russians.

What solitude! I tell myself it could be worse: for example, I could be taken to a concentration camp, where I would die of hunger and filth. Or I could be shot. I can see myself being taken to the site of execution. I'm not afraid, really, but I am moved at the thought of leaving my wife and my son. May they know that their faces were imprinted in me. May their sadness be without suffering. I brush off this absurd rumination. But it's not so absurd. Other people have been executed, not only in Poland but in France, who had no more logical or legal reason than I do to fear being shot by a firing squad.

"I smoke pipe after pipe." Flaubert says this a number of times in his correspondence. This increases my privation. Flaubert should have thought of me and not shouted it so loudly.

Déat:* "The Bolshevik stampede." Europe is lost if the Wehrmacht doesn't contain it. What can he possibly have in his head, this man with a degree in

---

[16] Laval was promulgating the full Compulsory Work Service [Service de Travail Obligatoire, STO], which drafted men in three age categories, workers and nonworkers, for two years. 650,000 of them would leave to work in the Reich.—J.-P. A.

philosophy who went into politics and then into treason? What mechanism? What passions?

February 18

Kharkov. But the Germans are gaining ground in Tunisia. The detail of these rounds is exasperating: I can't stand the art of pugilism or of strategy. Just give me the final results in one piece!

Goebbels's speech: "Victory is within our grasp." But there are times when you can't even move your pinky.

The birches jostle each other to get to the foreground; they're so silvery and white they look like imitation birches painted by an amateur who messed up his trompe-l'oeil.

February 21

Russians advancing. Americans and the Allies retreating in central Tunisia. The Mahatma is continuing his fast.[17] India is throwing the problem of colonization at England's legs. In everything that concerns colonialism the common historical truth is closer to a lie. How many contradictions. England, the country of individual liberty, is a great colonizing people, and colonization is a primitive form of fascism. The people in colonial countries firmly believe in the civilizing virtue of colonization. The purest moralists who, in Europe, abound in scorn for the civilization of quantity fall on their knees as soon as it's a question of justifying colonialism by the connecting rod and the faucet. On the terrace in Choëx a few years ago,[18] I was talking with a young Englishman, a free spirit, cultivated, who navigated through all the moral systems, Christian as well as Communist. We got to talking about India. Gone was the Englishman who juggled with moral systems. India belonged to him, his personal property, part of his family estate. He defended himself as if I had wanted to steal his watch. All the English are like that . . . No: Huxley isn't like that. See *Jesting Pilate: An Intellectual Holiday.*[19]

February 23

For Flaubert, the bourgeois was stupid as well as base. He railed at stupidity; he was obsessed by it.

---

[17] Gandhi was arrested on August 9, 1942; to obtain his liberation and enable him to continue his struggle for the independence of India, the old nationalist leader began a hunger strike on February 10, 1943. He would interrupt it at the request of his disciples on the grounds of the risks inherent in his age (he was seventy-four).—J.-P. A.

[18] Choëx was a property in Switzerland of a friend of the Werths'.

[19] Aldous Huxley published *Jesting Pilate* in 1926.

There isn't a single crook who doesn't denounce the immorality of another crook. It's rare that an imbecile denounces the stupidity of another imbecile. There is a lot to think about here.

February 24

English radio. It makes me impatient; I have a hard time listening to it all the way through. And yet it flatters my preferences and stokes my hopes. But I'm fed up with vast strategic plans, the heroism of the masses, the power of the war industries. It takes so long to kill Germany and Nazism, or just Nazism! Let them go faster, let's get it over with! Leave us with other worries!

I think of that friend who's extremely frightened of insects. When she sees a spider on the wall of her room, she calls the whole house, shouting "Kill it fast! Kill it fast!!!" Many of the French are like her. They shout to the Russians, to the English, the Americans . . . "Kill fast!"

For the idiots who don't believe there's a difference between regimes and only see an illusory façade in that difference. In the middle of the war, because of Gandhi's hunger strike, some Englishmen and Americans can protest English policies in India.

Sometimes I can hear the silence of thought in France and Nazified Europe, the way you can hear the silence of the countryside at night, or rather the silence of a cemetery.

In Flaubert's letters in 1876, I find a vague allusion to Ingres and Delacroix. Not a word about Manet, Monet, or Renoir. He respects Bonnat and in July 1879 writes to Zola: "As for Manet, as I can't understand a thing about his painting, I recuse myself."[20]

February 25

Yesterday, Hitler declared he would mobilize the whole population of occupied Europe for the German war and would proceed to exterminate all the Jews of Europe. One might have supposed he would seek a new solution to the complication and the increasing scale of unforeseen events. But Hitler doesn't try to understand events. He perseveres in himself. To events, he opposes nothing more than Hitler himself. He is a mythological monster, blind and deaf. He acts like the monster shooting out its tentacles, like a persecuted man killing his imaginary enemy.

---

[20] The academic painter Léon Bonnat (1833–1922) is largely forgotten today.

Panorama:

A hen is sold at seventy francs a kilo at the farm. That's not the black-market price; it's a friendly reduction.

Yesterday Hitler announced that men in the occupied countries are being drafted into the German army.

According to Radio Algiers, seventeen patriots were executed by firing squad yesterday in France.

Arrests are multiplying in Tournus.

From the town, seven departures for the Reich. (Austria and Upper Silesia.)

The Russians are advancing.

England and America make radio announcements about the invasion of Europe, sometimes far in the future, sometimes very soon.

"We will have no scruple," said Hitler, "about the life of foreigners." The paper—that is, Vichy—waters down Hitler's text and doesn't give it as it is. That would be premature. But if the war lasts another two years, Vichy will be able to speak and act like Hitler, without dissembling. Just consider what has become possible since June 1940.

February 27

I've already said the university elite has lost the spirit of protest completely. As for writers . . . Was it really so hard to show disapproval or scorn? And couldn't even the most academic, the most academician of them protest in the name of the most ordinary, the most temperate traditions of the academic world? It's a lie to say they couldn't have done so. It's hypocrisy to invoke the enslavement of the press. They wouldn't have been arrested. Witness Claudel's letter.[21] It was circulated and reprinted in underground newspapers. Vichy didn't dare arrest the poet Paul Claudel, an ambassador of France. They didn't dare. But today? Their consent by silence has created another environment; their silence has made them Vichy's accomplices, Germany's accomplices; their silence has made speech more dangerous.

Coincidence: Radio London is treating the theme of silent writers. However, it cites two of them who haven't given in to Vichy: Bernanos and Maritain. One of them is in Mexico, the other in the United States.[22]

[21] At Christmas 1941, the Catholic poet Paul Claudel, despite his admiration for Pétain, wrote an extremely explicit letter to the grand rabbi of France: "I must tell you the disgust, horror and indignation all good Frenchmen—and particularly Catholics—feel about the iniquities, confiscations and ill treatment of which our Israelite compatriots have been victims . . ." J.-P. A. Paul Claudel is one of the major French poets of the twentieth century.—D. B.

[22] Not quite: Jacques Maritain did go to the United States (he taught philosophy at Columbia and Princeton), but the novelist Georges Bernanos went to Paraguay and then Brazil as early as 1938. Appeasement at Munich, French collapse in 1940, and the policy of collaboration affected him deeply in his exile and inspired his *Lettre aux Anglais* (Letter to the English).—J.-P. A.

"They'll make an arrangement with Turkey and go through Bulgaria," says the bailiff.

"My idea is, they'll land in Greece," says the butcher.

February 28

"The Russians," says Riffault's wife, "they're people like anyone else."

March 1

Claude will be here next Sunday. Unfortunately, I'm already thinking he'll only stay for a week. In January, Suzanne only stayed a week. I still suffer from the shortness of that stay, like a kind of strangulation.

Madame L——, a stylish bourgeois lady, tells me: "I don't believe in history." "What about physical chemistry?"

On the side of the last house in each village, they've painted some strong sentence of the marshal in monumental letters. As far as I know, in the whole region, only one of those posters had cow dung thrown at it.

March 2

"On the black market," Laurent tells me, "there were ten calves, but there were fifteen guys from food-supply control."

Cornu, who was a café owner, and Crespin, the former gendarme, were replaced in the food-supply service. It is said that they were dealing with a horse-trader, they were replacing fat animals by thin ones, they bought animals cheap and sold them dear to the Food-Supply Office, they bought one sheep and counted several; what do I know? These are only unverified rumors.

March 3

Brun, the cabinetmaker, is leaving the day after tomorrow for Carinthia, in Austria. He's sad and full of anger. I can't help being hard on him. "French workers made guns for Germany without turning a hair, so long as it was in France. They only began resisting or groaning from the day they were forced to make them in Germany itself. It's the passivity of the workers that allowed Hitler and Laval, working progressively, to get some 200,000 workers to leave for Germany. At least that's the figure going around." No doubt I'm being unfair and I'm supposing workers hold an eternal revolutionary power they can use whenever they like in all circumstances.

He believes it's possible to sabotage production. "Are you sure?" "Yes, when the heart resists . . ."

Will they reach the level of constructive, effective hatred?

What poor things we are. I'm drunk: I ate white bread from the farm.

A few years before this war, a Paris newspaper published a photo showing Goebbels giving a lecture to German professors. I asked: "Would it be possible to see French professors docilely listening to a French Goebbels in a fascist Sorbonne?" I was already imagining that through the combined tracks of academicism and cowardice, this could become possible. Our Goebbelses in 1943 haven't spoken to professors. They chose journalists; they suppose they're made of softer dough. "In the big amphitheater of the Sorbonne, a hundred French journalists will hear Brinon,* Marion, and Bonnefoy and participate in seminars . . ."[23] Among those who Fargue called "Nobel Prizes in Blackmail."[24]

March 4

The gendarmes are going into the farmhouses of Bresse or the mountains, asking if they're hiding a man called up to go to Germany. They're not putting their hearts into this kind of work. "We're quite ready to close our eyes," they say. "But the day the Gestapo goes with us . . ."

There's a rumor that in Lyon the police are picking up the drafted workers in their homes at night, along with young people who're supposed to register.

They say five thousand people have been arrested in Lyon.

They say in Champagnole, not one worker obeyed the order to leave.

March 11

A failed attempt on Déat's life.[25] They say some thirty German soldiers were either killed or wounded by a grenade or a bomb in Lyon. (All the men of the commune between twenty and sixty are supposed to be on sentry duty on the railroad line for six hours.) Workers leaving for Germany, workers not leaving.

March 14

At the little café stand at the station. Told by a man in blue work clothes, an escaped prisoner: two gendarmes of Louhans arrested two escaped French prisoners, took them to Seurre, and handed them over to the Germans. "Those gendarmes," he says, "I'd like to hang them, not by the neck—they wouldn't suffer long enough—but by the ears or the hamstrings, like calves."

[23] Paul Marion was minister of information from 1941 to 1944, a powerful figure in the regime; he was sentenced to ten years in prison after the war.—D. B.

Thirty-odd journalists accredited by Vichy were invited to visit Paris, along with eighty Parisian journalists, to participate in seminars on documents about "Prisoner Relief" and the fight against Bolshevism. René Bonnefoy, a faithful servant of Laval, was general secretary of information.—J.-P. A.

[24] Léon-Paul Fargue was a poet who also chronicled Paris life in prose.

[25] Marcel Déat was in fact attacked by *résistants* with submachine guns in Arlebourse, his village. He escaped without being injured.—J.-P. A.

March 16

Kharkov has been taken back by the Germans. The radio announces that in Upper Savoy workers evading the draft hid out in the mountains. Will Vichy have its civil war?

State of siege proclaimed in Upper Savoy. They're announcing the arrival of the Italian infantry.[26]

"Did you hear the radio today?" a shopkeeper in the town asks me. A piece of news is troubling her, worrying her, oppressing her among all the news of the day. She has to pour it out. Is it the capture of Kharkov, the deportations?[27] "What can this mean? In Algiers, they took down the pictures of Pétain." (An order of Giraud's made the portraits and slogans of the marshal disappear from the shops.) She only has two ideas in her head today. One, the war is long, and the other, "They took down the pictures of Pétain."

March 20

Twenty Alsatian intellectuals sentenced to death. Others to long prison sentences. On Radio France, a man with a university degree is lauding the benefits of collaboration.

La Nouvelliste has two columns on the events in Upper Savoy, denying that they have any importance. Just a few young people were misled by some detestable propaganda for a few hours. They soon gave in to the paternal admonishments of the gendarmes. But either the facts are multiplying or the legend is growing everywhere. Yesterday, a train was derailed near Saint-Usuge (near Louhans). They say that in Lons, the young men who were drafted assembled in front of the war memorial and swore on the dead whose names are engraved on it not to leave for Germany. They say the rebels in Upper Savoy are being supplied by English planes, they have one machine gun for fifteen men, and three generals have joined them in the mountains. But rumors and news, true or false, don't spring up in the sleepy town the way they spring up in lively cities. They don't even spread out like water on a slope. They appear for a moment the way an insect comes out of a hole and goes back in.

March 22

At the grocery where they sell everything. A few old ladies. The kingdom of old ladies. "What about your son?" "He's in East Prussia." "A lady from Lyon, her son came back from Germany and she said he ate better than in Lyon."

---

[26] Fascist Italy occupied parts of southeastern France, including some Alpine regions, until September 1943.

[27] Werth is probably talking here about the draft of workers to Germany, not deportation to the concentration camps.

"If the English delay too long," says Laurent, "the ones who're for them are going to be against them."

The two schoolteachers who were on sentry duty when the train was derailed at Saint-Usuge were taken to Chalon. The gendarmes told the men from here: "If there was a derailment while you were on duty, don't go back home. Get the hell out . . . Hide out in the mountains."

March 23

A train from Bourg, another from Lons, were each to bring three hundred men leaving for Germany to the Saint-Amour station. The six hundred boys were to be grouped together at the station. The two trains brought in a little over a hundred in all. And they came in extremely late, because the young men drafted for Germany had sabotaged the brakes and it took time to repair them. French riot police were spread out from the station to the first houses of the town. The youths locked in the cars were singing the Marseillaise, the Internationale, and shouting "Long live de Gaulle! String up Laval!"

Is this one lonely spark? Are there a lot of sparks like that? Will they light a fire?

March 26

The pastorals of late 1940 are over and done with, no more back-to-the-land, when the marshal scratched the peasant's necks. In this as in other things, the men of Vichy proceeded gradually.

In Aubépin, their inspectors sent to check on stocks of wheat searched the beds. (They found eighty kilos of wheat in one bed and a hundred kilos in another.) Riffault says he has to supply six hundred pounds of butter in the course of the year. It seems that's an absurd figure. "The ones in charge of requisitions never saw a cow." Why don't they pick up their pitchforks? They're in the museum of historical props. "Where are your pitchforks?" "All of us would have to agree. But there're always some who're scared."

Riffault thinks the rebellion in Savoy is serious. "Yesterday at the Cuiseaux fair I met a Savoyard I used to do business with." (It's the first time I hear this expression in the mouth of a peasant.) "This Savoyard . . . I used to sell him pigs, he told me: 'If you want to travel in Savoy, don't dress like a gendarme.'"

March 29

Monsieur Abel Bonnard is inaugurating the exhibit "Bolshevism against Europe" in Lyon. Among the important people surrounding the minister: Dr. Westerik, an adviser at the German embassy; Baron von Wrangel, who directs the anti-Comintern department; Major Hoppach and Oberleutnant

Graf Schönfeld. Added to these names we see Monsieur Polosson, deputy mayor of Lyon; Monsieur Gain, rector of the university; Monsieur Rougier, dean of the law school; Monsieur Doin, dean of the faculty of sciences; Monsieur Dugas, dean of the faculty of letters; and Monsieur Luc, director of technical education.

Anti-Communists? Pro-German? Or both? Cowards, in any case.

Abel Bonnard declares that he "does not miss the society of yesterday, which is finished" and "prefers today's society, where bodies are hungry but souls can be fed." This academic crook has a low-caliber soul and a small appetite.

March 30

Rabaud, a café owner and a truck driver, used to be one of the patriots of the town. Ideas turned in his head without hanging on to anything. His head burned like an empty pot on the fire. That gave him the appearance of anger and conviction. When he was drafted for Germany, he asked to enter the Militia. He's living on borrowed time.

How many times have we said, speaking of Pétain or Laval, "It's not that simple: they aren't traitors like traitors in the movies." Our critical sense, our desire to be fair critics, our feeling that things were complex, or rather our obsession with complexity and our fear of being simplistic fooled us. The cunning brutality of Laval and the cynical hypocrisy of the sinister old man aren't as complicated as all that. It is like in the movies.

A German soldier down from Lons walked into the farmhouse and asked for eggs. They gave him two. "To hear him talk." And talk he does, freely. All the more so as he speaks French rather well with not much of an accent. Drafted three years ago, and he's only nineteen and a half. He was in Russia, got a minor arm wound. "Many dead," he says. "If they send me back there, I'll raise my arms and go 'Comrade.' I want to save my skin. I haven't lived yet. When they took me I was still a kid." His parents are farmers, and he wants to be a baker. "It's the world upside down," he says. "The Germans are in France, they're sending the French to Germany." "Who'll win the war," Laurent asks him, "the English or the Germans?" He answers: "I don't care, as long as there's peace." "Hitler, Churchill, Roosevelt?" asks Laurent. The German answers: "They play cards and we die."

In the space of an hour, this account was transmitted to me almost in the same terms by Laurent and his wife. Their two versions coincide. It would be vain to comment on the German's words. A mad pacifist, a total anarchist? An agent provocateur? And then perhaps his anarchism and stay-at-home wisdom have no more importance than a scatological joke in the mouth of a priest.

Protests from the Vatican and from prelates against the deportations and persecutions. But the Church offers its ceremonies to the persecutors. A fluid church,
more solid than ever. A changing Church, an immutable Church, which works
the miracle of being both the Church of the persecuted and the Church of the
persecutors.

Patriots or jokers pasted a sheet of paper on the door of the town hall. It reads
"Sentenced to death" and, under it, the names of twelve inhabitants of the
town. Ten are avowed collaborators and the two others, timid collaborators.
A sign of repressed rage, a village joke, or a form derived from anonymous
letters? Symptom, forerunner, joke? Depending on the overall outcome, history will unify, organize, and clarify these scattered, obscure signs—or simply
drop them.

April 1

"Decree concerning the attestation of employment. It is forbidden to leave the position mentioned without a transfer order . . . etc." A desperate bureaucracy, delayed-
action Nazism. Already, they can hear the sound of bagpipes in the distance.

April 3

I turn the dial on the radio. I hear a confused noise; it comes from Paris.
Something from Paris has entered my room. The noise becomes an enthusiastic
clamor. It's a soccer game. For what freedom for what Europe are these sports
voyeurs, these stadium screamers? Their homeland is a soccer ball.

April 4

Pétain on the radio. "Later, history will tell what you have been spared.—
Eliminate the proletarian condition.—The rebels have taken shelter by leaving
the country.—The genius of our race.—Bolshevik barbarism."[28]

He lists all the clichés from his preceding radio addresses. The clichés parade by,
but without flexing their legs or plunking down their rifle butts. They file by like a
ghost army. All you can distinguish clearly is their regimental numbers.

The text is so flabby we can suppose it was written by the marshal himself. It
makes no reference to current events. You'd think the marshal is already dead
and his spirit is speaking in a séance. His words are as vague as the words pronounced by spirits who answer through a table. Incredible that these flabby words
should be pronounced at the same time as the fighting in Russia, the fighting in

---

[28] All points in Pétain's message, a lengthy defense of the legitimacy and advisability of his
"authoritarian regime" (*régime d'autorité*). See Philippe Pétain, *Discours aux Français: 17 juin 1940–20
août 1944*, ed. Jean-Claude Barbas (Paris: Albin Michel, 1989), 299–302.

Tunisia . . . and the same time that France, as inert as she may seem, is focused on the hope of an Allied landing.

A few minutes later, an Alsatian was announcing on English radio that fifty Alsatians were sentenced to death for resistance to Germany and fifty thousand men from Alsace and Lorraine were drafted by Germany and sent to the Russian front.[29]

April 6

Half a page in the paper on the bombing of the Renault factories. Supposedly three hundred dead.[30] The total pacifist rejects everything concerning war. But, for the people, the dead in Billancourt are simply the ransom for destroyed tanks.

Some do not accept this difficult balance sheet. They don't even want England to be responsible for these dead through ricochets. Thus the legend is born that the dead in the apartment houses were not hit by English bombs but by German bombs. While the English bombers were attacking the factories, a few German planes were dropping bombs on the houses.

B—— gives me this version. I express doubt. This doubt hurts him. This doubt destroys the fine edifice of a story after his own heart.

A few posters of the Combat organization were pasted on the walls of the town late Saturday night. "Don't leave for Germany. Resist Hitler, resist Laval. Disobeying Laval means obeying France."[31] One was soiled with cow dung. The others, after three days and three nights, are still intact.

April 7

I thought the town knew its informers and there were hardly a dozen of them, roughly ten cowardly little civil servants or overheated shopkeepers. But a policeman in Lons told M—— there are fifty-two of them, and each one has a submachine gun.

It seems there are towns and villages where nobody left for Germany, where they made life difficult for the agents who do the checking. Nobody had anything

---

[29] Alsace had compulsory military service [in the Germany army] since August 25, 1942. The census and drafting of those born between 1914 and 1919 began in January 1943; some 200,000 men from Alsace and Lorraine were mobilized into the Wehrmacht. Thirteen young draftees from the commune of Ballersdorf in Alsace were executed on February 17, 1943, captured as they tried to flee to Switzerland.—J.-P. A.

[30] The second British daytime bombing of the Renault factories, which were working for the German war machine, took place on April 4. It was a Sunday, and the numerous victims—328 dead and more than 500 wounded—were people out for a stroll or inhabitants of Boulogne-Billancourt, just outside Paris. Vichy organized a state funeral.—J.-P. A.

[31] Combat was one of the main Resistance movements, the largest from 1943 on, with its own underground newspaper. Albert Camus was the editor of its newspaper *Combat* from 1943, when it was published and distributed clandestinely, to 1947.

to do with them, nobody talked to them. They couldn't stand living in silence and asked for a different posting.

The power and dignity of silence. But the cashier of a hotel in Bourg has no idea of that power and that dignity: yesterday she was playing the coquette with a German officer, who was plying her with heavy compliments.

Overcast sky. It's going to rain. The flowering cherry trees have taken on the shade of dirty laundry.

April 10

Three youngsters have been arrested. They admitted spattering an inscription of the Legion on a wall with red paint and hanging in effigy the grocer-sergeant, the supplies checker, and the renegade who joined the Militia. One is the son of a ragpicker, the other of the owner of a little café, and the third, of a railroad worker.

I sound out peasant opinion. "You can't do things like that now," Laurent says, "It's too soon."—"They're just kids," Riffault tells me. "It was easy to find them, they blabbed about it all over the place. They don't even know how to hold their tongue." They're thought of as imprudent little boys. One of them is supposed to be a little crazy. Nobody feels sorry for them; they're judged on their prudence.

April 15

Old mother Imbert's she-goat gave birth to four kids, two alive, two dead. She has a fallen womb. The veterinarian said the goat had to be put down. "He didn't cure her but he took our *sous* anyway." They hung her up in the cellar to get the blood. "Now she's cooking. At Louise's farm. I won't eat any. Like they say, it wasn't a cow but a goat. But a good goat. I won't find another like her. She gave five liters of milk. And good cheese."

She speaks in one breath, as if all her thoughts were one sentence, as if that sentence were one word. I don't know by what transition she goes from mourning for her goat and the miseries of the times to her own miseries: "I'm pretty old . . . I don't mind dying."

Belgian patriots seem firmer in their certainties and less prudent than French patriots. They're not waiting for the Germans to be driven out to punish traitors. The radio informs me that Paul Colin was shot dead in Brussels.[32] I was told he'd

[32] Paul Colin was a well-known Belgian journalist from the French-speaking community (the Walloons). Active in the far-right Catholic Rexist Party and editor in chief of a daily paper and a weekly, he supported the Nazis and attacked opponents of collaboration. There had already been an attempt on his life in 1942.

been linked to Belgian fascism for years. But in the twenties, he was one of those European travelers who were rebuilding the world on internationalism and the painting of Matisse. He wrote a book on Germany right after the war, and a book on Van Gogh. These books are not without merit.

I can see his pale eyes in his whitish, round face, a face surrounded by the fuzzy moss of a curly beard and sideburns, which seemed fake. I would have enjoyed conversing with Colin, were it not for his voice. It was high and yelping. You could hear it from one end of an apartment to another, like the whistling of a bullet.

How did he become a Nazi?

April 16

They don't separate out questions. Like the grocer-sergeant blaming the mother of one of the boys who hanged him in effigy for "not watching over her kid" and her answering: "And you—you'd do well to watch your daughter a little more, she's been seen in the fields with this one and that one."

April 18

Riffault's brother, a prisoner returned to France because of illness. His memories bubbled up in him, separately, unconnected, like air bubbles on the surface of a pond.

We talk about the ex-grocer-sergeant, the head of the local Legion. "He's strong," says Riffault's wife, "The government's for him." "No, he's not strong," Riffault's brother says. "Everybody's against him."

Yesterday he bought something or other in the grocer-sergeant's shop. "You're the one who's making him strong. You're incapable of going to another grocer. There are at least ten of them in town." "That's because you find things in his store you can't find in the others, he has more stuff." He doesn't understand, or doesn't want to understand.

In Paris, Suzanne refused to shake hands with Raymonde D——, whose husband is a well-paid Doriot* supporter. "I can't be friends," she tells her, "with people who're killing my friends or getting them killed." "She's impossible," Raymonde says all over town. "She believes in Nazi persecution and cruelties—pure inventions!"

April 19

There are many fine distinctions between the traitors who truly want to be traitors and the ones who were carried away by treason before they recognized its face. A few weeks ago, German radio put the case of Chateaubriant in front of me. I had read nothing by this writer. The last few days, as I rummaged in the library, I found his novel: *Monsieur des Lourdines*. I read it. It's not unreadable at all. The story of a country gentleman ruined by his son, a "partier." The peasants glide through a rustic atmosphere, above the laws of the earth and the economy.

The story is set in 1840. The old gentleman and his boots are 1840. The psychological analysis, like the boots and the old servants, is 1840. But this 1840 has the tinny sound of a music box.

In his life as in his book, Chateaubriant probably has the gift of avoiding the shocks of the real world. Thus do sleepwalkers, people used to say, walk with their eyes closed and avoid obstacles. Chateaubriant the sleepwalker didn't bump up against Germany or against Nazism. Any idea is fine for him, as long as it's sung. Thus a literary sleepwalker, a bookish, feminine man is led to treason.[33]

The paper. They have allegedly discovered, near Smolensk, the corpses of ten thousand Polish officers, shot in the nape of the neck by the Russians in the spring of 1940. The Polish government in London is allegedly asking for an investigation by the Red Cross. (For the German press, this dissident government becomes respectable and trustworthy if it does something that could be used against the Russians.) But there's one detail too much here, something comical in the macabre story: "At the Führer's request, the German Red Cross has already contacted the Geneva organization." Hitler has become the Führer with a tender heart.

It is surprising that it took three years to discover a mass grave of that size.[34]

April 21

I haven't seen a Parisian paper or magazine since July '40. Febvre* gave me a few issues of *La Nouvelle Revue Française*.[35] I vaguely knew it was controlled by the occupying authorities. (I had also been told that the Soviets were majority stockholders in it before the war.)

Today the great man of the journal is Drieu la Rochelle. So I read Drieu. How many commonplaces and upside-down commonplaces with their heads down

[33] Alphonse de Chateaubriant won the Prix Goncourt in 1911 [the most prestigious literary prize in France] for *Monsieur de Lourdines*. He had published agrarian, mystical novels and thought he saw in Hitler, whom he met in 1936, a redemptive bard: see his novel *La Gerbe des Forces* (The sheaf of forces). He launched into cultural-political collaboration, founding the group of that name and developing its themes in the weekly *La Gerbe* (The sheaf), founded in July 1940. He was a member of the Central Committee of the Légion des Volontaires Français contre le Bolchevisme.—J.-P. A.

[34] More than four thousand corpses of Polish officers were discovered in the Katyn forest near Smolensk on April 13. This decapitation of the Polish military elite was the work of the Soviet NKVD [precursor of the KGB]. Moscow denied it and broke off relations with the Polish government in exile. Note Werth's skepticism: more than anything, he distrusts German propaganda, and he had been a Communist fellow traveler. He will not be the only one to doubt Soviet guilt in this affair.—J.-P. A.

[35] Founded in 1911, the *Nouvelle Revue Française* (NRF) was one of France's most prestigious literary magazines, and still is. It is published by Gallimard, which became synonymous with those three letters. The Nazis allowed it to continue publishing under the editorship of Drieu La Rochelle,* a novelist, essayist, and poet who was also an ardent fascist. He committed suicide after the liberation of France.

and their legs in the air! I think of the comedy of ideas that Flaubert dreamed of. One wonders if this Drieu could be the Homais of an already out-of-date fascism.[36]

Imagining the hypothesis of an Allied victory, he writes: "Switzerland will be the last bastion of Europe against the Slav invasion."

A certain Marcel Jouhandeau rolls at the Germans' feet like a cat in heat.[37] Back from Germany, he writes: "At last, I was able to live for a few days in the intimacy of people who yesterday were our enemies and whose delicacy toward us astounds me."

April 23

People are saying the Germans used their revolvers to shoot at someone distributing leaflets in Bourg. First they hit him in the shoulder. He kept running. Then, wounded in the leg, he fell. The Germans threw him into a truck. The truck took off toward Lyon. Some say the man died on the way, others say the Germans finished him off.

April 24

Suzanne is to arrive this morning after a night's traveling. I wouldn't be any more tired if I had made the trip myself. All night, my head hit the walls of the car of the train. I dozed on and off, my body completely dried out. The station buildings and the trainmen on the platforms looked like beings out of absolute limbo.

April 27

The Germans came for the mayor. He had left yesterday.

"News reports on the radio," Febvre says, "have no apparent connection to each other and often resist any attempt at interpretation." The American legation left Finland. News from Turkey, news from Italy: Mussolini is making another purge of the fascist cadres.

April 29

At three in the morning, the Germans returned to the mayor's house.

They went to Chadel's, banged on the door with their rifle butts, and then broke a window. During this time, Chadel was able to disappear by going out behind the house, through his garden. They went to the town clerk's; he

---

[36] Homais is a pompous character in Flaubert's *Madame Bovary* who spouts clichés in every sentence.

[37] Marcel Jouhandeau was a writer whose *Chroniques maritales* are still read today. In 1941, anti-Semitic articles he had published in 1938 appeared in a small volume called *Le Péril juif* (The Jewish peril). He accepted Goebbels's invitation to visit Germany with other French writers.

was able to escape on his bicycle. The town is accusing the grocer-sergeant of denouncing them. According to the town, he'd said he would "get them."

The farmer's wife, who knows nothing of France, Europe, and the world except that they're taking some of her wheat, hens, and eggs and whose husband and son stand guard for six hours on the railroad line every third week, said: "It's because some people get into mischief; it's because of the trains they derailed."

Thus the old Parisian shopkeeper, as I was telling her about the execution of Rivet's colleagues in the Musée de l'Homme,[38] answered: "There always are people who do stupid things."

La Jeune Europe—Review of European university youth—Publisher: Inter-university Exchanges.—Managing editor: Dr. Rupert Rupp, Inter-university Exchanges, Berlin W 35, Friedrich-Wilhelmstrasse—Address in France: *Jeune Europe* (President: Monsieur Albert Villot), 8 Rue Jean Goujon, Paris 8e. Printed by: Buchgewerbehaus, M. Muller und Sohn, Berlin, S.W. 68.

Luxurious brochure. The text is in French, but there are German, Italian, Finnish, Norwegian, Dutch, Spanish, Portuguese, Hungarian, Romanian, Bulgarian, and Greek editions.

Dr. Hans Claui, of Saint-Gall (Switzerland) establishes the scientific foundations of Nazi Europe. So Nazism was founded on the exact sciences; a few philosophical props are thrown in for good measure. Thus Jacob Burckhardt (1818–97), Joseph Goerres (1776–1848), Professor Louis Le Fur of Paris, Marshal Antonescu, and Antisthenes, "Greek philosopher (445–365)," and Rodin. And then at last, with his given names and his nobiliary particle, Johann Wolfgang von Goethe.

Through its juxtaposition of names, the table of contents for 1942 is no less enticing: Déat, Adolf Hitler, Victor Hugo, Plato (Plato's text is entitled "A Heroic Sacrifice for Europe"), Alphonse de Chateaubriant, Jacques Doriot, Blaise Pascal,* Benito Mussolini...

I'm not entirely sure if there isn't a college student somewhere in Europe who thinks Doriot, Plato, and Goethe all had the same Nazi solution for the problems of the earth.

April 30

The local squire. Suzanne reminds him that he publicly declared his wish for German victory. "I don't get involved in politics," he says blandly.

---

[38] Paul Rivet was a doctor, anthropologist, and ethnologist who founded the Musée de l'Homme (Museum of man) in Paris. The resistance network he formed there was one of the first in France. Many of its early members were arrested and either executed or sent to concentration camps.

"Who would have thought it, in a little town like Saint-Amour?" This is what several shopkeepers are saying about the home visits by the Gestapo. For them, it's an injustice, a mistake of fate. A problem like this is for city people.

However, anger is growing against the grocer-sergeant. He wants to leave the area and sell his business; he placed an ad in the *Indépendant de Saône-et-Loire*.

They say that in Beaufort, the Gestapo pulled out the toenails of the county clerk to make him talk.

The Mireau farm, on a hilltop. "Someone wants to talk to you." The room on the second floor with whitewashed walls. We find Chadel there. It was still night when he arrived. First he'd hidden in Laurent's haystack. He was barefoot, just wearing a shirt. In the nick of time. The Germans fired their revolvers when he was still in his garden. The Mireaus are sheltering him. They didn't hesitate. The Mireaus are "bizarre." Laurent is critical of them for putting pleasure before work. Last year at this time, they gave us strawberries and cream . . . and the cows weren't groomed yet.

Here's Chadel, smiling, moved. I feel very strongly that I am in France. I tell them so.

Night had fallen when we left. We walk by the Laurents' farm. Prudent, provident people. They probably would have taken in Chadel. But just the time for him to find a better hideout. The new bourgeois. France is with the Mireaus—France, which is what you make of it.

May 1

The paper. "A diplomatic event of the highest importance for France. Chancellor Hitler received Prime Minister Laval."

Over the last three days, in the communes between Lons and Bourg, the Germans have arrested a hundred and fifty, say some, two hundred persons, say others.

At the Mireaus'. Chadel still in hiding. "Before this war," he says, "I was pretty much an anti-militarist. Today . . ." He doesn't finish his sentence.

People who wanted a peace less stupid than the war in 1914 accept a war less stupid than peace today.

That vague feeling of waiting, that search for safe places to hide some compromising papers. Before going to bed, I note the exact spot where I put my shoes. So as not to run out barefoot into the night.

May 2

The departure of Suzanne and Claude leaves me in a state of semi-somnolence. There is a traumatism of departures.

Léon Werth, ca. 1943. *Centre de la Mémoire, Médiathèque Albert-Camus, Issoudun*

The paper. The marshal has spoken. The Charter of Labor will solve the problems that neither capitalism nor communism can solve.[39] Why do they make this old man speak when no one listens to him anymore? Why this macabre game of making a corpse talk?

"The marshal tasted the soup of young people in the Chantiers."[40] A fine idealized image.[41] There is no great leader who does not taste the soldier's soup.

May 3

The marshal has spoken again. "My heart would bleed if I were to go through the streets of Paris when there are so many difficulties to be overcome and so much hostility. But be reassured, I am thinking of you . . .". He doesn't seem to have any illusions.

At the Mireaus'. Chadel is still hiding. In a kind of attic. A swallows' nest hangs from a beam on the ceiling. The weather is cool: they closed the window. But from time to time, the women open it so the mother swallow can get in or out.

[39] Adopted on October 4, 1941, this charter suppressed unions and the right to strike and set up guilds and "social committees"—that is, committees of workers—under government control.

[40] The Chantiers de Jeunesse were compulsory eight-month youth camps established by Vichy, where young people were supposed to work on roads, forests, harvests, etc. It replaced military service.

[41] "Idealized image" translates *image d'Épinal*: eighteenth- and nineteenth-century prints of idealized French life.

A friend of Chadel has come to the town. He says he accepted a pack of cigarettes from a German officer, and another day he shook the hand that a German held out to him, and he still feels ashamed of it.

M——tells about the work his group does: fabricating fake identity cards and destroying railroad lines.

May 4

Some German soldiers came by, accompanied by a woman in boots. They asked to buy eggs. They didn't demand and didn't pretend they had the power to requisition anything. The Riffaults told them they didn't have any eggs. But at Touraud's, they sold them half a dozen eggs. They were afraid. They thought they would gain favor with all Germany forever.

"*Signal* is selling less," says the newspaper vendor.[42] "I sell twenty-eight *Candides* and thirty *Gringoires*. But the people who buy these journals . . . it's more for the paper."

I'm skimming through *Conversations of Goethe with Eckermann*. No doubt I'm unable to place them in their time. But I can't get interested in it.

May 5

The town seems inert. But hatreds are hiding in it that could flame up in a historic bonfire. On one side, men in the Legion and the Militia. On the other, a few "patriots" who are all or almost all socialists or close to it.[43]

Madame Debeau goes around saying that if the mayor doesn't come back, the Germans will take eleven hostages. Eleven—not one more, not one less. Where did she get this figure from?

It's not enough to call the pastry maker, the pastry maker's wife, and their son (who they say is a homosexual) collaborators. Through a strange transfer, they've fallen in love with Germany. They believe in the regeneration of France and the world through Germany. They love it mystically.

I saw the baker's wife on her doorstep. She gave me a stiff little wave and a furious glance.

---

[42] *Signal* was an illustrated bimonthly—in reality the French edition of the *Berliner illustrierte Zeitung*—which first appeared in July 1940.—J.-P. A.

[43] One of many allusions to the possibility of civil war in France, a prospect also frequently evoked in Jean Guéhenno's *Diary of the Dark Years: 1940–1944* (New York: Oxford University Press, 2014).

It's rumored that the grocer-sergeant diverted tons of food intended for Supply Control and sold them in his grocery. And also that his daughter slipped some chocolate to a boyfriend.

"Must there always be, in France, so bizarre a mixture of what is best in the world and what is most contemptible?"—(Voltaire, *Correspondance Générale*, vol. 11, second part, Letter to Monsieur le Chevalier de Chastellux, December 4, 1776.)

In the town. Chadel's brother, a bike mechanic, is shaking my hand: "I'm fine . . . fine . . . fine . . ." He gives my hand a shake between each fine. And the fines multiply and grow in intensity. He finally announces that Bizerte and Tunis have been taken. "Scraped out, cleaned up."

Met young Clerc, who belongs to a group in the Resistance. "The organizations," he says, "don't agree with each other. The English Intelligence Service realizes this. In the region, you can't hope for much from the young people in maquis. They want to hide out and that's it. In Haut Jura, where they say there are eight hundred of them, it's a different story. As for the peasants, whether it's a question of helping or hiding, almost all of them are prudent, prudent . . ."

They're saying a woman in Saint-Étienne-du-Bois is a spy and she gets seven thousand francs a month from the *Kommandatur* in Bourg. That's the naked news. There are pieces of news that remain skeletal or disappear without a trace. Others snowball into bigger news. What law governs the proliferation of details and the development of scenarios?

After the Allied victories in Tunis and Bizerte, the town is full of hope. But once its hope is realized, what will the conflict between the *résistants* and the others be like? Will the others smother the *résistants* with kisses? What about the dead weight of people who're inert? And won't the *résistants* begin killing each other, among themselves?

The figure of de Gaulle is far away. But Gaullism means all forms of Resistance, whatever they may be. The legend of de Gaulle is not being fabricated with advertising methods. It's making its way all by itself. It will burst into the light.

May 15

According to the Hitler and Mussolini's messages to General von Arnim, the German-Italian troops only gave in to numerical superiority. According to the same messages, this African campaign was rich in advantages for the Reich, despite the defeat: instead of gaining glory and ground, it enabled the Reich to gain time. So the Duce and the Führer are shouting like kids: "You big coward!" and "You didn't hurt me at all."

The French had the debacle. The Germans surrendered in droves before Bizerte and Tunis, sometimes in serried ranks, marching in rhythm, obeying the discipline of the debacle. Will a common tradition of flight be born in these two military peoples? A tradition through which war itself will die?

May 16

General Giraud's daughter and her children arrested and deported to Germany.[44] The German enjoys multiplying sorrow by anxiety. This sadism seems complementary to the tenderness he shows to children. So his taste for the macabre is complementary to his appetite for *Gemütlichkeit*.[45]

A former minister is speaking on Radio London. Banality of clichés, vulgarity of voice. Will nothing rid us of that parliamentary vulgarity? A strange phenomenon: the Parliament takes a crafty but uncommunicative provincial and transforms him into a garrulous lout in a few months.

May 20

The station café. Someone from Champagnole told Madame Marie the Germans were completely deforesting that part of the Jura and they'd requisitioned the men of Champagnole, particularly the shopkeepers, to cut down trees. (It seems requisitioning shopkeepers is more intolerable than requisitioning workers or even peasants. The store counter is a kind of inviolable altar.) These improvised loggers are allegedly penned up in the mountains, barely nourished, and driven like slaves.

May 22

Do I really have, inside myself, any other desire but to nibble bits of happiness?

But today there's no question of high drama of the spirit. The radio is throwing the hard facts in my face. In Belgrade, for two German officers who were killed, four hundred hostages were shot. In Warsaw, the Jews, penned in the

---

[44] Renée Granger, daughter of General Giraud and the wife of Colonel Granger, who had gone to fight against the Germans, was arrested in Bardo [Pyrenees] on April 2, 1943, by men of the PPF [Parti Populaire Français, the French fascist party founded by Doriot] and then transferred as a hostage to Berlin with her four children—J.-P. A.

[45] From gemütlich: nice, cozy, cheery.

Nalewki quarter, are being killed by artillery fire. I feel more stupor than indignation.[46] An act only provokes indignation if it has retained some human proportion. I think about the cruelty of the German, his taste for atrocity. And suddenly I remember that in the first quarter of the nineteenth century they were killing Protestants in the Cévennes.[47]

The Communist International has been dissolved, the Third International.[48] "The national sections will no longer receive directives from Moscow." A brief commentary from Moscow: centralization in Moscow has no reason to exist in today's world. Unity in the common goal, the destruction of German fascism.

A political act to reassure the bourgeois democracies? The natural outcome of Stalin's policies? Indeed, as soon as Lenin died, Stalin was against the Trotskyist thesis of "permanent revolution," the universality of revolution. However, Trotsky, hounded, exiled, and persecuted by Stalin, wrote one day that if Russia were threatened by "imperialist villains," he would fight, even with Stalin as the ruler, in the ranks of the Red Army. Moreover, at the beginnings of Nazism, Trotsky favored a war against Germany. We may suppose that if Trotsky hadn't been assassinated, he would agree with Stalin today, for the time being.

But where is the time when Russia, Holy Russia, was the ideal homeland of the workers of the world?

May 23

English radio gives us a letter from General Giraud to General de Gaulle. He sets out the terms of an agreement between two dissidences. Too many words, too many stiff legal legalisms, too much chicanery. Giraud forgets that while he did make a glorious escape from Germany, he took his time escaping from Vichy.

May 26

Yesterday, English radio: "The France of Joan of Arc, of Napoleon, Foch, Péguy, and Clémenceau."*[49] With this enumerative, recapitulative method, one can construct as many Frances as one likes.

---

[46] When, on April 19, the Waffen-SS surrounded the Warsaw Ghetto, which still counted seventy thousand Jews not yet deported to Treblinka [where they were immediately gassed], it encountered strong resistance from groups of Jewish combatants. They fought on in an extraordinary manner until May 19, despite the scale of the military force deployed by the Nazis.—J.-P. A.

[47] Though the massacres of Protestants during the sixteenth-century Wars of Religion are well known, there were also mass murders of Protestants in the Cévennes Mountains during the White (Royalist) Terror of 1815.

[48] The Third International (the Comintern) was officially dissolved on May 15. This reassured the Anglo-Saxons and gave the war the Russians were waging a character that was more patriotic than ideological.—J.-P. A.

[49] Marshal Foch was the commander of French forces on the Western Front during World War I.

These historical homelands are all too easy to manufacture. They like to trot out the men of the constitutional convention or the forty kings of France. But those who manufacture these kinds of homelands only know academic or textbook history. It's more than they need for their political jobs.

Do you love a woman only because you know her great-grandmother was beautiful?

May 28

Trains full of troops and materiel went by toward Lons and Belfort. The rumor's going around that the night before last, rifle shots were fired from the tracks. Croatian soldiers enrolled in the German army are supposed to have jumped onto the tracks and run off into the countryside. The Germans allegedly fired at them.

No rifle shot was fired.

Le Nouvelliste reports the marshal recently received a writer of the name of René Benjamin and gave him a few sanctimonious maxims. I remember this René Benjamin: in the middle of the war, in his nice warm room, far from the danger, he manufactured a joyful soldier, an irresistible Gavroche.[50] A few foot soldiers, my buddies, sentenced him to be publicly spanked after the war. We forget quickly. But just look at the line, the filiation: the fight-to-the-ender of 1914–18 becomes the man of the marshal and Nazism in 1940.

June 1

The plain of the Saône, panorama. A heavy sky, heavy clouds, heavy earth. Atmosphere of a steam room, a room where herbs are kept. Panoramic platitude, heavy platitude of the Lyon suburbs. But under the dirty canvas of clouds there's the region around Tournus and Mâcon that I love.

The Vichy civil servant and people like Madeleine B——, who don't know, don't want to know about the concentration camps, the executions, the massacres. You'd think contemporaries know the present less well than historians know the past. During the Terror, in 1793, there were probably many people who didn't know it was the Reign of Terror.

It's not that those who don't know are deprived of information. It's because they don't want to know. Delicate people who close their eyes before a rough world. They need a smooth, sandpapered world. Thus, academic painters

---

[50] A journalist and novelist (he won the Prix Goncourt in 1915 for *Gaspard*, a book about the war), René Benjamin, a pamphleteer for the right-wing followers of Maurras,* turned into a eulogist for Pétain in a manner that often bordered on the ridiculous.—J.-P. A. Gavroche is Victor Hugo's gutsy street kid in *Les Misérables*. – DB.

produced polished nymphs at the end of the century. Thus, during the 1914–18 war, academic writers described comfortable trenches and gaily heroic soldiers.

June 2

Out of critical scrupulousness, I often attributed nuanced motives to journalists and writers who took the German side. I rejected the explanation of pure treason as too simple, too gross. Perhaps that way I was manufacturing literary traitors. Now I know there truly are traitors like in melodramas. In the second issue of an underground paper, *Bir-Hakeim*, I read a few quotations from articles published in 1940. A few journalists (Chaumeix, Béraud, and Benjamin) were then denouncing the ignominious Germans with the same energy with which they are now denouncing the infamy of the English. "Germany is the enemy of the human race" (Chaumeix, *Candide*, 1940). "This enemy, the German, is implacable and ignominious . . ." (Benjamin, same paper, same date). Traitors who deliver documents for money are less revolting, because they don't wait for their country to be defeated to commit treason.

The same paper recalls Laval's words in the Chamber of Deputies on May 17, 1935: "I traveled to Moscow because I firmly believe that Franco-Soviet collaboration is indispensable for European stability." " . . . I firmly believe . . ."

June 3

At the Riffaults. They "baked something." They offer me a piece of flat cake made with curdled milk. Someone from Chalon told them: "Last week, two women were out walking with German soldiers, two women from Chalon. Two students passed by the group. One of the students says, 'We'll remember those women.' The officers come over, grab them, and take them to a police station. One of the students was badly battered; they crushed his feet and broke an arm. When they released him, he was unrecognizable. His eyes were coming out of his head, everything was swollen, his eyes, his head."

"There are women . . ." said Riffault's wife, "they had a bed, a table, sometimes even two chairs. Now they have a wardrobe with a mirror and a nice rug."

"The ones who were with the Germans," Riffault says, "I'd hang them up by the toes. And if we had to dig their grave I'd do it for nothing."

For three years now, France has only had underground thoughts.

Deprived of meat, deprived of tobacco, deprived of thought. Thought deprivation is the one people bear most stoically.

June 5

The French Committee of National Liberation. Speech by de Gaulle and speech by Giraud. There were reasons to be afraid Giraud was "national" like our national substitute coffee. Afraid there was a grain of Pétain in him, a grain of Vichy. But the agreement has been reached. I was going to say Giraud is a Gaullist. Indeed,

French men and women leaving for Compulsory Work Service in Germany in April 1943. *Bundesarchiv, Bild 183-N0619-503*

to want liberation is to be a Gaullist. The two fuse, they're interchangeable. Here seniority counts. It was in June 1940 that de Gaulle became a Gaullist. That is: he chose France. And denounced treason. Since then, it's become easier.

According to English radio, all of occupied Europe is resisting Germany. In France itself, I can't measure anything. How many workers in the cities tried to escape deportation?[51] How many peasants whose false declarations and skimpy deliveries to the authorities are motivated by something other than immediate self-interest?

Jeanne Riffault, back from the market. Out of eight young men from Coligny drafted for Compulsory Work Service, she says, only two took off. The six others had no house where they could hide out.

In Beaupont during the night, a bomb exploded in the shop of a cloth merchant, a leader in the Legion. After the debacle, he said the German soldiers had done less damage than the French soldiers. (Actually, that's quite possible. The conquering army was well fed and its discipline intact.) "Sure," says Laurent, who can't content himself with an idealistic explanation. "He was a collaborator, but maybe they wanted to get back at him because when he sold his cloth he had his favorites. All that gets mixed up."

---

[51] Werth is talking about the Compulsory Work Service in Germany, not deportation to concentration camps.

Laval at the mic. "Politics finds its roots in the permanent necessities of history and geography." He invokes "the natural laws of the evolution of peoples." He knows them. He sleeps with them.

At the same time Laval was proposing Edenic German peace to France, the Gestapo was making a raid in Lyon. They picked up Rochard, the former garage owner of the town. They were driven to the Monluc Prison. They were made to march around the yard in a line, like common criminals. It would be nice if a few fat Lyonnais bourgeois collaborators had been picked up in the raid. For example, one of those who say "The curfew doesn't bother us at all. We never go out at night."

A crook like Laval is disconcerted before a man devoid of impurity, with a noble ambition. He may even accord him a kind of respect, provided he seems to move on another planet—if he is, for example, an archaeologist or a mathematician. But when a de Gaulle is winning the game and winning it against *him*, someone like Laval gets dizzy, and, like a cheater losing at cards, he feels he's the victim of an intolerable injustice.

The Moulets, in Paris, are stinking rich. They keep a magnificent table. They bought paintings; you walk over Renoirs at their place. They made a fortune by having German uniforms made by seamstresses working at home, uniforms they sell to the occupying army. "At the same time," Suzanne writes me, "other people are dying for an ideal."

June 9

Station café. Madame Marie, who takes in the groans or bad mood of the people the way you take in a popular song, tells me: "My son's not going to leave and neither is my son-in-law. I forbid them to leave."

June 11, 12, 13, 14

Chalon, Tournus, le Villars . . . Suzanne tells of the courage of Hany Lefebvre and Noémi.[52] They take in English aviators who parachuted into France. False papers, crossing France, to Spain, Portugal, London.

Something overheard by Suzanne, in Paris: Around a radio set, a few men, a few women, who all, men and women, are risking their lives. The radio enumerates

---

[52] The daughter of Hany Lefebvre, a friend of Suzanne and Léon Werth, Noémi would be arrested for acts of resistance and imprisoned. She published her testimony in *Six mois à Fresnes* (Six Months in Fresnes).—J.-P. A.;

destructions and gives statistics on the weight of the bombs that were dropped. A woman says, "Oh, when the war is over, I only want to hear about love." One of the men who risked the most—who is risking the most—answers: "Aren't we here out of love . . . ?"

June 17

"In Cormoz," Riffault says, "they threw a bomb into the stable of a guy who's for the Boches." Cows were killed and injured. "That's not right," he says. "It's the man you have to aim at and not the animals who didn't do anything wrong."

In Lyon, the Germans, accompanied by French police, are hunting down young men and going into houses at night.

"June 17, 1940," writes *Le Nouvelliste*, "three years ago tomorrow, the marshal was giving his first message to the French. . . . I am making France, he told them, the gift of my person." That seventeenth of June 1940, only the marshal's close friends knew about that magnificent present. I was part of the caravan moving forward at a snail's pace over the main roads. Neither the city dwellers nor the peasants of that exodus knew anything of the events. Vague rumors were going around. No certainty except that of the debacle. That historic sentence was only known much later.

The next day, June 18, we did not know any more than that about General de Gaulle's proclamation. Skimpy rumors were going through the traffic jams on the roads and in the barns. We were shipwrecked. We knew nothing, except that we had been shipwrecked.

I do not know what day we were able to learn, through a local paper, about "the text of the armistice contracts."

Armistice—it sounds sharp and short. There is a notion of duration in this word—short duration. Armistice: the time to pick up the dead and sign a peace agreement. The armistice is an interval between two periods of hostility or between the state of war and the state of peace. We didn't realize that the Armistice can be a regime. A Parisian shopkeeper, sleeping on the same straw as I was, told me toward the end of June: "It's bound to take three months before we get back to normal life."

Between June 11 and the middle of July, we had no newspapers. In June, we heard an extremely weak radio once or twice, connected to batteries. During the two weeks we spent in Chapelon, we couldn't get English radio; we were surrounded by German soldiers. And besides, did we know there was an English radio? How did we find our bearings, day by day? Was the disgust we felt at Vichy's lies enough? Those official lies, lies in the uniform of a lie? I rather think it was through a mysterious process of osmosis.

The Labour Party Conference has declared the distinction often made between Germany and the Hitler regime false and dangerous. Labour means a people is responsible for its government. Without the support or consent of the great majority of Germans, Hitler would not have existed. That seems very simple. It seems more complicated if we take another example. For example, "You are responsible for Pétain and Laval." "But the Germans were there, we could only oppose Vichy by an inner refusal." The anti-Hitlerian German will say: "The Gestapo was there, we could only oppose Hitler by an inner refusal." It's a problem of historical metaphysics. You can get lost in it. For the moment, I think that if a people does not succeed in vomiting out a government it detests, it's because it didn't stick its finger far enough down its throat.

June 21

News from Paris: education in the French State under Bonnard. Teachers and professors have been asked to use great discretion when talking about Galileo.

Could Pétain have been in touch with the German embassy in Madrid from the very beginning of the war? Is it possible that he was told about the German attack of May 10 before it happened? And he said nothing to the French government?[53]

June 24

I don't have a radio anymore. It's rather restful. I only receive the war drop by drop now.

Essay topic for the Bac in Lyon: "Compare Voltaire's idyllic (*sic!*) enthusiasm for the Revolution he saw coming (!) and for which he worked (!) with some of the clearest results of that Revolution."

It goes without saying that the journalist commenting on this topic will develop the theme of the failure of the Revolution. In language that would make him fail the Bac—at least I hope so. Will the examiners in Lyon fail the candidates who dared to claim the Revolution was not merely heads on pikes and knives between the teeth?

---

[53] The German invasion of France began May 10, 1940, putting an end to the "Phony War" that had begun more than eight months earlier.—D. B. The rumors Werth relays here illustrate the discredit of "marshalism." Appointed ambassador of France to Burgos, Spain, Philippe Pétain was no doubt on rather good terms with the ambassador of the Reich, but nothing supports the thesis of any complicity whatsoever.—J.-P. A.

Madame Solomon, Langevin's* daughter and a colleague of Rivet in the Musée de l'Homme, are in Germany.[54] We know that the deportees are forced to do unhealthy jobs and turn into nothing more than skin and bone.

The university doesn't say a word. "What could it do?" I have no idea. But priests have spoken against Nazism from the pulpit and were not even threatened.

June 25

Underbrush. The blue of the sky cut into pieces of stained glass and set in the branches. Yes . . . but often I close my eyes to block out this countryside I've seen a thousand times. Oh! for cities and the unexpected, cities and their mobility.

June 26

One of the town's hairdressers has been arrested. "They arrested her . . ." I am told. But I can't find out if "they" is the Gestapo or the Vichy police.

"Just let it end . . ." says an old woman. "Let it end any way at all . . ." says another. "How will it end?" an old peasant says.

June 28

"The government has extended the authority of the 'special sections' to all acts with a goal of provoking or stirring up a state of rebellion against the legally established social order, against the domestic and foreign safety of the state . . ."[55]

Upper Savoy and the Massif Central.

July 2

Lervet, a carpenter in the workshops of the railroad, arrived from Paris this morning. An attack on a busload of Germans at the Porte de Clichy. Sometimes Frenchmen show the Germans who committed the attack. They're Doriotistes, he says. On the whole, all the workers are pro-English. Not in any group, no attempt to group. As for the Charter of Labor, "We laugh at it."

---

[54] Hélène Solomon, Paul Langevin's daughter, was deported to Auschwitz, and her husband Jacques was shot in Fort Mont-Valérien in May 1942; both were Communist intellectuals. As for Rivet's colleague, she is probably Yvonne Oddon, the librarian at the Musée de l'Homme convicted for belonging to the Museum of Man Resistance Network there.—J.-P. A.

[55] The *sections spéciales* were special courts created in August 1941 to repress the action of "Communists and anarchists" (actually *résistants* of any stripe) without using normal legal procedure. Nine death sentences were pronounced by these courts in the provinces.

July 3

The marshal in Auvergne: "I've said it very often and I repeat: the French people carries its future in itself, in the depths of the sixty generations which preceded us on our land."

Too bad Flaubert didn't have the marshal.[56]

July 5

Eight AM. The sky is a foggy blue. The light on the plain is all spread out, pressing down with its weight of light. The plain has swollen with summer and war.

Gauleiter Sauckel has spoken to French workers.[57] He suddenly feels an immense pity at the thought that "new combats could take place on French soil" and French workers could be subjected to the horrors of Bolshevik slavery.

Gauleiter Sauckel's words have the same outdated tone as the marshal's. They come from the same past. The child-of-Mary-with-a-kepi style meets the Nazi style.

July 6

Febvre gave me a copy of the January 1 *NRF*. Drieu Rochelle's article can hardly be called triumphal. He envisages the Russian stampede and no longer seems to believe in German Europe. He's dressing Goebbels's propaganda in a tight-lipped (and tight-assed) style. Jean Giono describes Marseilles in a chewing-gum style.

Claude has arrived. I was drying up. I'm the dry earth that receives some rain and opens to the rain in all its hollows, all its bumps, and all its cracks.

July 8

L'Indépendant de Saône-et-Loire (a weekly manufactured with scissors) is reproducing a declaration Laval made to the press. It can be reduced to the following four points: 1. America has grabbed Africa.—2. Germany will win.—3. I will strike the French who help the English.—4. I am a French peasant.

The same *Indépendant* (a German paper) reproduces an article from *Pays libre* (Free country): "A victory in September 1940 would have been more dreadful

---

[56] Flaubert's mockery of pompous mixed metaphors by public speakers is famously displayed in a memorable scene in *Madame Bovary* (the *Comices Agricoles*, the farm fair).

[57] Fritz Sauckel, the *Gauleiter* [Nazi Party regional head] of Thüringen, was appointed "general plenipotentiary for the general recruitment of labor" [on] May 21, 1942. His nickname in occupied Europe was "the slave trader of Europe."—J.-P. A. He was sentenced to death at the Nuremberg trials and hanged.—D. B.

than a defeat. It would have delivered France to barbarity; Joan of Arc refused this and sent France the great soldier with no fear and no reproach, who . . ."

To speak like this journalist: the German boot has extremely bad pens at its service.

July 9

"The railroad man, you know," Madame Marie says, "that railroad worker from Dijon . . . the Germans executed one of his sons by firing squad, a boy of eighteen; someone threw a bomb into a hotel. His other son was interned in a camp and he escaped. The Germans go to his house every day. He was in his garden. A neighbor came to tell him the Germans were waiting for him in front of the door; he answered that there was no reason for her to trouble herself, he was leaving his door open now and nothing was locked in his house. He showed me the snapshots of his son. He used to come around here to see if he couldn't find a little food to buy."

Everything's all mixed together in this doleful tale: the railroad man's food basket, the snapshots. Everyday people don't separate out emotional pain in a dramatic way.

July 10

Allied landing in Sicily. The town's saying, "They're really banging away."

Ban on threshing without a government food-supply checker in attendance. The peasants thresh with a flail and hide as much wheat as they can. Men belonging to all draft years and all professions have received the order to leave for Germany. According to Joseph B——, only 6–7 percent of these men obeyed. This, in his canton. In Bresse, they're saying nobody left. The men who refused didn't take to the maquis; they're hiding at home. They work in the fields but don't take their meals with the family and don't sleep in their room. "In the country, that's possible. But people in the cities—except for rich people—they can starve them out. They all leave." According to Joseph B——, out of the two thousand inhabitants of the town, there are fifty-one Militia informers and seven or eight women affiliated with that police.

July 12

Speech by Laval. I've seen the peasants in their farmhouses, I've met some on the paths. None made the slightest reference to it, all of them talked about the landing in Sicily.

"Everybody always told you I was a fanatical enemy of England, an anti-Englishman. I'll tell you the truth. I'm 100 percent French and so you can really understand me, I only love my country." Does he mean that if he only loves his country, it's for the sole reason of being really understood? Is syntax taking its revenge?

Poor signs, but signs all the same. Someone like Laval soils both the patriotism he puts on and the anti-patriotism he practices. Patriotism and internationalism must be instilled with a new meaning. They're dying from tricked, truncated history, academic history, history that lies. They're dying from a history that isn't history.

July 16

The paper. The government admits it's not obeyed and announces that it will use coercion.

July 17

"The Legion of French Volunteers . . . , proud of the Franco-German brotherhood in arms . . . , is calling the young people of France to combat."[58]

Nietzsche et le problème européen, by Jean-Édouard Spenlé. An example of Nazi criticism adapted for France. The philosophy of history in the service of the policy of collaboration. The Sorbonne smiling nicely at *Mein Kampf*. A distinguished, flattering Nazism. This Spenlé isn't writing for ex-boxers but for the daughters of the lovely ladies who sat in on Bergson's lectures.[59] This book poses just one problem: "How are Spenlés made, and who makes them?"

July 19

The Germans searched Chadel's house again this morning. He's hiding out in Lyon. They arrested Guerlat. "In the street, with no hesitation. So he must have been denounced and pointed out."

"They searched everything in Guerlat's bedroom," Madame Marie says. "My daughter saw him in handcuffs. She came back all upset. Think of it . . . To see men in authority going into houses . . . I can tell you everybody in Saint-Amour is scared . . . Chadel, Guerlat—they're men who were active in politics."

Riffault tells me Guerlat said to the German policemen: "Kill me if you like, I won't tell you a thing." We hear they found papers and a submachine gun in his room.

---

[58] Next to anti-Muslim slogans scrawled on a village wall after the Paris terrorist attacks of November 2015 was the phrase "LVF NOW!"—the abbreviation of Légion des Volontaires Français (Legion of French Volunteers), a French fascist militia.

[59] The philosopher Henri Bergson gave public lectures in Paris.—D. B. Jean-Édouard Spenlé was reputed to be a good specialist in German literature and philosophy. Léon Werth is quite right: in this book, Spenlé attacks "rationalist, humanitarian ideology" and exalts the model of Nazi Germany in veiled terms as the guarantor of "the regeneration of Europe by means of the selection and education of a strong race."—J.-P. A.

July 21

In Dommartin, a bomb thrown into a grocery owned by a member of the Militia.

I think Laurent is still ready (as he told me months ago) to give up one of his cows for an English victory handed to him on a silver platter—his least productive cow. But he disapproves of sabotaging railroad lines. (A train was recently derailed in Sainte-Croix.) "Who's risking jail time?" he says, "The men who watch the tracks. If I saw a guy who wants to derail a train, I'd stop him with a club. I don't feel like going to prison or being shot. Run away, join the maquis? I've got other things to do, I've got my work . . ."

Who will think of collecting the finest gems of Goebbels and Vichy propaganda after the war? It will all be forgotten, thrown into the trashcans of history. Gustave Dupin (Ermenonville) collected the gems of the French press between 1914 and 1918. Who remembers his *Collier de Bellone* today?[60]

July 26

Mussolini has resigned.

What did he trip on? Who pushed him? Will he be assassinated or will he write his memoirs?[61]

July 31

La Nouvelliste: "Marie-Louise L——, sentenced to death June 9 by the High Criminal Court of the Seine for performing an abortion, was executed this morning in the Prison de la Roquette."[62] Who will guillotine the judges?

August 5

Tons of bombs on Hamburg, Catania, Orel. On German radio, General Dietmar declares: "The Axis powers have decided, with full knowledge of the facts, to remain on the defensive this summer—a mobile, very elastic defensive, but carried out in an offensive spirit." This dialectic is less elastic than that defense.

[60] *Le Collier de Bellone* was a satiric attack on wartime propaganda published in 1921 by Gustave Dupin, using the pen name of Ermenonville.

[61] King Victor Emmanuel III dismissed the Duce and then arrested him. He made his decision after Mussolini had been thrown into the minority of the Grand Council of Fascism the day before by a vote of 19–7. Most Italians were weary of the fascist regime, its alliance with the Reich, and military setbacks such as the loss of Sicily and the bombing of Rome on July 19. Mussolini would be executed by a group of partisans near Lake Como on April 28, 1945.—J.-P. A.

[62] According to the terms of the law of February 15, 1942, attempted abortion was a crime that could lead to an appearance before a state court. Several midwives were sentenced to hard labor; a washerwoman, Marie-Louise Giraut, née Lampierre, was guillotined on July 30, 1943.—J.-P. A.

They say Guerlat was tortured in Dijon. And tried to cut his throat with the lid of a can of sardines.

August 6

At the Laurents', in the evening, they have their radio on constantly—an old radio that only gives them Lyon, Vichy, Paris. It's for the sound; it's pleasant to have sound in the background. The Radio-journal de France announces the fall of Orel, the retreat of the Germans to "prepared positions." The prepared positions make them laugh, even the women, even young Georgette; we didn't imagine that she could ever have thought about war, armies, nations.

The newspaper's lying on the table. The marshal is exhorting a group of schoolteachers. I don't read it, I know nobody read it. Never have words fallen into such an absolute vacuum, with no resonance whatsoever.

August 7

A train derailed near Louhans. They say a fuel train is on fire near Chalon. A train has been waiting in the station for three hours for the line to be repaired. Something of Catania and Orel managed to get into the station café. A few weeks ago, Madame Marie would have seen the sabotage and derailments as the effect of clumsy anger. Today she says: "It's instructions." As if the schedule of derailments was being prepared and it was also the schedule of peace.

On a path in Bresse, two gendarmes run into a young farmer who didn't want to leave for Germany; they've been ordered to him hunt down. The young man, frozen with fear and surprise, doesn't run away. He's motionless on the side of the path. The gendarmes come up to him: "You're a good Frenchman? . . . Well, so are we." And they walk away.

It sounds like a legend, a fabricated story. And yet I got it from Laurent, who got it from the two gendarmes themselves.

August 9

The number of derailments is increasing, perhaps according to a coordinated plan.

August 16

At four in the morning, the Germans arrested Clerc (wine merchant), Martin (garage owner), and "little Marie,"[63] who runs a microscopic grocery. Clerc's face was badly beaten in. The girl who helps Marie in the store ran away. They fired

---

[63] "La petite Marie," Marie Béreziat, would die in a concentration camp.—J.-P. A.

their revolvers at her but missed. Clerc, Martin, and little Marie worked with Chadel (the Beaufort-Cuiseaux-Saint-Amour circuit).

The shopkeepers in town—like the farmers, in fact—explain everything by denunciations. When will I be denounced or turned in? The rich bourgeois and the local squires think I'm a Communist. But they'd probably still hesitate to write an anonymous letter. As for the sewer informers, the place they assign me isn't the one where they keep their hatreds, corroded by contact and macerated in seclusion.

They're saying the grocer-sergeant, the stool-pigeon hardware owner, the baker, and the baker's wife were standing in their doorways with beaming, radiant faces. I don't know if that's true. What is certain, at least, is that they had nothing to fear from the Gestapo.

Spent the evening at the Mireaus'. In their place, as in ours, an atmosphere of vague menace. A whole region like that. The nation created and re-created.

"These days," says Riffault, "you can't talk in front of just anybody." It seems the arrests have provoked more fear than rage in the peasants. Before the continuous German defeats, the effect of terror would have been still stronger. But perhaps the peasants are accumulating their hatred, slowly, like the people of the Far East.

"The Germans," Riffault says, "went all the way to Andelot. They interrogated the gardener of the chateau, hit him with their rifle butts, and broke his jaw, then they threw him into a truck."[64]

Riffault asserts that the gardener was denounced by the son of the baker. "And he's still alive?" I say. Riffault answered something or other, which was vague.

When Lormier, the son, was told of his father's arrest, he jumped out of bed and grabbed his submachine gun. They stopped him from leaving his house: they proved he couldn't deliver his father and he'd expose himself to still more rigorous treatment. What a debate between holy wrath and resignation to prudence!

August 17–18

English radio is giving horrifying details about the life of French men and women in a camp near Katowice, in Silesia.[65] Once the war is over, how will those who

---

[64] Andelot is a village on a hill ten kilometers from Saint-Amour. The gardener of the chateau would die in Buchenwald.—J.-P. A.

[65] This is probably Auschwitz (Oświęcim in Polish), in Upper Silesia, thirty kilometers away from Katowice. Werth has already referred to it. Jewish organizations and Polish *résistants* sent precise information to London about the concentration and extermination camp.—J.-P. A.

ordered those crimes and those who executed them be punished? And those, whether German or French, who consented through their silence? Those who denied the horror because it was dangerous or intolerable to know about it and look at it squarely? Will torture be punished by torture? By death? Will cruelty be unleashed by punishing it? Will a new form of reprisals be invented that debases neither those who gave the orders nor those who carried them out? Or will everything be forgotten, lost in the concern for economic reconstruction, in the rage to live and eat, in the frenzy of dance, swaying to new rhythms that will be neither the foxtrot nor the tango?

August 23

This is a sign of the spirit of the population, not an excerpt from a report of the Prefect: "The Americans will bring me chocolate." I heard it from the mouth of Anne-Marie, who is four.

The hatred some bourgeois have for de Gaulle is of the same order as the hatred that assassinated Jaurès.[66]

August 27

One face of France in this month of August 1943. A tableau of the bourgeoisie. An old garden, an old house, antique furniture. Families cut in half: some, most of them, conservative, strongly Catholic, on the brink of fascism or creeping toward fascism; the others, who have kept the taste of freedom, even creeping toward some kind of timid socialism. The women are ladies. A judge from Paris, on vacation.

A notable of the town: "I won't hide that I thought the Germans had won and it was best to get along with them. I can see they've lost. So we have to get along with the Americans and the English."
  "You call that a man?" says Laurent.

August 30

Lunch with Febvre. Appearances: a Côte du Rhône, the back-and-forth of conversation. In our hearts: unease and impatience. "When will they land in France?"

September 3

Allied landing in Calabria. De Gaulle's committee announces that after the Liberation, Pétain and all the members of his government will be tried in

---

[66] Jean Jaurès (1859–1914), one of the great figures of French socialism, was assassinated because of his pacifist views about World War I. His assassin was acquitted at the end of the war.

court.[67] What a fine trial to grasp the passions and political logic of professional occasional politicians! What a range of men, from a Laval to a Carcopino* to a Chevalier![68] And all of them, with their hands over their hearts, will swear to their patriotism. Perhaps that will clarify this word, which sorely needs clarification.

September 4

Effects of terror. A piece of news traveled the fifteen hundred meters that separate us from the town: "The Germans raided the town yesterday." It's transmitted to me just like that, without delay, without any indication of the source. Andrée François has returned from Saint-Amour. Nobody heard of a raid. Nobody saw a German.

September 7

I hear steps on the path, which is hidden by the trees. I strain my ears to hear. But I recognize the sound of wooden shoes, not of boots. I'm reassured. Thus I make the subtle calculations usually attributed to savages.

September 9

The unconditional surrender of Italy.[69] I was listening to English radio last night at the Mireaus'. The news was first given raw, without preparation or comment, with a Marseillaise as the last period. One would have thought the speaker was reading a lapidary inscription. A vanquished Germany was being hatched in this farmhouse room.

Liffré (seventeen kilometers from Rennes). A Jewish Czech by the name of Behar had taken refuge there in 1941 with his wife and their two children, eight and six. In the month of August 1941, the Gestapo appears. An officer walks into Madame Behar's bedroom, sits down in an armchair, settles in with his legs stretched out, and tells her: "You have ten minutes to get ready."

---

[67] On September 3, 1943, the Comité Français de Libération Nationale decided to try the leaders of the Vichy régime after the Liberation: 108 ministers, junior ministers, secretaries general, commissioners, and governors general as well as the head of state and the prime minister would be judged by a high court from 1945 on.—J.-P. A.

[68] The Catholic philosopher Jacques Chevalier was a junior Vichy minister from 1941 to 1942 who put God into the curriculum. After leaving the government, he became a dean in Grenoble, where he tried to shield students from the Compulsory Work Service. He also called for the repression of the "Communist" Resistance. Chevalier received a sentence of twenty years of hard labor in 1946, commuted to four years in prison.

[69] The Allies did not trust Victor Emmanuel III and Marshal Badoglio, heads of the Italian government, and imposed an armistice on Italy without giving them a chance to discuss the details. It took effect September 8, when American and British forces landed near Naples. German forces then occupied three-quarters of the peninsula, not without massacring part of the Italian army.—J.-P. A.

The Germans take Madame Behar to Rennes, leaving the husband and children in Liffré. The next day, she's released. In October or November '42, the Gestapo returns and takes the husband and two children to the camp in Drancy.[70] Madame Behar tries to kill herself. She is stopped.

In December, Behar and the children are sent we don't know where. A few days later, Madame Behar receives a small suitcase containing her children's clothes. Imagine this: a woman opening the suitcase, recognizing those clothes, touching them, unfolding them. Were the children murdered? German administrative sadism lets a mother hesitate between the picture of her children in a camp or her children dead. Since that month of December '42, Madame Behar lives without knowing anything about her children. That's how she lives.

And always the same contrast. German soldiers hold out their arms to every child. The German is full of tenderness for the child and tortures him and tortures his parents through him.

I've given the Gestapo a timetable. They once came into the town at nine thirty, another time at four in the morning. When I get up in the morning, I tell myself: "It's past four in the morning, I can relax until nine thirty." And after nine thirty I tell myself *they* won't come this day, at least.

September 13

The thundering Führer bleats and moralizes like the Pétain of 1940. You'd even think he was inspired by Pétain or Pétain's scribes. "I gave my country the gift of my person," Pétain used to say. "For a long time now," says Hitler, "my personal life has ceased to belong to me."

September 21

A message from the German generals captured at Stalingrad. They say Germany is now defeated and is no longer fighting for itself but for Hitler. A shady business: it makes me think of the confessions and great penitence of the October 1917 Bolsheviks accused by Stalin. The most determined anti-Stalinists did not explain this—or explain it only—by torture or threats. They invoked some kind of mystical faithfulness to the Party, to the revolution—the aberrant revolution, but the revolution nonetheless.[71] If this piece of news is true, what mystique or what calculation did the Stalingrad generals follow?

---

[70] The site of a large transit camp about seven miles outside of Paris. Most prisoners there were Jewish and deported to Auschwitz.

[71] In show trials (1936–38), the main leaders of the 1917 Bolshevik revolution all confessed to treason and were executed. Arthur Koestler's novel *Darkness at Noon* (1940) dramatizes such explanations by "anti-Stalinists." Werth's account seems closer to George Orwell's (and the truth): the confessions were simply obtained through torture.

September 23

Sick, in bed. No news of current events. Two days in bed were enough to remove me from the war. And from everything, except my body. I belong to the civilization of the bed, of books (reading mechanically), and drugs.

September 24

I haven't had any contact with the town for a long time.

"We were sold out," says the butcher. "The bullets didn't fit the rifles, the shells didn't fit the cannons. All they thought about was chowing down, stuffing their faces. France was in anarchy. Workers were paid too much, to do nothing and occupy the factories. The bosses were good at paying but not at commanding."

He's anti-German and quasi-Gaullist. He gets English and Swiss radio.

The old hotel keeper doesn't put together such complex thoughts. He just repeats: "It's the fault of the big guys, the fat cats."

September 29

Claude says, "I can't wait for the time when we won't live with the fear of being arrested! Because we're twenty, or because we're suspects."

Two faces of the Occupation. A few weeks ago, eighty French stationmasters or their immediate underlings were leaving for Germany. A propaganda excursion. Everywhere, they were well fed and cordially received. Each one got a fifty-mark bill for pocket money. At the same time in France, the German firing squads were hard at work.

September 30

A train derailed between Saint-Amour and Coligny. The old Parisian shopkeeper who took refuge in town makes a kind of joke: "Children must have fun." And, with no transition: "It's appalling . . . You just can't find maids anymore."

Laval's speech to the mayors of some region or other. He still wants to save us from Bolshevism.[72] But he doesn't understand that—a strange phenomenon—the military success of the Russians has lessened and perhaps eliminated the fear of Bolshevism. The best horse-trader in the world can't pass off a dead animal for a live one.

---

[72] On September 29, before the "representatives" of Paris and its suburbs, Pierre Laval declared: "If German power were to disappear, Communism would take over in our country."—J.-P. A.

October 4

Autumn sun over Bourg. The white-cheese city is as if transfigured. Young women go by in light dresses. Cyclists slide along. Bourg has taken on a kind of substance. Bourg breathes a whiff of city in my face.

It's at the bottom of a column in *La Nouvelliste*, in small type. It hardly strikes the imagination. It doesn't make any noise. It interferes with no one's habits: "On the order of the *Höherer SS und Polizeiführer*,[73] fifty Parisians were shot on October 2."

Same source: the captain of the gendarmerie in Annecy was killed by "terrorists." Eight lines for the execution of the "terrorists." Fifty lines for the murder of the captain.

October 5

The assembly of the cardinals and bishops of France affirms the legitimacy of the Vichy government and disavows those Christians through whom "French consciences are directed toward attitudes of personal judgment and independence, from which only anarchy and the division of minds can emerge." One would think they're taking aim at the editors of *Cahiers du Témoignage Chrétien*. As for us, nonbelievers that we are, we almost felt tenderness when they started talking about a Christian Church, an Evangelical Church. And those young, fervent Catholics, for whom the Church was not merely one power among temporal institutions, those who said they were fighting all Nazism with all their Christianism—tomorrow, the Church will force them into silence or tolerate them, depending on the situation and the political turn of events. For the moment, depending on the occasion, it offers its faithful the double example of prelates who resist and prelates who consent.

October 9

Le Nouvelliste: Forty-six "terrorists" sentenced to death. A train derailed at Saint-Ambreuil. Attacks by the Resistance. The authors of these attacks and derailing of trains are all, according to Vichy, Communists. Their goal: "disorder and anarchy."

Through what mechanism does the university produce men like Déat and Pucheu*?

Claude is on duty tonight, guarding on the tracks. "Hey . . . you're not telling him not to go there?" Andrée François says. She's right. I should have gotten the peasants

---

[73] The title of Karl Oberg, also responsible for deporting over sixty thousand Jews from France, most of them murdered in Auschwitz. Twice sentenced to death, he was pardoned and released in 1962.

together and organized our refusal. Ten years ago, I should have organized universal resistance to war. A hundred years ago, I should have . . . a thousand years ago, I should have channeled history in the right direction.

October 13

I'm not capable of waiting any more, of waiting for the Allied landing, for the new era after the landing.

Poulette teases Jean Bouvard (he's six): "You're only a baby, you're only six." "Six," answers Jean Bouvard, "six is already something."

The atrocities in Poland and in Drancy.

I would like to know the process through which the German of legend, the tender and naïve German (as we see him in Balzac, for example) became the Nazi German. Was everything false in that legend?

October 18

Alone. Claude has been gone for three days. No light on the platform, dark train.

A letter from Suzanne tells me, with no details, that Vildrac* is in prison: Fresnes.[74]

And me? Hiding in my hole.[75] A coward. No doubt, but you, Vildrac, you are blamed for acts you're supposed to have committed; between your judges and you, there is a wisp of legal procedure. But I'm condemned in one block, guilty of an original sin with no redeemer, guilty in my soul and flesh, my guts and skin.

October 23

Today I yearn, not for the quays, not for the perspective of the Place de l'Étoile. What I am deprived of today is the Boulevard and the Faubourg Saint-Denis, the Boulevard and the Faubourg Saint-Martin, those places that bear so little resemblance to Haussmann's boulevards or to old prints, where strange, stunted people used to walk.[76] Will I ever see that tabac-café again, where poor singers would gather for an audition . . . ?

October 21

A failed attempt on de Brinon's life. "It is through an effect of the heavenly power, so to speak, that I was protected." This heavenly power did not protect

[74] Charles Vildrac was a playwright and poet, active in the Resistance.

[75] Since Werth was Jewish, he was a prime candidate for arrest by Vichy's police and deportation to Auschwitz.

[76] Baron Haussmann was responsible for renovating Paris from 1853 to 1870. Many old neighborhoods were demolished. The style of the five- or six-story apartment buildings erected in this period and beyond give central Paris the look it has today.

three informers for Germany in Cuisia. (Cuisia is about fifteen kilometers from here.)

October 26

I'm like everybody else, like the worst of them: I'm finding it long, I'm finding it slow. And this world, now nothing more than strategy!

The noble gesture. Laurent is sowing wheat. He has no idea how to go about it. He never looked at the pictures, or he didn't look at them hard enough. Out of that largo he is making a presto. His rather brusque, automatic movements lack ampleness, unction, and solemnity.[77]

A deputy is speaking. One of the first to join the Resistance, says the radio. But still that parliamentary vulgarity that turns uplifting words into dirty words.

October 28

Fog. You can seek out all shades of pink, yellow leaves and red leaves in it. But autumn has given me indigestion. I dream of asphalt, of a Paris façade under the rain, like a face under the veil of a hat.

In Saigon, I asked a European woman what kind of pleasure she felt in smoking opium, and she answered: "I don't know . . . I smoke to deaden my mind."

That's how I feel. But I don't have opium. So I read.

England, Russia, America, China, Communism, Nazism. They're just entities for café philosophers—but also the real world, the reality of the world.

October 29

Saint-Amour to Tournus by bike.[78] Fog thick as in a polder. In a schoolyard, I can't see the children, but their colored sweaters, like flying sparks in the smoke.

Le Villars. They successfully derailed some trains, except for the last one. They miscalculated the timing for removing the bolts. It wasn't a German train that was derailed but a passenger train. There were dead and wounded.

A bank employee in Paris: "Well, the war hasn't changed anything in *my* life . . ." Someone else, about Laval: "He'll swindle everybody."

---

[77] Werth is debunking a famous line of Victor Hugo's about "the sower" (*le geste auguste du semeur*). He is also alluding to the well-known painting by Jean-François Millet (1851) and to similar, debased images illustrating one of Vichy's propaganda themes: the nobility of the Eternal Peasant and the Soil, in contrast to the "decadent" city.

[78] Werth pedaled close to twenty-seven miles one way.

November 3

A German truck bumped into the horse-drawn wagon of the local squire—a collaborator—and sent it flying into the ditch. Aside from a wound on his nose, he wasn't badly hurt. The Germans got out of the truck, examined their hood and fenders, and, finding them more or less intact, went on their way without a glance at the wagon, the horse, or the driver. "The locals," says Andrée François, "tell the story with a laugh."

November 4

Auschwitz. One would like to respond with equal tortures, by a death whose torture lasts forever. And then we're crushed, anesthetized by that ultimate horror, by that infinite sadism. Never will the punishment equal the crime. Animals suffer less and die more quickly. And nothing can prevent this from having existed.

A train derailed a hundred meters or so from La Bifur. The Germans arrested two railroad guards but left them at the gendarmerie.

The Moscow conference is promising an idyllic Europe.[79] Hitler was promising a new order. The language of politics is like the language of love in that the same words have different or contrary meanings. The vocabulary of the lie and the truth are the same. But lies and truth are not identical for all of that.

In dreams, there are brand-new characters you never met when you were awake. Are they created or transformed by the dream, or simply not identified by the memory?

Culture. During his school years, the young bourgeois is confronted with Racine, Pascal, and Bossuet.* As soon as he gets out of school, he turns to Maurice Chevalier and crime novels, or worse: Giraudoux or Montherlant.*[80]

November 9

Hitler has spoken. He roared. He had prepared a putsch against the universe. The putsch is failing.

"I am a deeply religious man," he said.

---

[79] The joint statement of the Allies who met in Moscow in October 1943 promised to pursue the war to a victorious conclusion, punish perpetrators of atrocities, and work through the UN to limit armaments after the war.

[80] Jean Giraudoux is generally considered the most important French playwright between the two world wars, and the playwright and novelist Henry de Montherlant is still read today. Both had pro-German attitudes during the Occupation—particularly Montherlant. This probably influenced Werth's judgment.

November 10

In the station café. The cantilena of Madame Marie: life is hiding in this cantilena. A liter of *vin ordinaire* costs 50 francs. A liter of white, 65 francs. A pound of butter, 100 francs. A liter of marc, 200–500 francs. You have to sell a little glass for 10 francs. But the cheaters on the black market don't care about 10 francs. The shopkeeper said he'd gladly give you a tire, but for five pounds of butter and two liters of cooking oil. A German got off a stopped train. He was a doctor. He knocked on the window, he asked if he could come in, he said he was cold. He had a coffee. He was very polite. He was a Boche, OK, but he was very polite. There were railroad men there. They asked if the war would be over soon. He told them: "I'm neither Hitler nor Stalin."

November 11

On the station platform, two officers walk up and down, taking down the design of something or other. They seem swollen with lard. And they're not acting important for us; they don't see us. There is nobody on the platform. They're acting important for themselves. They smack down the heels of their boots and raise their heads. There are contradictions between those larded faces and that muscular tension. But that's the way it is.

NOTICE

The French nationals: 1. Hubert Arnaud, student in Toulouse; 2. Edmond Guyaud, student in Toulouse; 3. Jacques Sauvegrain, student in Lardenne; 4. André Vasseur, office worker in Toulouse, were sentenced to death October 24, 1943, by a German military court for participating in terrorist acts.

The condemned men had gathered in a mountain camp to fight German troops, where they were given weapons and military training. They fired to prevent the capture of the camp and caused losses among the German troops.

The verdict was carried out by firing squad November 9.

Der Kommandant des Heeresgebietes Suedfrankreich.

Those days, those nights between the sentence and the execution.

They killed Bergère, because she went out wandering and killed four of Balanod's rabbits. She used to visit us often at lunchtime. We won't hear the sound of her tail hitting against the walls anymore. They took her somewhere and hanged her. And during that last trip, she probably jumped up on their shoulders and nuzzled them.

"You see that man," says Madame Marie. "The Germans executed his son by firing squad in Dijon. He was eighteen." (I remember. A bomb thrown into a café. Four young men sentenced to death, on vague clues.)[81] The man goes by, carrying one of those baskets railroad men use to hold their provisions. "He was like a dead man," Madame Marie says. "He's a little better now; he has another son in the maquis and another one who's younger."

I learn from Suzanne's letter that the Militia arrested André Berney in Villars. He defended himself with his revolver. But he's the one who was wounded in the arms and legs. A few hours after I had left.

When Laurent's daughter brings back news from the town, you'd think she's humming a few bits of a song. Does it come to her just like that? And if they ask her for more information about a detail, she repeats her bit of song as is.

The station café. Madame Marie stumbles if her heart isn't guiding her. She doesn't know how to filter things out, to examine things closely. And so, talking of the Lormiers (the father was arrested by the Germans), she repeats different versions and doesn't even dismiss the ones that are revolting calumnies. "There's espionage at the bottom of all this," she says; "they got a lot of money." I protest but I'm not sure I've persuaded her. And she answers immediately: "They shouldn't have hidden that Englishwoman." (I don't know who that Englishwoman is.) "You can't do things like that. Now, I love France more than anything. But you can't forget the Germans are here and they have ears." And now a third theme: "Those young people weren't serious-minded enough, they were imprudent." All that is vague for her, with no clear outline.

I've already said jealousy seems to play a more important role with the peasants than it does with city dwellers. Laurent tells me about a farmer the Germans arrested in a village. "He might've talked too much," he says. "All it takes is a glass of wine and he starts talking. Besides, he's a fisherman and a poacher. There are Militiamen everywhere. Someone might've informed on him. And not just because of politics but out of fishermen's jealousy. All that . . . it gets mixed up."

---

[81] The total number of French *résistants* or hostages executed by the Nazis during the Occupation is estimated at twenty-five thousand. Roughly six thousand more were killed in collective massacres, such as Oradour-sur-Glane (June 10, 1944).

The radio. A letter written by a young man of sixteen, a few hours or a few moments before going before the firing squad. It hurts so much you don't know if it hurts. Authentic or not? Or modified by a few added touches?

In 1914, most French soldiers left for the front to kill war. In 1918, they set down their victory at the feet of their rulers, saluted, and trotted home like the last of the three little pigs. Except for the dead. We know what the rulers did with the victory. Today millions of men are fighting to kill Nazism. What will be done with their victory? And already I can read or hear the same lies we read before 1914 and 1939 about Lebanon or Indochina.[82]

Marshal Smuts has declared that as France has collapsed, it will disappear as a great power at the same time as Italy and Germany.[83] He suggests that peoples, nations, will be worth only what their industrial power might be. He seems to confine himself to strict historical materialism. As if the morals, sciences, and arts—"superstructures," as Marx called them—were directly dependent on the economy and military power. As if they didn't have their own free play, once they're freed from their economic straitjacket. We don't know beforehand what blood will circulate in the veins of a victory or in the veins of a defeat.

"Why fight?" the shoemaker says to me. "Why not all be brothers, without devouring each other?"

I saw one of them, a real one, on the way to the station. With rolls of fat on the nape of his neck, a real pack of booted lard, big ears, and a face like a snout. But the one who drew him and hates this kind of German more than anyone is George Grosz, a German.

The blue eyes of the female Siamese cat. Nothing human in them, nothing animal either. They're mineral.

---

[82] Indochina (Vietnam, Laos, and Cambodia) was then a French colony; Lebanon, a French mandate.

[83] Jan Smuts, the strongly pro-English prime minister of South Africa, had made a speech that was denounced by Vichy propaganda.

December 7

The meeting in Tehran between Churchill, Roosevelt, and Stalin. Perfect agreement for a terrible war and an idyllic peace.[84]

Mornings in Paris (a letter from Suzanne): "We wash without soap, we can't polish our shoes, and for breakfast we have some watery concoction."

Grenoble. Five hundred hostages sent to Germany. A bomb in a barracks. Close to a hundred Germans killed.[85] (Radio.)

A train derailed at Moulin-des-Ponts. Just one car left the rails. "They arrested the railroad guards," Laurent's son tells me. "They searched them. One of them was smoking a cigarette. A German ripped it out of his mouth and threw it on the ground. He called the guards 'French filth.' Another one was drunk; he grabbed a Frenchman by the neck and almost strangled him."

I meet Debeau, who was on duty here that very night. "We were keeping warm around a coal fire," he says. "We were having a bite to eat. A German patrol went by. They said something we didn't get and then: 'Au revoir, Messieurs.'"

Why this contrast between the Germans' brutality in Moulin-des-Ponts and their good manners in Saint-Amour? According to Debeau, the ones here are gendarmes, the ones in Moulin-des-Ponts are from the Gestapo.

December 8

"I think of the ports I loved so much," Suzanne writes, "in Marseilles and Toulon. On some days, I'm not sure what I feel and I wonder if Clavel might not be completely right this time."[86]

Clavel wouldn't have known how to build ports. And we're forgetting that in 1914, rightly or wrongly, Clavel became a soldier of his own free will. Then he despaired and rejected everything about the war and all things of that kind.

---

[84] The three Great Powers met for the first time in Tehran from November 28 to December 2. The atmosphere was indeed quite cordial, all the more so as Roosevelt tried to charm Stalin. They reached an agreement on military strategy (the Anglo-Saxons would land on the Channel coasts) and political questions (the United Nations would be founded; Germany would be punished; Poland's borders would be changed to enable the Soviet Union to recover the territories it lost in 1920).—J.-P. A.

[85] The Germans arrested hundreds of Grenoblois demonstrating on Armistice Day (November 11) and deported 450 of them. In retaliation, the Resistance blew up the artillery of the German garrison on the night of the thirteenth; the Germans then executed a new batch of hostages. Thanks to the complicity of a Polish soldier forced into the Wehrmacht, the Resistance was able to blow up the barracks in Grenoble: there were a few French victims, more than fifty German soldiers killed, and two hundred wounded.—J.-P. A.

[86] Clavel is the protagonist of Werth's two semi-autobiographical novels about World War I. He is a soldier who is utterly disenchanted with war.

Today, if Clavel rejected everything about war and denied everything about war, wouldn't he also be rejecting what makes him hate war?

The station café. "What about the men in Dijon?" Madame Marie asks the conductor, who's from Dijon. "There are five of them . . . and a woman, too. All sentenced to death." "Why?" "The Resistance . . ." "People shouldn't get involved in politics today. This is no time to show what you think."

As soon as they heard about the death sentences, the engineers decided to go on strike for two hours. "For two hours," says the railroad man, "not one locomotive left the depot. If they execute them, there'll be a general strike. Or two depots will go on strike at the very least."

Sometimes social passions, conscious or not, are revealed in an intonation. When that railroad worker was saying "not one locomotive left . . ." you could feel the power of his group in him, his own power and the anger of the people.

Similarly, when the old Paris shopkeeper who has taken refuge in town says "the terrorists, those hoodlums," her throat tightens and her face goes tense with hatred.

The legend of the marshal is still crawling along, dying, in a few heads. The wine merchant believes in a captive marshal, with the people around him blocking sounds from the outside . . .

An order from the Régie[87] to the town's tobacconists: immediately turn in December's tobacco. "Because of the terrorists, who loot the tobacco shops." A strange new conception of order. To avoid revolutionary requisitions for the maquis, it orders the tobacconists to empty their shops. As if, after a bank robbery, an order were given to depositors to withdraw their money.

The Germans are defeated. The war will end when they agree to stop acting like conquerors. They are defeated. The problem is, they don't want to recognize it.

German Europe: the people who're imprisoned, the people who're hungry, the people who sleep on rotten straw mattresses, the people who are beaten, the people who are killed. I think of the minutes between the time they left their cell and the order of the head of the firing squad, that order—the last human sound heard by those adolescents killed in Besançon.

---

[87] The Régie française des tabacs, then a monopoly, is the French national tobacco company. It still exists, privatized and under a different name.

According to the ILO, the transfers of European populations have affected 30 million people.[88] This figure seems unlikely. In any case, with murders and transfers, they're giving me a sum of suffering that is too strong. It is well known that big traumatisms are less painful than light wounds. They go beyond one's sensibility. The sum of sufferings they're giving me to absorb is too strong. I can no longer feel them. I have nothing more sensitive than my egoism; I no longer feel anything but my own suffering.

December 10

Laurent, who went to the market in Gigny, learned that armed, masked men forced the tobacconist in Montagna to give them his stock of tobacco. "The men in the maquis need tobacco," they said.

What's surprising here is that Laurent, a prudent peasant (and a friend of the tobacconist) judges the masked men from Montagna indulgently, even sympathetically. His smile, which is not disapproving, is a sign.

December 13

The DNB[89] announces that "about four thousand Polish children, deported by the Soviets and separated from their parents, have died of neglect. According to witnesses, the children who were able to leave the Soviet Union were veritable skeletons dressed in rags, covered with eczema and wounds from head to foot."

The writer for the agency gives no place names. He didn't have the time to pick up an atlas and choose the name of a far-off locality. However, he doesn't fail to state that these children "were separated from their parents." Through a trick of bookkeeping, a trick of macabre accounting, he's made a transfer: he's put the children of the Vel' d'Hiv into another column.

December 17

Three Germans killed in Oyonnax. Five hostages shot. Two hundred people arrested.

Since the debacle, L—— has preferred Goethe to Shakespeare. As for the vulgar themes of propaganda, with what astonishing skill, worthy of a magician, does he relieve them of their weight! Manipulated by him, they are no more than nuances and reflections. Whatever the outcome of events, at least one of his

---

[88] Established by the League of Nations after World War I, the International Labor Organization is now a UN agency. The figure of displaced persons cited here is probably a conservative estimate, despite Werth's doubts.

[89] One of the main German propaganda agencies under the Nazis.

shimmering ideas will prove his uninterrupted loyalism to the winner, whoever he may be.

December 24

German cruelty and sadism. Torture to make people talk, torture to make people suffer. Mass murder. How can one measure the extent of the responsibility each German shares? The cruelty of the French colonists is, no doubt, of an infinitely weaker order. And it was never a system, a doctrine (except in groups of corrupt administrators). And always, almost always, it was dissimulated, hypocritical. But it existed. So consider the extent of the responsibility each Frenchman shares in those acts of cruelty. Consider, too, that most of those acts were not known to the French. Evaluate the number of Frenchmen for whom this ignorance itself was a crime—people who wanted not to know.

Who, considering the Germans' acts of cruelty, cannot hate Germans? Look that hatred straight in the face. You have to look that hatred straight in the face. Must one give in to it completely? Can you believe that a new world, a less despicable world, can be born from that hatred? What should one do with that hatred when the motives for it are only in the past? The worst would be to forget. The worst would be to subordinate everything to that hatred. And how should punishment be meted out? What punishment would be effective? Yes, how should we act, with our hatred? With our hatred of Germans, who killed and tortured, with our hatred of the French who were their accomplices?

December 27

A literary program on Radio-Vichy. It is disconcertingly stupid. If a moon dweller dropped from the sky or a Huron landed in Europe today and heard that, they would have thought France is going to have a very hard time getting back on its feet.

Hopes. A German battleship sunk. The Russians west of Kiev have advanced forty kilometers along a front of eighty kilometers.

Philippe Henriot.* The tightening of his voice at the tip of his lips and above the palate, a tough-guy intonation. It's not natural. He's playing at playing the traitor.

The idea the peasants have of the maquis is stronger than all the ideas that German or Hitlerite-Vichy propaganda try to impose on them. Without exaggerating at all, we can say that the maquis merges with their France and with their freedom (in the rawest, most material sense). Whatever the maquis may be, it's their maquis. If they talk about it, it's in an affectionate tone of voice.

In Nantua or Annemasse, the men of the maquis punished a woman who was denouncing the men evading the Compulsory Work Service. They didn't kill her. They threw her into the street in her shirtsleeves after smearing her with colored paint.

December 30

"They stopped the van near Coligny," Laurent says. "They took the tobacco the tobacconist went to get in Bourg." And he says that to me with a smile.

He should be afraid for his cows and his wheat. He should be cursing the Communist bandits. But he tells me this like a good joke. The way the peasants see this is a sign.

Those tortured men and women who don't divulge any information for a week, two weeks, and give in to physical pain and exhaustion after a week or two weeks.

Suzanne and Claude have left. I can see their faces—as if through a higher faculty than the memory of the eyes—reduced to the most fleeting, most moving, most immaterial quality of their expressions.

1944

January 5

I've decided to leave for Paris tomorrow.

January 6 and 7

Ghostlike Louhans, the Seille River, the trees on the banks of the Seille caught in the hard, cold night's hard mist, filtered through the moonlight.

A waiting room. A gendarme traveling by train, magnificent as a Napoleonic general. Three gendarmes on duty are inspecting luggage (for butter or meat) with no particular zeal. One of them, smiling, acts like a man of the world, above this task. He has the smile of a society lecturer. The two others have heads of extraordinary thickness, the heads of flattened monsters.

Train. The corridors are full of travelers standing, sitting on the floor or on a suitcase. Considered as a mass, you'd think it was a bunch of immigrants. One of them looks like Gandhi. The cap of a German soldier appears and disappears. A movement of the crowd brought me nearer to Gandhi, who says, without a preamble, "They won't be here for long." It's joyfully obvious for him, and he can't imagine that it would be less agreeable for others. And he adds: "The noon communiqué was good . . ."

A little before Dijon, a dark-haired woman, not ugly, rather elegant, speaks to me over a few shoulders and heads. She has chosen me. She asks what side we get off at when we reach Dijon. I've been standing throughout the trip and my body is stiff; my skin feels rough. I'm somnolent; I rock my body to the music of Harmonika Zug, as Larbaud* wrote.[1] But I make myself young, lively, and positively perky. I answer with gallant, noble courtesy. She's a foreigner. She speaks with an accent I take for English. But Gandhi whispers: "She's German. She's coming from Chamonix."

---

[1] German for "harmonica train," from a line in Valéry Larbaud's 1913 poem "Ode"—an ode to a train.

I'm sorry for my politeness to this member of the occupying forces. I'm ashamed of it, as of a betrayal. In Dijon, she calls through the door window to German soldiers standing on the platform. She speaks to them for a long time in a loud voice. She seems to be preaching through the door: she has no manners. One of the soldiers comes into the car and takes her suitcases.

Seven o'clock in the morning when we pulled out of the station in Lyon. It's night now. Strange Paris. A dark block, punctured by narrow reddish lights from the sky to the ground. I haven't seen Paris for three and a half years. It has turned into this dark block. The blind frenzy of the corridors in the metro. But right away, I feel the warmth of the city.

How sweet and tender the asphalt is to my feet! How beautiful the façade of the house on the other side of the street!

January 9

In the Nalewki quarter in Warsaw, I saw those old Jews with their *peyes* walking with their heads down, as if eternally pursued by the kick in the ass fate would give them.[2] Sometimes the Chosen People, the people prefiguring Christianity, sometimes the people constructed by the anti-Semites: temporally all-powerful or a virus in the healthy body of other peoples.

(See the first chapter on the Reformation in Michelet's *History of France*.)[3] The anti-Semitism of the fifteenth century can be superimposed on the anti-Semitism of the tsars and the anti-Semitism of Hitler.

Sometimes doctors were heard to complain that the Jews were cluttering up French medicine.[4] I have never heard a Sorbonne professor complain that there were too many Jewish philosophers in the Sorbonne. Must one accept a grossly materialistic explanation for this? One hesitates. And yet . . .

January 15

A walk with Suzanne. A walk in the night. I go out only at night. The shops are oases of discrete lights. In the shops, there are men, women, and not shades. A few little islands of life and light: those shops, those scraps of apotheoses in the darkness.

---

[2] From 1940 on, the Nazis had crammed some 400,000 Polish Jews into the Nalewki quarter, which became the Warsaw ghetto.

[3] The great historian Jules Michelet denounced anti-Semitism, although, perhaps unknown to Werth, some of his statements about Jews are highly anti-Semitic.

[4] A pertinent remark. During the 1930s, a good many French doctors openly professed their anti-Semitism. Pretexting the arrival of Jewish doctors, refugees from Germany, the medical profession pushed through the Armbruster Law as early April 1933: it limited the exercise of medicine to those who were born in France.—J.-P. A.

On the Boulevard Saint-Germain, a people of shadows slips through the darkness. We're at the bottom of the sea. We are grazed by the fauna of the abyss, by the fauna of vertical shadows, the shadows of seahorses.

Basch (eighty-one) and his wife killed in Lyon by the Militia. One of the generation of professors who believed in justice. Births and abortions from the Dreyfus affair.[5] I stayed away from him because he was just too eloquent. I felt submerged by it. Committee for the Defense of Freedom of Expression. One afternoon, between 1913 and 1914, I was at his place on rue Huysmans, with Mirbeau.[6] Two or three years ago, I accompanied my friend Latarjet to the library in Lyon. Basch was sitting at a table, reading, working. He got up and walked across the room. His step was lively and his back straight. He didn't see me; I did not make my presence known. These chance encounters draw the life of Victor Basch for me, an "activist" and a professor, devoted to what was then called social idealism.

January 16

The Seine at night, the Seine invisible. I look in vain for the colonnades of reflections, the colonnades of enchanted palaces that the lights on the bridges used to project on it. I look in vain for the Seine. Between the two banks, I can't even make out a hollow.

January 17

From the letter of a woman in the middling bourgeoisie: "They're talking about evacuating us! I hope it's just a tall tale like so many others. I can't see myself abandoning my whole house. And go where, for God's sake? Well, what will be, will be. But above all we've got a good chance of seeing some very ugly things happening. Because Communists and other people will come in with the English and that will be utterly charming for bourgeois like us! Who can trust people like that? Anyone who does is quite mad! To tell the truth, I trust no one, except for our dear marshal. But perhaps he isn't surrounded by the people he wants and isn't free to do what he wants. The poor man is having a sad end to his life, and I feel for him with all my heart."

This is propaganda made flesh. As for the tender feelings for the marshal, that has more distant, darker sources, in the spaces where historical

---

[5] Victor and Hélène Basch were arrested in Lyon on January 10. They were assassinated outside the city by two Militia leaders in the presence of a member of the German police. A professor emeritus at the Sorbonne, Victor Basch publicly supported the Popular Front in 1935 and was president of the Ligue des Droits de l'Homme (League for the Rights of Man). A militant anti-fascist, he was also Jewish, another reason the Militia hated him. For Dreyfus, see p. 167, note 69.

[6] Werth was so close to the novelist Octave Mirbeau that he became known as "Mirbeau's secretary." Luis Buñuel's film *Journal d'une femme de chambre* (*Diary of a Chambermaid*) is based on Mirbeau's novel of that name.

legends are created and real characters are transformed into stage characters, actors in a melodrama, with a simplified mechanism. Already, on the roads of the debacle, a Parisian shopkeeper was telling me: "I feel so sorry for Pétain, the victor of Verdun, getting into the railroad car in Rethondes as a defeated man!"[7]

I quote again: "Soviet practices are becoming more and more common here and give us a taste of what the Russian victory holds in store for us. Poor France, in what an appalling turn of events do we find ourselves! And what will we be forced to see? We tremble a bit more every day."

January 28

Vague rumors. As soon as the Allies land, any civilian going through the streets of Paris will be shot immediately. Women and children will also be forbidden to walk around the streets. So the Parisians will have a choice between dying from a submachine-gun bullet or dying of hunger. The day before yesterday, the police rounded up people in front of the Montparnasse station. Every day seems to add another drop of defeat to the Germans, but they seem more fearsome than in the time when they held all the reins of victory.

"It's not happening quickly," says Andrée François, who listened to the radio.

The atmosphere is heavy, time is heavy. In twenty years, it will all be summed up in two pages of a textbook, reduced to calligraphic facts, with downstrokes and upstrokes.

January 30

Last night, dinner at Febvre's,* with the Marc Blochs.*[8] A fine tablecloth and crystals under the light, the glasses bathing in watery light. We don't talk of what's happening right away. There is a time for supple conversation, without pushing it. You'd think it was the prewar years. In the course of the evening, we do touch on the war. Churchill is the Clémenceau* of this war. His cabinet is a war cabinet. A few years ago, Churchill showed his sympathy for Mussolini and his hatred of Bolshevism. The Americans have a childish fear of Communism. They still see Pétain as a guarantee of order.

---

[7] When Pétain agreed to the Armistice, Hitler demanded that it be signed at the same spot as the 1918 Armistice that ratified German defeat in World War I. Pétain's delegates signed it in a train car at Rethondes in the forest of Compiègne on June 22, 1940, in Hitler's presence. The car was then sent to Berlin as a trophy.

[8] Marc Bloch's memoir of the June debacle, posthumously published in 1946, is a brilliant analysis of the "strange defeat" (its title in English translation) by a combatant who was also an important historian.

As for me, I get lost in those clouds of high politics. And I know nothing about America and even England. I'm hanging on to that Allied landing, which will transfigure everything.

Madame V——. As Suzanne tells her about German cruelty and "atrocities": "I don't know anything," she says. "We don't know anything. I don't know any victims of German cruelty." There is a certain kind of lady who *doesn't know*. Bitch.

"How about Jeanne, how is she reacting? How does she feel about the war?" "Jeanne," answers Madeleine B——, "Jeanne isn't interested in politics."

January 31

A moonlit night, yesterday. I didn't find the Seine heavy and black again, with its columns of reflections: the Seine was pale; I was going to say blonde. These past evenings, I wandered through thick darkness, without contours. But the moonlight draws spaces; their extent and the façades that limit them. So that Paris, without pedestrians, without cars, resembles a huge architectural project, an enormous urbanist's model. I walk for a long time in this solitude and this emptiness. At last I meet a few passersby. I hear their voices. Five or six pedestrians are the only sound in a Paris with no background noise—the sound of clogs, which reminds me of the nights in Indochina. Then silence once again and solitude all the way to Saint-Sulpice, where there's a long line of candidates for the audience in front of the Cinéma Bonaparte.

Nobody has said a word to me about Hitler's speech. François, who was in the line in front of the grocer's, said nothing to me about this speech. The street didn't listen to Hitler. The street didn't try to guess the future from Hitler's speech. As if it thought he was out of the picture. I only learned of it through an issue of *Paris-Midi* that was used to wrap herrings.

"If the Bolshevik colossus were to win, ten years later the oldest civilized continent would have lost all its characteristics."

Two comments. Hitler has funny notions about the age of civilizations. And then he'd boasted several times of having destroyed the military power of the Soviet Union, and today he recognizes its "colossal" character. It's his only concession to events, to reality.

February 2

Dined with Hany Lefebvre. Noémi gives us a sober account of her stay in Fresnes. The prisoners communicated through the heating vents. They sent each other messages, bread, sweaters. A magnificent clandestine commerce between a woman with an advanced degree in history, a practicing Catholic, a woman of "high Protestant society," a factory worker who earned her living at eight and lived through years of hunger and slums, and her. What kind of spirit animated and united those women, so different, so separated through their origins and class? But what will happen to their unity and friendship once the war is over?

Noémi is sleeping at her mother's tonight. Her husband called her (with no explanations, of course) to say it was more prudent. The Gestapo arrested Prenant. A letter from Louise tells us that the mayor of Villars, who is seventy-two, was arrested along with his son.[9]

Meanwhile, F—— keeps doing his little jobs for newspapers and the radio. If I told him of these facts and the tortures and executions, he would say: "Oh, yes . . . Are you really sure? It is quite hard to know the truth." Perhaps he would even show some small distress, a vague unease. But as for prison, deportations, torture, and death, he'd drive them far away, he'd write them off. He, too, would more or less say, "I'm not interested in politics." Besides, didn't he pay his dues? In 1940, as he had left Paris, didn't workers repairing a drainpipe get into his apartment through the balcony and steal a brand-new pair of pajamas from him?

Hitler's latest speech. He's not fighting the English or the Russians anymore but the Jews and the Bolsheviks. (True, if we're to believe the core of Allied propaganda, the Allies are no longer fighting the Germans but the Nazis.) That way, Hitler can think he won't be defeated by the English or the Russians, since he's not at war with them.

The wife of the Jewish tailor on rue Vavin had obtained permission to go with her granddaughter to see her son-in-law in Compiègne. As they were leaving the camp in Compiègne, they were arrested and sent to Drancy.

What struck me right away about Noémi, who was so flighty in the past, is her simplicity, without the slightest vanity or romanticism: she lives this new, dangerous life as if she had always lived this way, as if it were quite natural for her to live this way.

February 3

The maquis in Upper Savoy. Squadrons of well-armed police. The mass of French people is torn between hope and the impatience for an Allied landing, which even leads to a dull anger at England. A strange declaration (or interview) by General

---

[9] Marcel Prenant, a renowned biologist and a Communist activist, joined the Resistance when he got out of *Oflag* [officers' prison camp] at the end of 1941. He became chief of staff of the military committee of the FTP [one of the main Resistance groups in France] from 1942 until his arrest on January 28, 1944. He was tortured and deported but returned from the Neuengamme concentration camp. Louise was a cousin of Suzanne Werth's.—J.-P. A.

A French gendarme guards inmates at the Drancy concentration camp. Drancy, originally a modern housing complex fifteen miles from Paris, was a stop on the way to Auschwitz from 1941 to 1944. *Bundesarchiv, Bild 183-B10919*

Montgomery. It can be summed up like this: "I'm beginning to get sick of this war . . . But I undertake a strategic operation only when I'm sure it will succeed."

February 4

I think of the sign in front of old inns: "Lodging on foot or on horseback." Every night, the sofa of the big room is transformed into a bed. Our guests sleep there for one night, two nights, go away, return. Thus Colonel Vendeur, who commanded a regiment of Moroccan riflemen, and Aymé-Guerrin . . .[10]

"The Jews," says Madame N——, "held all the reins of power. They should understand that Germany's obliged to defend itself, after all. The Jews should just keep quiet. We have Jewish friends. They have nothing to complain about." (It's hard to say where vileness ends and stupidity begins.)

Suzanne has given a bed for a few nights to a young Jewish woman hounded by the Gestapo. Timid, fearful. Her voice is dim. Her husband is a prisoner. Her

---

[10] Colonel Vendeur was a *résistant* who would often stay in Suzanne Werth's apartment on rue d'Assas. Aymé-Guerrin was a *résistant* who worked with Suzanne Werth.—J.-P. A.

brothers were deported, her sisters are being hunted. Her father's a tailor and has no work, since all work is forbidden to him. He's sick, worn out. He took refuge in a hospice in Saint-Cloud where the Gestapo has already arrested elderly people.

Until a few days ago, she worked as a milling-machine operator in a factory. She wasn't home when the Gestapo knocked on the door of her place and smashed it in. The neighbors looted the apartment and shared the linens and the pots and pans. Some nuns found her a position as a maid in Tours. She's supposed to leave tomorrow morning. She hesitated. Should she leave or stay near her father? She wanted to take him with her; she thought she could hide him in Tours or around there. But he won't budge. "I'm too old," he says. "If they want to take me, they'll take me. I'll suffer with the others, if I have to suffer."

Today she went to see some friends. They'd been arrested an hour before. The door was shut with official seals on it.

All she owns is a little underwear, which she carries half in a bundle, half in a shopping bag.

It seems to me collaboration and resistance are as different as black and white. And it's true that a few people found certainty deep inside themselves as early as June 1940. But how many have wavered! And it's impossible to know if they gave in to self-interest, to the pressures of propaganda, or if they were reeling from the shocks of the times.

But the N——s and the P——s, those who swung this way and that, bounced around, those flaccid bodies who don't even own up to their cynicism—who may not even admit it to themselves—those collaborators who turned an eye to London, those Gaullists who sometimes still turned an eye to Vichy, those faithful friends waiting, without wanting it, for the return to a world where I would have the right to live, who have no problem tolerating a world that excludes me . . . to take up the slightest comradery with them again would be to deny the little I believe in: it would mean dying.

February 8

Father Perrenet has just been arrested by the Gestapo. He's the head of the Ollier youth center, with his brother. From our windows, we can see the building and the courtyard of the center.

Neither the peasants nor the people of the town knew the name of Déat.* But on the walls of Paris, I saw his name in letters almost as big as the name of Mistinguett.

I go out only at night.

February 10

In 1939, Madeleine B——, a patriot 1914 style, wore a fine military tunic, a split skirt, and a military cap. In those days gone by, when she heard the account of an aerial dogfight on the radio where German planes crashed burning to the ground, a flame of lust flickered in her eyes, and she salivated abundantly. Then came the time when she said: "We can't forget we're defeated." And, as one says "I don't have the heart to deprive old women of the faith that consoles them," she added: "You have faith in England; I don't want to deprive you of your illusions." She also said: "France is rotten: Germany, a young people, can regenerate her." Today she's a Gaullist, a fervent Gaullist. But she wouldn't hide an English parachutist for five whole minutes.

B—— has forgotten that after the debacle he was saying, "If Europe is constructed by Germany or another people, it doesn't matter. As for me, I prefer Goethe to Shakespeare, and the English are neither philosophers nor musicians." He has totally forgotten that. And if someone reminded him of it, he would deny it in all good faith. Memory is a strange faculty.

February 13

Everywhere you hear the word "Gaullist." You hear the name of de Gaulle less frequently. There is a contrast between the immense historical role which was—which is—his, and a certain eclipsing of his personage. He spoke when all was silent, when everyone was silent or spoke like cowards. He acted when everyone had given up. He made France enter history when she had been evicted from history. But no one made him a legend, and he didn't make himself a legend. He doesn't dispense justice under his oak tree. He doesn't pinch the ears of enlisted soldiers.[11]

Mandouze* brought me a few issues of the *Courrier Français du Témoignage Chrétien* ("A Connection to the Front of Spiritual Resistance against Hitlerism").[12] Its theme is that urgent things must be done first. The present danger is Hitler. "Perverse" as it may be, and alarming in its materialism,

---

[11] The image of King Louis IX (later, Saint Louis) holding court under the oak is legendary in France, and Napoleon was famous for affectionately pinching the ears of his officers.

[12] Werth mentions the *Cahiers du Témoignage Chrétien* as early as October 1942. See p. 169, n.72. This offshoot could be called "The Christian witness mail." Both were, of course, underground publications.—D. B.

The first issue of the *Courrier Français du Témoignage Chrétien* (fifty thousand copies) appeared in May 1943, launched with the full consent of Reverend Father Chaillet; André Mandouze was the editor in chief. With this new publication, they hoped to increase the readership of the *Cahiers*, whose presentation was austere.—J.-P. A.

Bolshevism is only a potential risk. And besides: "We are not opposed to every-thing in the complex movement that is Communism. We are not against the desire to lift the working class out of its undeserved poverty . . . and to elimi-nate certain privileges that no longer have any justification . . ."

And now here's the archbishop of Toulouse using a language that has a quasi-Marxist sound to it: "The scourge of the proletariat must disappear." "It is scan-dalous that abundance should produce poverty and that technology, instead of liberating the worker, should enslave him."

Catholics and Communists work together in resistance organizations.

February 16

Night. Light rain. Boulevard Raspail. So many memories buried in that dark mass! I can only see fragments of façades and poor lights, lights as dull as shad-ows. My eyes grope along the boulevard. Thus do the dead, if they go out walk-ing, vainly try—with invisible signs, scattered and not anchored in space—to reconstitute their memories, which flee from them.

February 22

Rumors these past few days: evacuation of the 6th and 7th arrondissements. Already the rumor has vanished. Another one: they're preparing the Vel' d'Hiv to pen in the Masons, Jews, and "left-wingers."

February 26

The radio. Broadcast of the Special Commission on Jewish Questions. The read-er's voice, an unwashed, filthy voice.

There are common elements in all the systems of the Cagoule,[13] whether they're made from rigid ideas or ideas in liquefaction. Thus, before Hitler and the French post-Hitlerites, Maurras* denounced Jews, Masons, immigrants, and Protestants in the same breath at the beginning of his career.

February 28

From Lyon. Twenty-two corpses of young men from eighteen to twenty-two deposed at the Pavillon d'Anatomie. All killed by a pistol shot to the head. A German soldier had been killed. They were taken as hostages.

Rumors. "There won't be a mass landing by the English. They'll set up a beach-head in Belgium, like the one they have in Italy. Two motionless fronts and we'll never see the end of it. As for the Russians, they'll ally themselves with the Japanese against England."

---

[13] The Cagoule (literally, "the balaclava") was a violent far-right organization active in the 1930s.

La Gerbe, February 24. I had never seen an issue of *La Gerbe*, *Au Pilori*, or *L'Œuvre*.[14] Nothing unexpected.

An article by Robert Vallery-Radot: Spiritualist civilization, which came from Egypt, India, and China, led to Christianity. It is threatened by materialist rationalism. The article is called "The Beast and the Gods." The beast: the eighteenth-century authors of the *Encyclopédie* and Marx. Hitler is among the gods. The author is obviously retarded.[15]

March 2

Le Matin.[16] The technique of an agent provocateur applied to the news.

Headline: "They wanted to blow up the Sistine Chapel. The Reds put an Anglo-American bomb inside it." "Rome, March 1. The papal guard discovered a time bomb in the Sistine Chapel on Thursday, February 17." (The news item, like the bomb, has a delaying fuse.) "An expert investigation established that the bomb was of Anglo-American origin. . . . Ecclesiastic circles are persuaded that it's a Communist terrorist attack."

An astonishing identity: Reds, Anglo-Americans, and Communists.

March 3

Goering* spoke on "Aviation Day." Laval* spoke to "120 presidents of Craft and Trade Associations, the elite of the French craft industry." Goering's proclamation has the style of a military man. Goering speaks, Laval speaks. No one listens. Laval's speech counts no more than the speech he would have given twenty years ago at the inauguration of a hospital or a brothel. I read it anyway. "If I cared about my person, I wouldn't be here! I don't need to be here! I love the countryside . . . I love the fields like a peasant loves his fields; I love the life of the earth; I love the simple life . . ."

---

[14] Respectively, "The sheaf" (the original meaning of the word "fascist"), "To the pillory," and "The task."—D. B.

Werth is discovering the collaborationist press of the Northern Zone: *L'Œuvre*, a daily that reappeared in September 1940, was politically controlled by Marcel Déat; *La Gerbe*, a weekly that appeared in July 1940, was founded by Alphonse de Chateaubriant,* the head of the movement called Collaboration. *Au Pilori*, a weekly created in July 1940, specialized in the propagation of extreme, murderous anti-Semitism.—J.-P. A.

[15] Robert Vallery-Radot, a Catholic fundamentalist, specialized in combatting the Masons; he was the editor in chief of *Documents maçonniques*. The article in question does, in fact, have no interest whatsoever.—J.-P. A.

The *Encyclopédie*, whose editor in chief was Denis Diderot, is one of the great documents of the Enlightenment.—D. B.

[16] "Morning." One of the main daily newspapers in Paris—violently collaborationist, of course. Another was *Le Petit Parisien*, mentioned further on.

In yesterday's *Le Matin*, a photo where we see Chateaubriant, de Brinon,* Philippe Henriot,* and Dr. Eich all together.[17] They're creating a "press club for the French, the Germans, and foreigners." (In de Brinon's France, the Germans are no longer "foreigners.")

March 4

Noémi in a field at night. Was the plane able to land? Where is she? In London? Or in the sea? I see her floating, drowning in a white dress, in a long white dress. Why a white dress?

The trial of Pucheu.*[18] A few fragments from the radio. He wasn't a collaborator. He tried to save hostages. He had nothing to do with the repression in France, in the organization of a police state. It was Darlan's* fault. He was playing a double game. From these slivers of a report given news-agency style, we can't tell if he's lying, using a subtle dialectic, or even if there's a particle of truth in his defense.

March 6

I hardly feel impatient at all anymore. Wake me up when it's over. The most magnificent military operations of the Russians leave me cold. Now I can accept only definitive results.

A few of our most recent friends sleep in a different bed every night.

March 8

"Pucheu must be shot," says Colonel Vendeur. "No legal formalities or philosophical considerations. As long as the Germans are here, I want to be a military brute, I want to be nothing but a military brute."

An armed detachment of German soldiers is marching by my window. They're singing. But they're following orders. The day the marshal visited Bourg, that's the way a detachment of his cops were singing.

When I was doing my military service, we would sing lovely obscene songs on the road. But not following orders.

Le Petit Parisien. Aspects of Paris. A kid who jumped through a fourth-story window to escape from the police, collectors who have 1 million gold pieces and 2 million in stamps in their apartments.

From the same *Petit Parisien*: "Several women and an old man were killed by terrorist attacks.—Nine terrorists have been shot.—Philippe Henriot, talking

---

[17] Sonderführer Eich was the head of the press group of the German propaganda services.—J.-P. A.

[18] Pierre Pucheu was being tried in Algeria, now under the control of the Free French: the country was liberated by Operation Torch, the Allied landing in November 1942.

on the radio from Annecy to young men in the maquis, implores them to think of their duty before they let themselves be dragged into crime."

But here's something that has another ring to it:

> The fight against traitors and organized crime.
> Marcel Gerbas was executed February 14 for spying, attempted treason, and theft of ten thousand francs from a craftsman in Coligny.
> Gustave Lacroix was executed in Coligny February 19 for 1. Denunciation of a patriot, who was odiously tortured; 2. Complicity and fencing ten thousand stolen francs; . . .
> The maquis had to bring order to this crime, which so often goes along with treason.
> —Les Francs-Tireurs et Partisans Français.[19]

This was copied by Old François. He sent us the copy with no comment. He simply added only: "Papers distributed Saturday morning February 19, immediately after the execution, at 8:00 p.m."

No town in France seemed less destined for tragedy than that one. There are passions that may be awakened in the depths of these towns. They have been awakened.

March 10

Russian military operations. The Allies are not landing. I wonder if they haven't decided to limit themselves to a war of attrition through the air. But I just don't get problems of vast dimensions. I have no taste for strategy.

March 11

Pucheu sentenced to death.

"I don't feel sorry for him," I say.

And instantly I see the man in his cell facing death. His calculations, his schemes, and his crimes have fallen into the depths of his being, a deposit where nothing moves. He has forgotten the brilliant student turned into a businessman, intoxicated first by money, then by politics. After the trial, he is empty and light, like a child, like the criminals in high court, who talk indifferently about their crime—stale, no longer theirs.

---

[19] Les Francs-Tireurs et Partisans Français [or FTP—"French Free Fighters and Partisans"] were the military branch of the Front National, in which the underground French Communist Party was the driving force. From fall 1943 on, the resistance movements showed less and less reluctance to execute people they thought were traitors, while striving to fight against crime, which developed under the cover of resistance actions.—J.-P. A.

March 14

The historian Marc Bloch was arrested in Lyon.[20]

March 15

A visit from Altman, who "worked" with Marc Bloch.[21] How fresh he is, how confident! He has kept the flower of youth. Risk steadies him. I give him a few of my notes for an underground paper. I'm capable of nothing but writing. If you can call it writing, one might say.

March 18

At the same time the Russians are approaching the Romanian border, Germany "addresses the French" through the voice of Gauleiter Sauckel and affirms that "the terrible power of the Jews" is the only cause of the war and the only cause of all the evil and unhappiness on earth. "The Jews are trying to carry out their plans for universal hegemony. But Providence has given the German people, for its salvation, a leader gifted with grace."

Delirium of a persecutor persecuted. An erotomaniac delirium, too, which we even saw in the soldiers of the occupying forces: the German thinks he is loved. He thinks that even in the present circumstances he can be loved, loved by the French.

In Saint-Étienne, three high school students who distributed a few leaflets are denounced by the Militia and arrested by the Gestapo. The men of the Gestapo break the wrists of one of them in a vise. Another gets pounded by a blackjack fifty times. The third one has a testicle ripped off. They send his bloody underpants to his parents.

March 20

Altman knows, through some hidden communication with Lyon, that Marc Bloch was seen in a corridor with his face bloody and swollen. They think he may not be executed.

March 21

Pucheu was shot yesterday at dawn.

---

[20] The great medievalist, who entered the Franc-Tireur Resistance movement in March 1943, was arrested in Lyon on March 8, 1944. He would be executed June 16.—J.-P. A.

[21] Georges Altman, a journalist who was an activist for the French Communist Party until 1929, wrote in left-wing newspapers and then became an editor of *Le Progrès* [the main Lyon daily until November 1942, when the Germans occupied the Free Zone]. In March 1942, he agreed to enter the Franc-Tireur movement and edited their paper, cited above.—J.-P. A.

National sensitivity. "I don't know how to express this feeling," Suzanne says. "The words change it and give it a solidity and clarity that it really doesn't have. When the Germans kill someone, I feel sadness first; hate comes only later. But Pucheu's execution doesn't sadden me; it leaves me with a feeling of unease. I feel responsible."

"This execution means that the Bolsheviks have become the masters of our empire." (*Le Petit Parisien*, signed Claude Jeantet.)[22]

March 22

I have often tried hard to put myself in a traitor's shoes, not to explain treason simplistically, not to transform traitors into the traitors of melodrama or movies. I rejected the single explanation of self-interest, of money. "It's-more-complicated-than-*that*" may have become a kind of method: no, it couldn't be true that the traitor, sitting face to face with a German at the same table, just held out his hand and pocketed a stack of bills. And I would invent a convoluted psychological explanation. Much more complicated, but not less naïve. And perhaps still more arbitrary. I had constructed a Chateaubriant whose treason was the effect of some literary poison or other. Now I'm told this same Chateaubriant founded *La Gerbe* with a capital of 45,000 francs and sold it for 9 million.

Christian tells me German directives to the press authorize, in fact order, some "objectivity" in anything concerning the Russian advance, even in the headlines. Thus, we read in *Le Petit Parisien*, March 21: "Between the Dniester and the Bug, Soviet attacks have grown still more violent." The Germans think increasing the fear of Bolshevism is to their advantage and compensates for the admission that their troops are giving way. It's strange they can be so completely mistaken.

Sometimes German psychology is more accurate. A few days ago, for example, an express train was derailed by sabotage. About fifty Germans were killed. The press is forbidden to make the slightest allusion to this derailment. Fifty German corpses are not, in today's France, good propaganda. The news would add to the sense that they're slumping into defeat.

In Nîmes, the Germans indulged in spectacular repression.[23] But most often they wrap it in mystery. They don't announce the transfers to Germany, the death sentences, the executions. Terror is complete only if worry and fear have

---

[22] A classic theme in the collaborationist press and in Philippe Henriot's talks on the radio: de Gaulle is, at best, a Kerensky.—J.-P. A.

Claude Jeantet was a far-right journalist; he received a life sentence at the Liberation but was released a few years later and continued writing for anti-Semitic, far-right causes.—D. B.

[23] On March 2, 1944, more than a dozen resistance prisoners were publicly hanged and their corpses exposed to view with signs on them reading "This is what we do to terrorists." The ropes used to hang them remained in place until Nîmes was liberated on August 24.

no limits, if they can't be circumscribed in space and time, if the threat is indefinite, if the threat is everywhere.

Max Jacob died in the camp at Drancy.[24] The papers not only announce his death but publish an obituary that resembles, in tone and length, the one they would have published before the Occupation. "Max Jacob was there at the origins of Cubism, wrote hermetically for a small public, and displayed gouaches and ink drawings that revealed a gift that his whimsical nature refused to exploit."

They suppress Heine.[25] But they announce the death of Max Jacob. They announce the death of Max Jacob and order newspapers to talk about him as if he weren't Jewish. They announce his death but don't say he died in Drancy.

They try to create a state of oscillation and imbalance, to make us go from doubt to certainty and from certainty to doubt, to add more effective nuances to brute terror. Nazism has perfected the technique of terror.

NOTICE

All inhabitants, particularly doctors and other caregivers, who treat in any way whatsoever wounds caused by firearms or explosives are required to declare this fact without delay to the nearest *Feldkommandantur* or *Kreiscommandantur* or to the nearest service of German police, indicating the name and present address of the wounded person.

Whoever does not submit to the obligation to declare the wounded persons treated by him will be subject to the severest penalties, to the death penalty if need be, in accordance with paragraph 27 of the edict of December 18, 1942 concerning the safety of the German army. (*Der Militaerbefehlshaber in Frankreich.*)[26]

March 27

Hany Lefebvre is trying to save the prisoners on death row Noémi knew in Fresnes. Two Frenchmen, one married to a German woman, are in contact with a German general and Gestapo officers. One of these Frenchmen is supposedly

[24] The Modernist poet and artist Max Jacob converted to Catholicism but was arrested as a Jew in the medieval Abbey of Saint-Benoît-sur-Loire, where he had retired. On February 28, 1944, the sixty-eight-year-old poet was transferred to the transit camp of Drancy, where he died of pneumonia on March 4.

[25] The work of the great nineteenth-century German poet Heinrich Heine was removed from anthologies and textbooks during the Nazi era because he was Jewish.

[26] Neither Werth nor the Germans saw any reason to translate *Der Militaerbefehlshaber in Frankreich*: the Military Occupation Authorities in France. The words would have been common knowledge.

intervening out of generosity; the other, before any intervention, is supposedly being paid now forty thousand, now twenty thousand francs and sharing these sums with the Germans.

A speech by Déat. "Germany is heroically bearing up under a prodigious effort, because it pushed its revolution far enough, because that great nation forms one material and moral block without a crack . . ." And then a paraphrase of the "I want Germany to win" of Laval, a paraphrase supported by the Militia.

Now and then, I wish—oh, I'm well aware it's a very faint wish—that I were deported to the depths of Poland, to be with the people who are suffering, with those suffering the most. Just as during the 1914–18 war, a soldier in a trench in Woevre once said to me: "I don't believe any of the arguments our masters use to justify the war. I'm not fighting against Germany. I'm sharing suffering. That sharing justifies my being here."

March 29

Le Petit Parisien. Nine dangerous terrorists sentenced to death by a French court-martial in Lyon. Every day, the press gives us massive doses of "dangerous terrorists."

"In Upper Savoy, the terrorist bands in the Glières plateau have been cleaned out."[27] Then the same old stuff about youth who have gone astray, thinking they were saving France and realizing they were playing the game of the international brigades, the Communists, and common criminals.

For a few days now, a campaign has begun against the indulgence of the courts. The German press offices are instructing the papers to preach rigid virtue.

Goering wants to buy "the biggest diamond in the world."

A man who was deported and escaped from Germany says the batch of deport-ees he was in was locked into a railroad car for two weeks. For two weeks, the doors of the car were not opened. Their food was passed to the prisoners by an air hole, and they relieved themselves in a corner of the car.

When they arrived at their destination, another train was in the station. It was Russians, whose trip had lasted for twenty days. They were forced to get off. As soon as they set foot on the platform, many of them fainted. The ones who fell were finished off by the Germans, with bayonets.

---

[27] *Résistants* went up to the Glières plateau to make sure they could receive parachuted weapons. They were surrounded on February 13 by some 1,500 men in Vichy's forces of order; the attack was launched by the Wehrmacht and the Militia on March 26. Two days later, most of the maquisards were killed or captured (and earmarked for torture).—J.-P. A.

At the Sèvres-Babylone metro station, an old man is selling a map of the Russian front, not a nice colored card but a poor black-and-white diagram on bad paper. His stock is exhausted in a few minutes.

March 31

In Lyon, the Militia or the Gestapo arrested Dr. Weil's widow, eighty-seven, and her daughter. (Dr. Weil was a famous doctor; a street in Lyon bears his name.) How can this possibly be useful for them? Absurdity seems to go beyond cruelty here. A mistake. Uselessness and absurdity are the conditions for usefulness here. To hurt and kill those who act, struggle, and resist is simply to be rigorous. To create terror, you must strike without any apparent rule. Everyone feels threatened. No one escapes the threat. Not even the child, not even the old man, not even those who "aren't interested in anybody" and shut themselves in their apartments.

April 1

It seems de Monzie, like Madame V——, is astonished and skeptical when people tell him about German tortures.[28]

The tailor's worker who cut a jacket for Claude is Greek. He lives in an attic room on rue de Charonne. He was living there a few weeks ago with his wife. But she's Jewish: the Gestapo came, took away his wife, and sent her to Poland, he thinks. He has no news of her.

Néomi related the end of Médéric. For a long time, he escaped the French police and the Gestapo. The French police arrest him and discover his identity. Then he risks his all: "You know who I am . . . Release me." The policemen were hesitant and inclined to release him. But a police officer was against it. "Thirty seconds later," Néomi said, "he was dead." To be sure he wouldn't talk under torture. What poison? I don't know. You can only get it from "the other side" (in England).[29]

April 4

Le Petit Parisien. Main propaganda theme: "Block the Soviets' road," work, or fight "for Europe."

---

[28] Anatole de Monzie was twice a minister between the two world wars.

[29] Gilbert Védy ("Médéric" was his resistance name), one of the leaders of Ceux de la Libération (People of the Liberation), was arrested March 21, three days after landing on a beach in Brittany. The police chief Dufour . . . delivered him to Commissaire David, head of one of the special brigades. That is when Médéric chose to commit suicide by swallowing a dose of poison. He died in l'Hôtel-Dieu [then the biggest public hospital in Paris].—J.-P. A.

I forgot to note a text put out by the Commissariat aux Questions Juives a few days ago.[30] However accustomed we may be to its most delirious manifestations, it is still astonishing. They wanted to achieve a tone of apocalyptic lyricism: the Jews want to kill all the Christians to feed on the golden calf; they want to destroy the cathedrals. They want to dig up the dead. The opposite of the imprudent tolerance of the Christians, who never touched their synagogues.

Before the debacle, I was familiar with the fascism of one part of the French bourgeoisie: "Mussolini saved us from Bolshevism." But I knew nothing of the Nazism of the "intellectuals." Men like Drieu* and Montherlant* were no more than insolent brats to me. I lived so far removed from ordinary politics that I didn't know Hitler had been financing French Nazism for a long time. I knew no more than the peasants among whom I was living, and in fact I was thinking like a peasant.

Five "terrorists" sentenced to death by a German war council sitting in Paris. And executed.

Speech by de Gaulle. Necessity for unity, from the moderate to the Communist. The voice insists but never swells through an oratorical trick. He soft-pedals it.

April 6

I don't know how the Germans are proceeding through the intermediary of the papers in the Southern Zone now. I haven't seen one of those papers for three months. But in December of last year, the propaganda of the papers in the south was less crude than the propaganda of the Paris papers today. The latter use the method of obsessional advertising, and its simplicity is disconcerting. They don't seem to have more than one idea now, one single theme: the Bolshevik peril. And the most surprising thing about it is their perseverance in this monotheistic advertising despite its obvious inefficacity. Are Goebbels* and his men stupid? Out of arguments? Are they automatically, hopelessly persisting in trying to ward off fate by casting spells in which they no longer believe?

Or are they raving mad? Or do they think one mad idea works on the people as well as another? I read in *Le Petit Parisien* that according to von Ribbentrop, "it's thanks to the Reich that England still has gasoline." Simulated ravings, or the real thing?

---

[30] Vichy set up its High Commission on Jewish Questions in March 1941. It was responsible for anti-Semitic propaganda and for confiscating Jewish property (such as apartments and businesses) and selling it cheaply to "Aryans." A commemorative plaque can be seen on its former headquarters, 1 rue des Petits-Pères, Paris 2ème.

This, from a draftsman at the Compagnie du Nord, from a quasi-direct source. A train derailed about a hundred meters before the station of a town near the Belgian border. Two cars of the train were occupied by German soldiers. No one dead, no one wounded. The officer in command of the soldiers knocks the station-master to the ground with his rifle butt, then shoots six or seven workers in the station with his pistol. In the town, he assembles all the men on the town square, turns machine guns on them, and gives the order to fire. Over a hundred dead.

The news spread through Paris in a few hours, from shop to shop and from concierge's loge to concierge's loge,[31] amplified in cruelty and dimension. One of these secondary versions is odd because it expresses an unconscious need on the part of the crowd: the murderous officer was supposedly executed by the Germans "themselves." Thus the crowd, attributing the reprobation of atrocities to the Germans, satisfies itself through a vengeful ending and calms its fear of limitless repression.[32]

April 7

Two parachutists arrived from London. But R——, who was harboring them, has been arrested.

Completely shut in, even at night. It stays light out very late, and Christian advised me to live cloistered like this. Suzanne brings me news and rumors from outside. I have the strange illusion that she makes them good or bad at will, that she's responsible for them. It makes me understand the custom of princes who sentenced the bearer of bad tidings to death.

April 10

The Americans don't recognize the French National Liberation Committee in Algiers, or recognize it without recognizing it. I hear a group around Chautemps is working away at America.[33]

---

[31] Paris concierges used to live in a small apartment next to the building entrance (the loge) and sometimes still do; they functioned as janitor and doorkeeper and distributed the mail.

[32] During the night of April 1–2, a train carrying the SS Adolf Hitler Jugend division was stopped in Ascq (near Lille) by an act of sabotage that derailed three cars without claiming any German victims. The SS then killed eighty-six civilians in Ascq, who were buried the next day before a large crowd. The carnage was stopped by the arrival of higher German officers alerted by the stationmaster, but no SS officer was executed.—J.-P. A.

[33] Of the three Great Powers, the United States was the one that adopted the most restrictive position on the CFLN [Comité Française de Libération Nationale]: the White House "recognizes the CFLN as the organism governing the overseas territories which recognize its authority." Nothing like full legal recognition. Camille Chautemps, the former leader of a center-left political party, then a refugee in the United States, was actually anti-Gaullist. But Washington's position was above all inspired by Roosevelt himself: he was deeply distrustful of Charles de Gaulle, whose presumptuous nationalism might stand in the way of American policy.—J.-P. A.

The radio. I hear the end of a text about the Jews: I'm sorry I didn't hear all of it. But the end is an odd document in itself. "The Jew, hot-tempered and bloodthirsty, is accumulating his assassinations of us. He wants to destroy the human race." The speaker talks in a furious tone, inspired by rage and fury. As for the text, it doesn't even pretend to present the listener with fallacious arguments or fabricated documentation: it's not about the Jew who holds the reins of power, the Jew who is a ferment of societal decomposition, the Jew with his hooked fingers, the traitor of high finance. Rather, it sounds like verse from an Apocalypse, the verse of a propaganda Apocalypse. The intention is to provoke a state of frenzy.

April 11

Dead and wounded through English bombings. Two voices: "The Parisians are admirable. They understand that terrible things are necessary in war."—"They couldn't care less . . . they don't care about anything that doesn't immediately affect them."

"The Paris of 1941," Suzanne says, "was so different! People thumbed their noses at the Germans. Women combined blue, white, and red in their outfits. They wore the Lorraine Cross as a brooch. The police intervened. Then you saw women grouped in threesomes, one wearing blue, the other white, the third red, and they walked along holding each other by the arm. And then there was that day Noémi biked down the Champs-Élysées with three veils on her shoulders, a blue, a white, and a red one, and when they were lifted by the wind, they floated behind her like the veils of a Loïe Fuller.[34] Maybe all that was a bit childish. We didn't take full measure of the situation. Terror was only going to come later. But the street was still alive."

And today, there's the maquis.

April 12

At eight in the morning, the bell rings. The colonel asks Suzanne to put him in touch with Father Fanget *today*.

Meeting arranged for the afternoon. As they were waiting in the sacristy, a priest who had nothing to do with this kind of thing comes over to them and says: "You're probably here for a wedding?"

Father Fanget is unbelievably daring. For night "work," he takes off his cassock and puts on a jacket.

Andrée François is back from Saint-Amour. In Louhans and Bruailles, she saw two locomotives lying on their sides past the embankment. And all through her trip,

---

[34] Blue, white, and red are the colors of the French flag, in that order; the double-barred Cross of Lorraine was the symbol of de Gaulle's Free French forces. Loïe Fuller was the stage name of Mary Louise Fuller, an American dancer known for whirling veils around her as she danced.

railroad cars on their sides and the debris of railroad cars. At Vernay, between Saint-Amour and Coligny, the saboteurs carried off the railroad guards and kept them in a safe place during the time required to set up the derailment of the train.

In Paris these past few days, I've hardly seen anything but weariness and disappointment. And even a kind of resentment toward the Anglo-Americans because of the postponed landing. According to Andrée, the townspeople and the peasants are much firmer. For example, despite the orchestration of the papers and the radio, the dead in Villeneuve Saint-Georges and Lille are acccpted by them as war dead. (True, they're distant dead.) But as for the Resistance, they can touch it, they have direct pictures of it. The maquis is not just a strange and far-off country for them: they know the woods and the refugees hiding in them. When there's the slightest derailment, they know the spot and the effects. Some of them could observe them from a field at the side of the tracks. When a train is late, the town is informed. Arrivals and departures used to be markers of time, like the sun rising and setting. A station in a big city is an HQ. All you hear is sounds of steps and whistles of locomotives. Travelers and railroad workers slip through it without knowing each other, like ants. But the station of the town is like a café and a salon. On the platform, at the station bar, people talk. The railroad men bring news.

April 13

The newspapers did not announce the derailing and the massacre near Lille (Ascq); that goes without saying. The same papers devote whole columns to the victims of the RAF, when we know very well they weren't targets and their death was unintentional. To each his own dead, his propaganda dead.

But wouldn't it be high time to give up these dissections of the newspapers, these commentaries about nothingness? Could these glosses possibly retain the slightest interest twenty-four hours after the end of the war? Those articles, those distorted news stories (and so crudely distorted), those typographic tricks and fireworks are symptoms. As thin and slight as they are, they are symptoms.

April 16

The life of a French family in April 1944. The father (a road worker) is hiding out in the woods: he got his order to leave for Germany a few months ago. The son is in Germany. The son-in-law just got his departure orders.

April 17

During the war of 1914–18, a woman told me: "The war doesn't interest me. What I want is not to be bothered."

Many collaborators aren't really so keen to collaborate. They hate Communism, the rebels, and agitators (especially women) but don't care about the Europe of

Hitler or Laval-Déat. What they want is not to be bothered. They're not Nazis through ideology or passion. The Nazi Germany of 1939 was burning with Nazism. But their Hitler is emptied of Hitler, their Nazism is emptied of Nazism. They made a sterilized Nazism for themselves. No matter the acts of cruelty and sadism you can cite, they erase them, they repress them. They've created a Nazism in bedroom slippers. This is the mass of soft collaborators.

But there are also soft resisters. They hope for deliverance through the evaporation of the Germans and a landing in bedroom slippers.

A nineteen-year-old high school girl, Nicole Kritter (so fresh, Suzanne told me, and quivering with emotion), came here yesterday: "I would like to be useful. Help me to be useful." "You know what the risks are?" "I do know." "Prison and even death." "I know." "But what about your parents?" "My parents know I'm here."

April 18

Le Petit Parisien: "Twenty-seven terrorists sentenced to death by a German court."

"Notice. The population is once again reminded that any inhabitant who treats wounds caused by firearms or explosives is required to declare this fact without delay to the nearest *Feldkommandantur* or *Kreiscommandantur* or to the nearest service of German police, indicating the name and present address of the wounded person."

April 19

A photo with this caption: "Adolf Hitler will celebrate his fifty-fifth birthday tomorrow." Hitler is leaning out of the door of a railroad car toward a little girl. A bad photo: the perspective is jumbled. Hitler is stretching out his arm, and his hand seems to land on the child's throat. You'd think he was strangling her.

April 20

"Rouen and its suburbs: 1,200 dead. Paris and its suburbs: 556 dead. Seine-et-Oise: 184 dead."[35] "Six false policemen rake in 27 million." "Olek won't be able to box in Belgium."

Philippe Henriot last night: "The English bombings have no military significance. So the English have no other goal than the goal of savage destruction. They want to wipe out Berlin, Budapest, Bucharest, Rome and its art treasures." In a

---

[35] During the night of April 18–19, a thousand planes of the RAF bombed the railroad yards in Juvisy, Noisy-le-Sec, Rouen, and Tergnier; it was one of the deadliest British or American raids before the one at Pentecost.—J.-P. A

furious voice, like someone in a trance, he refutes English radio, which accuses him of being "controlled by Germany." It seems difficult to grant him the kind of sincerity that comes from automatically repeating the same arguments—the sincerity of the get-dumb.

April 21

The radio. Philippe Henriot: "The murderers are attracted by the scene of their crime. . . . The English came back to light the stake of the saint once again."[36]

The first column of the *Petit Parisien*: "April 20, 1429, Joan of Arc summoned the English to raise the siege of Orleans. And as they did not obey, she made them do it. These are things the English cannot forget." Bolshevism has been forgotten. The directive is to evoke, lyrically, "the massacre of the French by the Anglo-Americans" and Joan of Arc.

The people of Paris no longer believe in the newspapers. The people are impermeable to newspapers. They know who inspires them and who directs them. They know they're lying. The people checked the map with the news about the war in Russia. They compared the idyllic Europe promised by Hitlerite propaganda and the reality of occupation.

But when it comes to the dead in Rouen and Seine-et-Oise, people know they aren't invented dead. People in the street, in the concierges' loge, in the shops have lost their strategic impassibility for a moment. They were firm, and they used to say, "That's war." But the bombings, the fires, the ruins, and the dead are making them waver.

A new type of man: the man with a suitcase. The sheepskin jacket, the beret, the crude colored shirt. That's the way the colonel is dressed. But he has no identity papers in his suitcase. His papers are hidden in his tie.

Young women ring the doorbell, stay a few minutes, and disappear. There is a labyrinth, a network into which they are directed by the colonel and Father Fanget. This woman looks like a girl in a park from 1930 photos. Who could suspect her? That one is elegant, like a typist. Another one is a salesgirl in a department store. Another looks "common." Still another can look at will like a Parisian college student or a young Russian woman at the time they were throwing bombs at archdukes.

Near the Torcy station. Working-class neighborhood. Three houses at the edge of the tracks were hit. In the fourth floor, a woman and her six children, buried under the ruins. To save them they had to bring them to a lower floor through a hole they made in the ceiling. "You wouldn't have thought they were people. They were like packages."

---

[36] "The saint" is Joan of Arc, burned at the stake by the English in Rouen (but sentenced by the French).

The firemen are working. The tenants are rummaging through what was once their apartment, looking for something or other, underwear, a snapshot. "That's where we lived," says a woman hugging a little girl to her, "It's sad, really; you feel friendship for your furniture."

Not an angry word, no tears. No stupor either. They are calm, astonishingly calm, a grandiose calm.

From daybreak on, Father Fanget worked on saving people, risking his life a hundred times over. That black spot in the dawn light, agile in the ruins, surprised a fireman who took him for a thief, a looter of ruins.

April 22

The papers never say anything about the police roundups.

Despite a bed and running water, the men and women who sleep in a different place every night look like they've just spent the night on a train. Their eyelids are narrowed and gray.

April 24

Le Petit Parisien. Contradictions. "A recently opened, pretty cabaret, the Boîte à Cocktails, really went to town Saturday to welcome the smart set of Paris on the Champs-Élysées."—"Yesterday afternoon, in a café on the Place du Tertre, twenty couples were happily dancing away. Police raid. A group of Militiamen taught them a lesson they'll never forget."

Georgette R——writes us from Coligny. "After the railroad was sabotaged several times, there was a thorough 'visit' of Coligny. Police raids, etc. My aunt's house was turned completely upside down. All her jewels were stolen."

You have to admit the Gestapo displays a certain impartiality as far as the theft of jewels is concerned. Georgette R——'s aunt is a pure, unadulterated collaborator.

Women belonging to the Gestapo are visiting houses in the Clignancourt neighborhood and taking note of the unoccupied apartments.

The street, the shop, the concierge's loge, and the office:

Overheard dialogues: "Just to take the bolts out of four rails, it wasn't worth causing so many deaths . . ."—"They're savages . . ."—They're waging war against Germany, and Germany is in France,"—"I'm telling you, they're savages."—"If we sabotaged more tracks ourselves, we wouldn't have to fight with bombs."—"What about the women . . . and children?"—"Forty people were buried in one cellar. In another, seventy . . . They can't get them out of there. They'll die of asphyxiation."—"And yet . . . If only we could be sure they were coming . . ."

"Savages . . ."—"When it was the Germans, you didn't say things like that. "That's not the same thing."

"That's not the same thing. And yet . . . If only we could be sure they were coming." Outbursts of passion. The fluctuation of a passion of the masses. The anger and bitterness of a love which thinks it has been betrayed. "And for *him* to do that to me . . . And yet, if only I could be sure he was coming back . . ."

April 25

De Gaulle is disconcerting for the average bourgeois. When they were wallowing in defeat, de Gaulle said to them: "You are not defeated." When a distant picture of victory is emerging, he disconcerts them even more through his calm. He doesn't enlarge the picture and he doesn't bring it closer. And when the picture takes on a firm outline, he refuses to give the bourgeois the oratorical effusions they were expecting, and deliberates with Communists. And a few of them, who trusted Pétain for a long time, are saying: "A general—now that's really worrying."

Many of the men who work in the Resistance are imprudent. They often neglect useful precautions, and the precautions they take aren't much better than illusory attempts to ward off danger. Thus, they think they're safe if they turn around three times before they go down into the metro. Or they grow a mustache, as one might appease a barbaric god through sacrifice.

"Tonnerre et rubis aux moyeux . . ."[37] Last night, during the air raid alert, I was reading Mallarmé in bed. If a bomb had fallen on me, I would have died reading Mallarmé. It would have been quite literary.

I'm afraid I gave an inexact image of the emotional effect produced by the bombs that fell on Paris. I'm afraid I exaggerated people's heroic resignation to the necessities of the war. Today I've been given examples of revolt, of total rejection. But those who reject England this way are among the untouched; they received no damage. And the disaster victims—through stupor, consent to fate, or the feeling of deliverance that follows catastrophes once they're over—say nothing.

April 26

Doriot's* posters in the metro. The Communists are connected to the two hundred families.[38] The association of Communists and capitalists has been one of the common themes of German and Vichy propaganda since 1940. But why do they arrest the Communists and leave the capitalists at liberty?

---

[37] Literally "Thunder and ruby at the hubs," a line from "M'introduire dans ton histoire," a poem by the esoteric nineteenth-century poet Stéphane Mallarmé.

[38] "The two hundred families" were supposedly the biggest stockholders in the Banque de France between the two world wars and, by extension, the reigning financial elite of the country.

April 27

Dream. I'm in some room or other with Jean Guéhenno.[39] Suddenly a voice comes out of nowhere: "Jean Guéhenno has been killed." He cries out and falls. I think I remember falling too. But I see he's dead, *he died from having learned of his death*. Aside from the presence of Guéhenno, whom I haven't see for ten years, all the matter of this dream is made of recent, banal memories.

Neither the papers nor the radio announced last night that Pétain and Laval were coming to Paris for the ceremony of Notre Dame. Idlers, a few shouts given under orders, and a few cries of *Vive la France* with intentions impossible to evaluate. This at the Hôtel de Ville.[40] Then on the Boulevard Saint-Germain, total silence. One might have thought it was a newsreel where they forgot the sound track.

The radio follows the marshal to the hospital. He asks: "Where were you wounded?" As the wounded man answers, weakly, the announcer intervenes, fills up the silence, raises the tone and repeats a few times: "Spine . . . spine . . ." in the same professional voice, rolling and insistent, as if he were reporting a soccer match.

An anachronistic marshal wheeled his dead legend and his old imagery through Paris.

April 28

Photo: meeting of Hitler and Mussolini.[41] The Führer is greeting Mussolini when he gets out of the railroad car. They're smiling at each other with a radiant, total, victorious smile. If I were in their shoes, I would have looked serious. That smile seems bad propaganda to me. Won't it seem out of place to the families with dead in Russia and to people who live in the bombed-out cities? But perhaps this photo is for export only.

Mussolini is thinner. He smiles blissfully, like the pictures of old snuff users tapping their tobacco pouch you used to see in old color prints.

The street reflects the combats in the Jura Mountains.[42] Suzanne was on her bike in Paris this morning. (Her license plate displays "Jura.") Three times, there

---

[39] Jean Guéhenno was an important left-wing intellectual. He did not die until 1978.

[40] The Hôtel de Ville, in the center of Paris, is the city hall. It houses the municipal offices, including the mayor's.

[41] Hitler officially received Mussolini on April 22–23, in the presence of Joachim von Ribbentrop and Marshal Keitel.—J.-P. A.

[42] The occupying forces used strong measures to bring down the maquis in the Jura. In Upper Jura alone, fifty-six inhabitants of the Jura were executed and 456 were arrested, 307 in the city of Saint-Claude on April 8; 172 of them would die in deportation.—J.-P. A.

were shouts of *Vive le Jura!* And it wasn't a kind of cordial joke. It came, as Pétain would say, "from the heart of Paris." Two pedestrians and a young woman on her bike hailed Suzanne as an ambassador of the maquis.

The colonel told me a German soldier was killed in the Bois de Vincennes. The park was surrounded. The men they arrested were executed. Almost all of them were teenagers.

April 29

I recall what I wrote about colonialism. And this evening, I'm expecting the colonel, from our colonial infantry. And there is harmony between us. What will remain of that harmony after the war?

April 30

The colonel. "He was an honest man, frank, true, and of simple virtue, all of a piece, military."—Saint-Simon.* The Africa he loves is an Africa where French and Arab leaders deal with each other nobly, as warriors. "No," he says, "no, I can assure you they don't look like defeated people, and we're not insolent conquerors." The dignity of the leaders. Their equilibrium, which doesn't come precisely from peace, nor from war. As far from empty pacifists as from heroic showoffs. But don't they belong to a world inside the world, an old world of duels, of traditions, which doesn't grasp the nature of the present at all? I can see the fine pleats of the noble burnoose. But what about the colonists, the poor Arabs, and the economy?

On the walls of the metro, a poster for *Germinal.* Among those contributing to the journal, Challaye, Giono, Hamp, Céline, Delaisi, Montherlant . . .[43]

May 2

The colonel was to have lunch with us. He didn't come. On a mission? Arrested? We learn through Mademoiselle G—— that Hélène (we don't know her by any other name) is in Fresnes. They know her spirits are excellent. She sings. They know she was denounced by a young man she met in a group of friends. A fake identity card had been manufactured before his eyes. If Hélène talked, we would all be caught.

---

[43] *Germinal,* "the weekly of French socialist thought" named after Zola's novel about coal miners, appeared for the first time on April 28, 1944. It was founded by left-wing pacifists and socialists who converted to Hitler's National Socialism. Three writers in the above list are well-known names in French literature: the novelist Louis-Ferdinand Céline was violently anti-Semitic and pro-Nazi; neither Jean Giono nor the playwright and novelist Henry de Montherlant actually contributed to *Germinal,* despite their collaborationist sympathies. Werth found all of them beneath contempt.

Eight o'clock in the morning. Doorbell rings. "Who's there?" "Security." "But who?" "Police headquarters."

Suzanne is speaking behind the door and, of course, does not open it. "Just a moment," she says. "I'm in my nightgown . . . I'm getting dressed." She hands me her purse and a few papers. I go out on the balcony. (We live on the second floor.) I walk over the zinc roof of a little shed and climb down by a metal pole into the church youth center. Solitude of the yard. There are the toilets. But I don't like the idea of hiding in the toilets. I prefer the shed. But I get bored. I take a few steps in the yard, look into the empty classrooms, the school benches. One of the rooms was transformed into a room for playing billiards.

What will I say to the priest if he comes in? I prepare a fine legendary sentence, the sentence of the refugee who invokes the sacred rights of the guest. But the priest does not come.

Alone in the yard. For days, I haven't felt so light, so open to the air. I'm freed from a weight, the vague threat of the storm that has weighed on me for days. In a word, I feel relieved. What will be will be. I submit to fate. I don't prepare any response to the event. It's the event that will respond. The event's response will be immediate, it will come all by itself.

Ten minutes or so go by. A "Yoo-hoo!" from Suzanne. Her head appears in the window. She motions to me. I climb up the pole of the shed by doing a pull-up. Memories of gymnastics in my whole body, forgotten since my years of lycée; up the pole like rope climbing, and a pull-up onto the zinc roof. I go from the zinc roof to the balcony. I notice I still have my pipe in my mouth.

The man from police headquarters hadn't come for me but for Claude, and he was only instructed to check the work-service registration of the class of '45.

Andrée François comes back from doing her marketing. "I couldn't find a thing," she says. "It's high time they came."

Le Petit Parisien. "Nine leaders of the dissidence have been sentenced to death by a court-martial in Annecy. Five of them were immediately shot."—"Monsieur Sacha Guitry's film *From Joan of Arc to Philippe Pétain* was presented yesterday at the Opera."

All you have to do is put the two headlines side by side.

The radio. Philippe Henriot invokes eternal morality. Accelerations and decelerations of rhythm in the delivery, skillful changes in tone. The voice goes from confidential serenity to aggressive violence and back again. But the timbre is coarse. A voice for selling dirty postcards.

May 6

Atmosphere and color of the times: "Quimper. The German military tribunal sentenced twenty-three Frenchmen and a Spaniard affiliated with resistance groups to death. The sentence was carried out. The thirteen bandits, who had attacked the police station of Saint-Dié, were executed. Because of the difficulty of transporting the guillotine, will everyone who is sentenced to death be shot?"

A letter from Febvre. The Germans searched a few houses in Saint-Amour. (They say there's a maquis in Saint-Jean d'Étreux.) The mayor of La Balem d'Épi was executed because they found an old one-shot hunting rifle in his house. They can say: "We execute snipers." But this is characteristic, specifically "totalitarian": they executed a surgeon in Lons who, after removing a bullet from a young work-service evader, did not denounce him.

"Let them come quickly!" said Andrée François. "Let them come quickly!" says the street, the concierge's loge, and the shop. "Let them come quickly!" we all say. It is high time. We're living a life reduced to waiting, wavering between fear and rage.

May 9

"The funeral of the Militia leader Élie Penot was held in l'Hay-les-Roses. We recall that he had been murdered in the most cowardly way as he was coming out of his house. Monsieur Joseph Darnand* attended the ceremony."

Madame X——, who knows the family, says: "That Penot was a traveling salesman. Not a criminal, but simple-minded, a fanatic. Any violent propaganda would have turned his head. His whole family is against the Germans, they're all Gaullists. A violent man. A short while before he was assassinated, he was arguing with his younger brother and hit him. His funeral was a parade of armed Militia to protect Darnand. Six women, friends of his mother, were there. Not one man, aside from the Militia."

Yvonne saw Hélène in Fresnes. She sings. The Germans couldn't get a single name out of her.

The colonel has lunch with us. His wandering life. He's been wearing the same khaki shirt for days.

There are five of us in the apartment now, five sheltered by the same walls. Each of us is living under a menace, more or less.

Suzanne for the last four years. She's helped, hidden, and saved people who were being hunted down. By the dozen. She crossed the Demarcation Line thirteen times, illegally. Sometimes in a freight car, sometimes through the fields. Once, to get through Seurre, she went from Navilly to Saint-Jean-de-Losne lying on a board slipped under the locomotive, between the front wheels. She got hit by stones that bounced up from the roadbed between the rails. She was covered by a cloud of steam.

And every time, she came into the Saint-Amour station smiling, with her features hardly drawn, as if she were getting out of a sleeping car.

Suzanne and Léon Werth, ca. 1945. *Centre de la Mémoire, Médiathèque Albert-Camus, Issoudun*

May 10

"The marshal is moving to the Northern Zone." But they don't say where.[44] His place of residence: somewhere in occupied France. Strange, a head of state with no fixed residence—that angel, that genius, who is everywhere and nowhere.

The bakeries of the Paris region open and close in rotation.

"Any attempt at a landing will be turned into a bloody adventure," Marshal Rommel declares.

The Russians have recaptured Sebastopol.

Average collaborator: a product of propaganda. His politics are anti-Communism and anti-Semitism. Full of old legends, well before Hitler: the Jew, the only financier and a destructive "redistributor of wealth." Unable to formulate a thought about Communism and its variations, nor about anything at all.

How did narcissistic nationalism become Nazism? Hypnotic power of the conqueror, fear of the people.

The average *résistant* has, for the moment, no doctrine at all. He feels the weight of the occupier. He feels the simplest freedoms, like spiritual freedoms, wounded inside him. He can feel freedom wounded inside him. He doesn't need to define it to know it. He has a freedom ache, as you can have a toothache.

A black cat is hunting through the trash can. In the past, occasionally dogs (and then through sheer perversion) hunted through the trash cans. Never cats.

The cat's gone. An old woman replaces it, and she's not a ragpicker.

May 12

120,000 Frenchmen executed, 70,000 in the Paris region.[45] (Figures given by English radio.)

May 17

What will tomorrow be made of? Tomorrow, what will become of those systems, religions, and passions that signed an armistice or were reduced to silence by oppression? How, once the occupier has disappeared, will Christians, fellow travelers, Communists, and patriots act toward one another? What will their new feelings be based on? What will the men of tomorrow be, not the whore-men,

---

[44] Under pressure from the occupying authorities, Philippe Pétain stayed in the chateau of Voisins in Île-de-France from May 7 to May 28.—J.-P. A.

[45] Exaggerated figures, without the slightest doubt: it is estimated that the occupying forces shot nearly thirty thousand French men and women; some eighty thousand others met a violent death inside France, but most of them perished under German or British-American bombs.—J.-P. A.

but the men? I reject the idea of an exhausted world, in which there will be nothing more than whore-men and sleeping men.

And what about the collaborators? I don't mean those who betrayed us publicly but those who betrayed us in desire and thought, or the poor morons who stammered out the legend of the marshal to the very end. No doubt they'll disappear into the mass. But in what part of that mass? And will their poisons be resorbed?

Jacques Decour, who founded the underground journal *Les Lettres Françaises*, was shot by the Germans on Saturday, May 30, 1942.[46]

What, tomorrow, will be the fate of the Célines who are more or less Drieus, the Drieus who are more or less Célines, the Montherlants who are more or less Thérives?[47] And what will be the fate of those painters, sculptors, and musicians who were banqueting in Germany at the same time that the Germans were shooting men like Jacques Decour? Will they be forbidden to publish, exhibit, or stage their works?

May 21

In Italy, the Adolf Hitler Line has been pierced.

"The Russian soldier," a Waffen SS war correspondent writes in *Le Petit Parisien*, "is a fanatic." However, "he stops fighting as soon as he no longer feels the Jew behind him urging him on with his revolver . . ." Moreover, "he is poorly fed, poorly dressed, and isn't able to give himself a good wash." The soldier who "isn't able to give himself a good wash" is beating the German soldier. Do Goebbels and his French Waffen SS correspondents (this one's name is Lousteau) still believe in their victory, in a chance for victory, in the miracle of a victory?[48] Or does some propaganda litany or other rise from their depths automatically, like a child's prayer on the lips of a dying man?

On the fifty-third anniversary of Pope Leo XIII's papal encyclical *Rerum novarum* on the condition of workers, Cardinal Liénart, the bishop of Lille, defined once more the position of the Church on social problems. The cardinal

---

[46] Daniel Decourdemanche, alias Jacques Decour, was a Communist activist with an advanced degree in German who did exemplary work in mobilizing intellectuals into the Front National des Écrivains (National Front of writers). He was one of the founders of *Lettres Françaises* [an underground journal that published writers of the "intellectual Resistance"]. Arrested in January 1942, he was shot May 30 of that year.—J.-P. A.

A lycée in Paris bears his name.—D. B.

[47] André Thérive (real name: Roger Puthoste) was a right-wing man of letters who collaborated less actively than Drieu or the virulent Céline.

[48] Jean Lousteau was one of three journalists on *Je Suis Partout* ["I am everywhere," a pro-Nazi, anti-Semitic daily] who wore the uniform of Waffen SS war correspondents.—J.-P. A.

He also worked for Radio-Paris. Sentenced to death after the Liberation, he was later pardoned and went back to journalism.—D. B.

has no hesitation in reconciling opposites. "Work," he says, "belongs first of all to the worker." One must "truly emancipate the worker." But one must leave it to the marshal's Labor Charter for this emancipation.[49]

"The production of the National Theater of Hamburg that was given last night at the Odéon Theater was a message of friendship to France." The incarcerations, the deportations, and the registration of the class of '45 are another message of the same friendship.

A friend of D—— who was mass-producing fake identity cards has just been arrested.

May 23

Contradictory rumors. Contradictory propaganda arguments.

A "worker back from Germany" said the German cities were terribly bombed, but countless factories were intact. The factories spared by the Anglo-American planes supposedly function with mixed English and German capital. Could this war have its Briey coalfields too?[50]

But this morning's *Petit Parisien* declares, on the contrary, that French factories are being targeted. (Signature: André Algarron.) "The orders aiming to asphyxiate our economy and destroy our society come from London, Washington, and Moscow. England and America have every reason to smother competition from French industry in the postwar period."

But German propaganda (through the voice or the pen of the same Algarron and Roujon of the radio or press) ceaselessly repeats that English and American aviators aren't targeting or hitting our factories and railroad centers but innocent populations, churches, hospitals, and nurseries.

London, Washington, and Moscow . . . Perfect agreement between Moscow, high finance in the City of London, and Wall Street. The City and Wall Street want the contagion of Communism. The City and Wall Street sacrifice (the newspaper says) "on the Judeo-capitalo-Marxist altar." This can only surprise those who are unaware that Marxism and capitalism are two faces of the same Judaism.

Police roundups on rue de Rennes. These are French policemen at work. Suzanne saw two police vans go by, full.

[49] Werth is ironic: Vichy's Charte du Travail of October 1941 abolished unions and the right to strike.

[50] The Briey coalfield, where François de Wendel possessed many factories, was occupied by the Germans immediately after the strategic retreat ordered on July 30, 1914. Right-wing and especially far-left voices accused the ironmaster of intervening to prevent the bombardment of his factories, which worked for the German war industry from then on. The accusation has no foundation in fact, although it has had a long life.—J.-P. A.

The Vir—— deny the deportations, the executions, the tortures, the children of the Vel' d'Hiv'. There are two distinct, watertight worlds: ours and theirs.

"Let people who're for the Germans," says a bank clerk, "fight along with the Germans. Let people who're for the English fight along with the English. Me, I'm for the French. I have no reason to fight."

I learn of Brossolette's death. The German version is he tried to run away and a sentinel fired.[51]

Father Fanget is a man with two alternate personalities . . . The man in a cassock, the man in a jacket. The man in the jacket was denounced twice. Three of his fellow workers tried to kill a Gestapo officer. He was hit but not killed. You'd think he was wearing armor. Two were arrested. The third was able to get away. The priest organizes groups of twenty to thirty men. They speak of the ones who were executed, S—— tells me, without pity, without effusions. They take note, they record. The risk was known and accepted. Perhaps that acceptance gives one a great peace.

The priest teaches the catechism to the children of a working-class neighborhood, takes corpses out of the ruins of bombed houses, gets identity cards for people on the run, organizes groups and gives them their assignments. What is his France? What is his God? Is his Christ the Christ of workers' neighborhoods in naïve paintings? Is he a more mystical Christ, or more learned? Perhaps he has found him so completely he has no more reason to look for him or define him.

What drives Suzanne to help people, save them, and risk her life? What drives the priest? What drives the Communist who's a believer?

Everything is threatened, everything is affected, the belly and the soul. Young people hunted. Hostages twenty-four years old. And no refuge except disgust or rage, a rage as powerless as disgust.

When the Militia was created, I thought, and the peasants thought, it was a residue of the Legion, a Legion reinforced by policemen and the unemployed who volunteered "for the bread." We didn't see the reign of Darnand coming, the Militia guiding the Germans or killing people themselves, supplying them

[51] Pierre Brossolette was arrested on February 3, 1944, as he was trying to get back to England on the boat *Jouet des flots*: first imprisoned in Rennes, he was recognized on the nineteenth and transferred to Fresnes the next day, brought to Gestapo headquarters on Avenue Foch the twenty-second. Afraid of giving up information, he jumped out of the window of the sixth floor that evening and died in the Hôtel-Dieu hospital during the night without regaining consciousness.—J.-P. A.

As he was a leader of the Resistance, a street in Paris bears his name. — DB.

A smiling member of the French Militia guards prisoners, undoubtedly Jews or members of the Resistance. *Bundesarchiv, Bild 1011-720-0318-36*

with Frenchmen to kill, like presidential gamekeepers flushing game for invited sovereigns.[52]

May 29

We grasp at anything. "If," Madame C—— said, "there's a rhinoceros or hippopotamus in a message, it means the Allied landing is imminent. In one of last night's messages, I heard the word 'hippopotamus.' But there was no landing this morning."

The ghost of Papa Ubu, speaking in Nancy, envisaged the hypothesis of an Allied landing and advised the French to remain neutral, not to get mixed up in other people's business.[53]

May 30

"The prefect of police has banned the production of *Andromaque* in the Théâtre Édouard-VII. The Militia informed him that it would oppose the present production at the theater, because of its concern for the intellectual protection of France as well as public morality." The Militia defending Racine, an official interpretation of Racine according to the Militia.[54]

"Over five thousand French citizens massacred in two days by the Anglo-Americans.—Indignation of the French episcopate." Once again, we wonder why the French episcopate doesn't get indignant when the Germans shoot Frenchmen or imprison Frenchmen of twenty-four as hostages. True, the newspapers wouldn't publish testimony of that indignation. We would know about it, however, if only by the arrest of a few prelates.

June 1

Claude, class of '45. Should he run away, hide? In Paris, in Saint-Amour? There is talk of wonderful farms, logging enterprises. The newspapers are spreading rumors of dissidence in the dissidence. As it is constantly delayed, the Allied landing seems to be a myth, a distant allegory of deliverance into the other world. Disgust, torpor. And then we become reinvigorated by this simple idea: "If they

[52] Young people of modest condition, particularly farmworkers, did volunteer for the Militia, especially its armed branch, the Franc-Garde; they were attracted by the amount of the pay, among other things. But the heads of the Militia, especially its general secretary Joseph Darnand, were activists, almost all from the far right, with a political project of establishing a totalitarian regime. By 1944, Vichy had become a paramilitia state.—J.-P. A.

[53] Werth is obviously talking about Philippe Pétain, who went to Nancy on May 26. The neutrality he demanded amounted to forbidding the French to help the English and Americans.—J.-P. A.

[54] The actors Jean Marais and Alain Cuny were putting on *Andromaque*, one of Jean Racine's classic tragedies in verse (1667). Aside from their "interpretation," they were known homosexuals, which no doubt added to the Militia's wrath.

didn't have the intention of landing, why would they insist on bombing factories and railroad lines and hitting inhabited neighborhoods by mistake? Simply for the pleasure—as German propaganda has it, when it doesn't say the opposite—of killing women and children?"

June 2

The paper: "Rouen and its cathedral ravaged by flames. The downtown area is nothing but a huge furnace." "The German military tribunal sentenced fifteen young people from resistance groups to death. . . . The youngest of them is eighteen."

What are our idealized images worth? The Anglo-Americans land in France. Germany surrenders. An attempt to make a "democratic" world. But what democracy? Churchill is not an apostle, and Roosevelt is not Walt Whitman. We know nothing more about Stalin, except that he's a marshal. What will be the role of high finance, of heavy industry and the old politics of diplomats? What about the peoples, the masses? Weary masses, or masses dreaming of justice? And what meaning will they give to the word "freedom"?

From her window on Boulevard Arago, the daughter of the laundress on rue Vavin saw a Militiaman shoot a young man with his revolver. No one knows anything else, except that the rumor went around that the young man had taken his Bac that very day.

June 5

The Anglo-Americans are at the outskirts of Rome.

Chronicle of our civil war: "Three doctors assassinated in d'Eymoutiers . . . A postman and his daughter kidnapped and killed . . . A bandit shot by a farmer . . . Militiamen victims of aggressions," etc.

The current's cut off from 7:00 a.m. to 1:00 p.m. and from 1:30 p.m. to 10:00 p.m. That breaks the bridges between what's happening and us. We can no longer listen to the radio whenever we want, depending on our little habits and our availability.

An issue of *Je Suis Partout* and an issue of *Au Pilori* from the beginning of last year were wrapped around some packages. Do the people who write in these papers believe what they write? Wrong question. Habit is conviction.

Madame Ph—— is back from Saint-Amour. Two hundred Militia have moved into this town of two thousand inhabitants. According to the mayor, a compromise was reached: they don't show much opposition to the peasants' supplying the maquis with food provided the peasants supply them too. They questioned a few of the inhabitants who were denounced as suspects. They killed a refugee in a narrow, sunken path. His identity could not be established.

They've landed.

At eight-thirty this morning, American radio wasn't announcing anything. At noon, Claude returns from the lycée. A vague rumor of a landing had gone around, but nobody believed it. They were saying barges were going up the Seine. "Sure," a joker said, "the Americans are marching along the Quai Saint-Michel."

Suzanne comes back a little later. The event came closer to her. She met Car——, a cool, prudent man. "Swiss radio," he said, "announced the landing at several points along the coast. I heard it, I heard it myself, with my own ears." But he was shaking with fear: "How will we get food? Are they going to fight in Paris?"

Durel was swelling with joy, with hope.[55]

At one, we get Radio London. I would like to tug at the words to get them to say more, as if the words had the power to create events. I feel unbound, lightened. As if I'd been carrying all the weight of the war on my shoulders, as if I were just delivered from it.

A Vichy program. The marshal issues "a solemn warning." The voice of a ghost.[56]

The street is like the preceding days: asphalt, decently dressed pedestrians, housewives with shopping baskets, cyclists.

"One of the patients in my department," says Henri Febvre, a med student, "threw away a cigarette he'd hardly smoked. As I expressed my surprise, he answered: 'No need to hang on to the butts now.'"

For the first time, I hear Hérold-Paquis.* He sounds like an agitated monkey, a monkey breaking words.

Let's admit it: we're not happy and filled with joy, as we had hoped. "We've waited too long . . ." said someone or other. But it's something else, I think. True, the landing no longer appeared to us like the exterminating angel who would destroy the enemy in one breath and give us victory and peace. But nonetheless, deep down, we were waiting for some sort of immediate change in the way things feel. They're in Le Havre and Caen—so near. And for us, everything is just as it was. No more than if they had landed on some Pacific island. We're disconcerted by the contrast. It's a tremendous event, but it is only a mental object. Nothing palpable connects it to us yet. We're trying to

---

[55] Auguste Durel was a colleague of Suzanne Werth in the BNCI (Banque Nationale pour le Commerce et l'Industrie), where he worked in the advertising department.—J.-P. A.

[56] At 2:15 p.m., Radio-Vichy broadcast a "message" written February 19, 1944. The occupiers, foreseeing an English-American landing, had recorded it over four months earlier. The message ends with these words: "Frenchmen, I implore you to think above all of the mortal danger that our country would be risking if this solemn warning were not heeded."—J.-P. A.

find perceptible evidence for it, the way you hold out your hand before a storm to feel the first raindrops.

Nothing has delivered us yet from our monotonous daily anxiety. What do the Germans mean to do? Assemble the men and send them off to Germany? Round them up and put them in a camp in France? Use them to build defenses? I hear they've gone through the census cards in city hall. The baker saw three trucks go by full of young men guarded by German and French police.

Le Petit Parisien: "Most of the troops who landed have been pushed back . . ." And: "Almost all the paratroop units between Le Havre and Cherbourg have been annihilated."

A statement has force, whatever it is and wherever it comes from. It's enough to give me a brief feeling of doubt and disappointment. Perhaps in my heart of hearts I was thinking that when the first Englishman landed, the offices and presses of the newspapers would go up in a burst of flame and be reduced to a heap of ashes.

Suzanne and the colonel are surprised by the calm in the streets, a grave calm, they say, which is not indifference but a feeling of tragedy. Aren't they projecting their own feelings?

June 9

Bayeux. Caen. Cherbourg. I can't think beachheads. All I can see is tanks clashing and, in the sky, paratroopers.

The war correspondent of the *Petit Parisien* follows his directives with disconcerting naiveté. Thus he has a "good Normandy peasant" speaking like this: "Can't the English and the Americans leave us in peace? This invasion business won't last very long, thanks to the defensive strength of the Germans. I hope they soon repel the invaders of our beautiful, peaceful France, and then we can live in peace again."

June 10

Normandy. Italy. The algebra of tanks and planes. Bayeux, the first city that's become French again. Paris is motionless. The four years of occupation have acted like an injection of curare that doesn't anesthetize, but paralyzes you.

In the market, fifty women line up in front of a few heads of lettuce. At the fruit seller's stand, the boards are bare. Nothing to see, except two or three bottles of wine at 196 francs. No more packages home sent by rail or truck.

Rumors: the first regiment of France, the regiment of Vichy, joined the maquis. The maquis is master of a few cities in the center of France: Tulle,

Limoges. Giraud* and de Lattre de Tassigny are now commanding our forces there.[57]

De Gaulle declares that for the moment there is no agreement between the Liberation Committee (in Algiers) and the Allies about the administration of French territory as it is progressively liberated. He protests the proclamations by General Eisenhower, which "seem to announce a kind of takeover by an inter-allied command in France."[58]

De Gaulle protests. What's more, he protests sharply, clearly, without holding back, without skirting around the issue in thought or language, without interposing a mattress of ambiguous precautions between the English and him, without padded precautions. Could de Gaulle be the statesman who finally breaks with diplomatic style, the style that puts a people to sleep?

Electricity and gas in dribs and drabs. Telegraphic and telephone communications, regional and intercity, suspended in part of the Occupied Zone. What do they mean by Occupied Zone? According to the radio and the rumors going around, the armed forces of the interior are holding several cities.

A state of war—less depressing, less degrading than the lethargic state of occupation.

"Douai. The criminal court has sentenced Marcel Sidrac, aged fifty, from Sin-le-Noble (North) to four months in prison for having stolen a dog in order to eat it."

---

[57] Paris was effectively buzzing with rumors. The only true piece of news here: June 7–8, the *résistants* took Tulle; but on the morning of the ninth, the city was controlled by elements of the SS division Das Reich, which hanged ninety-nine hostages from the balconies and trees of the city. As for the first regiment of France, part of its three thousand men were fighting the occupying forces.—J.-P. A.

Jean de Lattre de Tassigny (1889–1952) was a much-decorated officer in World War I, wounded five times. In 1940, the youngest general in the French Army, he distinguished himself in tank battles. Arrested by Vichy for refusing to fight the Allies, he escaped to join de Gaulle in London in 1943. He was the only French officer to command a large American unit in 1944–45.—D. B.

[58] On June 6, General Eisenhower addressed the Norwegian, Dutch, Belgian, and Luxembourgian peoples, telling them he wished to work together with them. But since the White House judged there was no representative government in France, Eisenhower asked the French to "follow his orders," while adding that they would "choose their representatives and government themselves." To protest what he considered intolerable interference in purely French business, Charles de Gaulle refused to give a speech after the American Supreme Commander of the Allied Forces. He would speak only at 6:00 p.m., on the BBC. In a June 10 declaration to the AFI news agency, he officially protested American policy, particularly their putting "so-called French money" in circulation in the liberated territories.—J.-P. A.

Déat broadcasts an appeal to French workers.[59] It's all Hitlerian orthodoxy. An astonishing fidelity at the very moment Hitler's armies are retreating everywhere. "Before civil war lights its torches," Déat says, "before a crazed assault is launched against national unity, before pitiless and irresistible repression imposes order on seditious and dissident forces, their duty must be clearly defined for those (the workers) who have incontrovertibly suffered the most and will continue to suffer."

So Déat declares that whatever may happen, "the workers will continue to suffer." So Déat joyfully accepts "pitiless and irresistible repression," a new Versaillais repression.[60]

Neither the Siamese cat, nor Riv——, nor Bel—— know there's war, the Occupation, the Resistance, the maquis, and, depending on the outcome of the war, the mind (that's what one is forced to call it, there's no other name) will either retain a few chances to exist or lose all of them.

On Suzanne's dressing table, mixed in with brushes and perfume bottles, there are identity cards, rolled-up papers, maps, and sketches. In one of those sketches, I see the name of La Clarté. La Clarté . . . the memory of a happy vacation with Gignoux.

A maid at a hotel where German officers are staying relays information to Father Fanget. Thanks to which, two informers were caught like rabbits in their den.

June 14

I'm in hiding. I don't go out. I'm a spider in the center of its web. From time to time, a rumor gets caught in it.

The people of Paris. Since the Allies landed, German trucks go by camouflaged with branches. Out of mockery, cyclists and pedestrians plaster leaves between their cap and their neck. The same ones, no doubt, who in 1941 made swimming motions in the metro. (There were rumors at the time of failed attempts to land in England and German soldiers drowned or burned by flaming sheets of oil on the water.)

June 15

De Gaulle spent a few hours in France.[61] Will de Gaulle's full, pure glory rise from the heart of the masses? The bourgeoisie has a reticent attitude toward him.

---

[59] While continuing to live in Paris, Marcel Déat had been minister of labor and national solidarity since March 1944.—J.-P. A.

[60] This refers to the bloody repression of the Paris Commune by government troops from Versailles (the "Versaillais") in 1871.—D. B.

[61] Charles de Gaulle landed from the destroyer *La Combattante* on the beach at Courseulles the morning of June 14. He walked around the little portion of liberated France, particularly Bayeux and Isigny, which gave him a warm welcome. He installed François Coulet as *commissaire de la république* in Bayeux before returning to England that night.—J.-P. A.

He's not exactly a safe soldier. When the bourgeoisie were asking for someone to guard their deposit boxes, when they were wallowing in defeat, he was proposing nothing but victory, a victory the bourgeoisie did not desire. So they accused him of ambition. Poor souls, who can't conceive of a point where ambition fuses with a great goal and is absorbed by it. And that's exactly what makes someone destined for greatness.

June 16

Immobility and inaction have brought me to a state of bizarre torpor. It seems to me I left my self in storage somewhere, I don't know where. If I were arrested, it seems to me it wouldn't be me they were arresting.

Christian de Rollepot has been arrested.[62] No one knows anything, except that he must have been transported to Vichy. His wife just told us this. As soon as she left, Suzanne said she was afraid he'd be tortured. "No, no, of course not . . ." I said, as if rejecting the word, brushing it off, were enough for Christian to be saved. But I quickly realized Suzanne was right, and I'm ashamed I yielded to that optimism. It's merely a way of evading other people's misfortunes. In actual fact, the French police often use the same methods as the Gestapo.

June 17

They've created courts for maintaining order, for crimes against military duty or discipline.[63] No preliminary investigation, an appointed defense attorney, sentences immediately pronounced and enforced. Civil servants who perform acts against the enforcement of the laws or government orders will be handed over to courts-martial constituted as extraordinary criminal courts.

The historian Marc Bloch was tortured in Lyon: repeated immersions in ice water, the soles of his feet burned, three ribs broken. He just got bronchial pneumonia.[64]

June 19

Last night Radio London played their recording of the call General de Gaulle addressed to the French people June 18, 1940.[65]

---

[62] Christian de Rollepot was Suzanne Werth's cousin.—J.-P. A.

[63] This new measure of June 16 reinforced the Militia's control of the judiciary. These courts, whose mission was to punish "antinational activities," were set up within the jurisdiction of every appeals court.—J.-P. A.

[64] Marc Bloch was shot on June 16, 1944.

[65] Incorrect: it can't be the original recording. The BBC did not keep the record of the historic call of June 18.—J.-P. A.

For the full text of de Gaulle's "Call of June 18," see Appendix 1.

I was not familiar with the text of this appeal. On June 18, 1940, I was on the banks of the Loire. Noise of the road and incoherent snatches of false news items were all that came to me, through a poor radio connected to a car battery. So on June 18, 1940, I did not hear de Gaulle. In those hours when everything in France was decomposing except treason, de Gaulle announced the future and forced it. Why didn't London radio detach part of this Call of June '40 and repeat it every day, like a slogan?

In the first half of July when we were refugees in Chapelon at the Delaveaus', all we had in our hands were two newspapers: a Montargis weekly and an issue of *Paris-Soir* hastily written by the Germans. There was a radio set in the Delaveau's kitchen, but German non-coms ate there, and soldiers came in at all hours. And yet something of de Gaulle, the main point of de Gaulle's words, did reach us. In what mysterious way? Today I would be unable to say.

Butter costs 850 francs a kilo.[66]

Proposal for the postwar period:

Establish all the acts of torture or cruelty following the most rigorous, critical rules of evidence. Ask German professors and scientists to participate in the fact-finding mission. Ask them to confirm, without comment, the reality of the facts they helped to establish. If they refuse, contrast their refusal with the quantity and obviousness of the evidence.

Publish the whole thing in pamphlets, books, and posters. Those books and pamphlets would be published in Germany; those posters would be displayed in Germany.

But I was forgetting that the Gestapo and the SS were not alone in torturing: in France, the police and the Militia . . . Well then, let it all be published, and let's bring these chapters in human bestiality to light and compare them.

June 22

"Young men of France, Captain Darmor says to you: 'The Kriegsmarine is opening its ranks to you and to the elite of European youth. German is the uniform, European and French is the cause . . .'"

A hundred similar texts were published in the papers and still are, multiplied by posters. No one pays attention to them.

Immediately after the debacle, despite the Anglophobia of part of the French bourgeoisie, this text would have seemed the work of a madman. German propaganda was hiding behind the masochistic moralizing of the marshal. Then

---

[66] In the following weeks, the price of a kilo of butter would reach 1,300 francs. The monthly salary of a skilled worker in the Paris region was 4,500 francs.—J.-P. A.

came the period of the "policy of Montoire" and collaboration.[67] "Collaborator" has remained in common speech, where it's the opposite of "Gaullist." But who remembers Montoire? Is it a man, is it a village? Then came the period of anti-Communism. The theme is the defense of "our old civilization," of "Christian civilization." The accent is on Europe; its old and Christian characteristics become secondary.

Christian was released. The man and woman he'd been working with didn't talk.

First night (in Paris), handcuffs on his wrists, the chain of the handcuffs attached to a radiator. Paris-Vichy trip, courteous police officers, not louts. Vichy. The casino is used as a prison.[68] He is first led down to the basement, under the kitchens. No light, oozing with water. They don't leave him there. They take him into the movie theater. He spends the night in an armchair. Militia wander through the room armed with submachine guns. One of them shows him his weapon: "Move, and I fire." Thuggish faces (a lot of former soldiers from disciplinary regiments among them). Two young men, teenagers really, seem lost there. The head Militiaman, who's supposed to interrogate him, is not to be found. Two days of waiting. Questioning: "To me, you seem an out-and-out liar." Then, at the end, giving in to some unease or other: "If what you say is confirmed, you will be released immediately." No food during those two days. Taken back to the movie theater. Instead of an armchair, they give him a loge. So he will have one night of sleep. As they went by the offices to the movie theater, he saw a Militiaman with a rope around his neck and his legs tied, stripped to the waist; other Militiamen were beating him with belts. His flesh was bleeding. On the one hand, Nazi sadism, transplanted sadism. On the other, in the offices, the incoherence of the improvised policemen. It was obvious that Christian was "guilty."

People are saying that in a town of some fifteen hundred inhabitants near Tulle or Limoges, the SS drove the men into barns, the women and children into the church, and burned them alive.[69]

---

[67] Pétain shook hands with Hitler during their meeting at Montoire, October 24, 1940.

[68] It was in the Petit-Casino of Vichy and the nearby Château des Brosses that the Militia interrogated and tortured the men and women they arrested.—J.-P. A.

[69] This is Oradour-sur-Glane, some twenty kilometers from Limoges; it was occupied on June 10 by 120 men of the Third Company of the First Battalion of the SS division Das Reich, whose mission was to sow terror in its wake before it reached the Normandy front. Taking as a pretext the disappearance of an SS officer fifty kilometers away, the murderers machine-gunned or burned alive 642 men, women, and children (including fifty-four refugees from Lorraine) and then burned down the village.—J.-P. A.

June 24–25

This may be a legend, but it's a fine one. They say after the Occupation, the Germans called Paris the city without a gaze. They meant that the Parisians, without even turning their eyes away, seemed not to see them.[70]

Yesterday, I saw two very young German soldiers in the metro, the colonel told me, disconcerted by that refusal of anyone to gaze at them. I have often seen the crowd "grave and absent" before the occupiers.

Grave and absent, but sometimes, too—especially right after the debacle— without any decency or modesty. I can still see that beautiful girl in Chalon on July 14, 1940, walking forward with a royal step, smiling, surrounded by several German soldiers who composed her court.

In *Deutschland-Frankreich*, Albert Buesche, "after analyzing the contemporary tendencies in painting, sculpture, decoration, and illustration," notes a surprising resemblance between French and German art, in which he sees "the presage of a community to come, etc."[71]

Hardly had I gone through these excerpts from *Deutschland-Frankreich* than Hany told me fifty young men taking refuge in the woods near l'Isle-Adam have been shot.

The Americans are in Cherbourg.

June 26

In *Le Petit Parisien*, André Salmon "pays homage to the intelligent zeal and the patriotic goodwill of the railroad workers busy repairing the harm done by terrorist criminals."[72]

Cynicism? The conformism of a journalist? A clause of style?

"The workers," V—— told me, "only want their aperitifs." He bases this scorn on the reactions of the typographers who work for the newspapers. "When the bombs

---

[70] This is not exactly a legend. The day the Germans entered Paris, June 14, almost all the Parisians who had remained in the capital chose to remain behind closed shutters, even after the curfew was lifted. German reports speak of "a city without a gaze" (*die Stadt ohne Blick*). True, on the following days, some Parisians watched the Wehrmacht parades and were filmed by German propaganda services.—J.-P. A.

In an essay on the Paris Occupation in *Situations*, Sartre describes Parisians looking "through" the occupiers and not at them, much as Werth does above.—D. B.

[71] *Deutschland-Frankreich*: "Germany-France." Albert Buesche, who had written a book on Arno Breker, Hitler's favorite sculptor, covered art and literature for the *Pariser Zeitung*, the Paris newspaper of the German occupiers.

[72] The "terrorist criminals" were resistance saboteurs. André Salmon was a poet, art critic, and writer, a friend of Guillaume Apollinaire and other giants of Modernism in art and literature. After

fall twenty kilometers away from them, the English are liberators; when they hit their houses or fall in their neighborhood, they hate the English, those murderers." I think V—— is being short-sighted. What a typographer says is one sign among thousands. The soul of the masses is more discreet. It is not entirely in one statement of fear or anger.

And here's a contrary sign. It was in the metro, during an air raid alert that lasted almost an hour. A woman says she had nine children, her husband died in 1940, and houses right next to hers were destroyed by English bombs. She spoke without anger and without whining. She simply repeated: "That shouldn't be . . . That shouldn't be . . ." Then she said: "My oldest son—he's nineteen—I don't understand him. He says that's fine, that's the way it has to be. And if the bombs fell on his house he'd still say it's fine . . ."

June 28

Philippe Henriot killed. It wasn't an impulsive act but an organized expedition.[73]

When Pucheu was sentenced to death, there was not unanimous approval. People said: "Blood calls for blood," or: "We shouldn't make martyrs." Many reasons for this, the simplest being that the people hardly knew Pucheu's name, while they knew Henriot as the man who spoke for the Germans. Henriot's death is welcomed by the street and the shop with an odd, smiling lightness— and this neighborhood isn't a working-class neighborhood. "Well done," they say, without emphasis. A curious reaction, with no apparent hatred. This death seems satisfying to people, with no tragic dimension.

Laval, in his eulogy, laments the civil war. His text is ambiguous. You can't tell if he's deploring a civil war that's already here or if he fears the threat.

But Henriot's murder is not an act of civil war, not yet. It's one of the last episodes of the foreign war.

"It's not an assassination," says the colonel, "it's an execution." No . . . let's not look for a euphemism or a legal justification. It would be very close to hypocrisy.

In La Ferté-Saint-Aubin, near Orléans, twenty young men from eighteen to twenty were shot. They were in the maquis, except for two of them, who were arrested by chance with the others.[74]

the Liberation, he was sentenced to five years of "national indignity"; one consequence was that he could not publish using the pen name he had used before.

[73] The expedition was, in fact, organized. The Groupes Francs du Mouvement de Libération Nationale planned the kidnapping of Philippe Henriot and his assassination if he resisted, since he was one of the symbols of collaboration: minister of information, editorialist on Radio Nationale, and a member of the Militia. On the morning of June 28, sixteen men overpowered the Ministry of Information. This execution created a huge stir.—J.-P. A.

[74] A few additional facts are necessary here: dozens of students in the classes preparing for the competitive entrance exam to the "grandes écoles" left Paris to join the maquis, with a meeting

June 30

The image of the day according to the paper: "Germany is achieving important defensive success on all fronts." English prisoners going through Paris. "There was, for a long while, an uninterrupted line of prisoners, under the jeers of the crowd, born from unspeakable anger."

The street and the shop are optimistic. "At the grocer's, everybody says we'll be rid of them by August."

The Dominican monastery near rue Sarrette. A group of Militia and Germans demand to see one of the priests. He appears. He is shot.

I have no other details. But this was transmitted to me by a witness, someone with a critical sense.

July 2

"If I'm not back in three days," the priest says, "it's because I won't have succeeded."

What's the connection between this kind of activity and Christianity? And Catholicism? Watertight barriers, like between science and religion with priests who do scientific research? Or is he defending the freedom to be a Christian? Does he identify France with Christianity, as others identify France with revolution?

In the calm tone of a technician, the priest talks of the superiority of the machine gun over the submachine gun.

In a few days, if he returns, he'll get Claude and a few other boys together and instruct them in the use of the revolver and the submachine gun.

July 5

In a bookstore on rue du Four, Hérold-Paquis is dedicating his books today, to whoever comes. (When I lived with the peasants—and they listened to the radio—I didn't hear his name once.) When I came to Paris, I had no idea who he was.

It doesn't seem people in Paris have the same hatred for Hérold-Paquis as they had for Henriot. They think he's a funny guy. I've just heard this voluble radio peddler. His words spin like a squirrel in a cage, in its cylinder.

point in Sologne at farms around La Ferté-Saint-Aubin. But they did not go unnoticed: thirty of them, arrested on the morning of June 10 at La Ferme du By, were shot on the spot; twelve others met the same fate a few kilometers from there, and fourteen more would be deported to Dachau.—J.-P. A.

Not a street rumor but a story a young man who was there told Hany. He was watching railroad traffic in the station at Lagny-Pomponne. A freight car on a siding. A hand at a window. He walks over. He tells the maquis. In the car, a hundred and twenty-five men, locked in for three days with no food, without even a glass of water. And twenty-five corpses.

July 12

The priest is back. He traveled on a locomotive. In a station, he was arrested by the Germans. Four hours of questioning. A miracle: they examine the food he's carrying and not his documents. But a woman of the Gestapo is more mistrustful than the men. "The worst," she says, "are the ones who have their papers in order and the ones who look the most natural." Four Germans take him to the road. Then he walks forty kilometers.[75] He was setting up a liaison between several thousand parachutists and the maquis.

Riv——has reached the stage where he openly admits his support for Déat, for Henriot, for de Brinon.[76] How can we explain that in 1943 a man so familiar with all the subtleties of the political jungle could have gone hand in glove with the Berliners, who were already defeated? Victory, defeat, resistance, and collaboration—he probably calculated them in the same way he would have calculated the electoral distinctions between two politicians. Perhaps he thought the rules of thought and even those of the heart have no other value than the rules of a game. It is not degrading to respect the different rules of different games.

He didn't understand that there are moments when no idea is inoffensive, when the poorest idea carries with it shreds of reality and flesh, men's flesh. He thought he was playing with poker chips. He was playing with his soul and his whole being.

July 13

A young English aviator was brought to us for lunch (a navigator). He parachuted down near Rambouillet on June 1 (his plane shot down by a fighter). Three of his flight crew were killed, two taken prisoner. A Canadian was able to escape, and as he knows French, he may have gotten away.

Bobby has burns on the nape of his neck, his hand, and his left wrist. The scars are reddish but not horrible. They don't say "crippled."

Claude went to pick him up at the Denfert-Rochereau station. He came from Chevreuse, where he was taken in by Cherbonnier. Cherbonnier, who runs a

[75] About twenty-five miles.

[76] Werth is very likely referring to Paul Rives, a mildly socialist politician before 1940 who became a collaborator. Oddly enough, he was also a militant anti-racist.

bookstore in Chevreuse, was sheltering five other aviators. It's almost unbelievable. Six aviators hidden in an apartment above the bookstore, a little shop that sells newspapers. And this in a small town. What precautions to bring them in at night, and so that nothing reveals their presence during the day! But Cherbonnier is an admirable specialist at these jobs.

This Englishman is a big boy of twenty-five. Baby-faced. Gentle, calm. There are thousands like that, who the political powers and process of history are offering to death. Thousands, but far off. But here he is, with us.

He doesn't like tea or jam and doesn't smoke.

Antoinette (her real name is Anne-Marie de Dudzeele) brought him from Chevreuse to our place. In the metro, someone asked the young Englishman for the time. He doesn't know a word of French. Antoinette glances at her watch and says, "I just looked at the time . . . Have a look . . ." And she shows her wrist. The Englishman lowers his head and pretends to be sleeping.

In the afternoon, Claude and one of Aymé-Guerrin's daughters take him to the Gare de l'Est station and from there to Rainey, where he'll be taken in by a safe house. They're used to those transits and escorts. In Paris, the Englishman walks behind his guides.

Bobby told us this, and perhaps it's true: an aviator who'd jumped from his burning plane was able to approach the Spanish border. He gets into a train. He has no papers, or at least no fake ones. A policeman comes into the car and asks for ID. The aviator takes a sheet of blank paper out of his pocket and writes these three letters: RAF. The policeman gives him back the paper, makes a little bow, and disappears.

July 15

For a few days now, the rumor has been going around (from the street to the shops, from upper floors to the street, from the shops to the street) that Georges Mandel and Jean Zay were assassinated by the Militia.[77]

This morning we read in *Le Petit Parisien*: "Death of Georges Mandel . . . During his transfer to a detention camp, the car transporting him was attacked on the road, and Monsieur Mandel was killed during the skirmish. A judicial inquiry has been opened." They kill, they don't dare admit they kill and lie with such crude ingenuousness that it's disconcerting. That attack, led by unspecified assailants, by an abstraction of assailants. That "skirmish . . ."

---

[77] Jean Zay was assassinated on June 20. For the far right, he had two things against him: he was minister of education in the 1936–37 Popular Front government and remained until 1939, and he had a Jewish father; the Paris dailies repeatedly demanded the arrest of "the Jew Jean Zay." Georges Mandel, a minister in conservative governments, was also Jewish and anti-Nazi. Deported to Buchenwald, he was returned to France, imprisoned in Paris, and delivered to the French Militia, which shot him July 7 near Fontainebleau.

The Russians have taken Grodno.

That couple: the man solicited young men for a fictive passage to Spain; his wife, a gatekeeper at a railroad crossing, would hide them for a few hours, the time to tell the Gestapo and hand them over. She was assassinated.

Shop rumor. German soldiers in Paris disarmed the Gestapo. An idealistic, dangerous rumor tending to suggest the image of two Germanys, the good one and the bad one.[78]

An attempt to kill Hitler. No details.

The Führer speaking to the German people: "If I am talking to you today, it is so that you can hear my voice and know that I am safe and sound . . ."

A German soldier went into the shoemaker's and asked him to make some small repair or other. Suddenly: "We're sick of it . . . We're sick of the war." He leans on the edge of the table with his fingertips, drooping, insubstantial. "Just look how we're dressed," he says. And he shows his torn sleeve with its worn-out fabric. The threads can't hold it together anymore.

I know . . . months ago, German soldiers would strike up a conversation with peasants, telling them "We're sick of it." And we didn't know if it was a soldier's confession or bait from an agent provocateur. And every soldier in every army in the world is sick of it. But there are a hundred different ways of being sick of it.

Two English aviators have been brought to us. There was an incident on the way. They came across a German truck stopped right on the sidewalk. Soldiers were changing a tire. The two Englishmen stop, reluctant to mingle with the soldiers scattered along the sidewalk. Their guide turns around and says, "Come on . . ." And one of the Englishmen answers "Yes," in English. It all went very well. The word was lost in the noise of voices and tools.

One of the Englishmen is tall, elegant, and blond. What's surprising is the harmony of blond and pink, a pink spread over his whole face like a pink light

---

[78] The rumor was premature: in the hours following the announcement of the July 20 attempt on Hitler's life, units of the Wehrmacht did arrest SS and Gestapo officers, but they would have to release them immediately.—J.-P. A.

from the inside of his head. The young lord of English novels of the past century. The other is dark-haired and stocky. Much less "showy" in transit. He doesn't know if he's a father or not. They told him the child would be born at the end of June. But since then, he's been deprived of news.

Their plane was hit by a fighter at 2:00 a.m. They were flying at two thousand meters. One or two minutes in a parachute. (I calculate that corresponds to twenty-five minutes on foot.) Chappie, the dark one, injured his nose against the floor of the plane. The wound scarred over, and the scar zigzags between his eyebrows and his nostrils. They walked for forty minutes. Then met some farmers. Chappie was able to wash his blood-covered face.

I don't feel too ashamed, because now the risk we're taking is as great as theirs.

I surprise them alone. They don't look happy anymore. Not sad either. They look like soldiers in a war, with the bad tempers of men who have nothing to do. I'd hardly come in when their smile appeared again. I'm bringing them something from life, something that isn't war.

They've been offered a safe refuge in a house near Paris surrounded by a big garden. They refuse. They want to get back to their squadron. And the young lord makes the gesture of dropping bombs on an imaginary city.

Suzanne, Claude, and I think as simply as they do. May the world and politicians be obliged share a little of that simplicity.

This letter sent by pneumatic tube from Aymé-Guerrin to Suzanne. The text seems clear to me. I have a hard time believing the Gestapo would be fooled by it. But, true prudence being just about impossible, they try to ward off detection by whatever means they can. "Dear Madame, three of our little puppies were already taken outside Paris yesterday. To transport them rapidly in little groups, I need to know how to reach them rapidly. Would you be good enough to set up the necessary emergency liaisons? To avoid any loss of time . . ." etc.

"Note on an informer: height: 1.75 m, light-colored eyes, balding head. Killed and robbed a German who was carrying a large sum of money. Accused a Frenchman of this murder, who was executed. Informed on several work-service evaders or résistants."

Suzanne doesn't like to transmit this sort of message. Besides, I think it's the first of its kind.

July 24

At 8:00 a.m., someone knocks on the door. It's not a worrisome knock, authoritarian or professional. It's not the hasty, not very rhythmic knock of the little telegraphist either, nor the hesitant knock of an old lady lost on the stairs.

This knock doesn't much worry me. I'm pretty sure I can identify it. It's the two Englishmen who spent the night in "the big room," one on the sofa, the other on a mattress on the floor. No doubt their time of departure or their place of destination has been modified. It was almost that, or at least the same kind of thing: documents to be transmitted.

July 24

Allied landing, bomb for Hitler ... Will there never be the event that sweeps everything along with it—the event that shakes up the rhythm of events? The war is like a dead dog in the water that kids are vainly trying to sink by throwing rocks at it.

Suzanne is arranging the transport of a radio transmitter.

A paper that's worth more than an identity card. It's not counterfeit; it was stolen: "Demobilization card. Discharge Center of the Département de la Seine. *Stets bei sich tragen!* Always keep it on you! *Entlassungsschein.* Discharge document."

The two Englishmen—our Englishmen—have left. How light they were, how discreet!

July 25

Jeanne V—— is back from Saint-Amour. A week ago, about 250 Germans arrived. They didn't do much in town. Above all, they visited the villages and isolated farmhouses. "In Chantemerle,"[79] she says, "we saw them come from all over, from the path of Ch'Coulot, the path of Vauceneau, the Besson woods. Goudeau was in his vineyard, looking at everyone who was coming by the road down below through his binoculars. They shot at him. He got back to his house. Crawling."

In Bel Air, they searched through the chests of drawers. When they got there, old Perrot, venerable like an old man in a play and twisted like an old vine, was reading a letter from Raymond (his grandson). They ripped it out of his hands.

In Balanod, after a simple examination of their identity papers, they killed a Jew hiding there and two unknowns they'd brought from somewhere. Papers were not found on their corpses.

They came into our house; friends were staying there. They stole a watch. They looked under the beds, ripped off the sheets and blankets. In Billet's place, they took the rabbit and the piece of pork that were on the table.[80]

[79] Chantemerle was the summer home of Suzanne and Léon Werth.—J.-P. A.

[80] Marius Billet [called Laurent elsewhere] was Suzanne Werth's tenant farmer, here cited using his real name.—J.-P. A.

They took men under forty to Salavre, about fifteen kilometers away, to check their papers. The commanding officer gave them a harsh speech, telling them to make sure they "obey marshal Pétain."

One of the Germans said they'd burn down every house (like at Moulin-des-Points and elsewhere) if the maquis appeared there again.

I was forgetting this: on the terrace of Chantemerle, a German leaned over our friends' youngest, a child of two, picked him up in his arms, and spoke to him tenderly. That illuminates everything with German light. A volley of machine gun fire isn't completely German if the gunner can't lean over a cradle.

July 26

We learn Masiée was arrested. I never saw him. But I know, through Suzanne, of his courage, his nobility, his purity.

A gala down in the youth center. Accordions, sketches, monologues. The priest, who just got out of Fresnes, gives a short speech: "In that particular place I'm coming from, I saw the most complete optimism, the finest devotion, and the most complete unity." He says that standing on a little platform in the courtyard of the youth center. He's not afraid of informers. But after the war, what will become of that total unity?

In Saint-Amour, the maquisards did some damage to the shops of the grocer-sergeant and a pastry maker. But the collaborationist bourgeois and squires were not harassed. Perhaps they were more prudent in the way they expressed themselves.

A Canadian who parachuted out of his plane near Chevreuse wandered about for four days. He pushed away people who wanted to help him, hide him. He said he was sick of it all, and he had only one idea in his head: to turn himself in to the Germans and be done with it.

July 31

A truck is transporting *résistants* sentenced to die to the place of execution. A group of maquisards stops the truck, delivers the condemned men, and ties up the Germans. You need more adventurous strength and difficult courage for this than for regular warfare.

Claude biked across Paris with a radio transmitter for Father Fanget in his saddlebag.

The colonel wears maps of fortifications sewn into his tie.

August 3

Speech by Churchill in the House of Commons. Damage caused by the V-1 rockets (4,735 dead, 14,000 wounded, 17,000 houses destroyed, 800,000 damaged) and the possibility of unpleasant surprises. It's not a victory song. But, several times already, we've seen that Churchill imitates those parents who pretend to their children not to know if Father Christmas has "brought something." To announce successes, he uses the same precautions the Germans use to announce setbacks.

The Allies are in Rennes and Dinan.

Sometimes, in Indochina, I was ashamed of being white, ashamed of being French. Every German is responsible for Germany, for the Gestapo.

But we must learn to measure this kind of responsibility. Tolstoy lived at the same time tsarism was organizing pogroms.

Riv—— played, as they say, the wrong card. He defends himself in this way: "Germany is losing. I'm with the collaborators, with those who are defeated." (He forgets to say that the defeated are still holding on to their positions, and he has one of some importance.) "Collaborator I remain; because I have no other passion than music, and Germany is a musical country, because Germany is the country of Mendelsohn (he doesn't say that the music of the Jew Mendelsohn is banned in Germany), "the country of Beethoven, the country of Wagner."

August 6

Radio-Paris is making fun of the credulous *résistants* who think the Americans are already approaching Brest and Nantes. In what court are these lawyers arguing? They can no longer sway public opinion, and they know it. Do they think they can sway what's happening?

Mandouze is hiding in Paris. His library in Bourg was destroyed.

August 7

German propaganda is admitting defeat but affirming that defeat contains a hidden victory.

The street, the shop, Aymé-Guerrin, and Father Fanget: "They'll be in Paris next Sunday."

August 9

Eleven at night. I'm vaguely listening to the radio. Suddenly I hear: "The French pilot de Saint-Exupéry,* who belonged to a dissident unit, was reported missing after a mission over France."[81]

The historical events are indifferent to me. I see a crippled plane falling, I see a plane burning. I see his face.

I think of so many hours of friendship. Sometimes he would arrive late at night. Serious problems and card tricks. And the inn at Fleurville—those hours we spent at the Fleurville inn, where life seemed to have the taste of perfection to us.

I weigh the words "reported missing." I look for reasons to hope. Suzanne has hope. But it's to reduce my sorrow.

Silly thoughts: it's doubting him, it's betraying him to believe in his death. I hope. He fell, wounded. He's being taken care of by peasants.

August 10

I mechanically go on keeping this diary. All I have inside me is sorrow. Would he be happy at the absoluteness of my sorrow? Would he ask me to be wise enough not to shed childish tears? As he said of Mermoz, I cannot see him "in the perfection of death."[82]

August 11

Rumor of a general strike on the railroads.[83]

Buses go by full of German wounded, standing, squeezed together.

An escaped prisoner, a friend of Alain Bourdon's,[84] saw Poles hanged in a Warsaw station. He saw Jews pushed into train cars with rifle butts. When a car was full to bursting, the Germans machine-gunned the Jews clinging onto the steps who were vainly trying to enter the car.

The train was taking the Jews a few kilometers away. The soldiers made them get off and mowed them down.

---

[81] Despite his forty-three years, Antoine de Saint-Exupéry managed to get himself assigned to an air reconnaissance unit. He did not return from a mission over Annecy on July 31: his P-38 Lightning was hit as he got ready to land near Bastia (Corsica) on the Bongo airfield. Werth would tell the story of his death in a little book he devoted to his friend (*La Vie de Saint-Exupéry*, Éditions du Seuil, 1948).—J.-P. A.

[82] The pilot Jean Mermoz was a pioneer of civil aviation. He disappeared over the Atlantic in 1936.

[83] It was effectively on August 10 that union members in the Resistance set off a strike with patriotic watchwords as the order of the day. The movement progressively gained all railroad workers in France.—J.-P. A.

[84] Actually the poet Armand Robin.—J.-P. A. Robin, a multilingual anarchistic writer, poet, and journalist, was a pupil and friend of Jean Guéhenno, too.—D.B.

The Germans gave the notorious collaborators who write in the papers (the Lousteaus, the Brasillachs, the Luchaires,* etc.) passports for Wiesbaden.[85]

Trucks are parked in front of the hotels occupied by the Germans. Soldiers pile mattresses, rugs, and sewing machines in them. "The circus is moving out," I hear. They work night and day.

At the Senate building, on top of the mattresses, the blankets, and the most varied utensils, they piled a few "gray mice."[86] I've heard that at the Gare de l'Est, from which trains were no longer leaving, they began fighting among themselves.

P—— said to Suzanne: "You're thinking like a carpenter, you're as sentimental as the masses. You don't understand a thing about political interests. The Americans and the Germans agree. The Germans are intentionally letting themselves get beaten in Normandy and Brittany. They'll abandon Paris. Laval will receive them. They'll deal with him. After that, he'll hand over power to Jeanneney, who'll hand it over to de Gaulle."[87]

Who's talking like this? Some simpleton, someone in the early stages of madness? No, a cultivated bourgeois, whose library is full of expensive editions.

In a bookstore. A customer: "I'd like a map of the front."

The saleslady: "I would advise you to get a map of France."

The radio. A German combatant addresses his "French comrades." Thanks to new weapons, Germany will win the war. "Stalin, Churchill, and Roosevelt spend their time looking at their watches in terror: every minute is bringing them nearer to the fatal disaster. They know it's all over for them."

Is de Gaulle loved by the people? There's not the slightest trace of an attention-grabbing Boulanger in him.[88] The love of the people for de Gaulle is still silent. Tomorrow, it will surge from the depths of the crowd, like a huge sigh, like a tidal wave.

---

[85] Robert Brasillach was a novelist, essayist, and poet whose wartime journalism strongly supported the Nazis, including their deportation of the Jews. He was tried for treason after the liberation of France and executed, despite appeals for clemency from leading intellectuals.

[86] *Souris grises*: literally "gray mice": German women in the military or Gestapo auxiliary. They wore gray uniforms, and the French word for "mouse" is feminine. Werth puts the term in quotation marks.

[87] Jules Jeanneney presided over the Senate. He would be a minister [in the provisional government] set up by Charles de Gaulle on September 9, 1944.—J.-P. A.

[88] The extreme nationalist General Boulanger was so popular that it was feared he might become the dictator of France toward the end of the nineteenth century.

August 14

Fighting between maquisards and Germans in Le Rainey. The Germans machine-gunned people in the streets.

On the Esplanade des Invalides, three trucks have stopped. They're filled with prisoners people say are Canadian. The crowd formed a circle around them. The men lift up the women in their arms so they can kiss the prisoners. The Germans guarding them don't intervene, seem indifferent. A few moments later, they disperse the crowd that's beginning to form. By firing in the air, some say, without firing, say others.

The metro's not running anymore. Electricity from ten to midnight. They say gas is going to be cut off. A hundred grams of bread a day instead of three hundred.[89]

August 15

There's a rumor that the police are on strike.[90] No details.

Message from the military governor of Paris, General von Choltitz, about order, food, and security in the capital. A strange text, written in uncertain French and full of involuntary admissions.[91] General von Choltitz admits fearing terrorist—that is, resistance—activity. Recognizes the proximity of the front, sees the approaching Anglo-Americans awakening a hope that could even result in a riot. A few clear images remain after reading: an invincible Germany, whose means of transportation are hardly bothered by sabotage, a kindly Germany that provides Paris with electricity . . . An implacable Germany, determined to exercise "the severest, even the most brutal, repression." But also a hesitant Germany, which "pleads" with us.

Not one policeman in front of the police station on Place Saint-Sulpice. The station is closed.

Where is Tonio? Now I think he's alive. The certainty he's alive has taken hold of me. But how anxious that certainty is!

---

[89] 100 grams is roughly 3.5 ounces.—D. B.

A significant remark, because Léon Werth rarely complains about his lot. Daily life was effectively getting more difficult every day.—J.-P. A.

[90] The call for a strike by the three resistance movements of the Paris police did take effect on the morning of August 15. The Paris insurrection was near.—J.-P. A.

[91] Hitler appointed General Dietrich von Choltitz, who seemed to him sufficiently safe politically, commander of *Gross-Paris* on August 3. The general affirmed that, despite everything, order would be maintained "at any price."—J.-P. A. Later, von Choltitz would disobey Hitler's order to destroy Paris when the Germans were forced to abandon it. He had, however, obeyed his order to liquidate the Jews in the Soviet Union, as he said in a postwar conversation secretly taped while he was in captivity in England.—D. B.

Dinner: a few carrots, a few noodles with a piece of pork rind.

August 15

English radio is officially announcing that French troops commanded by General de Lattre de Tassigny, English, and American troops have landed on three beaches between Nice and Marseilles.[92]

How is Hitler reacting inwardly to this accumulation of hard knocks? He undeniably believes in himself and perhaps in his mission. Each hard blow seems to him like an injustice.

August 16

Twenty to thirty people are lining up in front of the bookseller's, hoping to get a newspaper, hoping to interpret the headlines.

In a Breton village near Plouguernével, the Germans hanged seventeen young men. They forbid anyone to take down the corpses. The parents who came to ask for the bodies were whipped. (Witness, a friend of Alain Bourdon's.)

The gas chambers, the torment of the mothers who don't know if their children are alive or dead. It's possible the German people don't know of these systematic atrocities, as the French people don't know of the sporadic acts of cruelty of its colonists. The people must be informed.

August 17

Revolver shots in the street last night. They say the Germans fired because the door of the requisitioned hotel where they sleep wasn't opened quickly enough.

Big headline in *Le Petit Parisien*: "Intense fighting in the Chartres-Dreux region." But the people say: "*They're* in Chartres, they're in Dreux."

A poster on the façade of the police station at Saint-Sulpice. The police are with the population of Paris. They've joined three centers of resistance. Ninety-seven percent of the policemen are no longer obeying Bussière, the Gestapo agent.[93] (Told to Andrée François by the shoemaker.) Hard to explain why the Germans haven't destroyed these posters.

Rumor: the Americans will be in Paris tonight. Another rumor: postal strike.

At five o'clock, the poster is still on the wall of the police station.

[92] Second entry for August 16. — DB. Operation Dragoon [the landing in Provence] was completely successful. French forces under the command of General Jean de Lattre de Tassigny made up seven out of the eleven divisions involved in the operation.—J.-P. A.

[93] Amédée Bussière was, more precisely, the last prefect of police of the Vichy government. As for the strike of the Paris police, it was effectively followed massively.—J.-P. A.

Groups squeeze in and huddle around it. I'm surprised. I think it's an extraordinarily important sign that neither the Gestapo nor the Militia have torn it to shreds. "If someone tried to rip it up," Claude says, "he'd be ripped up himself."

"Someone who works in city hall" told the director of the École Saint-Sulpice, who told the concierge, that Paris had been declared an open city.[94]

The soldiers of the anti-aircraft battery on the roof of the house on the corner of rue Madame lower a machine gun and crates with a pulley. They line them up on the sidewalk. It looks like poor people moving out of their apartment. Children watch them from the sidewalk across the street.

At seven o'clock, we're all convinced the Germans will evacuate Paris by midnight and the Americans will enter the city. The Germans are fleeing, routed. And the most urgent problem for us is the occupation of Berlin. At five we'd all decided that the Wehrmacht was leaving Paris but the Gestapo was staying. At seven, we were saying it was leaving. However, no new piece of news had reached us. The news in our midst had cooked and stewed in its own juice.

They say the Germans shot 140 political prisoners, as they did in Caen. And shot a hundred Frenchmen who were working for the Gestapo.[95]

August 18

No paper.

The commentators on Radio-Paris are gone. It's rumored that a Gaullist government, including seven Communists, has been constituted in the Hôtel de Ville. I ask Andrée François who she got this from, if the news was on a poster, and who signed the poster. "Madame Bigot (the concierge) is the one who told me," she says in an irritated voice. She lives from minute to minute, and I exasperate her by trying to make sense of the news and eliminate the most absurd reports.

We don't know anything, except that the police went over to the Resistance, and the soldiers in the anti-aircraft battery moved their machine gun elsewhere.

People are saying law and order in Paris will be given over to an SS regiment. They're also saying the Americans will be here Sunday.

People are saying the American police will replace the German police, the political prisoners in Fresnes and the inmates of Drancy were freed, and a Chautemps administration has been set up already. What confusion! How many spontaneous rumors, how many intentional rumors.

News items remain suspended in space for a moment and fall like snowflakes.

---

[94] This news is obviously false. General von Choltitz's mission in Paris was to fight.—J.-P. A.

[95] A certain number of political prisoners were executed in the Paris area, but an agreement between the Swedish consul Nordling and men around General von Choltitz enabled a large number of political prisoners to be saved.—J.-P. A.

August 19

A few isolated shots in the night, fairly near us. Radio at half past midnight: Montgomery declares the Battle of Normandy has been won,[96] the Germans are in flight, and the Allies are "at the outskirts of Paris." Meanwhile it does seem the Germans are leaving Paris. But what's the connection between this departure and the rumors that have been going around for two days about the agreement making Paris an open city? Were these rumors merely a prefiguration? Did they foreshadow, if not a surrender, at least the Germans' inability to defend themselves in Paris?

We don't know where the detachments that occupied Paris are going. We don't know if the Gestapo is leaving Paris too. We don't know who'll be in power in Paris tomorrow. We don't know anything, but, just as you can smell the sea before seeing it, we can scent freedom.

They're saying Pétain and Laval followed the Germans to Nancy.[97]

Speaking of de Gaulle, I'm told V—— said: "I don't trust generals." Sure, but just try and find a civilian whose thought was as lofty and far-sighted as his from 1940 to 1944.

The French flag is raised over the Hôtel-Dieu and the Prefecture of Police.

Fighting at the bottom of Boulevard Saint-Michel. The concierge of the building where the Krehers live was wounded in the leg while she was closing the carriage entrance. She was taken to the hospital. Madame Kreher (her husband, a lawyer, was deported) went down to the courtyard where the wounded had hidden and dressed their wounds.[98] She's the only one of the tenants of the building who opened the door to the FFI (who would then fire from her windows).[99] They were nice enough not to force the doors of the tenants who had locked them.

August 20

Shots fired from Boulevard Montparnasse last night, and from rue de Rennes.

---

[96] Operation Overlord was put under the command of the British general Bernard Montgomery.—J.-P. A.

[97] Hitler wanted the fiction of a French government acting in its official capacity to be maintained. Pierre Laval was to reach Belfort, where Philippe Pétain would join him, forcibly brought there from Vichy on August 20.—J.-P. A.

[98] Madame Kreher was a distant cousin of Suzanne Werth; her husband would return from deportation.—J.-P. A.

[99] The FFI (Forces Françaises de l'Intérieur) was the recently formed, armed and uniformed Resistance under the command of General de Gaulle.

Around 9:30, shots at the corner of rue Vavin. They say a German patrol fired at a man who was out for a late walk and killed him. This morning, you could see blood and a cap on the sidewalk.

Yesterday, London radio was announcing that the liberation of Paris was "imminent." But for the past two days Paris has thought it was liberated. The last German was supposed to have left Paris by midnight.

Yet there are still sporadic battles between resistance fighters and German soldiers. Real fighting on Place Saint-Michel and around the Prefecture of Police.

Nothing is clear. We don't know to what extent the Germans have left Paris. They fire from street corners but seem incapable of a massive demonstration of military force. A few days ago, the general who commands Paris was announcing that if "riots broke out," "brutal measures" would be taken. Is this general still in Paris, or has he been transferred east to Nancy? Did the Resistance take up arms too soon? Without the agreement of the heads of the Allied troops advancing on Paris? London seems to have no knowledge of what's happening in Paris.

Around 11:00 p.m., Christian phones to confirm the news of an agreement between the Resistance and the Germans. The Americans are in Mantes, in Fontainebleau, in Versailles. Why don't they enter Paris? When will they parade, with a band in front of them?

I don't know what the news is on the street. But the street is different from the way it was the other nights.

Not excited and tense, but in a state of calm beatitude. Groups gather in front of the doorways, larger than usual, and denser too, as if swollen. The children aren't playing and don't disperse; they're waiting for the great event to appear in the flesh, the visible flight of the Germans, the passage of an American tank.

A phonograph is playing the Marseillaise. Flags pop out at the windows, briefly hiding a chest or a face, which disappears instantly into the darkness. Applause spreads and glides along like flowing water between the asphalt and the façades of the buildings. A flag has been raised on the roof of the house where the German anti-aircraft battery used to stand.

The evening of this summer Sunday is warm and sultry. It feels like a July 14 risen from the grave. There's a sudden drop in the tension of my four-year-long wait.

August 21 (10:00 p.m.)

A sound like a roll of far-off thunder, breaking the silence. The whole street says: "It's them."

August 23

Two tanks were captured on Place Maubert by the FFI.

Something's changed; we don't analyze every ring of the doorbell anymore.

"Sure we'd like to fight," says a man in line in front of the baker's. "But we'd need weapons . . . On rue du Louvre, there were two hundred of us, and we had five rifles . . ."

An image of these days: the return of the barricades and a swarm of little Baras attacking tanks with grenades.[100]

A sheet of paper (is it bigger than a standard sheet of typing paper, is it printed or stenciled?), a ripped paper, on a wall. It's the "last message" of Pétain. It seems to have come from the depths of time. Two bourgeois, two bourgeois ghosts: "There are people," says one, "who did worse . . . He did what he could."

A principal of a Catholic school, non-collaborator and quasi-Gaullist. But he's afraid of "the dregs of the people," Communists and foreigners. He's worried. He knows, through the manager of a factory, that "the workers and even the white-collar employees are just dreaming of a great upheaval."

Only a week ago, Riv——'s wife, to a friend who was discreetly worrying about his fate, answered: "But the game's not over. The V-2s are going to come out soon."

August 24

Roux and Claude spent five minutes at the house. They immediately went back to Place Saint-Michel, to their post in the FFI. In jackets and with blackened hands.[101]

We're told Militiamen and Doriotists are firing from the rooftops.[102]

Are the Americans at the Porte d'Orléans or aren't they?

Two German armored cars with machine guns mounted on them go down rue de Rennes toward Boulevard Saint-Germain. The gunners are looking up at the façades. Ready to fire. Tense, nervous faces.

A tank is stopped by a barricade in front of the Hôtel Lutetia. It maneuvers, backs up, and fires three cannon shots, at the barricade no doubt, and

---

[100] Joseph Bara (1779–93) was a drummer boy in the republican army of the Revolution who met a heroic death, the subject of several paintings. Streets in Paris and elsewhere bear his name.

[101] The "blackened hands" undoubtedly came from building a barricade with paving stones; there was a big one on the corner of Boulevards Saint-Michel and Saint-Germain and others not far away.

[102] The number of collaborationist snipers—Militia and others—has been exaggerated, but they did exist.—J.-P. A.

On August 26, 1944, in the Place de la Concorde, crowds of Parisians celebrating the entry of Allied troops into Paris scattered for cover as a sniper fired from a nearby building. Although the Germans had surrendered the city, small bands of snipers—Wehrmacht or French Militia—still remained. *NARA, 111-SC-193008*

disappears. The noise of the explosions filled the sound corridor of rue de Rennes.

As soon as the noise stopped, the groups in the doorways, who had gone back inside, reappear. We can see bouquets of faces at the windows again.

We go back home around seven. We go to the window. A man walking by in the street raises his head toward us and shouts: "Do you hear the bells of Notre Dame?"

I don't know how we learned that two tanks of General Leclerc had pulled up in front of the Hôtel de Ville.[103]

---

[103] General Philippe Leclerc de Hauteclocque was one of the few officers to join de Gaulle's Free French. He had a distinguished career commanding the Second Armored Division: it landed in Normandy and went on to Germany. With de Gaulle, he persuaded Eisenhower to let the French liberate Paris themselves. Considering Werth's hatred of colonialism, it is ironic that two Free French generals, Leclerc and de Lattre, died defending French colonial rule—Leclerc in Algeria, de Lattre in Indochina.

I didn't know history existed. I didn't believe in history. And now everything is full of historical resonance. My chest swells with history.

Around 8:00 p.m., D—— and his wife ring our bell. D—— takes us to the Hôtel de Ville. He doesn't want to wait till tomorrow to breathe the air of a delivered Paris in the street. Breathe in Paris, but not see it. To see Paris is out of the question. It's pitch-black out.

We follow rue Madame to Saint-Sulpice, rue Madame normally inert, with dead façades, with windows that seem to look out not on a living street but on a courtyard. The street is pitch-black. But in the street and on the sidewalk people are singing the Marseillaise. Tight-knit groups that don't mingle with each other, don't melt into one mass. Separate groups, like people who haven't been introduced to each other. But these groups are singing, and in the houses, they're singing too. All the repressed Marseillaises unfurl over the street or fall in cascades from the windows. We can only see masses of shadow. It's the street and the houses that are singing. Rue de Buci is almost deserted. When we reach the corner of rue de Seine, gunshots burst out. The Germans are probably firing at the Senate building. People whose faces we can't see take shelter in the entrances behind the porte cochères. A man from civilian defense advises us to go back home and avoid main thoroughfares. We turn around and go back. Everything is turned off, lights and songs.

We hear cannon and machine-gun salvos until dawn.

August 25

The Germans are firing from the Luxembourg Gardens. Machine-gun fire and rockets. In the afternoon, the shelling grows more violent.

Beneath our windows, three passersby are wounded in the feet and legs. They take shelter in the bookstore. When I walk into the store, two of them have their wounds superficially dressed, and they're lying on blankets spread out on the floor. Phone call to a first-aid post. A few minutes later, stretcher-bearers take them away.

Five young men wearing jackets and armed with revolvers jump from doorway to doorway and advance toward the Luxembourg Gardens. Two others with a more military look, wearing helmets and armed with rifles, take up position at the corner of rue Madame, out of the line of fire along rue d'Assas.

Meanwhile, a Leclerc tank emerging from rue Vavin fires at the blockhouse on rue Guynemer. It destroys it in two shots. Right after the explosions, the windows are filled with faces. And from every window, people are shouting "Bravo!" They're clapping as if it were shooting practice or an orchestrated performance. Applause bursts out from the corridor of every street. My nose is glued to the window. I see the line of a tracer bullet light up and go out.

The tank rolls up rue d'Assas, stops at the corner of rue Auguste-Comte in front of Lycée Montaigne, and fires at the sandbags piled up at the corner.

A German throws a jerrycan of flaming gasoline at it. But it doesn't reach the tank, which has already started moving.

The young men (FFI) I'd seen from my window have advanced by leaps and bounds and reached rue Guynemer. They hurl grenades at the blockhouse and kill a few Germans. But one of them falls face down on the street.

A white ambulance has arrived. Men in white helmets and clothing are waving white flags, as if they were performing a ritual. They place the dead youth on a stretcher, slide the stretcher into the car, and disappear into the empty street.

Each tank is covered by a human swarm. German prisoners are standing, squeezed flank to flank, belly to back, all with their hands on the back of their necks.

Never will I forget those men with their hands clasped over the napes of their necks, those caryatids in faded uniforms, in the posture of the damned. One of them, hardly an adolescent, has let his head fall on his neighbor's chest. He's sleeping.

Victory. Tears come to my eyes, tears of deliverance. But I am moved by the obvious, striking contradiction: these terrible, heavy machines did the work of justice. Through them the nuances of human thought have been preserved. No, I'm not afraid of these big ideas, and I don't care if they make some people smile. These tanks going by are giving me my share of victory, my share of

General de Gaulle leads a victory parade after the liberation of Paris. August 26, 1944. *NARA, 196287*

freedom. My joy is too strong, it's a joy I can't keep inside me for long without spoiling it. But the humiliation of those men makes me suffer. It is necessary, it is even justice itself. I approve of it, it satisfies me, it soothes me, and I cannot rejoice at it.

Is this feeling really so complicated, so difficult to grasp? Everyone I confessed it to told me: "You're forgetting what they did, the murders, the tortures . . ." I'm forgetting nothing. But when a man is humiliated, his humiliation is in me.

August 26

A few houses down the street. They just cropped the hair off the heads of four women. The hair is in the gutter. They're going to parade these four women through the streets. A procession accompanies them with a kind of dignity, without shouting. But an old man spits in their faces and wants to hit them. He is prevented from doing it.

The shaved heads of those women . . . And one of them had a clayey face and dilated eyes; I once saw them on a condemned man they were taking to the guillotine.

De Gaulle is walking down the Champs-Élysées. A lapping of shouts and murmurs rises from the waiting crowd. When he appears, all those cries and all those murmurs fuse into one wave, hardly oscillating at all and filling the whole space between earth and heaven.

BIOGRAPHICAL DICTIONARY

Abetz, Otto (1903–1958). Hitler's ambassador to Vichy France. He was a lifelong lover of French culture—cleansed of all anti-Nazi or Jewish elements: the long list of books banned from 1940 to 1944 (called "La Liste Otto" in his honor) included works by Freud, Jung, Heinrich Heine, Thomas Mann, André Malraux, and, after 1941, American authors such as Hemingway and Whitman.

Bloch, Marc (1886–1944). A distinguished medieval historian, cofounder of the Annales school of history, a twice-decorated combatant in World War I, and an officer in World War II. (His posthumously published *Strange Defeat* is a brilliant analysis of the reasons for the French collapse in May-June 1940.) A member of the Resistance, arrested and tortured by the Gestapo in March 1944, he was executed in June.

Blum, Léon (1872–1950). A political leader on the moderate left, three times head of the French government, and the author of a dozen books. He headed the Popular Front—the Socialist-centrist-Communist coalition that governed France in 1936–37—and introduced paid vacations and the forty-hour work week. Arrested and imprisoned by French authorities in 1940, he was put on trial in 1942 (embarrassing Vichy with his speeches against collaboration) and deported to Buchenwald in 1943.

Bossuet, Jacques-Bénigne (1627–1704). A bishop whose sermons and other writings are classics of French prose.

de Brinon, Fernand (1885–1947). A leading collaborator, he was Vichy's ambassador to the occupying authorities in Paris. Executed in 1947.

Carcopino, Jérome (1881–1970). A historian known for his work on ancient Rome, he was the director of the École Normale Supérieure from 1940 to 1942 and secretary of education and youth from February 1941 until April 1942. The "Carcopino Law" established a quota limiting the number of Jews in the universities.

Chateaubriant, Alphonse de (1877–1951). A writer whose "regionalist" novels won critical and popular acclaim. He sang the praises of the Occupation, and when it ended he fled to Austria, where he died under another name. He was sentenced to death in absentia in 1945.

Clémenceau, Georges (1841–1929). An important figure in French history for many reasons, he became prime minister toward the end of the First World War and earned the nickname "Père-la-Victoire" (Father Victory).

Daladier, Édouard (1884–1970). Head of the French government in 1939–40, he resigned in March 1940, but not before signing the Munich agreement along with Chamberlain, Hitler, and

Mussolini to "appease" Nazi Germany. He was arrested by Vichy nonetheless as a leader of the republic and eventually deported by the Nazis.

Darlan, François (1881-1942). Admiral Darlan was second only to Pétain in the Vichy government from February 1941 to April 1942, when Germany insisted that he be replaced. He urged close military collaboration with the Nazis, but they preferred Laval. In December 1942, Darlan was assassinated by a member of the Resistance in Algeria after the Allies had invaded.

Darnand, Joseph (1897–1945). Darnand had a long history in far-right groups before founding the Service d'Ordre Légionnaire (SOL), a paramilitary organization supporting Vichy. It became the French Militia in 1943, and Darnand was named secretary for the maintenance of order in 1944. He joined the Waffen SS, fled to Germany in August 1944, and was executed for treason in France.

Déat, Marcel (1894–1955). A man of modest origins who succeeded in getting into the elite École Normale Supérieure. A socialist until 1933, he then became enthusiastic about the National Socialists (Nazis) and was an indefatigable propagandist for their cause. He founded a political party to the right of Pétain and became Vichy's minister of labor in 1944. Sentenced to death in absentia at the liberation of France, he died in an Italian monastery.

Drieu la Rochelle, Pierre (1893–1945). A novelist, essayist, and poet. A "prophet" of French doom and decadence, he was an ardent fascist and wrote of his hopes for the new (Nazi) order in Europe. He committed suicide after the liberation of France.

Doriot, Jacques (1898–1945). A Communist politician of working-class origin who became a fascist. He founded the Parti Populaire Français (PPF) in 1936, and his newspaper *Le Cri du peuple* took the name of a nineteenth-century revolutionary journal. He also helped create a unit of French volunteers in the German army and fought with them on the Russian front. After D-Day he fled to Germany, where he was eventually shot and killed by an Allied plane.

Febvre, Lucien (1878–1956). A specialist in sixteenth-century France and one of the most influential historians of the twentieth century. With Marc Bloch, he was a cofounder of the Annales school of history—the study of history from the bottom up, with particular emphasis on the history of *mentalités*—attitudes and values.

Franco, Francisco (1892–1975). As a Spanish army general in 1936, he led a revolt against the elected republic, won this civil war with the massive help of Hitler's air force and Mussolini's troops, and from 1939 until his death was the caudillo (a translation of the German *führer*) of a fascist dictatorship in Spain. His government remained neutral during the Second World War.

Giraud, Henri (1879–1949). For a time, General Giraud led one current of the anti-German French. A favorite of US diplomats, he distrusted de Gaulle and, despite his nationalism, withdrew his support from Pétain only in 1943.

Goebbels, Joseph (1897–1945). As Hitler's minister of propaganda from 1933 to 1945, he was the most important political figure in Nazi Germany after Hitler (and ultimately in charge of all publishing in occupied France). Fanatically devoted to the Führer and violently anti-Semitic, he incited Germans to violence before the war and to fight to the bitter end during the conflict. After Hitler committed suicide in his bunker in May 1945, Goebbels followed suit, along with his wife and his six children, whom he killed or had killed.

Goering, Hermann (1893–1946). A Nazi from the earliest days, he was the head of the Luftwaffe, Hitler's air force. His collection of artworks stolen from German-occupied countries and his taste for luxury were notorious. He committed suicide after the Nuremberg trials to avoid being hanged.

Henriot, Philippe (1889–1944). A recurrent voice on Vichy radio from 1940 on, appointed minister of information and propaganda in January 1944. His violent attacks on de Gaulle and the Resistance were notorious.

Hérold-Paquis, Jean (1912–1945). A pro-Nazi propagandist, routinely ending his radio commentaries with "England, like Carthage, will be destroyed." He was executed after the Liberation.

Langevin, Paul (1872–1946). A world-class physicist and a left-wing anti-fascist. He was arrested by Vichy on October 30, 1940.

Larbaud, Valery (1881–1957). A major modernist poet, critic, and translator who signed his most famous collection of poems with the pseudonym A O. Barnabooth.

Laval, Pierre (1883–1945). Pétain's prime minister except for one short period (December 1940–April 1942). He came to personify the policy of collaboration, publicly declaring "I want Germany to win the war" (see entry for June 22, 1942). Unlike Pétain, he was widely hated in France, as he was held responsible for the Compulsory Work Service and other unpopular measures. He was executed for treason at the Liberation.

Luchaire, Jean (1901–1946). A prominent journalist who urged support for Nazi Germany, he fled there just before the liberation of Paris and was executed for treason afterwards.

Pascal, Blaise (1623–1662). A Catholic philosopher whose *Pensées* is a classic of world literature; he was also a mathematician of the first order and a physicist.

Mandouze, André (1916–2006). A Catholic historian, he was an early anti-fascist, editor of an underground Catholic resistance paper, and later an activist against France's Algerian War.

Maurras, Charles (1868–1952). An influential right-wing writer—often cited by T. S. Eliot, for example—who was intensely nationalist, anti-democratic, and violently anti-Semitic. A leading figure in the monarchist movement Action Française, he was an enthusiastic collaborator (famously describing Pétain in power as "a divine surprise") and was sentenced to life imprisonment at the liberation of France.

Montherlant, Henry de (1895–1972). A writer whose plays are still performed in France. Some of his novels are still read too.

Pucheu, Pierre (1899–1944). Like Marcel Déat, he was of working-class origin and rose in society through the École Normale Supérieure. As Vichy's minister of the interior—the ministry responsible for maintaining order—he created the "Special Sections" to try and quickly execute "terrorists" (members of the Resistance). He himself was the first member of the Vichy government to be executed by the Free French.

Saint-Exupéry, Antoine de (1900–1944). Although he is best known in the United States as the author of *Le Petit Prince* (1943), his novels won literary prizes in France, and *Terre des hommes* (*Wind, Sand, and Stars*) won the American National Book Award in 1939. A pilot in the Free French Air Force, he died on a reconnaissance mission in 1944.

Saint-Simon, Louis de Rouvroy, duc de (1675–1755). His *Mémoires* were much admired by Proust and other writers and are still read today. Werth often quotes them in his diary, but most of these quotations have been cut in this edition.

Vigny, Alfred de (1797–1863). One of the French Romantic poets. He was also a playwright and a novelist. Proust particularly admired his poem "La Maison du berger" (The shepherd's home).

Vildrac, Charles (pseudonym of Charles Messager) (1882–1971). A left-wing poet. His work was included in *L'Honneur des poètes*, an underground anthology of resistance poetry published by Éditions de Minuit in 1943.

CHARLES DE GAULLE
"THE CALL OF JUNE 18"

Léon Werth heard Charles de Gaulle's radio address of June 18, 1940 four years later. When he did, he wondered why English radio did not "repeat part of it every day, like a slogan." De Gaulle became, increasingly, one of Werth's rare heroes. Moreover, as this brief speech is now a classic and one version of it is posted all over France every June, it seemed useful to include the full text here in English. In French, it is known as the "Appel du 18 juin," usually translated as "The Appeal of 18 June," but it is far more a call than an appeal. This translation is based on the official text (found, among many other places, at http://archives.charles-de-gaulle.org/pages/l-homme/dossiers-thematiques/1940-1944-la-seconde-guerre-mondiale/l-appel-du-18-juin/documents/l-appel-du-18-juin-1940.php).

The leaders who have been at the head of French armed forces for many years have formed a government.

This government, alleging the defeat of our armies, has contacted the enemy to put an end to the fighting.

Certainly, we were—we are—overwhelmed by the enemy's mechanical force, on land and in the air.

Infinitely more than their number, it is Germany's tanks, planes, and tactics that have pushed us back. It is the tanks, the planes, and the tactics of the Germans that surprised our leaders so much it brought them to the situation they are in today.

But has the last word been said? Must all hope vanish? Is our defeat definitive? No!

Believe me: I know whereof I speak, and I am telling you that nothing is lost for France. The same means that have defeated us can one day bring us victory.

For France is not alone! She is not alone! She is not alone! She has a vast empire behind her. She can join forces with the British Empire, which holds the sea and is continuing the fight. She can, like England, make unrestricted use of the immense industrial power of the United States.

This war is not limited to the unhappy territory of our country. This war has not been decided by the battle of France. This war is a world war. All our mistakes, all our delays, all our suffering do not alter the fact that there are, in this universe, all the means necessary to crush our enemies one day. Struck down today by mechanical force, we can win by superior mechanical force in the future. That is where the world's destiny lies.

I, General de Gaulle, now in London, call on the French officers and soldiers now in British territory or who may come here with or without their weapons, I call on the engineers and workers in the arms industry who are in British territory or who may come here, to contact me.

Whatever may happen, the flame of French resistance must not and will not go out.

Tomorrow I will speak on London radio, as I have today.

INDEX

Figures are noted with an *f* following the page number.